JOHN NEVILLE TAKES COMMAND

THE STORY OF THE STRATFORD SHAKESPEAREAN FESTIVAL IN PRODUCTION

ROBERT A. GAINES

WILLIAM STREET PRESS * STRATFORD, ONTARIO

"What legacy shall I bequeath to thee?"
The Rape of Lucrece 1192

For Bobby, Elizabeth, Denny, Chester, Laurie, and Patrick

Published by:

The William Street Press
53 William Street
Stratford, Ontario
Canada, N5A 4X9

Printed and bound in Canada by:

Webcom, Ltd., Toronto, Ontario

$13.95

Canadian Cataloguing in Publication Data

Gaines, Dr. Robert A.

John Neville Takes Command:
The story of the Stratford Shakespearean
Festival in production.

Includes index.

1. Stratford Festival (Ont.). 2. Neville, John. 3. Shakespeare, William, 1564-1616 -- Drama Production. 4. Theatre -- Ontario -- Stratford -- Production and Direction.

I. Title

PN2306.S7G35 1987   792'.09713'23   C87-094180-1

ISBN 0-9691075-3-6

"You speedy helpers, that....
Appear and aid me in this enterprise."
1 Henry VI V.3.5-7

I wish to acknowledge with grateful appreciation: the Canadian Embassy in Washington, D.C., for a stipend under its Faculty Enrichment Grant Program, Auburn University at Montgomery, The Arts Council of Montgomery, and two donors who wish to remain anonymous for subsidizing this research.

"There are the whole contents."
Henry VIII IV.2.154

Contents

"This paper is the history of my knowledge."
Cymbeline III.5.99

Foreword

Historians spend their professional lives searching for missing pieces. The theatre historian, like his counterpart in any field of history, has few tools to help him unlock the past. Working with prompt books, reviews, the physical theatre itself, or the memories of those involved in a particular production may prove difficult enough, but frequently one or more of these records have disappeared, making the reconstruction of the past that much more difficult. Consequently too often historians can agree on the facts relating to a certain event but cannot tell why the affair unfolded as it did. History provides so many facts--so many names, dates, and places--and so few of the "whys" surrounding the occurrence. Yet the "whys," when known, frequently translate these empty facts into a compelling narrative.

Therefore, historians must record contemporary events of significance at the time when they occur so that an accurate account, not only of what happened but of why those persons most closely associated with the event believed it happened, can become a part of the permanent record. As one of the Festival's 1986 Associate Directors, Douglas Campbell, explained while watching The National Film Board's presentation of *Stratford Adventure* in Rehearsal Hall 2 of the Festival Theatre in mid-February, "History isn't just about the past. The historian preserves the past for the future." For this reason, I have chosen to document the story of a great theatre in action at a time when it seeks a new direction with a new artistic team. In order to capture the story of this season, I have interviewed the persons most directly involved in the process and have observed the process first-hand by entering into that crucible, the rehearsal hall, where plays come off the printed page and assume distinctive personalities before their public openings. This permanent record is intended to communicate this Stratford season, as presently understood, to fellow professionals and interested partisans, and to establish a contemporary chronicle whereby others may assess what happened here.

In the late winter of 1985, I wrote to John Neville asking for and receiving permission to observe the rehearsal and performance process during the

5

1986 season for the purpose of writing this history. But because rehearsals constitute a very private exploration that actors must undertake to develop their characterizations, no one can simply sit by and observe without disrupting that very process which he/she came to record. The 1986 company chose to support me in the writing of their history despite the difficulties my presence at rehearsals sometimes caused them. In addition they gave most graciously of their time to answer numerous questions in informal sessions with me. No one ever denied a request for an interview, refused to answer a question, or sought prior approval of what I wrote. Therefore I take immense pleasure in expressing my thanks not only to John Neville but to the entire Stratford organization, which for the whole nine months of the 1986 season accepted me not only as an observer and historian but also as a member of the family. While I had the good fortune to write this account, because those company members created it, this history more properly belongs to them. Unless otherwise noted, the quotations and paraphrases I have used come from both formal and informal interviews or comments made during rehearsals and performances from the sources cited.

I have attended the Festival's productions since 1970, but the impetus for this book came out of an intensified study beginning with the 1982 season. In the four seasons before 1986, I had become a reasonably well-informed person studying the Festival from the outside. Nevertheless crossing over that demarcation to the inside proved a Brobdingnagian step for a number of reasons, not the least of which was the immediate shift of perspective which it engendered. As a result I did not begin writing immediately. Rather, from February through May, I watched the process and made notes. The writing of the manuscript began in June after the opening of the first round of plays in mid-May. One has only to watch a morning's rehearsal and then hear it recounted over lunch in the Green Room of the Festival Theatre to tally the many separate interpretations that it receives. Which interpretation proves the right one? Each one does, at least to the person proposing it. That some involved in the 1986 season will differ with interpretations offered here shows the subjective nature of all writing, history included. And importantly, because the purpose here is to tell the story of Stratford's creative process, this is not a recounting of reviews and particularly not of controversies or behind-the-scenes politics but of artistic decisions and their results. In fact, it was a season as I observed it that was remarkably free of dissension.

A number of other people made the writing of this history possible and I take pride in acknowledging my debt to them. Mrs. Toni Burke shared my excitement over this project from the beginning. Dr. Guin A. Nance and Dr. Marion C. Michael, Vice-Chancellor for Academic Affairs and Dean of the School of Liberal Arts, respectively, at Auburn University at Montgomery, arranged for my leave of absence. Dr. James T. Kenny, Vice-Chancellor for Development at the same institution, provided some valuable assistance. Mrs. John G. Kimbrough, Mrs. John Allen Jones III, and Mrs. J. LeRoy Bosko of Montgomery, Alabama, worked hard in locating additional aid. Dr. Norman T. London and Dr. Ginette Chenard of the Canadian Embassy in Washington, D.C., as well as Suzanne Cormie and Jeffery Smith of the Canadian Consulate in Atlanta, contributed much help in working with the Canadian Embassy. My thanks go to Mrs. Nancy Anderson for proofreading the text.

A large group of people supplied constant assistance and encouragement once I arrived in Stratford, Ontario: Mr. and Mrs. Alfred Bell, Mr. and Mrs. Jack Chessman, Mr. and Mrs. Don Farwell, the Rev. and Mrs. John Spencer, Mrs. Lorne Brothers, Mr. and Mrs. Nick Giannakopoulos of the Cafe Mediterranean, and Sir Rudolph Betweenjobs. My sincere thanks go to my editor and publisher, Patricia A. Wilson, for her continued faith in the value of this enterprise and her ever-helpful suggestions.

Finally, I wish to give special thanks to my wife, Elizabeth Blair Riepma Gaines, for her never-failing support for me and her patience and constant good will in managing the family and household without me. She has also served above and beyond the call of duty as editor for this project.

Robert A. Gaines
Stratford, Ontario,
21 October, 1986

"...the prologue to their play"
2 Henry VI III.1.151

The Prologue

Chapter One: The Election

The history of the 1986 Stratford Shakespearean Festival began with the search for its seventh artistic director, which terminated in the appointment of John Neville in September 1984. The genesis of that process grew in turn out of a decision by the Board of Governors of the Festival, when it hired John Hirsch as its sixth artistic director in December 1980, to sign him to a three-year contract. Board member Ronald Bryden, who serves as director of the graduate programme at the University of Toronto's Drama Center, explains that while in theory the board considers a five-year term of office as the norm for an artistic director, in practice it prefers to issue a shorter contract and then extend it for an additional two years if both parties agree. But because the board could not assume that Hirsch would agree to such an extension, Bryden says, he first began compiling a list of candidates to succeed Hirsch in the latter half of 1982. When Hirsch did accept the offer to extend his contract, says 1985 Board President Peter Herrndorf, who publishes *Toronto Life* magazine, both the board and Hirsch agreed at that time he would not serve in that capacity beyond 1985. Therefore, Herrndorf says, the board decided to move as quickly as possible to line up a successor to Hirsch. Herrndorf explains that because the new artistic director might have come without a working knowledge of either the Festival or the community, both Hirsch and the board wished to make an appointment a year in advance of the time the new director would assume responsibilities for the 1986 season. Not only did such a strategy solve the problem, but it had precedent. The long transition period between the administrations of Sir Laurence Olivier and his successor, Peter Hall, at The National Theatre of Great Britain provided the most striking example of such an arrangement, explains Herrndorf. Yet the Stratford board had brought Robin Phillips from England so that he could tour the country meeting the theatre community in advance of his undertaking the Stratford artistic leadership role in l974. In order to meet its schedule, the board wished to make the appointment during the summer of 1984.

Festival General Manager Gary Thomas describes the search committee as a permanent standing committee of the board called the Continuity Committee. "Some years it has more to do than in other years," says Thomas. 1984 proved one of its busier years. But before the committee could get down to work, it had to establish its internal working methods. Herrndorf explains that he joined Bryden as co-leader of the search committee in early 1984 to assist in compiling lists of qualifications and candidates. By this time, he says, Bryden had worked for over eighteen months preparing the résumés of possible candidates for submission to the full committee. Bryden says the résumés consisted of biographical data, lists of roles performed and/or plays directed, and reviews of the work of each candidate. Because the board's 1980 search for a new artistic director had drawn so much criticism from so many sources, Bryden explains, this search had to proceed very slowly and in full consultation with a broad range of interested parties, such as funding arts organizations' personnel, prominent theatre people, and concerned government officials, as well as Stratford company members. (For a full account of the board's 1980 search, see: 1.) Knelman, Martin. *A Stratford Tempest*. McClelland and Stewart, Toronto, 1982 and 2.) Pettigrew, John, and Portman, Jamie. *Stratford: The First Thirty Years*. Macmillan of Canada, Toronto, 1985, Vol. II, pp. 187- 227.) Herrndorf remembers that he and Bryden, as well as other committee members, interviewed about fifty "interested parties" who gave the committee both lists of the qualifications that the new artistic director should possess and names of persons who fulfilled such requirements.

Herrndorf begins the discussion of the search by stating that the committee's intent lay in finding a Canadian. But he stresses that the use of the term did not constitute a "narrow test of nationality" but rather reflected the committee's desire to find someone who: 1.) was a Canadian citizen, 2.) had landed immigrant status, or 3.) was a long-term resident. In addition, he says, the committee sought someone who had or would make a long-term commitment to Canadian theatre, as opposed to the "mercenary" who might stay in the country only for a few years. The committee agreed at the outset that every possible Canadian candidate would have to be interviewed and eliminated before the committee began looking at any non-Canadians.

As a result of their extensive consultations, Herrndorf says, he and Bryden began with a list of fifty candidates, most of whom they interviewed, many a second time. He remembers with a smile that others would say, only partly in jest, that if a person moved and had so much as read a Shakespearean play he got an interview. Bryden points out that in addition to finding someone acceptable to the Canadian theatrical community, he and Herrndorf looked for someone with experience both in directing Shakespeare and in running a major theatre. Herrndorf says that out of that process came the short list of twelve and then four candidates (in alphabetical order): John Caird, John Neville, Christopher Newton, and Robin Phillips. One of the candidates on the list of twelve, Des McAnuff, had directed the Festival's 1983 production of *Macbeth*. After a Toronto interview, Herrndorf says, although he and Bryden believed McAnuff "well on his way to being one of the premiere directors in North America," he did not yet have the credentials of the other four. Bryden acknowledges the difficulty involved in cutting the list to four but also points to the relatively few people within the Canadian theatrical community who have both extensive experience in directing Shakespeare and in running a major theatre company. Herrndorf explains that the abbreviated version of the short list also tallied with the names most frequently mentioned by those with whom they had consulted earlier in putting together the complete list.

While the committee had an interest in Phillips' candidacy, says Herrndorf, it did not pursue "the Robin Phillips option" because it had strong indications from several sources that, because of the large number of other commitments which he had undertaken, Phillips could not see his way clear to returning to Stratford as artistic director at that time. For quite a while, Herrndorf continues, the committee did not pursue John Caird, either. When first approached Caird said that due to job commitments he could not come to Canada for an interview at that time, explains Bryden. Although native-born, Caird had spent almost all of his professional life in England, where in 1984 he served as an associate director of the Royal Shakespeare Company.

Bryden and Herrndorf, says the latter, then interviewed Neville and Newton. Herrndorf says that Neville "was a known quantity" who brought a lot of advantages with him: a terrific theatrical background, wonderful acting talent, experience as a Shakespearean director, a high degree of credibility within the theatrical community across the continent, and a demonstrated investment in the Festival and in the community. During the interview with Newton, explains Herrndorf, the candidate expressed an interest in the job but also stated that a 1984 appointment would come at the very worst time because, as artistic director of the Shaw Festival, he believed that everything he was doing at Niagara-on-the-Lake was setting the stage for a twenty-fifth anniversary season (which The Shaw Festival celebrated in 1986). Newton went on to explain that, because of the timing, if the job were offered to him, he was not at all sure he would accept it, says Herrndorf, who explains the objection on Newton's part as the biggest factor weighing against him. Herrndorf also points out that while Newton did express a desire to make some big changes were the job at Stratford his, John Neville also from the beginning took the position that he would do things differently. Knelman contends that the board at first shied from Newton's ideas for change

(Knelman, Martin. "My Deeds Upon My Head,"*Saturday Night*, March 1986, p. 60), but Herrndorf contends that the point was insignificant in negotiations because each new leader initiates change, including Hirsch in 1980.

Bryden points out that at this point some committee members began to question whether an artistic director of Neville's background would represent a generation of classical tastes rather than a more radical approach. So fairly late in the process, the possibility of Caird's candidacy again surfaced in the committee, explains Bryden. Herrndorf says that he wanted to "cast the net as widely as possible" for candidates, and he and Bryden went to England "to see whether or not we had a candidate." He recalls their trip.

> *Bryden and I flew to England on one of these amazing whirlwind trips, leaving Saturday....We had breakfast with John Caird from 9:30 to 11:00 and at 12:15 we were on a plane back to Toronto. From that (meeting) we had an indication that Caird might be interested and that led to Caird's being considered.*

Once Bryden and Herrndorf had returned and had had time to review all of the qualities that they wanted in the new leader--including experience, leadership, creative skills, and flair--they decided that they would recommend to the full committee two candidates, Caird and Neville, from which to select the next artistic director. Caird's candidacy further delayed the process because he could not come to Stratford to interview with the full committee until the end of August. The committee wanted to interview the candidates back-to-back, setting up a luncheon interview between Caird and the committee on a Monday and one with Neville on a Tuesday, says Herrndorf, who lists the committee members attending, in addition to Bryden and himself, as Bill Somerville, Gerry Eldred, and Oliver Gaffney. Bryden says that although Caird appeared impressive at his interview, he had not managed a large company, rather leading a protected life within a larger organization and working with other directors. As a result, explains Bryden, the committee still did not have a sense of what kind of director he was in his own right because it had reviews from only two Shakespearean plays he had directed by himself. On the one hand, Bryden goes on, his *Twelfth Night* done at Stratford-on-Avon got rave reviews, while on the other hand, many thought that his *Merchant of Venice* done there might deserve the label of "the worst production anybody had ever seen." (Bryden believes he could not answer his question about Caird as a director until he saw his production of Ben Jonson's *Every Man In His Humour* at the RSC's newly-opened Swan Theatre in Stratford-on-Avon during the summer of 1986, with which he pronounced himself well pleased. He singles out as particularly praiseworthy Caird's sense of detail with every character during each scene.) Caird also told the committee, relates Bryden, that he could not come to Stratford until after the opening of the RSC's *Les Miserables* in November 1984. In the final analysis, says Bryden, the committee did not know after its interview with Caird if he would leave the RSC if the position were offered to him.

Neville, by contrast, during his final interview presented the committee with a most detailed plan for running the theatre which combined, Herrndorf says, his vision for the kind of Stratford Festival which he foresaw with a very practical and yet meticulously planned approach to controlling such a large organization. Neville describes this plan by stressing his commitment to the Festival's mandate to present the whole Shakespearean canon, including the "less popular" plays, and increasing the number of non-Shakespearean plays done, ranging from ancient to modern classics. "I do not wish to do boulevard theatre," he reiterates.

The committee then decided almost immediately that for any number of reasons, relates Herrndorf, it wanted to offer the position to John Neville. Herrndorf staunchly defends the integrity of the process, saying that until the back-to-back interviews neither he nor, he suspects, any other member of the committee knew which way he would vote. Bryden believes just as strongly in the validity of the process, but he thinks "the majority was always sure it was John (Neville) they wanted." But, he adds, considering what happened in 1980, the committee wanted to move very slowly. Bryden explains that the vitae which he had assembled for almost two years at the time of the appointment consisted of one page for most of the candidates, while the one on Neville ran four pages. "If one had never heard of John Neville," Bryden continues, "looking at his vita one would have to say, 'Who is this man?' All the qualifications we could ask for and more." At that point "It became clear to a lot of us that our search need not go a lot further." After the interviews, a consensus formed very quickly around Neville, who, Herrndorf stresses, represented "a known quantity" in that he had lived and worked in Canada for the last twelve years. In fact Herrndorf reveals and Bryden confirms that the committee voted unanimously to recommend Neville. It then took that recommendation to an advisory committee, made up of representatives from Equity and the Stratford community, among others, which the committee had appointed early in the search process. Herrndorf explains that the advisory group endorsed the recommendation, which then went forward to the Executive Committee of the Board and finally to the full board in what amounted to a recommendation of John Neville by the search committee and a three-step process of approval for that recommendation.

One small complication developed, says Herrndorf, when on 13 September, the day of the announcement, the executive committee met in Toronto in the morning before a full board meeting in the afternoon. The press picked up

15

the information that Neville would get the appointment and sought confirmation from board members between the two meetings. No one could give them that information until after the full board had gotten its hands on the nomination and approved it. Board President Oliver Gaffney appeared later to make the expected announcement, just as white smoke from Vatican chimneys signals the selection of the new man.

Bryden had originally spoken to Neville about his interest in the position in the fall of 1983, and when Herrndorf and Bryden interviewed Neville early in the rehearsal stages for the 1984 season, the board still envisioned an appointment in the early summer. Because the Festival had incurred an operating deficit during the 1983 season, Neville strongly advocated early planning as one of the best methods for holding down operating costs. As the selection process dragged out three months longer than originally expected, Neville saw at least part of the advantage the new director would have for advanced planning eroding and he occasionally lost patience with the length of time the process took. "I saw the possibility of doing a good job slowly slipping away," he explains. (During the 1986 season many people spoke of the relationship between time and money, but *Cymbeline* designer Daphne Dare has best summed up the essence of the equation: "When you have time you can overcome the problems of a limited budget to some extent, but when you don't have time, you have to have money." Without either, almost all possibilities disappear, she concludes.) While acknowledging that Neville became impatient at times, both Herrndorf and Bryden express sympathy and support for his position. "He believed he was the best man for the job, as we wanted him to believe, and he wanted to get on with the work," Herrndorf says. But, he continues, the committee had to weigh the problems the delay caused Neville against the charge contained in its mandate to find and interview all qualified candidates. Bryden explains that in addition to having to proceed slowly, the committee had to consult with a wide range of interests at every point. As a result, Neville explains, when the job was offered to him, he took a brief time to assess the deficit he would inherit, the time left to plan the 1986 season, and his own resources (including his stamina and resolve) before accepting the board's offer. Bryden has a final thought on the search, which, he quickly acknowledges, represents only his viewpoint. The Stratford Shakespearean Festival has its roots in a long classical tradition of playing Shakespeare that comes directly out of the British tradition. Every now and then the Festival "needs a re-infusion" of that tradition. It cannot simply take the form of a British classical theatre because Canadians find that structure unacceptable. In looking at the tradition of choosing the Canadian Liberal Party's leader, which calls for the office to rotate between an English and a French speaker, Bryden believes the party has found the mechanism to ensure that it remains a national party. He sees the same kind of mechanism developing in the appointment of artistic directors for the Festival: Englishman Michael Langham followed by French Canadian Jean Gascon; Robin Phillips, schooled in the English tradition, followed by Canadian-educated John Hirsch. Of the 1984 search Bryden says, "It was time for another infusion of the English tradition," which he goes on to defend by pointing out that each artistic director, regardless of the culture in which he received his training, has tried to find new ways of making the Festival "more Canadian." But, he says, the Festival still needs at regular intervals to draw nourishment from the tradition which begat it.

"Instinct is a great matter."
1 Henry IV II.4.272

Chapter Two: Planning and Instinct

English-born John Neville, sixth successor to the Canadian mantle of Tyrone Guthrie, ascended to the Stratford artistic director's chair in the autumn of 1984. This appointment was the fortuitous result of intensive long-range planning and unerring instinct, capping a signal career as an actor, director, and theatre executive on both sides of the Atlantic. Neville was an admirer of Guthrie, who had directed him several times in leading roles; he was an advocate of the open stage, which Guthrie had help re-establish in the Twentieth Century; so he was thoroughly grounded in its traditions when the opportunity arose at Stratford.

Neville's early theatrical interests were nourished by two sources: trips to Stratford-on-Avon as a teenager and an English master with an abiding interest in Shakespeare. Neville ranked as top choirboy at St. Michael's Stonebridge, an Anglican church in Northwest London where he received a musical education, the full value of which was not immediately evident. He came to the attention of a church warden who invited him to go to Stratford-on-Avon with himself and his five nieces. Although Neville admits that the five nieces were the "immediate attraction," he quickly came not just to appreciate but to become what he describes as "very obsessive" about Shakespeare. He accepted the warden's invitation three years running, seeing twenty-four plays.

At the same time he felt the influence of an English master who had two passions in life, Shakespeare and Milton. While admitting that he didn't like Milton at that time, Neville welcomed the chance for a formal study of Shakespeare. He recalls, "These two channels fed into me from different sources instilled...a love of Shakespeare in the classroom and a love of the theatre...."

Neville remembers two of those productions especially well: Theodore Komisarjevsky's production of *The Comedy of Errors* in Victorian dress with the Dromios in bowler hats and "a rather marvelous Lear" by Randle Ayrton. While deeply impressed by seeing these performances, he believed himself unable to do much more than admire the theatre from afar because he came

19

from a poor, working class family. His father, an automobile mechanic, made bicycles out of spare parts for both his children. Such enforced frugality demonstrates how the family could not purchase the kind of education which Neville would need to lose his Cockney accent and train as a classical actor.

During Neville's late teen years, which he describes as "early wartime," London was bombed fairly regularly. The pattern of life called for an early supper, and when the air raid sirens went off, his family made its way to an Anderson Air Raid Shelter, a structure made of corrugated iron and buried deep within the earth, which in the case of the Neville family meant the garden. He remembers bombs that took out whole blocks as well as those that hit single targets, many falling quite close to his own home. Years later at the Bristol Old Vic, the first time he played the title role in *Henry V*, Shakespeare's and perhaps England's greatest warrior king, he characterized him as a warmongering tyrant, an interpretation based in part on Neville's painful memories of the ravages of war in London. This ploy, he acknowledges, won him few kudos but bore witness to painful memories.

But the war was also directly responsible for two events that launched John Neville's theatrical career. Youth clubs sprang up all across the country, and Neville organized a new one chiefly for the purpose of performing drama. But in order to gain the cooperation of the others whom he needed to stage plays, he also had to compete in other activities which were not appealing to him, "like table tennis and even boxing." But through his perseverance his new youth club entered the first act of *Hamlet* in an annual festival and won first place. This was Neville's first appearance in the title role that in 1958 would end his Old Vic career while winning him considerable critical acclaim. On the strength of this early Hamlet local borough and county councils offered Neville a scholarship to the Royal Academy of Dramatic Art.

That grant, coupled with his parents' offer to subsidize his living expenses, for the first time made a theatrical career a distant possibility. But after passing his entrance exams at nearly 18, he "was promptly called up into the Royal Navy." Neville had already displayed a sure instinct both for a field in which he had almost no schooling and a role in which he could excel. He has, he says, always trusted his aptitude and he still prefers to make most major decisions based on his instinct, a habit which has become a major facet of his personality.

Neville's naval tour of duty served as the second event which launched his theatrical career. To avoid marking time, he used his free hours aboard ship studying speech books to lose his Cockney accent, consciously using the officer's speech as a model for his own. "I'm a planner and always have been," Neville says. He laughs when recalling these times and describes the war years as a time of growing up. He sailed completely around the world and saw "some action" during his three and one-half years in the navy. He served as a signalman and as such was stationed on the upper deck, where he could see all that happened. He much preferred this duty station to that of the telegrapher, who was stationed below deck. He also remembers being stationed on an oil tanker made up of a mostly East Indian crew with British officers for an extended period of time. Listening to the conversation of officers and crew heightened his awareness of differing accents.

After being discharged from the Navy, Neville finally got the opportunity to attend the Royal Academy of Dramatic Art as part of a government-sponsored programme for servicemen whose careers were interrupted by the war. The RADA experience did not prove entirely successful. Neville recalls that he "was a bundle of inhibitions" and that "I wasn't good enough. I simply wasn't good enough to take advantage of what was there." The one technique that he still uses as an actor focuses on a system of speaking based on rib reserve taught him by voice teacher Clifford Turner at RADA. Neville attended RADA as part of its first postwar class, when the institution experienced an accelerated change from catering to young ladies who had no intention of going on the stage ("Perish the thought!") to aiding a generation of seriously aspiring professionals, many of whom had combat experience. To compensate for both his own and perhaps RADA's deficiencies, he reverted to an old habit of spending his spare time reading his way through the play collection of the public library by checking out a dozen plays at a time.

Despite his feeling that he wasn't "good enough," Neville believed that if he could get a start he would improve. That conviction he now explains as instinct; with a knowing look in his eye, he smilingly proclaims, "but since I always go on instinct...I was proved right. Once I got work I did improve." His first acting job consisted of a walk-on role in *Richard II* at the New Theatre in November 1947. Of that appearance Old Vic critic Audrey Williamson said, "No one at the time probably noticed the name of John Neville among six anonymous 'Soldiers and Servants'; and this speck of future Old Vic stardust vanished, as unobtrusively as it had arrived, for several years from the theatre's history." (Williamson, Audrey. *Old Vic Drama 2*. Loxley Brothers Limited, Letchworth, Hertfordshire, 1957).

The obscurity into which Neville vanished was the Open Air Theatre at Regency Park; this theatre offered a Shakespearean bill in which he played Lysander in *A Midsummer Night's Dream* and a small role in *King John* for the three summer months during which the theatre operated. The company manager, Robert Atkins, had run the Old Vic after the First World War and the Regency Park Theatre for 30 years. Neville remembers Atkins as a hard taskmaster who made him the company "whipping boy" but who, he willingly concedes, taught him an enormous amount about reading verse. Then followed nine months at Lowestoft, a weekly repertory theatre (a different play every week) on the east coast of England. Other than the rigors associated with playing a different character every seven days, he remembers being influenced by the example of Hermione Gingold's son, who attempted to be interesting as well as competent within the bounds of those very short rehearsal periods.

In early 1949 he joined the Birmingham Repertory Company, which did a different play every three weeks. There Michael Langham had taken over the company Barry Jackson had built into a major force. Neville recalls that Langham was raw ("We were all raw in those days") and only a few years out of the service, but "you knew he was something special." Langham was very specific about what he wanted: He "was remarkable...well on the way to being very remarkable, and I was too young to know why."

At times in his career Neville considered his boyish good looks a liability to serious acting ambitions, but he played "saints and the beautiful people" for Langham because "This was what Michael reckoned I could do," among them archangel Gabriel in a modern-dress production of *Everyman*. But when the season progressed as far as Ostrovsky's *Dairy of a Scoundrel*, Langham needed an actor to play the role of Kourchaev, a young, silly, effete hussar. He couldn't find anybody to do the role and then, as Neville recalls, Douglas Campbell, later to become a veteran Stratford, Ontario, Festival actor and director, said "I think you ought to give it to that young man." Langham replied, "Oh, no. He only plays saints." Campbell, "being the persevering soul that he is," finally succeeded in getting Neville cast in the role partly because Langham couldn't find anybody else to play it. (Campbell's wife, Ann Casson, also a company member, was quite pregnant at the time, and played the Virgin Mary that season.) The role "was great fun" and turned out to be a pivotal one in Neville's career, not just because it won him great acclaim, but also because "It was a character part, and that's what I am, a character actor." From this role on, he says, he knew when he had found that distinguishing flavor for each part that he undertook. He learned this lesson so well, in fact, that for the better part of the next ten years he would turn even the leading men he would play into character roles.

John Neville and Caroline Hooper were married in 1949; shortly thereafter followed a six-month period of unemployment which he describes as "a bit bleak, really" as they awaied the birth of their first child. Then at a London production of *Pericles* Neville met Denis Carey, who was auditioning actors for the Bristol Old Vic, tied to the Old Vic through the Arts Council of Britain. Neville's audition won him roles in the first three shows of the season; within three years he was the leading man of the company, having played the title role in *Henry V* and Gregers Werle in *The Wild Duck*, a role he still lists among his all-time favourites. Other roles there also included Dunois in *St. Joan*, the Paul Scofield twins in *Ring Around the Moon*, Valentine in *Two Gentleman of Verona*, Charles Surface in *The School for Scandal*, Valentine in *Love for Love* and even a fling at a pantomime comic. (Williamson. *Old Vic Drama 2*).

Then Michael Benthall of the Old Vic invited him to London for the 1953-54 season but warned him he would have to go back to playing the *jeun premier*. Neville decided to accept the offer and was hired for one season, but stayed for six. At the time Benthall had just taken over the Old Vic and with it a heavy debt. He proposed to do the whole First Folio of Shakespeare over the next five years as both an artistic challenge and a way out of further financial woes. In that Old Vic company during Neville's first and third seasons was Richard Burton, and the two became good friends very quickly. Burton had made several films by that time, and his name had more drawing power than had Neville's. During those years he and Burton "became the joint matinee idols, with a brace of girls each." Neville recounts that he and Burton fanned the flames of controversy on occasion, thereby using the newspapers to boost ticket sales.

At the Old Vic Neville was a part of the leading classical company in the leading centre for English-speaking theatre, doing the entire Shakespearean canon; he gained experience there both playing and observing that would have been available to him nowhere else. For that reason, a chronology of both his roles and some of the critical response to them is worth noting. Neville maintains his conviction that turning the leading men into character roles made playing them more interesting for him while at the same time making him a better actor because he demanded more of himself. The Old Vic opened the 1953-54 season with two plays in repertory, with Neville playing Fortinbras to Richard Burton's Hamlet as well as Bertram in *All's Well That Ends Well*. Burton later told him that he sensed when Fortinbras came on he, Burton, had better watch out. Neville also came to the attention of the London press with his characterization of Bertram. Critic and historian Mary Clarke said, "John Neville had no hope of making Bertram heroic but played him with considerable spirit aided by a handsome voice and presence." (Clarke, Mary. *Shakespeare At The Old Vic*. London, 1954, Vol. 1) He teamed with Claire Bloom, playing Ferdinand to her Miranda, in *The Tempest*. Neville's desire to portray the hero as something beyond the young man in love made an impression on the critics. (Clarke, Vol. 1) Bloom "had a noble Ferdinand in John Neville, and their scenes together had a beauty that was almost sad in its youth and trust...." (Clarke, Vol. 1) Next came Orsino in *Twelfth Night* to Gwen Cherell's Olivia. Cominius in *Coriolanus* brought comment from the critics about the beauty of his voice and verse reading. He also appeared as the Dauphin in *King John*.

When Benthall invited him back for the second year Neville opened as Macduff in "the Scottish play." (According to theatrical lore, neither the name *Macbeth* nor a line from it should be quoted outside of a rehearsal or performance because speaking either would provoke bad luck.) But the big role for him that season was to be Richard II. A week before the play opened, when Neville reported to work he was told Benthall wanted to see him immediately. Neville remembers being frightened that he was going to be replaced in the role. Instead Benthall, after acknowledging that Neville might lay a great big egg as Richard II, expressed his confidence in him and asked him to stay for the five-year plan. Neville accepted by shaking Benthall's hand. *Richard II* opened the following week and was a huge success. "It may have been the turning point of my career," Neville reminisces. After remarking that on opening night Neville played the first half better than the second, Clarke concludes her assessment of his Richard II: "Mr. Neville found confidence and without in any way losing the sharp temper of the early scenes he gradually found a deeper note of suffering in Richard's misfortunes; at the later performances there was pain etched deep in his face as well as his voice during the deposition, the farewell to his Queen, and the final scene at Pomfret." (Clarke, 1956, Vol. 2) Neville believes that the criticism that he was not at his best on opening night applied to several of his performances while at the Old Vic is "entirely fair" and admits that apprehension he still feels on opening nights goes back to some of those experiences at the Old Vic. Williamson also complimented Neville on his performance in the role:

> His Richard II was a fine one mainly because he realized that Richard is not just a matter of a beautiful presence and some musical speech-making, but is a character part demanding not romanticism but a shrewd and even savage insight into the complexities of tryranny and emotional instability.

Neville had convinced at least one critic that turning leading roles into character parts paid large dividends for audiences and actor alike.

Following the success of *Richard II*, Neville received a call from Paramount Pictures asking him to come to the London casting office. There he was offered a seven-year contract and a move to Hollywood immediately if Paramount were successful in buying him out of his contract, or, if not, a move at the end of the season. The first movie he was to have made was *War and Peace*. Neville declined, citing his agreement with Benthall to stay for the five years. Paramount asked if he had signed a contract and, when he replied he had not, wanted to know what the problem was. He replied that he had shaken Benthall's hand. So Neville stayed at the Old Vic and Jeremy Brett eventually played the role Neville had been offered in *War and Peace*, and Neville stuck to his ambition of RADA days "to become the best stage actor I could be." During the remainder of his second Old Vic season he played Orlando in *As You Like It*, Berowne in *Love's Labor's Lost*, Hotspur in *Henry IV, Part 1* and Pistol in *Henry IV, Part 2*. Neville drew comment from several critics who believed that his Orlando may have recognized Rosalind in her disguise as Ganymede. While he remembers having seen the criticism he laughingly admits that he cannot now recall if that were then his intention. But he remembers both his Berowne and Pistol with delight, for the imaginative use of language in the former and the chance to perform an avowed character role in the latter. Historian and critic Clarke recalls his Pistol: "John Neville, too long condemned to young and romantic parts, had a tremendous time with the swashbuckling Pistol, mocking his own wonderful voice as he roared out the mighty lines, and suddenly finding real flexibility of facial expression" (Clarke, Vol. 2).

He opened the 1955-56 season as Mark Anthony in *Julius Caesar* before getting another chance to play a character role as Autolycus in *The Winter's Tale*. This part allowed him to revert to the Cockney accent he had worked so hard to lose. Perhaps his most interesting assignment of the season again involved Richard Burton: Neville had been rehearsing Iago to Burton's Othello for about three weeks when he received a call from Benthall for what the latter called a "challenge." Neville was offered the opportunity to play Othello to Burton's Iago as well. Under Benthall's plan the actors would switch roles nightly. Neville immediately declined this opportunity, saying he had quite enough to work on with Iago. But when Benthall told him Burton had agreed, rising to the occasion Neville also agreed. When he confronted Burton the next day, Burton reported that Benthall had told him Neville had agreed. While Clarke judged his Othello better when Iago was absent, she also reported Neville had a "gift of poetry, and there were moments when the beauty of his voice set the theatre aching with a sense of poetic tragedy" (Clarke, 1956, Vol. 3). Williamson preferred his Iago to Burton's, noting that he was:

> a crew-cut mercenary with wind-reddened cheeks and a hint of the uneducated but able soldier "passed over" ...Neville brillantly showed this driving inescapability of evil inflated by success, and made each tentative return to the attack a gamble unresistible and unresisted.

Burton's Iago, on the other hand, "could hardly be said to exist," Clarke said (Williamson. *Old Vic Drama 2*). Robin Phillips, then an eleven-year-old-schoolboy, remembers Neville's Iago as both "wonderfully wicked" and "devastating beyond belief." Othello may have been the hero of the piece but, says Phillips, the evil bent Neville gave the character captured the attention of the schoolboys. Phillips continued to see Neville in many of the roles he played at the Old Vic during these years and describes him as "a huge hero."

Neville also played Troilus in Guthrie's renowned modern-dress version of *Troilus and Cressida* that season. Neville acknowledges idolizing Guthrie but admits that playing Troilus for him "wasn't the greatest fun because Guthrie's interests lay elsewhere." When the production was revived in New York later in the year, again with Guthrie directing, Neville played Thersites. Clarke complained that in the original London production Neville was constantly upstaged by one Guthrie quirk or another (Clarke, Vol. 3). Veteran critic J.C. Trewin says that the production "gave him (Guthrie) a wonderful opportunity to emphasize the satire at the expense of the love scenes." (Rossi, Alfred, editor. *Astonish Us In The Morning*. Detroit, 1980). According to popular theatrical lore Guthrie was famous (or notorious, depending on the point of view) for drawing attention away from his leading actors in order to highlight some idiosyncrasy. When asked if the Guthrie quirks upstaged or bothered him, Neville diplomatically laughs broadly and replies, "That's why I enjoyed playing Thersites and that answers that question." During that season he played Romeo in *Romeo and Juliet* and the Chorus in *Henry V*. He characterized Romeo by playing him as head over heels in love with Rosaline when the play started, an interpretation fully supported by the text but frequently ignored in production. Such a characterization forced Neville to show his love for Juliet in an even more emphatic fashion than he had for Rosaline.

During the 1956-57 season, he made his first North American tour with the Old Vic. He says that in those days there were only two places to play in Canada, Toronto and Montreal, because they were the only cities with large auditoriums. The tour also played in Washington, New York, Chicago, Los Angeles, and San Francisco. The six-month tour was presented by Sol Hurok, for whom Neville's admiration is still evident: "He put you in very big places but he also filled those places. He knew how to sell. I learned a lot from him." The same feeling of intimacy that existed at the company's London home, although itself a large house, could not be achieved on the tour because of the even larger houses. Therefore, as Neville recalls, projecting the character throughout the auditorium was a big job. "Those tours were a strain; they were a strain on the voice; they were a strain on the whole of your physical being; they were exhausting because of the travel; the playing itself was exhausting." Neville played the tile roles in *Richard II* and in *Romeo and Juliet*. He was also Macduff in *Macbeth*. In New York City the company added *Troilus and Cressida* as previously arranged because Guthrie was free to direct it after having finished directing *Candide* in New York. Williamson says:

There is no denying that there were serious weaknesses in the company that in the autumn of 1956 went to America....But the brillance of the male leads, Paul Rogers (who made an outstanding success) and John Neville, both in dominating roles in two productions and well-cast in the other two, helped give the company a fine artistic ballast, and with Coral Browne, Claire Bloom and Rosemary Harris in feminine support a large degree of success was inevitably achieved. Macbeth *and* Richard II, *too, were particularly good productions.... (Williamson. Old Vic Drama 2).*

Following the tour Neville returned to the Old Vic for the 1957-58 season, playing the title role in *Hamlet*, Angelo in *Measure for Measure*, and Sir Andrew Aguecheek in *Twelfth Night*. He finished the season riding the high tide of critical success. Clarke calls his Hamlet "one of the great achievements of the Old Vic's five-year plan." (Clarke, 1958, Vol. 4). Of his Aguecheek, J.C. Trewin (*Illustrated London News*. April, 1958) says, "But, over all, my thanks go to John Neville for a Sir Andrew likely to be definitive. The man is slow-witted but charmingly so. When he is addressed, it is some time before a glimmer of daybreak shows itself behind his eyes. But he can enjoy himself in his own single-minded fashion. He can be "a dog at catch and he will pursue the morning's jest with a child's concentration." Neville remembers his Aguecheek as "lovable but dim."

During the 1958-1959 season Neville again toured the United States as Hamlet and Aguecheek. He was scheduled as assistant director for *Pericles*, planned for production despite its absence from the First Folio, but instead he recreated his role in *Twelfth Night* because it was preferred to the lesser-known play for the tour. *The Importance of Being Earnest* later served as the vehicle for his directing debut at the Bristol Old Vic, an experience at which he chuckles upon recalling. "I didn't realize how difficult it was; I wouldn't recommend it as a first directing exercise." One of his early directing exercises involved staging *Henry V* for the Old Vic in 1960. Mixed reviews marked this early effort. Peter Roberts (*Plays and Players*. July, 1960) called it "merely dull" while T.C. Worsley (*Financial Times*. 31 May, 1960) judged it to have "the kind of merits which suggest that Mr. Neville has a considerable future in this branch of the art too." Phillips recalls that he first met Neville while the former was acting and directing for the Bristol Old Vic during this period. The two, he said, made a Shakespearean record about this time, and Neville's aristocratic manners and gentlemanly style impressed him.

Also during the decade of the 1950s Neville performed frequently with the Old Vic at the Edinburgh Festival, where as Neville recalls, there were "very few venues" for performance. Following Guthrie's example the Old

Vic played at the meeting Assembly Hall of the Kirk of Scotland, which provided Neville with the experience of playing annually on the open stage to which he, like Guthrie, also became a convert. Worsley (Financial Times. 31 May, 1960) also says: "Mr. Neville has declared himself publicly and vigorously in favor of the open stage as the only right way of producing Shakespeare; the stage at the Old Vic is not open (and rather curiously, in view of his predilections, he doesn't use the apron at all); but the open stage does lay its mark visibly on his style."

By the end of the second North American tour, Neville believed the time to leave the Old Vic had come. As he said, "I was longing to wear a pair of pants again....I had done six years and...I had never done a modern role." But just as importantly he had reached the conclusion of the five-year plan, and by leaving then he went out as a big success. As he muses, "By that time...I had come to the end. Hamlet was my apotheosis."

Once outside "the sheltered environment" of the Old Vic, he made his first film, *Oscar Wilde*, and he played in a musical comedy in the West End in which he took over the role of Nestor in *Irma La Douce* for six months. He had also reached the point in his career when he had acquired enough stature and maturity to speak about his profession publicly. A letter from Neville about actor training appeared in the *London Times* of 2 January, 1960, in which he says: "I refer to the continuing learning of the craft which...I maintain...can best come from reasonably permanent companies of actors working together on many different types of plays over a long period." This comment, added to those Neville made to a theatre conference in Cambridge a few days later, demonstrates that much of the philosophy behind Neville's 1986 Stratford season was already in place as early as January 1960. In a story in *The London Times* for 8 January, 1960, the Cambridge correspondent reported Neville's speech under the headline "Outspoken Actor as Critic." It said in part:

> We have no producers in our country....We have only Tyrone Guthrie, who is an experimenter. He is the only example we have of a genius at work in the theatre....What we want to get back to is giving the words of Shakespeare on a practically bare stage so that all the emphasis is thrown on the actor and the words....It should be very easy for an actor to make the transition from Shakespeare to musicals....But actors are not properly trained in this country. The kind of acting that is needed in musical comedy is good all-round classical acting. The musicals we have had recently...require proper acting and not this standing about we have been used to.

Neville explains that these ideas came from his concept of actor training.

From the time of his schooling at RADA, he has believed an actor should be able to to go from one end of the scale, classical acting, to the other, musical comedy. He remembers that his success on the musical stage in 1960 astonished some critics, to whom he explained his conviction that most good performers ought to be able to play roles across the whole acting spectrum.

Following his first film, Neville accepted the invitation of his good friend Frank Dunlop in 1961 to come to Nottingham and "spend a little time" in the three months before he was scheduled for some television work. Here he acted in two plays and directed one. He also went on a tour of Malta with the company, playing the title role in *Macbeth* and Sir Thomas More in *A Man For All Seasons*.

He left Nottingham to play in the first Chichester season in a company headed by Laurence Olivier. He played Don Frederick in *The Chances* and Orgilus in *The Broken Heart*. The theatre at Chichester was modeled on the Festival theatre in Stratford, Ontario, with two notable exceptions that both proved damaging to Chichester in his view. The stage is larger and the auditorium is shaped like a saucer so that it spreads out over a great distance, whereas Stratford's auditorium is shaped like a cup and all seats are closer to the stage. If the season was not judged as a critical success due in part to Olivier's play choices, Neville learned anew about playing on another open stage. Also during 1962, he made two more movies, playing the Second Officer in *Billy Budd* as well as a part in *Topaze* with Peter Sellers.

But because he had enjoyed working in Nottingham, he accepted an invitation to join a triumverate charged with running the Nottingham Playhouse. The other two members were Dunlop and Peter Ustinov; Neville recalled that he and Dunlop did most of the day-to-day work. After several years Dunlop left and Neville emerged in sole charge of the playhouse, helping to build the new theatre in addition to his many other duties. During 1962-63 he directed *Twelfth Night* and a musical version of *The Three Musketeers* that he also helped to write and in which he played a leading role. When the construction pace of the new theatre slowed, the British Council, which Neville describes as "the cultural wing of External Affairs," asked him to lead the company on a tour of West Africa. Again he played the title role of *Macbeth*, this time opposite Judy Dench; he also undertook the role of Malvolio in *Twelfth Night*. The tour, which Neville describes as "one of the most exciting things I have ever done," lasted thirteen weeks. The company played in Nigeria, Ghana, and Sierra Leone.

In June of 1963 and with the new Nottingham Playhouse still not ready, Neville created the title role in *Alfie*. He admits feeling somewhat guilty because all he had to do was revert to the native Cockney accent which he had used so successfully as Autolycus in *The Winter's Tale* at the Old Vic. "I had grown up among Alfies, so it wasn't that big a step for me, but the critics all thought so....I'm not like Alfie," he reminisces, "but I know what he is like." The success of *Alfie* again brought Neville a large share of public attention. He enjoyed the then-novel opportunity to speak directly to the audience at times during the play. At times as Neville recalls, "They would answer back, so one had to be a bit of a stand-up comedian...and that appealed to me enormously."

With the new playhouse at Nottingham finally nearing completion, Neville wrote to Guthrie offering him the premiere production. He also enclosed a long list of plays he judged suitable for the occasion, a list headed by *The Alchemist*. Guthrie had done this play several times and instead picked *Coriolanus*, a play not on the list, provided Neville agree to do the title role. Neville agreed and a *Coriolanus* set in the French Empire period opened the new playhouse.

Neville had come to Nottingham as an actor and while there built a solid reputation as a director as well. But as indicative of his future as any of the many roles he played or shows he directed at Nottingham was his success in making the theatre viable. He said that he did it by trial and error. But what he did grew out of his belief that the theatre should be a part of the community, that it should be "a part of people's lives." He constructed his own model for the welding together of the community and the theatre and consciously has attempted to use it, with necessary variations, in each theatre he has headed since that time. He started in Nottingham what he called a "theatre in education" plan, in which he bussed the actors out to schools in the city to interact with the students. Because Nottingham was a coal-mining centre, he invited the company to tour one of the coal mines and experience the reality of working in that environment. But also because Nottingham lay in the heart of industrial England, he arranged a tour of the Raleigh Cycle Factory for the company. They found the noise so deafening in parts of the factory that lip reading proved the only means of communication. With such manoeuvres he succeeded in bonding the theatre to the community, as attested to by the huge following he built with a repertory which included such plays as *The Importance of Being Earnest, Richard II, Oedipus Rex, Saint Joan, Moll Flanders, Measure for Measure* and *Death of a Salesman*. Neville explained that building that audience constituted not only "a challenge for us, but also a challenge for them. They don't want pap; it's insulting to them. I have more respect for them."

But despite the growing audience, he had mounting difficulties keeping both the artistic and financial sides of the house in order. By the spring of 1967, the playhouse faced the prospect of its third season, 1967-68, without an increase in its Arts Council grant. Neville recounts that the Nottingham

Playhouse Board had tried to get an increase and failed to secure it. During the first two years of the government's freeze on grants, Neville had supported the government's stand, since he had voted for the incumbents whose program was, as Neville recounts: "This is a time of restraint...hold on. The grant is not going to be increased...and eventually things will come right." But after several years things hadn't come right, and despite the board's intervention on behalf of the theatre not even a nominal cost of living increase was forthcoming.

The London Times of 20 May, 1967, carried a story about Neville's resignation: "Mr. John Neville...said in a statement released tonight...that his decision to leave his present post comes after an Arts Council refusal to enlarge their grant to his theatre. The playhouse is to get £50,000....Mr. Neville, who led a Playhouse deputation to London, insisted, on £57,000. This was rejected."

A subsequent story, dated 12 August, under the headline "John Neville to Stay At Nottingham," reported, "Miss Lee, Minister for the Arts, told Mr. Neville: 'You are staying in Nottingham and we are supporting you.' Mr. Neville said Miss Lee's statement was one of the major factors in his decision." At that point Neville expected to stay.

But by 14 August *The Times reported*, "Mr. Cyril Forsyth, chairman of Nottingham Theatre Trust, has expressed astonishment at Mr. John Neville's public statement that he has withdrawn his resignation as director of Nottingham Playhouse. Mr. Forsyth said he was 'shocked and amazed.' His board had agreed to accept the resignation and Mr. Neville had been informed by letter." Stories about the resignation and the board's refusal to let him withdraw it abound in the August issues of *The Times*.

Neville has filled in the gaps between the newspaper stories. After the original refusal by the Arts Council, Neville went to see Lord Goodman, head of the council, and told him that the playhouse would go broke without a nominal increase. There, over the table, Lord Goodman gave Neville the increase and he "went back to Nottingham thrilled". But "The board was mortified because they hadn't done it....They never forgave me." So Neville resigned and went back to London, where he again saw Lord Goodman, who said to him, "You mustn't resign. You are in a very important position in this country and...you must go back and retract your resignation." So Neville did go back and retract the resignation, but the board would not accept it. In the furor that followed, theatre administrator Peter Stevens and board member Alderman Charles Butler resigned their positions at Nottingham as well. The Playhouse Club, made up of Nottingham citizens who attended the productions, had swelled to number 3,000 and supported Neville to the extent that it called for the Arts Council to use its influence to fire the board. Some

31

of its members formed the Playhouse Action Group, which eventually issued a pamphlet in support of Neville and lobbied with Members of Parliament. The pamphlet, called *The John Neville Affair*, was written by G. R. Hibbard, who then worked in the Department of English at Nottingham University and has since immigrated to Canada, where he works at the University of Waterloo. Ronald Bryden, who then worked as a drama reviewer at the London-based *Observer* and regularly came to review the work of the playhouse, remembers that he came to Nottingham to help Neville after a call from Hibbard. "We sat around George's kitchen table, plotting revolution and eating cookies," Bryden comments, "but in the end things had gone too far." More importantly Bryden remembers telling Neville that if ever he could assist in getting Neville his own theatre again, he would be happy to do so. Nineteen years after the uproar, a typed copy of a "Statement From The Playhouse Action Committee" could still be found in Bryden's copy of the group's pamphlet. But eventually Neville went and the board stayed at Nottingham.

A 22 August *London Times* article headlined "Neville's Rich Legacy" assessed his success at Nottingham: "If John Neville...leaves the Nottingham Playhouse next July, he will leave behind the not inconsiderable legacy of a ready made audience. In the year ending last month, attendance averaged 83 percent, a figure unequalled at provincial repertory theatres." And Neville has assessed what Nottingham taught him: "I learned a lot," he said, including trusting those instincts which told him to forge the bonds between the theatre and the community. He remembers, "That was the first time I had run anything and I learned how to do it....I learned about having respect for the community and the fact that it is a relationship like a marriage that has to be worked at. You can't ever take it for granted and cannot cheat on them, not sell them short. I learned all those things in those six years."

But he also was quoted on 2 January, 1968 that he could deal with the business as well as the artistic considerations of running a theatre. Under the headline "John Neville Answers Back" he asserted "I am no airy fairie artsie tartsie artist with my head in the clouds," stating that he "never went over budget, so it is a mystery...why the local butcher, baker, and motor mechanic were held to know more about running the theatre than the professionals." But his most provocative statement about the controversy centered on theatre boards and came later. "Can there be an ideal board, small enough to be coherent, large enough to be representative; generous and wise enough to delegate comprehensively, but acute enough to rumble the phony; discreet enough not to interfere, but quick enough to respond to the wishes of its community; average enough to represent the ordinary theatregoer but specific enough to have an insight into the world of professional theatre?" *(Performing Arts in Canada.* Summer 1982).

After leaving Nottingham in late 1967, Neville did some acting in the legitimate theatre and "a great great deal of television...some of it good, like *The First Churchills*....It was a good series, classy, the BBC at its best, but I also did a lot of crap." While he earned a very good living in television, he longed to do something else but had reached the point in his career when he wasn't yet old enough to do the Shakespearean roles he longed to do and hadn't yet done--among them King Lear and the title role in *Antony and Cleopatra*. So he supplemented his television work with stage roles where he could. He played Garrick in *Boswell's Life of Johnson* and Benedick in *Much Ado About Nothing* at the Edinburgh Festival in 1970, as well as touring the United States as Humbert Humbert in *Lolita*, before returning to England for the tenth Chichester season in 1972. This last event was memorable because there he renewed his friendship with Robin Phillips. He played Captain Macheath in a production of *The Beggar's Opera* that Phillips directed and he played Ridgeon in *The Doctor's Dilemma*, a production in which Phillips played Dubedat. "Whatever happened to Neville was outrageously funny," Phillips remembers, including the time a set change revealed him in nothing but a shirt, with a stare for the audience. "Nothing small, nothing tiny" figures in Phillips' memories of Neville. Elspeth Cochrane, stage manager at Stratford during the Festival's early years, remembers a meeting with Neville about this time in which he was contemplating the next step in his career.

The National Arts Center of Ottawa invited Neville to stage a production of *The Rivals* that year. The venture interested him because the show was slated for the Third Space, which he described as "a square space in which you could rearrange these tiered seats in various configurations." The space forced Neville to give this play, so obviously written for a proscenium stage, an open stage treatment. This unusual opportunity intrigued him. He recalls having a superb cast of Canadian performers and a wonderful time: "I never went back to Britain." Neville also recounts being favourably influenced by the calibre of the work in both acting and directing he was offered in Canada, which was not being offered him in Britain.

Following the Ottawa production, he was invited to Winnipeg to do Judge Brack in *Hedda Gabler* and while there he was called back to Ottawa to do Prospero in *The Tempest*. While playing Brack in Winnipeg, he was offered the artistic director's position at the Citadel Theatre in Edmonton, but declined because he had already accepted the role of Prospero. But theatre administrator Joe Shoctor agreed to wait for him to finish his Ottawa engagement. So in May of 1973, he accepted the position at the Citadel, where he ran the theatre from an Old Salvation Army Citadel for three years, during which time the plan to build a new theatre was conceived and executed. He then ran the new theatre for two years before deciding the time had come to move on. He has said of Edmonton:

I feel of all the places I have been in Canada it is my home town. I can't say anything more about it than that. Marvelous people. It's Western. You see that makes a hell of a difference. I don't use the word pejoratively at all, but it was pioneer time and I mean that in the very best sense, in the sense that if you have an idea that's even half decent they are inclined to say, "Great, can we start tomorrow?" Whereas in Britain they are inclined to say, "I think that's been done" or "We don't have the money. Can you just wait?" That's really why I left (Britain), I guess. That's not an attitude that appeals to me in the slightest. I'm interested in doing things, not talking about them.

So Edmonton and Neville agreed with one another: a spirited city seeking an artistic identity, a resourceful administrator, actor, and director in the full zest of his artistic maturity. He and his family became Canadian citizens while residing there, but for Neville Canadian citizenship went beyond the formality of filing the necessary papers. All of the artistic opportunities he'd had since his arrival made Canada the place where he wanted to build his future. So deeply engrained are his feelings about his Canadian citizenship that he still bristles at any suggestion that he is a foreigner.

While the Citadel, in Shoctor's capable hands, had few financial problems, Neville doubled the subscription base from 7,000 to 14,000 by using many of the methods to bring together theatre and community that he had first developed in Nottingham. The old theatre could not accommodate the increased audience size, so he helped complete plans for a new theatre, which had long been the subject of much casual conversation. During the construction phase, he attended a site meeting every Monday morning and immensely enjoyed meeting "the labor force head on." The first production at the new theatre was *Romeo and Juliet*, with Brent Carver (Stratford Festival's 1986 Hamlet) playing Romeo. At Neville's insistence the very first audience invited comprised all the workers who had built the theatre, and a large majority of them accepted Neville's invitation and filled the auditorium on opening night.

Also during his Edmonton years Neville answered a call from his old friend Peter Hall of the National Theatre and returned to Britain in 1975 to play in *Happy Days* with Dame Peggy Ashcroft in a production that Neville then brought to Edmonton. Despite all the positive associations with Edmonton, after the completion of the new theatre Neville again grew restless, believing that he had accomplished what he came to do, and so he left.

He accepted the artistic directorship at the Neptune Theatre in Halifax, again without knowing much about the community before he arrived. The people of Nova Scotia had attitudes much like those found in Britain, Neville recalls. "Oh, I think that's been done," flourished in that older province. He also objected to the "almost arrogant pride in poverty, which I object to because I don't think poverty's good. I don't think it is to be admired at all."

Neville remembers that his repertory at Edmonton and Halifax constituted a mix of popular and classical works. At Edmonton, he says, there was only one theatre and only one card-carrying member of Actor's Equity. That situation called for a mix of plays because he was trying to appeal to a number of different audiences. One of his seasons at the Neptune (criticized as "crass, not class" in *Canadian Theatre Review*, Summer 1980) included *18 Wheels*, a new musical by John Gray, author of *Billy Bishop Goes to War*; *The Taming of the Shrew*; and *The Master Builder*; as well as more popular fare, *How the Other Half Loves* and *Butterflies Are Free*.

When Neville took over the theatre, the debt stood at $180,000. After one season he had reduced the deficit to $72,000. He eventually wiped out the entire deficit and faster than he let on because, as he laughingly acknowledges, when the debt disappears "you get your grant cut." He accomplished this feat, he says, by putting quality work on stage and by again working very hard to make the theatre a part of the community. He also brought in big-name stars for brief periods, such as Tony Randall, who directed *The Master Builder*.

During his second season at the Neptune, Neville had his first official contact with the Stratford Shakespearean Festival during the crisis of 1980, in which Robin Phillips' resignation as artistic director eventually caused a furor. He had been a frequent visitor to Stratford since his arrival in Canada eight years earlier. Neville was invited to interview for the artistic director's job by his old friend Ronald Bryden, of the University of Toronto. Bryden, a member of the Board of Governors of the Festival and a member of the search committee, invited Neville to Stratford to talk about the succession. Neville knew he had promised the Neptune he would stay until the debt was cleared and in his mind he was not free to accept the job should it be offered--a position he believed he had made clear before coming for the interview. The interview took place in May in the Toronto offices of then Festival president Robert Hicks and later in Stratford with various board members and Robin Phillips. All the guidelines for the job were not yet in place. The artistic director might head a committee charged with shaping the Festival's creative direction or he might have sole control. Hicks offered him a position, says Neville, who believes he was offered the top job. Bryden says that even if Neville had become a part of a committee to head the Festival, little doubt existed that Neville would emerge as the guiding spirit. Later at Phillips' home, the two reaffirmed their desire to work together again, both men relate. Discussions went so far as arranging for Phillips to direct some productions at Neptune should Neville decide to come to Stratford, so as not to leave that theatre in the lurch, says Bryden. Obviously, Neville reports, the offer tempted him. But he also reports that in the end, he did not believe he could leave Neptune, a position which he had accepted only a year before. He also points to that theatre's deficit, which he had greatly reduced but not yet eliminated, as the main reason he felt morally obligated to stay at Neptune. He then wrote to Stratford withdrawing himself from consideration. He acknowledges that talk of building a new theatre in Halifax resurfaced as a result of his decision to stay but reaffirms that keeping his word to Neptune played the only role in his decision to stay. But his connection with Stratford during 1980 did not end there. The four-person committee eventually named to replace Phillips, in the person of Martha Henry phoned to ask him to direct a show during the 1981 season, perhaps with William Hutt. Neville agreed, but at the 5 November board meeting, the committee was dismissed, and Neville heard nothing else about directing at Stratford during 1981.

While the issue of the new theatre or arts center to house the Neptune had come to the fore at the time of Neville's original appointment, he says that he believes his first job consisted of filling the old one, accomplished as the subscription base rose. Neville believes he had been assured that the support for a new facility was in place, but when the time came for a commitment, the political support turned soft, even antagonistic, *The Globe and Mail* of 14 September 1984 quotes a Nova Scotia cabinet minister as having said "he wasn't about to bankroll a new theatre just so Neville could caper about the stage in velvet tights." Having had time to assess the situation, Neville submitted his resignation in May 1982, a year before it would become effective. He says, "I wasn't going to go soldiering on in an old cinema building which was beneath my station, really." With the planning completed for the 1982-83 season, he went to New York to portray Pastor Manders in a production of *Ghosts* with Liv Ullman as Mrs. Alving. That production ended unhappily when Director John Madden left during the Washington, D.C., tryout and Neville, who had already refused to take over the direction several times, finally accepted it. But by that time, as his instincts had told him, the production was beyond fixing.

Following his last season in Halifax, he and his wife, unable to find housing in Tornoto, settled on Stratford, although he did not want the assumption made he would work at the Festival. But Michael Langham had been appointed director of the Young Company for the 1983 season, and he asked Neville to play Don Armado in *Love's Labour's Lost* and Leonato in *Much Ado About Nothing* and to assist in actor training. Neville accepted. He spent the 1983-84 season in Robin Phillips' company at the Theatre Grand in London, Ontario, where he directed *Hamlet* with Brent Carver and acted with William Hutt as the two elderly sisters in *Arsenic and Old Lace*, among other roles.

During the 1984 Stratford season, Langham was to redirect a highly successful production of *Love's Labours Lost* on the Festival stage and wanted Neville to recreate his Don Armado, which had so contributed to the play's success. Then when Neville was also offered Shylock in *The Merchant of Venice* and the dual male leads in *Separate Tables* to be staged at the Avon Theatre, he accepted. However, during the 1983 and early 1984 seasons, he became disillusioned with the overall quality of work being done and decided not to return to Stratford for another season when the interview with Bryden and Herrndorf caused him to re-think his plans.

"For 'tis a meritorious fair design...."
The Rape of Lucrece 1692

Chapter Three: The Season Design

Neville says he had stressed two related goals in his talks with the Stratford Shakespearean Festival Board in 1984: to restore both financial and artistic footing securely, since at Nottingham Playhouse and the Neptune Theatre he had inherited a considerable deficit. Although he would not take over the operation of the Festival until 1 November, 1985, he knew, barring a financial miracle during the 1985 season, that he would take over his third debt-ridden theatre. Because of his experience in dealing with financial problems, he specifically asked the board what could be done about this one, a question for which there was no answer, he says. "To that end, no matter who was responsible for it, the decifit is always yours." Festival General Manager Gary Thomas explains that the Festival held securities that could be sold at maturity in order to retire the liability. Columnist Gina Mallet reports: "Even the $2.8-million accumulated deficit was controllable because a $2.9-million endowment fund set up in 1980 could start being drawn upon in 1985." (Mallet, Gina. "As Stratford's World Turns." *Toronto*, April 1986, p. 96). (The Wintario program of provincial arts challenge grants had matched funds raised by the Festival).

In the meanwhile the interest payments on that debt would continue to hamper the artistic director by claiming a portion of the revenue that might otherwise go into the productions. Neville lost two productions from the 1986 season as a direct result of the budget crunch, Strindberg's *Dance of Death*, in which he had hoped to star with Liv Ullman, and a Molière play with which he had hoped to lure Peter Ustinov back to Stratford. While Thomas explains that neither star had agreed to appear in Stratford prior to the board meeting which approved the 1986 season--and the board did not want to approve the shows without the stars. Producer Richard Dennison, who handled contract negotiations for Neville while serving as director of production during the planning of the 1986 season, says that if the money had been available these stars or others would have been, also. But Neville agreed to withdraw the productions because he wanted to design a season that would come in at or under budget.

Neville acknowledges that he had a further problem in that the Festival had produced almost all of the most popular Shakesperean comedies in the previous five years. Yet while offering the plays with the biggest potential box office appeal, the 1981, 1983, and 1984 seasons had not produced enough revenue to meet expenses. So Neville proposed producing three of the four Shakespearean romances on the stage of the Festival Theatre during the 1986 season. Although he wanted to do *The Tempest* as well, that romance had been seen on the stage in 1982. Part of the appeal of such a grouping, he believes, stems from their seldom being produced anywhere: The Festival had last produced *The Winter's Tale* in 1978, but *Pericles* had not been seen since 1974 and *Cymbeline* since 1970. If that choice seemed daring given the Festival's precarious financial standing, Festival Archivist Dan Ladell puts the situation in perspective by saying that the only other Shakespearean choices Neville had before him included a season of tragedies or histories. Neville takes seriously the Festival's mandate to produce the entire canon because he believes people do not want to see the same plays done over and over again. In this light the romances made more sense from a box office perspective than did another repetition of the same war horses. Resident director Robert Beard says that Neville's decision to hinge his first season on the romances proved the most revolutionary choice he made. Beard contends that the romances compose a very difficult part of Shakesperean's work to produce successfully and that few companies tackle them for exactly that reason. If Neville's primary goals consisted of improving the Festival's financial picture and raising its artistic quality, in *The Winter's Tale*, *Pericles*, and *Cymbeline* he had chosen a season that would strictly test his artistic and administrative skills.

In putting together the season for the Avon Theatre, Neville explains the choice of *Henry VIII*, last produced in 1961 at the Festival Theatre, by maintaining that the play, although not a romance, comes from the same final phase of Shakespeare's writing as do the romances with which it shares themes of reconciliation and forgiveness. He decided on *Hamlet*, last seen at the Festival in 1975, because it had box office potential and because he knew a young actor to whom he wanted to extend another opportunity to play the title role. Once he had settled on these two selections, he remembers, coming up with the idea of adding a companion piece to play opposite each did not take long. *A Man For All Seasons* and *Rosencrantz and Guildenstern Are Dead* are products of contemporary writers but explore some of the enigmas in Shakespeare's plays.

Neville also took a different approach to producing the Festival's musical. Each year between 1981 and 1985 the Avon Theatre had been home to at least one Gilbert and Sullivan operetta: *H.M.S. Pinafore* in 1981, *The Mikado* in 1982, *The Mikado* and *The Gondoliers* in 1983, *The Mikado, The Gondoliers*, and *Iolanthe* in 1984, and *The Pirates of Penzance* in 1985. These highly successful operas had played to excellent notices and nearly packed houses, making them a triumph on both the artistic and financial sides of the ledger. Between 1982 and 1984, the productions bore the credits for direction and choreography by Brian Macdonald, musical direction and additional arrangements by Berthold Carriere, and costume and set design by Susan Benson. Macdonald and Carriere teamed up again in 1985 and again got rave reviews. Neville wanted to continue the musical tradition but says that he wanted "to give the Gilbert and Sullivan" a rest, and Ladell defends Neville's point by saying that the Festival had already staged all of the major G&S works. Neville wanted to switch not only the music but also the theatre, since he believes many of the music patrons who had attended the productions at the Avon had never seen the inside of the Festival Theatre. He contends that once inside that impressive theatre they might come back for the other shows staged there. Also, the Festival Theatre has more than 2,200 seats and the Avon fewer than 1,200. Some of the risk of doing three romances in the larger house could be offset by moving the musical there as well.

The next logical question involved what kind of musical to produce. Neville explains that, apart from the four performances of *Candide* staged at the Festival in 1978, no musical had ever been presented on that stage. Even *Candide* played the majority of its nearly thirty performances at the Avon. Neville thought it fitting that the first musical staged entirely in the Festival Theatre take its plot from a Shakespearean play, thereby linking it with tradition. *The Boys From Syracuse* and *Kiss Me, Kate* immediately suggested themselves because of their Shakespearean heritage. Neville says that he has always liked *The Boys From Syracuse* and offered the direction to Macdonald, who believed the play needed some major rewriting and preferred to do *Kiss Me, Kate*. As events worked out, the Royal Shakespeare Company took an option on *Kiss Me, Kate* and the play was not available to the Stratford Festival. Macdonald thought about directing *The Boys From Syracuse* for a long time before turning it down, says Neville.

The two plays that were to be offered by the Young Company at its headquarters in the Kiwanis building, known as the Third Stage, reflected the choices of 1986 Young Company director Tom Kerr. He also chose to match a modern play, Brecht's *The Resistible Rise of Arturo Ui*, with a Shakespearean classic, *Macbeth*, both of which explore the nature of tyranny. With the selection of these two plays the repertory for the season was complete. When interviewed at the end of the 1986 season, Beard recalls that Neville sought much more consultation from his associate directors and other members of his team about the 1987 season than he had about 1986.

Neville says that during the year in which he served as artistic director designate, he, Dennison, and Beard had to put the season together pretty much on their own because the other members of his ensemble were not yet available. With the repertory at least pencilled in place, drawing up a balanced budget became the next priority.

Thomas explains that the budget was planned by Neville, former producer Peter Roberts, finance committee chairman Murray Frum, and himself. He also acknowledges the help of John Hayes, who retired as executive producer of the Festival in 1983 but who has returned several times since to lend his expertise in the budgeting process. Thomas explains that much of the budget consists of fixed expenses--utilities, for example--so the biggest single area of flexible costs remains production. Neville had decided not to employ a separate musical company, a payroll saving, yet he stresses his view that a classical acting company ought to be able to sing and dance in a musical as well. Perhaps remembering his own West End success in *Irma La Douce*, and while acknowledging that not every classical company member has those additional talents, Neville says that using the same company to do *The Boys From Syracuse* and the three romances moved his beliefs concerning the versatility of classically trained actors from theory to practice.

If the smaller size of the company would reduce costs, the change from one administration to another--with different working methods and costs which arise from doing things for the first time--made building in money to handle these contingencies necessary, says Dennison. Both he and Thomas credit Hayes with helping to build these hedges into the budget. Hayes notes that costuming continually comes in as one of the most expensive units in production and that a costume budget is a fixed part of each designer's contract. In 1986 he estimated that costumes for all productions would cost on average $1,850 each to make. He judged that because the costumes for *Henry VIII* would have to be so much more elaborate than those for any of the other shows they would cost $2,200 each. Designers in 1986 were required to pull twenty-five percent of the costumes from stock, but even then, altering an existing costume cost $750. By adding a few more costumes to the production budget for each show than the designer would actually need to build, Hayes put a reserve into that budget, which nonetheless increased. Everybody connected with the budgeting process points out that the board requires a balanced budget be submitted. Because the budget makers knew the size of the various federal, provincial, and local government grants, and because the amount of money for the fund-raising arm of the Festival could be projected using its past record, they had to determine that the balance of money needed to operate the Festival would come in at the box office, says Hayes. The 1986 budget called for $14.2 million in expenses, which pushed box office projections to $9.9 million.

Neville also made another decision about cutting costs which impacted on the 1986 season. That decision grew out of conversations he had with designer Phillip Silver while the two commuted by train from Stratford to London to participate in the Grand Theatre's 1983-84 season under then artistic director Robin Phillips. Silver says that Neville asked him one day why production costs at the Avon Theatre were rising so sharply. He recalls telling Neville that fellow designer Desmond Heeley had been asked by John Hirsch to redesign that space; it had been used by Phillips during his tenure as a black box after a design by Daphne Dare. Heeley's plan discarded the raised stage, painted the proscenium arch a lighter colour, and embellished its walls with gold-painted trim work. Silver says that he believed such a design raised an expectation of a theatrical grandeur which designers sought to incorporate into their renderings, thereby increasing costs. Neville gave Silver the go-ahead to change the Avon in order to bring down the cost of building sets, using a simpler design that also featured the raised stage to improve sight lines. His black box concept called for four black "towers," including the walls of the procensium arch, to rise out of the floor in matched pairs on each side of the stage. These functioned like tormentors, or curtains, in that they masked the entrances and exits of the performers while lending a visual balance to the stage. Silver provided a choice of backdrop or cyclorama, given greater exposure when upstage towers were played in open position. The black covering for the stage floor, the towers, and the backdrop provided a uniform look to the stage that could be painted with coloured light on the cyclorama against the neutral black expanse of the stage. In addition, painting the walls of the proscenium arch and the house the same dark colour eliminated the traditional break between house and stage. Some of the gold trim work was added back to the proscenium arch to visually enliven it, Silver says. Although the black box concept was designed to serve as the background on which sets for individual shows could be mounted over a number of seasons, the money for the project had to come entirely from the scenery budget for the 1986 season, so the set designers at the Avon during the 1986 season had to operate with reduced budgets. While Silver says that he hoped to design in the space he had created in 1986, he also says he did not want to know what shows would be mounted there or for which ones he might have design responsibilities while working on this design because he wanted to concentrate his efforts on a plan which would work as the background for a broad range of shows. Recalling a quip about having to redecorate the palace for each palace revolution, Silver says that sensitivity to the issue of money kept the project under wraps until late August.

The issue of money also worried then board president Peter Herrndorf, who personally led a 1985 fund drive in addition to the one the Festival's campaign office conducted. On 8 August, 1985, about a week before the board meeting at which a vote would be taken on the budget for Neville's first season, Herrndorf mused on the problem in his Toronto office. Neville's know-how and ingenuity would take him about thirty percent of the way, Herrndorf reasoned, but for the rest he would need money. A few hours later and 161 kilometres to the southwest, Neville lunched on a bowl of vissychoise and summed up his view of the approaching season, "With so many problems, it's best not to be too optimistic." Neville describes this period as the lowest point in his year of waiting.

Mallet reports in hyperbole that Neville's 1986 plans "had jittery board members hanging off the rafters" (Mallet, p. 61). Herrndorf more circumspectly says that some board members questioned whether it made any sense from a box office point of view to do three romances in one season. They also questioned whether the expense side of the budget had been lowballed while revenue projections were set too high. As a result, according to Herrndorf, that budget got more board scrutiny than any other Festival budget "with which I have been associated." Herrndorf also says that he took "great pains" to point out to the board the series of assumptions that underlay the budget, including the possibility that Macdonald might not be part of the season as well as revenue projections based in part on the untested appeal of the romances. In the end the board approved the budget. Beard describes Neville's position with the board throughout their discussions of the 1986 season by saying Neville had a very clear idea about what he wanted to do from very early on. He kept emphasizing to the board his commitment to the lesser known plays, explaining that if they wanted him, they wanted this kind of season. Beard believes that his "unwaffling" persistence proved the decisive factor in winning the board's confidence.

Following the board meeting, Herrndorf says, he and Gerry Eldred had a lunch with Macdonald at The Old Prune, a popular Stratford restaurant, in a final and unsuccessful attempt to convince the latter that it made sense for him to work with Neville. An angry letter from Macdonald to Neville was not read at the board meeting by Herrndorf or given by him to any media; Martin Knelman later wrote about it in the April 1986 issue of *Toronto Life*. (Under terms of an agreement with the magazine, Herrndorf does not see articles about Stratford in his magazine until they are in print.)

In lining up his company for 1986, Neville stressed his commitment to Canadian theatre people. Indeed, eight of the nine directors hired for the season were Canadian, while the ninth, David William, had worked extensively if not exclusively in Canada. But, Neville adds, if he could attract some star performers from in or outside the country who would contribute to the quality of the work done at Stratford and at the same time provide box office appeal, he wanted to do so. When board members began to question him about the absence of stars from the season, Neville says, he prepared a list of stars with whom discussions about coming to Stratford in 1986 had taken place. In some cases the discussions had not gone beyond an initial contact, while in other instances they had been long and protracted. Neville provided a copy of that list for inclusion here. The persons contacted but not contracted include: Alan Arkin, Bernard Behrens, Salome Bey, Richard Chamberlain, Glenn Close, John Colicos, Donald Davis, Judy Dench, Peter Donat, Albert Finney, Jane Fonda, Mel Gibson, Ron Glass, Sir Peter Hall, Roland Hewgill, Anthony Hopkins, William Hurt, Jeff Hyslop, Jeremy Irons, Ray Jewers, Stacey Keatch, Kevin Kline, Barry MacGregor, Des McAnuff, Louise Marleau, Albert Millaire, Richard Monette, Kate Nelligan, Mike Nichols, Christopher Reeve, Kate Reid, Diana Rigg, Alan Scarfe, Maggie Smith, Donald Sutherland, Peter Ustinov, Ken Welsh, and Jack Wetherall. Dennison says that the Festival failed to lure some of the big-name performers because of the long-term contract and the larger salaries paid by the televison and film industries. Consequently, says Dennison, Neville devised a plan during 1986 which called for using a big-name performer in a show with a limited run, a plan which Dennison expects to see implemented in 1988. With a budget in hand, Neville, Dennison, and Beard began the process of hiring a company. Neville explains that because of the possibility of touring two shows playing at the Avon to Expo 86 in Vancouver during the season, separate acting companies had to be formed at the Avon and Festival Theatres, although the tour did not materialize. Neville, Beard, and Dennison started with the top people on their list, attempting, according to associate director Richard Ouzounian, who directed *Pericles*, to pair leading roles in each company with the assent of the directors involved. Beard explains that they put together what they considered an interesting list of parts for an individual and then waited to see if the performer found them as exciting. Dennison says that Neville left all contracting to him, requiring that the board's budget be met. Sometimes, he confesses, agreements failed over very small sums of money but believes that tiny amounts, when added up across all areas of the Festival, had the potential to become a big obstacle to Neville's plans for a balanced budget.

Neville and Beard concede that improving the quality of the artistic product becomes much more difficult to plan and measure than did improving the organization's fiscal standing. Beard compares directing a play to cooking a meal: "You can shop very well, have an exciting recipe, use only the best ingredients, and still cook a lousy stew," he laments. He says considerable time went into matching a director's strengths with the needs of the play and an actor's assets with the other two. That process proved more difficult when agreement could not always be reached with persons whose talents suggested them as the answer to the season's needs. But in the end it worked: Ouzounian, discussing his leading man, Geraint Wyn Davies, says "That I am big, blond, and outgoing, and that Gerr is big, blond, and outgoing is no accident."

Beyond finding the blend of talent, keeping an open and communicative atmosphere in the rehearsal hall is about all an administrator can do to ensure a quality product at the end of the processs, says Beard. Neville visited rehearsals and so, more frequently, did Beard. Neville gave his comments to each director and offered to talk over ideas and solutions to problems, thereby, says Beard, he hoped to avoid becoming known as the "hatchet man."

The period of more than a year between Neville's appointment as artistic director designate and his assumption of control as artistic director he calls "the worst year of my life." Mallet reports personal animosity between Neville and outgoing artistic director John Hirsch, who, she says, never wanted Neville to succeed him. (Mallet, p. 60). Neville simply says, "John Hirsch and I cannot be cast in the same play." While a number of issues caused tension, the planned American tour of the 1985 company taking two productions (*King Lear* and *Twelfth Night*) to six American cities proved a special irritant to Neville. Hirsch, who had originally directed *King Lear*, redirected both productions, originally performed on the Festival Stage, for the proscenium arch houses the company would encounter on the tour; on 1 November, 1985, when John Neville took over as artistic director of the Stratford Festival, his company was on the road 3,000 miles away producing two plays directed by his predecessor.

Herrndorf acknowledges that problems existed between the two men but believes that both behaved honourably. He sees no heroes or villains in the piece but rather two men caught in the pressures and circumstances of performing their roles within the Festival. He believes that having an artistic director designate in place for a year might work particularly well in a situation where the new man was a protegee of the retiring artistic director. That system does not work so well, he points out, in situations where the two men have differences in philosophy, leaderhip styles, and goals for the organization. Whatever the down side, the 1986 season was planned, approved, and announced earlier than any in his memory in the last ten years.

With his season, budget, and company in place at last, John Neville spent his winter vacation reading Dickens' *Bleak House* on the beaches of the Caribbean island of Grenada, where he escaped a particularly snowy portion of Stratford's 1985-86 winter.

"There it begins."
Cymbeline V.5.179

Act One: The Avon Company

HAMLET

BY WILLIAM SHAKESPEARE

DIRECTED BY	JOHN NEVILLE
DESIGNED BY	SUE LEPAGE
MUSIC BY	ALAN LAING
LIGHTING DESIGNED BY	LOUISE GUINAND
FIGHTS DIRECTED BY	JEAN-PIERRE FOURNIER

THE CAST

in order of appearance

Francisco	CHRISTOPHER THOMAS
Barnardo	JEAN-PIERRE FOURNIER
Marcellus	PETER DONALDSON
Horatio	LORNE KENNEDY
Ghost	DAVID SCHURMANN
Claudius	JAMES BLENDICK
Gertrude	ELIZABETH SHEPHERD
Laertes	SCOTT WENTWORTH
Polonius	RICHARD CURNOCK
Hamlet	BRENT CARVER
Ophelia	LUCY PEACOCK
Lady in Waiting	HAZEL DESBARATS
Rosencrantz	KEITH DINICOL
Guildenstern	WILLIAM DUNLOP
Player King	RON HASTINGS
Player Prologue	NOLAN JENNINGS
Player Queen	IAN WATSON
Player Lucianus	PETER DONALDSON
Player	JEAN-PIERRE FOURNIER
Fortinbras	PETER DONALDSON
Captain	LEON POWNALL
Osrick	DAVID BROWN
First Gravedigger	ERIC HOUSE
Second Gravedigger	IAN WATSON
Priest	MAX HELPMANN
Ambassador	DANIEL BUCCOS
Courtiers, Servants, Soldiers, Pallbearers, Ladies in Waiting:	KEVIN CORK, KEITH DINICOL, WILLIAM DUNLOP, MICHAEL FAWKES, JEAN-PIERRE FOURNIER, CHRISTOPHER GIROTTI, DOLORA HARVEY, RON HASTINGS, MAX HELPMANN, NOLAN JENNINGS, CAMILLE MITCHELL, JOHN NELLES, LEON POWNALL, CHRISTOPER THOMAS, ERIC TRASK, IAN WATSON
Stage Manager	MICHAEL BENOIT
Assistant Stage Managers	SUSAN KONYNENBURG, MARYLU MOYER
Assistant Director	MEG WESTLEY
Assistant Designer	JULIA TRIBE
Assistant Lighting Designer	ELIZABETH ASSELSTINE

Ophelia: "'Tis brief, my lord."
Hamlet: "As woman's love."
Hamlet III.2.162-163

Chapter Four: *Hamlet*

For some of the actors who stumbled into Rehearsal Hall 1 of the Avon Theatre for the beginning of rehearsals for *Hamlet* at 10 a.m. on 3 February, 1986, the first day on the new job felt more like an end than a beginning. These actors had returned from the American tour which had brought them to Stratford in the middle of the night, and here, less than eight hours later, they assembled to answer the first call of the infant season. Many of these returning veterans wore blue sweatshirts with the slogans "Lear for a year" and "The wonder is we have endured so long," on reverse sides. While some of these actors dealt with a sense of dislocation, at the other end of the spectrum others new to the Festival, veterans who did not go on tour, or those returning after an absence of several years searched for familiar faces. When John Neville strode through the door at 9:47 a.m., the 1986 season began in earnest for the acting company.

Neville moved about the room greeting people in turn before beginning the rehearsal by announcing two administrative promotions, which would affect the company. Robert Beard, former company manager, had been promoted to resident director. His new job, explained Neville, was to ensure that *Hamlet*, which would run three hours on opening night, would not close at three and a half hours. (Beard would later joke that in his new job he did everything but windows.) Neville then announced that Festival house manager Ron Nichol would move up to company manager as well. For Nichol, the addition of the new post meant a year-round job with the Festival. (Nichol held both jobs throughout the 1986 season.) Actors were then instructed to go to a series of tables set up around the room, with the resulting movement resembling that in a medieval play staged in front of "mansions." These modern-day mansions bore the names "wardrobe," where an actor's measurements were checked against those provided in his or her contract, so that costume construction could began in early January; "wigs," where head sizes were checked; "boots," where an outline of the performer's stocking foot was taken; "payroll," where the financial forms were filled

51

out; and "accommodations," where housing requests were taken. Stage manager Michael Benoit passed out cut copies of the script, the season brochure showing dates of all performances, and an in-house booklet containing useful information about the Festival and the town.

Neville and designer Sue LePage then introduced the production design to the cast, a model of the stage constructed to mirror Phillip Silver's black box design and to which LePage had added the scale-model equivalents of the series of platforms and set pieces she had designed for *Hamlet* and *Rosencrantz and Guildenstern Are Dead*. Neville explained that LePage's arrangement of the platforms should remind one of those on the Festival Stage. LePage mentioned the ease with which the platform setting would travel should a tour be forthcoming. At the mention of the word "tour," LePage had the full attention of the tour-weary veterans, who looked so startled that Neville laughed out loud. Immediately the whispering began.

"Does your contract say anything about a tour?"

"I don't know. We just got in last night. I haven't even seen my contract. I don't even know how much money I'm making."

"I don't know about you, but I'm not touring!"

LePage stressed that both plays will be set in 1905. Although *Hamlet* will stay very Danish, she said, the period before World War I captures that time just before the end of the Prussian military power at which she and Neville wanted strongly to hint with this production. Rosencrantz and Guildenstern, she said, will introduce the fencing gear when they arrive at court, and its continued association with this pair will properly prepare for the fencing bout at the end of the play.

To suggest through costuming the transition from the close of the Nineteenth Century to the opening of the modern era, the play will begin with very formal, elegant costumes but will begin fairly quickly to slide into the 1905 version of the three-piece suit. LePage and her design assistant, Julia Tribe, laid the costume sketches on the floor and the actors walked around them, looking first for individual costumes and then for a sense of the visual sweep of the whole show.

LePage, who took a degree in English with a drama major at Guelph University, says that on coming out of that program in 1973 she made application to Stratford and was immediately put to work with a glue gun in a season in which she also worked as a costume painter. She explains that she came to design out of a love of theatre, rather than through an extensive art background. She recalls that the designers of her first year at the Festival included: Desmond Heeley, Annena Stubbs, John Ferguson, and Leslie Hurry. After a year in Europe spent partly at the Edinburgh Festival, LePage came back to Stratford in 1975 to make boots and shoes. By this time she had begun to work as an assistant designer at other theatres and had spent an additional season at Stratford as a costume painter. Later she reappeared at Stratford as a costume painter and applied for a position as a designer by showing her portfolio to the then head of design, Daphne Dare. She assisted Dare on several shows and finally was asked to design costumes for *The Beggar's Opera* in 1980, with Dare designing sets and Robin Phillips directing. She came back to Stratford in 1983 to design Edward Atienza's one-man show, *When that I Was...*, which came originally from the National Arts Center in Ottawa, where LePage had done the original design. When the show appeared on the Festival schedule that year, she partly redesigned her original concept to fit her setting into Desmond Heeley's redesigned performance space at Third Stage, which was also new that year. LePage had also worked with Neville during the 1983-84 season in London.

Neville called her in late August asking her to attend a meeting with him and John Wood, who had drawn the directing assignment for *Rosencrantz and Guildenstern Are Dead* using the same set and the same costumes as Neville's production of *Hamlet*. She recalls that while Neville spoke in vague terms, he did ask her if she could take the early morning train to Stratford the next day for the preliminary conference. Once in Stratford a look at their schedules confirmed that they could work together. She suspects that having worked with both directors previously weighed in her favour.

The next major problem involved Wood's imminent departure for England. Since his directing assignment there would prevent his return to Stratford until after the Festival's deadline for design submissions had passed, LePage relates, most of the basic design work for both shows fell due within the next ten days. Wood and Neville had already had a series of talks about the plays before LePage's appointment. While she recalls she did not participate in those first discussions, because she had been an assistant designer on a production of *Hamlet* which Wood had directed at Halifax almost ten years ago and she had seen Neville's 1983 production of *Hamlet* at the Grand Theatre, she could enter into the discussion with a pretty good understanding of what each director saw as the essence of the major characters. She also enjoyed the give and take of the discussions, with any idea grist for the mill. Each went away and did homework; later discussions, she says, were so interesting that she sat "with her heart in her mouth." Only after she returned to Toronto and unrolled her drafting paper did she realize that while the conversations had proved invigorating she still had to translate very quickly all of that energy and vitality into a single approach toward designing the productions.

The two directors asked her to consider late Nineteenth Century style as somewhere between 1860 and 1914, and the library showed her what that span of years would mean for the look of each character. Eventually 1905 emerged as the year they would use because it set the play on the cusp "between the fall of old European chivalry and the rise of Twentieth Century efficiency." She also says that in choosing a period for the play they agreed that they wanted a period whose costumes would enchance the physical attractiveness of the characters. She points out that a Festival audience which also watched television should find these 1905 costumes make the characters look more appealing than the usual run of modern clothes.

LePage had not completed final costume renderings before Wood left for England, but preliminary decisions made about each character had given a definite shape to the whole of the design concept. LePage believed that Wood had a firm idea about what direction the final costume and scenic environment for the two productions would take. In considering the milieu, she remembers that Neville wanted to give the production a more contemporary feeling so that young audience members did not experience undue alienation from the look and feel of a world which seemed foreign to their own, especially when he believes the play centers on characters and emotions which directly relate to today's world, she says. On the other hand, they decided once they had agreed to update the piece that they would do a very straight production of *Hamlet* because playing *Rosencrantz and Guildenstern Are Dead* at the next performance provided a large twist of its own without adding another to the production of *Hamlet*. Partly for that reason, explains LePage, the production team decided not to do a "Woody Allen treatment" of the play, a study in modern neurosis that some productions attempt in the guise of contemporary relevance.

LePage says she got a peek at Silver's plans for the black box environment at the Avon very early in the design process and immediately embraced the concept as a method for both saving money and upholding the high standards of visual presentation for which the design arm of the Festival has earned its renown. The final design for the platform stage used in the two productions, says LePage, looks very simple, so in September, once the basic decisions had taken shape, LePage came back to the setting to see if she had accomplished anything more than solving the basic problems. Each time the question arose in her mind, she went back and changed the setting around and each time came back to basically the original setting with only a small modification or two. But while small, these changes justified to her mind the time spent rethinking her basic concept.

Because final design deadlines carried a November date, Neville approved most of them with an occasional letter or phone call to Wood to inform him of changes in the plan, says LePage. By December, Wood had returned from England and, even more significantly for LePage, much of the casting had taken place. She did not even want to think about colours, she says, until she knew if the production would feature a dark or blonde beauty as Gertrude. But once the casting reached completion she finished her designs quickly and she and Tribe went out to buy fabric before Christmas. Because the costumes in *Hamlet* create all of the elements of the world of the play while those in *Rosencrantz and Guildenstern Are Dead* create these two characters and their nightmares, designs for *Hamlet* remained her first concern, with modifications only needed for *Rosencrantz and Guildenstern Are Dead*. The costumes for the characters of Rosencrantz and Guildenstern went through the most changes, says LePage. The colours for *Hamlet* were blue, gray, burgundy and non-earth colours. When she moved to *Rosencrantz and Guildenstern Are Dead* she used the convention that the non-earth colours of *Hamlet* seemed very artificial, so the world of Rosencrantz and Guildenstern made greater use of browns and tans. She cautions that the concept could not be taken too far because she did not want a nice honeycomb-coloured world as the backdrop for the terrible events that happen in that play.

After the design presentation on the first day of rehearsal Neville dismissed the actors for the noon break; actor Michael Fawkes quipped that they would have to wait for the read-through after lunch to find out who gets the girl. But Neville never held a formal read-through of the play. He says that as an actor he found it helpful to move on the set as quickly as possible, especially in cases where everyone knew the script in advance. By the time the lunch break came, the general attitude toward a possible tour had softened to something resembling Scarlett O'Hara's "I'll think about that tomorrow," and by the end of the first day whispered opposition had melted away. Actors declared they knew they would appreciate the extra work by the end of the season even if they found the idea a difficult one at present.

Neville explained often to the company that although he and Brent Carver, who played Hamlet, had done the play before, they both considered this production a new voyage of discovery. To that end they based no decision on prior productions except to play Hamlet as if he were feigning madness rather than actually mad because it gives the character more options. But all other decisions had yet to be made, he assured the cast.

According to Neville, the disillusionment of youth formed the hinge on which exploration of other decisions about the play took place. When one grows older, one comes to expect a certain discrepancy between what others say and do; but, he says, the young feel the pinch of the inconsistencies more acutely than do their elders. He recalls that he had used this idea as the framework for his Hamlet at the Old Vic and appreciates its continued relevance. Neville's directing style featured showing the actors the part of the stage to be used for a particular scene and having them read the scene several times using blocking that he had given them as a starting point. This process gives actors a movement pattern wherein they can walk about the stage exploring the lines. He says that from his experience an actor needs the security of a set blocking scheme at the opening of rehearsals. Blocking must help the actors grow, he says, and after actors had several opportunities to explore each scene, he began to explain the shape of individual scenes to them, giving ample time for questions or comments about his interpretation. Often his choice for the individual scenes came from what the actors brought to the scene, rather than from a predetermined blueprint. Once an interpretation had been chosen, blocking and line readings were sometimes reshaped to match the agreed-upon plan. Neville remained open to actors' comments and suggestions, altering the shape of scenes several times to include what he regarded as valuable suggestions from company members. Early in the rehearsal process he would begin working a scene by having the actors read it first at a table in the corner of the rehearsal hall. At other times he used this technique when several days had passed between rehearsals. He explains that what emerges from a reading at the table can have a very different look and feel from what happens on the rehearsal hall floor, so he uses instinct as a guide about when to employ this technique.

After the play has taken on a physical shape, a blocking plan determined by the overall concept, Neville's next step consisted of giving the individual moments or beats within that scene a vocal shape by determining which parts will be louder or softer, faster or slower. At times during rehearsals for *Hamlet*, he says, the actors' instincts gave a proper shape and he did not have to say anything. At other times he asked for a particular reshaping of an individual beat. Once the vocal shape was set, he says, the rest of the process was smoothing out the rough edges.

For the first three weeks of February, the Avon company solely rehearsed *Hamlet*, although four actors had contractual obligations elsewhere. Devising a rehearsal schedule which allowed Neville to run consecutive scenes for Neville tested Beniot. At Neville's suggestion, by the end of the first full week of rehearsal, Wood began to work with the two actors playing Rosencrantz and Guildenstern (Keith Dinicol and William Dunlop) when they were not called for *Hamlet* rehearsal. Rehearsals for *Rosencrantz and Guildenstern Are Dead* would not open until 24 February, but Neville wanted the two actors to begin to develop their characters for that show so he could fit those conceptions into his production. Because *Henry VIII* opened rehearsals a week later, on 3 March, and because both actors had parts in that show as well, having Wood use the two actors during the early weeks when they did not have another call only made sense.

Interest ran high among the cast members in watching Carver's Hamlet take shape and develop. He concentrated his first three weeks on this work and says that he brought a number of different Hamlets to the rehearsal process but gradually reduced the number and fleshed out the remaining ones. As a result the Hamlet that eventually emerged on 25 March, seven weeks after rehearsals had started, was a carefully considered choice--Hamlet the actor, playing first one role and then another in order to mask his real intent until he finally performs it.

In 1984 Carver had played Hamlet for Neville at the Grand Theatre in London from January to May. A little over six months later, Neville was offering him the opportunity to play Hamlet again at Stratford in 1986, in a production which would not go into rehearsals for almost another fifteen months. Carver says he realized that he would then be two years older, with Hamlet having had two years to set. Also knowing that Neville's interests would change during that period caught Carver's inquisitiveness. Together they would have the opportunity to do the production from a fresh perspective. While waiting to start Stratford rehearsals, he had accepted the role of the pirate king in *The Pirates of Penzance* for the 1985 Stratford season. Over the course of that season, he became an admirer of voice coach Patsy Rodenburg and spent ten days in England working with her on speaking verse during the 1985-86 winter in preparation for doing *Hamlet* again. During the fifteen months between his conversation with Neville and the start of 1986 rehearsals, Carver says, he tried to put the role out of his mind until the time came when he knew he couldn't do so any longer. Even during the time he didn't think consciously about playing Hamlet, he says, "It was always there on the back burner, quietly simmering away." By late August of 1985, he knew he could no longer postpone a more active approach to the Danish prince. At that point, he read and re-read the script and the mountain of critical comment about the play and its title character, he explains. The play culminates in the famous fencing bout in Act V, Scene 2, which occupied a prominent position in rehearsal from the beginning of the second week when Jean-Pierre Fournier arrived to be fight master for *Hamlet, Pericles, Macbeth,* and *Cymbeline*. An affiliate member of the Society of British Fight Directors, Fournier has been a stage combat instructor for Canada's Royal Winnipeg Ballet and several Canadian universities, coming to Stratford from the National Theatre School in Montreal. With Fournier in place, the duel led off the morning's rehearsal on Monday, 10 February, and played a prominent role in the lives of the two actors--Carver and Scott Wentworth (Laertes)--through 18 October, the last performance of the play. Even after the actors learned the fight's many sequences, they always practised it prior to a performance. Fournier began with diagrams of the different fencing positions, from numbers one through eight, and demonstrated them for the actors. After having helped the actors select foils that properly fit their individual grips, he led them through the positions and eventually began to choreograph the duel for them. He had written the entire fight on paper with a vertical line down the middle: Laertes' moves were recorded to the left of the line and Hamlet's to the right of it. Fournier stressed that the fight, which would eventually go very quickly, would begin very slowly. Thereafter a part of each day's rehearsal was given over to the rehearsal of the duel, and Fournier's most frequent instruction became "Slow it down!" Because the fight was staged on the flat rehearsal hall floor where coloured tape marked the positions of the platform stage, concern soon surfaced about what would happen when the time came to play it on the raked stage and series of platforms which would form the set for *Hamlet*. Consequently Thursday, 13 March, the first day on the raked stage with the platforms in place, proved a great relief to all. The first part of the scheduled rehearsal involved the fight, and both Carver and Wentworth pronounced themselves comfortable with the duel, which had undergone only a few slight alterations under Fournier's careful attention as a result of playing on the actual set in the Avon theatre.

As rehearsals began the stage of the Avon Theatre had been occupied by a silent army of seamstresses, who relentlessly stitched it--stage floor and towers--in a rich black material to complete the black box concept to which one set would be added for *Hamlet* and *Rosencrantz and Guildenstern Are Dead* and another for *Henry VIII* and *A Man For All Seasons*. Once the seamstresses had completed their work, a not-so-silent group of technicians practised shifting scenery, setting lights, and testing sound cues. As a result rehearsals for the production after 13 March had to shift between the two spaces, using the stage when possible and the rehearsal hall when the technical crews needed the stage. The show also teetered between being too large for the rehearsal hall and too small for the theatre during this period. Toward the end of March, after a run-through in the theatre, Neville warned the company that the production was not yet ready. He asked for the energy and concentration from the actors to carry every line right straight through to its concluding syllable. In the rehearsal hall the actors had worked hard on creating the proper emotions and on the internal process necessary to produce and sustain them. Now in the larger theatre they had to learn again to project those qualities to all parts of the theatre. The auditorium of the Avon has a slight dead spot just under the balcony, and Neville often sat there to judge the effectiveness of the production.

Gradually the actors adjusted to the director's requests, and the production picked up assurance and polish as it headed into its first student matinee on 16 April. From there the production had the benefit of a run of thirteen student matinees before heading into its three public previews prior to opening on Tuesday, 20 May.

Two other members of Neville's production team, lighting designer Louise Guinand and composer Alan Laing, worked with the director over the three-and-a-half month preparation period. Guinand began her career with a degree from Queen's University before graduating from the National Theatre School. While working as resident lighting designer for the Blyth Festival in 1981, several of the designers who also worked at Stratford suggested to Guinand she meet with resident lighting designer Michael Whitfield and with another Festival lighting designer, Harry Frehner. The winter following that meeting Guinand remembers receiving a call asking her to come to Stratford to assist during the 1982 season, during which she served as assistant lighting designer for all four shows at the Festival Theatre because lighting assistants were assigned to theatres that year. She assisted on several shows during the 1983 season but got her first chance at lighting her own show with the Third Stage production of *When that I Was...* that season. During 1984 she lit *Henry IV Part One* at the Third Stage and co-designed lighting for *Romeo and Juliet* at the Festival Theatre with Frehner. 1985 saw her light both shows at the Third Stage, *Antigone* and *Beaux Stratagem*. She also worked at the Grand Theatre during the season Neville had first directed Carver in *Hamlet*. When she got her offer in December to light *Hamlet* at Stratford she calls that opportunity her best Christmas present ever.

In early February Neville and LePage had talked through each scene with Guinand, using LePage's sketches to bring the lighting designer current about the way they saw each scene, says Guinand. In early conferences, she reviewed ideas for scenery and LePage's ideas about the look and feel of the specific room in which each scene was played, explains Guinand. Because Neville began doing run-throughs of the show by mid-March, Guinand could spend time in advance of the specific rehearsal designated as the run-through for the lighting designer. In this way she got more than the customary one look at the whole play before hanging her lighting specials. Following the run-through for lights, she says, she talked extensively with Neville. She and Whitfield did the basic ''hang and focus'' for the Avon Theatre during the first week in March; this process did not relate to any one show, but put about 90 to 100 instruments in position to isolate main acting areas with front, top, and side light, adding some colour washes. This work prepared the theatre for specific lighting designs for all shows at the Avon: Whitfield would light *Rosencrantz and Guildenstern Are Dead* and *Henry VIII* while Frehner, absent from the basic hang and focus because he was on assignment in the West, would light *A Man For All Seasons*. After this preliminary work, each lighting designer had sixty additional instruments at his/her disposal. Guinand recalls that she used an additional forty-four for *Hamlet*. In lighting *Hamlet*, she says, creation of the mood and atmosphere was her first

59

priority; raising the level of light on the stage to where one could see without squinting was her second.

Laing describes his background as that of a musician, first as a pianist and then as a flautist in the Calgary Symphony Orchestra. He came to school in Winnipeg and stayed for eight years, picking up three degrees in statistics and joining the statistics faculty at the University of Manitoba. But he also played a bit of jazz piano in night clubs to keep his hand in music, he says. In the mid-Sixties John Hirsch, at the Manitoba Theatre Centre, asked him to play piano for a production of *The Hostage*, which would open in four days. Laing, who has a reputation as a quick study, bore down to learn the score in two days. From that experience he developed his interest in theatre and came to Stratford in 1967 at director Hirsch's invitation to do James Reaney's *Colours In The Dark*. He worked at Stratford for the next ten years under three different artistic directors, and was named music director for drama in 1971. In the off seasons he travelled across the country from the Neptune Theatre to the Vancouver Playhouse.

Laing says he agreed to do the music for *Hamlet* and *Rosencrantz and Guildenstern Are Dead* in September before Wood went to England. Both directors wanted the same composer and the same designer for the two shows, but Laing and Neville had not worked together. In their initial meeting, which took place at the end of the first week of rehearsal, Laing explained that he had an extensive background as a soundman as well as a composer. He asked Neville to list specific places he wanted music as he spotted them in rehearsal. Laing also turned up frequently at rehearsal to make a number of specific suggestions about places for additional sound effects/music. He says, "I like to do what is required and then a little bit more." He also began with the thesis that he wanted to relate the music of the two scores to each other so that hearing one also brought the other to mind. In the end, Laing says, the two scores wound up being similar because the two directors had taken such different styles in staging the two productions and he used the score as one way of connecting them. Had they been similar in style, he says, the scores might have been much further apart. He envisioned the title character's theme as played primarily on wind instruments. He had used a seven-foot Bolivian flute in a production of *The Tempest* to produce a very low, strange sound which he characterizes as "almost entirely breath." The theme ended up fairly atonal with a lot of fifths, which produce jumps and make it an uncomfortable sound, he explains. At the same time it contains a great many open spaces defined by the breath instruments played in a minor key and at a slow pace, he continues. *Hamlet* concerns itself with "air, wind, breath, and pipes," he says, clarifying his choices.

Three previous productions of *Hamlet*, all on the Festival stage, had used actors from the 1986 production: In 1957, Michael Langham had directed Christopher Plummer as Hamlet in a production which also featured Max Helpmann as the Ghost. In Neville's production, Helpmann appeared as both the Priest and a Courtier at Claudius' court. In 1969, John Hirsch had directed Kenneth Welsh in the title role in a production that also featured James Blendick as Horatio. In Neville's production, Blendick appeared as Claudius. In 1976, Robin Phillips and William Hutt had directed both Richard Monette and Nicholas Pennell as Hamlet in a production that featured Richard Curnock as Osrick. In Neville's production Curnock appeared as Polonius.

Benoit divided this production, which opened on 20 May, into thirty-eight scenes, each with its own title. All act, scene, and line numbers refer to the New Penguin edition of *Hamlet* used for this production.

Prologue

Without a front curtain for this production the lights rise on Hamlet, who sits facing stage right with his hands around his knees singing the second verse of Ophelia's song in her first mad scene:

> *He is dead and gone, lady. He is dead and gone. At his head a grass-green turf, At his heels a stone.* IV.5.29-3

Distant bouys sound; Laing used them throughout the production to reinforce the melancholy quality of the play and contribute a steady, rhythmic beat. During the song a high top light and a front light captured Hamlet's face and shoulders. Guinand says that a top light always makes for excitement because when the front light fades out at the end of the song, the top light catches the actor in a shimmering glow. The front light also creates some tension, she says, because it strikes him from such a high angle it sculpts his face in light and shadow, diminishing at the end of the song to the warm glow about him. Laing says that Neville wanted Hamlet to sing both because Ophelia sings and because Carver has an excellent singing voice. In casting about for something for him to sing, Laing came up with Ophelia's description of her dead father, which also works well as a description of Hamlet's father. But Laing chose a different melody for the two presentations of these lyrics, putting each version in the character's own distinctive style.

Act I, Scene 1

Following a blackout at the end of the song the lights rise very quickly, and the setting for Scene 1, ''Battlements'' (pp. 63-70) puts the familiar fog for the ghost scene over the stage. Neville explained during rehearsals that this scene shows the transformation of Horatio from absolute disbelief to total belief in the ghost. The guards first try to convince an openly skeptical Horatio, but once the ghost appears Horatio must be converted immediately and to the point that when the ghost leaves the scene Horatio takes charge by setting off to convince Hamlet of the truth of the ghost. Lorne Kennedy, who played Horatio, invented a biography for the character in which he and Hamlet often went to the pub together and perhaps played on the soccer team. While they knew Rosencrantz and Guildernstern at Wittenburg University, those two belonged to the stamp club, says Kennedy.

Guinand explains that if the director wants fog to rise and fill the air, designers use hot mineral oil fog machines. If the effect requires fog close to the ground, then the designers use cold liquid hygrogen fog machines, as in this scene, where fog was blown on to the set from several feet off the ground and slowly drifted to the floor. Guinand explains her lighting of the scene as one of the darkest she has been able to "get away with lately." The light carried medium blue hues broken up by gobos in the lighting instruments into pale patterns instead of concentrated pools. She also explains that the ghost had his own "theme colour," a purplish blue not used elsewhere. The guards wore gray military costumes and the ghost appeared in a white full-dress military uniform complete with plumed helmet.

Act I, Scene 2

Three separate scenes made up Shakespeare's Act 1, Scene 2, in this production: Scene 2, "First Court" (pp. 70-74), Scene 2A, untitled but composed of Hamlet's "O that this too too sullied flesh would melt" soliloquy (pp. 74-75), and Scene 3, "Fellow Student" (pp. 75-80). The "First Court" scene, says Neville, should have a slightly decadent edge to it. A bit too much drinking goes on, especially by Claudius, and the stage picture shows things beginning to slip, the director explains. Hamlet stands out by his disapproval of the goings on at court, Neville said in rehearsal, noting that the audience doesn't yet understand his perspective in this scene. He should sound rude and harsh in answering Claudius, and the members of the court must transmit that idea to the audience by their reactions to him. By contrast the king must appear smooth, polished, graceful, and charming to a fault. In turning his attention to Gertrude, Neville said the queen obviously enjoys her new marriage and goes out of her way to include Hamlet in the business at court. Neville wanted crowd reactions in the scene to support the monarchs and isolate Hamlet and his churlish behavior. When Laertes asks for permission to return to Paris, Neville told the company, the French capital had the same connotations for the Elizabthans as it has for a modern audience and they should react accordingly. Richard Curnock explained to the company that as youth Polonius had traveled to Paris and had mixed feelings about his son's returning there. Picking up on Neville and Curnock's statements, the members of the court gave Laertes a mixed reaction to his petition in this scene.

Servants stand to each side of the stage with trays of glasses filled with red wine. The monarchs wear their best dress clothing, Claudius in a military uniform with a powder blue coat and Gertrude in a formal purple dress, each with a red slash over the right shoulder. The members of the court wore blues, blacks, grays, and whites. To set the room apart as the throne room a set of maroon drapes played behind the thrones and as the rulers entered the room. Laing provided a military-sounding rendition of the Danish National Anthem while everyone stood at attention and faced the king and queen. Thank goodness, Neville said, the anthem did not last very long.

Carver explains Hamlet's apparent rudeness at the beginning of the play by saying that the character has come home to attend his father's funeral and is in much pain. On hearing of his mother's plan to wed Claudius, whom Carver acknowledges was never his Hamlet's favourite uncle, Hamlet wonders if they had been sleeping together while his father still lived. If so, puzzles Carver, "Did my father know about it?"

James Blendick as Claudius sees the character as a man of war, who believes his brother did not do a good job of running the country; he also wants to wed and bed the queen. Being a man of action in an age where murder paved the way to power for other successful men, Blendick says, Claudius has justified the deed by believing himself the better king for the Danish state. But while Claudius longs for Gertrude, he must also deal with Hamlet or with what Blendick terms the domestic side of his character's life. While his Claudius can efficiently handle affairs of state, when faced with a domestic crisis, he acquiesces to whatever Gertrude asks him to do, says Blendick. Although, the actor explains, his character has committed a murder, he believes no one knows of his guilt and therefore he can afford to placate Hamlet actively until he learns that the prince has somehow uncovered his guilt during the "mousetrap" or play-within-the play sequence. The other aspect of the character which Blendick developed concerns the "excessiveness" of the man. Because he has been second in command for so many years, says Blendick, when he finally gets the power he overdoes everything: He drinks too much, he eats too much, before the wedding he has been with too many women, and he carouses too much. While his Claudius may have had a penchant for overindulging before he came to power, the opportunity to explore it did not present itself until he became king.

Elizabeth Shepherd, who played Gertrude, says her character very much loved her first husband; as a woman who defines herself in terms of a man she finds herself comforted by Claudius' wooing and falls victim to both his charm and his passion. Shepherd adds with a smile that Gertrude has attained that certain age where she finds a man's romantic attentions doubly flattering. Seen in this light, Shepherd believes Gertrude guilty on only one count, not waiting the customary length of time before marrying a second time. But Claudius has made her feel nineteen again, declares Shepherd, and he has turned her head to the point where she does the same silly things as would a much younger woman in the same situation. Her decisons to play Gertrude as openly in love with and somewhat sexually aroused by the mere presence of Claudius, choices which quite rightly offend her son, put her on a collision course with him from this first court scene, says Shepherd. She explains that for the Elizabethans the word "adultery" meant any kind of sexual irregularity. Thus, later in the play when Hamlet levels the charge at her, he accuses her only of marrying too quickly, says the actress, who acknowledges that Gertrude lacks discretion in "parading her love life in front of Hamlet."

Neville stressed at one rehearsal that the soliloquy gives Hamlet a chance to speak his mind and that even if an audience will not totally accept his reasoning, at least it knows he has a strong point of view. When Horatio and the guards enter, Neville explained, Hamlet still wears the moroseness that defined his attitude during the soliloquy. While he experiences some joy at seeing his friend, his line about "the funeral baked meats" throws him back into his problem-filled reverie, an interior world, said the director, seated on the floor with the actors after running this scene one morning. Hamlet's line "I think I see my father" comes out of that very despairing soliloquy he has just given and the line only works if Hamlet bounces in and out of that mood during the scene, Neville pointed out. But this line gives Horatio his opening to explain the meeting with the ghost and Horatio's attitude must say, "Look, I didn't believe it either, but it's true," said the director. Neville explained that Hamlet moves to the attack using the same style of one-liners that began the play; when he becomes convinced Horatio is speaking the truth, he resolves to watch for the ghost. Kennedy points to the honesty which characterizes his relationship with Hamlet in this scene. When Hamlet asks him why he has come to Denmark, after a joke he tells the truth, in direct contrast to what Rosencrantz and Guildenstern will do when faced with the same question. Kennedy believes that the relationship between Hamlet and Horatio comes out of that friendship.

Guinand wanted to contrast the richness of the court with the shadows of the battlements in the first scene, so she poured the bright white light into the scene from the front and the sides. The side lights, she says, caught the glitz of the brocade on stage and also played nicely off the drapes beneath the throne. As the characters leave the stage and Hamlet begins his first soliloquy, Guinand pulled down the level of lighting to concentrate on him by stripping away the rest of the stage. She says she gave him his "theme-coloured light"-- a mixture of two different blues, one of which had just a bit of red in it so that he had a slight tie-in to the purplish blue of his father's theme. Guinand explains that the light has cooler qualities than the warm white light in the court scene because during the speech Hamlet says that things aren't going well. At the end of the soliloquy when Horatio and the guards join Hamlet the lights again come up on the full stage, but they are cooler because the overall situation has deteriorated.

Act I, Scene 3

Scene 4, "A Few Precepts" (pp.80-85), played as one scene in the production. Neville very much wanted the affection of brother and sister to shine through the scene. Because the text does not necessarily emphasize the point, he asked the actors to be sure that they did. Early in the rehearsal period Ophelia brought her brother a rose which she put into his lapel, but Neville suspected that this addition might turn the scene into one about a flower so he cut that business and the actors concentrated on demonstrating the affection that flourished between them. Neville asked Richard Curnock to play Polonius as a very efficent military man who demonstrates very little affection for his children. While Neville says he has never seen such an interpretation of Polonius, it forced the children to turn to each other while growing up. With Laertes in Paris, Ophelia must turn to Hamlet for affection. Neville explains that he was very anxious that Polonius not come across as a doddering old fool; rather, his humour must come out of the text, out of the way he operates. Neville also wanted Laertes to listen carefully to the precepts which Polonius gives him even if he is hearing them "for the eighty-fifth time." He loves and respects his father, says Neville, and must not even hint at disrepect during the speech. The director adds that this view of Laertes as the good son ties nicely into his violent anger at hearing of Polonius' death later in the play.

Curnock says he likes the idea of Polonius as a military man because it presents a very different look at the character, especially as Polonius relates to his family. Repeating the precepts to Laertes, for example, shows that Polonius has developed some formidable chinks in his efficient military manner. In discussing Ophelia, Curnock says that his Polonius never sees Ophelia as a potential bride for Hamlet. Polonius can fall back on the excuse that Hamlet as a prince cannot marry her but, acknowledges Curnock, the old man saw something in Hamlet's character that he disliked.

Wentworth explains that Shakespeare uses both Laertes and Fortinbras as foils for Hamlet in that all three have fathers killed and embark on courses of revenge. But in order to come across as an effective counterbalance to

Hamlet, Wentworth says he looked to Carver's Hamlet. The result was a stylish young rake, off to Paris to explore the world but keeping a very tight grip on his emotions. Wentworth says he and Lucy Peacock, who played Ophelia, explored what effect the behaviour of the stern father and the absent brother might have upon Ophelia. Peacock says she decided to play Ophelia as very young and in love for the first time, which explains the deep hurt she experiences. The character also developed out of the family that Curnock and Wentworth had created around her, says Peacock. When Polonius tells Ophelia to break off the relationship with Hamlet, she plays the moment as if she willingly and lovingly does what her father commands her to do without understanding why her brother and father fear Hamlet.

A large arched window rested on the top platform to form the background for this scene. (The small rectangle on the top platform in the illustration represents the window in those scenes in which it played.) Ophelia, dressed in white, contrasts with the grey morning suits of the two men. Guinand says the light for the scene supposedly comes through the window so the lighting filters in from that upstage source. But, she explains, the colouring appears more neutral in this scene because the blue light plays off the dark floor (painted to simulate a dark green marble), and the overall effect looks more like a normally lighted home than any other. The cyclorama, lighted for the first time with no drop in front of it, provided a gray backdrop for the scene, she explains.

Act I, Scene 5

The scene was divided into three: Scene 5, "Battlements II" (pp. 85-89), Scene 6, "List List" (pp. 89-93) and Scene 7, "The Cellerage" (pp. 93-96). The setting and lights played in much the same manner as they did in "Battlements I." Neville worked "Battlements II" to make the restraining of Hamlet and his subsequent breaking away credible as he follows the ghost. The absolute frenzy into which Hamlet has worked himself at the encounter with the ghost finally makes the difference in allowing him to break free. Kennedy says Horatio tries to restrain Hamlet because he fears for his friend's safety.

When in "List List" Hamlet finds the ghost, he falls to his knees and reaches up plaintively to receive the ghost's admonition. David Schurmann, who played the ghost, says he decided before rehearsals began to impersonate a tortured spirit. Although the first few times through the scene he held back, Schurmann says, he later began to explore the horrible pain implicit in his choice. Carver says of the second soliloquy, after the ghost exits, that Hamlet promises to let the ghost's "commandment" be the guiding principle and that the character will spend the rest of the play endeavouring to live up to that pledge. For the moment, says Carver, Hamlet has everything clearly in focus.

Later in "The Cellerage," when Hamlet meets Horatio and Marcellus and three times makes them swear to keep his secret, the ghost calls out "swear" each time the oath is proposed, but this pair does not hear the voice of the ghost, focusing all of their attention on a highly agitated Hamlet, who collapses into their arms. Kennedy reveals that when Horatio sees Hamlet return, the momentary joy is undercut by the realization that the situation could hardly get worse. Kennedy also says that Hamlet informs him in a scene offstage of what the ghost has said.

When Hamlet and the ghost meet in "List List," Neville, LePage, and Guinand decided that the scene should move from the battlements to a cellar. Consequently Guinand used a strong top light with a heavy metal gobo to make it appear as if light came in through a metal grate above them. By splitting the lighting gells into quarters, with two sections containing the ghost's color and the other two a greener blue, she was able to keep the ghost's presence amid the darkness.

Act II, Scene 1

During the scene in which Ophelia reports Hamlet's advances to her father, "Scene 8, Mad for Love," the setting returns to the bare stage with the window at the back and the lighting neutral. During rehearsals, Neville pointed out that Polonius feared he would be thought a fool if his daughter slept with the prince and Peacock says that during an offstage scene Hamlet has "literally frightened the hell out of her" by his strange appearance and behavior. She emphasizes that Ophelia must think that Hamlet has gone mad for love of her, a clue to her behavior when she herself goes mad.

Act II, Scene 2

This scene contained six sections: Scene 9, "Welcome R & G" (pp. 101-103), Scene 10, "Soul of Wit" (pp. 103-108), Scene 11, "Fishmonger" (pp. 108-110), Scene 12, "Good Friends" (110-114), Scene 13, "With Good Accent" (pp. 114-119), and Scene 13A, untitled but containing Hamlet's "Now I am alone." soliloquy (pp. 120-121). LePage and Guinand had decided that this sequence of scenes takes place in a throne room in another part of the castle from the "First Court" scene. The room, according to Guinand, had two windows down right that provide light across the thrones. The lighting was not to read as rich and bright as it had in the primary throne room, explains Guinand. During "Welcome R & G" Rosencrantz and Guildenstern arrive dressed in their motoring coats and goggles, with the fencing gear. Neville decided to inject some humour into the scene by having Claudius look at Guildenstern and address him as Rosencrantz, who bows even when called by the wrong name. But Rosencrantz also, bows and the pair exchange a glance of consternation from their bowed positions. The action then repeats on the name of Guildenstern, and they bob again when addressed by the queen.

Blendick says that the queen has suggested sending for Rosencrantz and Guildenstern and Claudius has bowed to her wishes. As rehearsal of the scene progressed, Blendick suggested moving through his explanation of their mission to this pair, one line at a time, to be sure that they did not miss the point that they have come to spy on Hamlet and report his conversations and actions. Heady with status, Guildenstern snaps his fingers for servants to pick up the luggage.

Keith Dinicol, who played Rosencrantz in *Hamet*, used what he terms a "fresh-faced approach" to the character, by which he means that Rosencrantz, despite the pains Claudius has taken, never quite understands. His Rosencrantz comes into this scene each night not quite sure what to expect. William Dunlop, who played Guildenstern, says that his character understands exactly what Claudius wants of them and that he would make it worth their while. Thus by the end of this scene the differences between the characters of Rosencrantz and Guildenstern have been sketched with a bold hand.

During the "The Soul Of Wit," Neville wished to establish Polonius' lines:

...that I have found/The very cause of Hamlet's lunacy. II.1.48-49

as the first time anyone had used the word "lunacy" to describe Hamlet in front of Gertrude. Consequently Shepherd gave Curnock an adverse reaction to his announcement at the beginning of the scene, a reaction that Blendick noted before he asked Curnock to continue his explanation. As Polonius advances his case that Hamlet has gone mad because of Ophelia's rejection of his love, and actually reads Ophelia's letter from him aloud, Neville points out, Polonius has reached his most self-serving point, even reading his daughter's private correspondance like a town crier with his customary lack of forethought as to how his behavior might harm his daughter. Curnock cites his character's desire to play the statesman with the correct solution to the problem as his motivation for not seeing the hurt he has caused Ophelia. Peacock, who still feels the horrible guilt of believing that she caused Carver's madness, worries about what the king and queen might do or say to her.

Neville also made another important choice in bringing Hamlet on stage a few lines earlier than the text dictates so that he hears the beginning of Polonius' plot, beginning with:

You know sometimes he walks four hours together
Here in the lobby.
II.2.160

Carver says that, while overhearing the conversation proves helpful, Hamlet has no idea when the plot will be sprung and that he must wonder why his mother would stoop to spying on him. Blendick says Polonius' device to discover the cause of Hamlet's madness again pulls Claudius back to the domestic world and away from the affairs of state. His Claudius agrees only to please his queen; Curnock believes that Claudius' willingness to undertake this plan, calling for him to go about the palace hiding behind the furnishings, demonstrates the extent of his weakness in handling domestic affairs. But he also points out that the more helpless Claudius appears at handling this situation the more Polonius has to gain by handling it for him.

When "Fishmonger" begins, Hamlet has just overheard the old man's contention that Hamlet had "from his reason fallen." Thus Carver's Hamlet chose deliberately to act as if he were on the edge of madness, from which he can chide Polonius, something he could not do if he dropped the guise. Neville asked Carver to describe Polonius with the passage beginning, "For the satirical rogue says here that old men have...." (II.2.197-198) as if he were reading it from the book. Polonius should respond as if he had noticed some of these things in the mirror while shaving this morning, explained the director. Neville also attended to a technical aspect of the scene by establishing some physical distance between the actors before Hamlet's asides so that Poloinus could begin his next speech immediately after the aside.

No sooner has Polonius left Hamlet than he points him out to Rosencrantz and Guildenstern, hidden behind their fencing masks. Neville, who has always enjoyed this scene, especially enjoyed the one in this production because as soon as Rosencrantz and Guildenstern leave this scene they play the one in *Rosencrantz and Guildenstern Are Dead* where Rosencrantz says "he murdered us." Neville went on to explain his production's plan for allowing Hamlet to do just that. Rosencrantz and Guildenstern come on wearing the masks, says Neville, which make them appear a bit sinister, and they come on specifically to question him. But they never succeed; he questions them instead, says the director, and the scene from *Rosencrantz and Guildenstern Are Dead* makes that point very nicely from underneath. In order to make that point visually, Hamlet grabs Guildenstern's sword and fences with Rosencrantz during II.2.267-276, the scene in which Hamlet asks if they have come to pay him a free visitation or if the king and queen have sent for them. To enhance Rosencrantz's awkwardness, Hamlet catches him off guard and scores off him with the foil. Fournier worked the brief fencing bout to time Hamlet's winning foil thrusts when his adversary let down his verbal sparring guard as well as his physical one.

Carver, Dinicol, and Dunlop agree that while Hamlet knows this pair, the friendship does not go very deep. Dinicol points out that Shakespeare never has the three of them speak of any past relationship. Carver says that Hamlet begins with a dirty joke about fortune but that after that nothing meaningful gets said. Therefore, Carver concludes that if Hamlet spent too much time with this pair he would quickly become bored. If the pair feels a closeness to Hamlet, why do they betray him by telling the king and queen the little they can learn from him? Dunlop's Guildenstern does see himself as a spy, and whatever the king wants of him, he willingly does. Dinicol sees Rosencrantz as a pawn of the king. Carver points out that everyone in this play makes a choice. If Rosencrantz and Guildenstern choose to serve the king, then he reacts with disappointment, but they still bear the responsibility for their choices as their deaths eventually demonstrate, he says. The entrance of the players begins "With Good Accents." Neville believes that Hamlet knows and has some affection for this troupe, since before the play within the play begins, he lectures one of them " Speak the speech, I pray you..." III.2.1. Polonius' entrance brings interruption and the famous soliloquy, often interpreted as showing Hamlet's indecision. Carver asks the question, "What can he do?" If he kills the king, how does he prove that Claudius has murdered his father? If he publicly accuses Claudius and has him brought to trial, where does he get the evidence to prove his uncle's guilt? Instead, Carver says, Hamlet hits upon a plot to test the guilt of the king and lead him to his course of action. Hamlet begins the soliloquy with lights pulled down around him to accent him in his blue colour.

Act III, Scene 1

This scene was composed of four parts: Scene 14, "Dangerous Lunacy" (pp. 121-124), Scene 14A, untitled but containing Hamlet's soliloquy beginning "To be or not to be -- that is the question;" (pp. 124-125), Scene 15, "Nunnery" (pp. 125-127), and Scene 16, "We Heard" (pp. 127- 128). "Dangerous Lunacy" again brings Rosencrantz and Guildenstern face to face with the king and queen for their report on the cause of Hamlet's behavior. The king and queen have split up the pair for separate questioning. As Dinicol says, the pair accomplishes very little in *Hamlet*, and this scene shows their ineffectiveness. The king, he says, asks, "Have you drawn him on to any pleasures?" and the answer is, "Well, there are some players coming and they are going to be involved with him tonight," which at least gets them off the hook for the moment.

For Carver, Hamlet's "To be or not to be" soliloquy paves the way for his character's entrance into the "Nunnery" scene. As a consequence, early in the rehearsal process when the "Nunnery" scene was scheduled separately, Carver asked if he might begin with the soliloquy, which gave him his mental set for the top of the "Nunnery" scene. Neville pointed out in rehearsal one day that Ophelia, under her father's injunction, must lie to Hamlet about her affections for him and that lying does not come easily for her. Hamlet, on the other hand, realizes at some point in the scene that Claudius and Polonius are hidden behind the arras, and he plays the scene for their benefit as well as Ophelia's. Therefore, says the director, in some ways this scene becomes one in which two people put on an act for one another. Each knows his/her own motives but incorrectly guesses at those of the other. When Hamlet believes Ophelia has proven untrue, he begins to read into Ophelia's behavior some of the inconstancy he finds in his mother's conduct, concludes Neville. Carver, taking his cue fom Claudius' line, "For we have closely sent for Hamlet hither," III.1.29, believes Hamlet comes into the scene because he has received a summons to appear. The famous soliloquy bubbles to the surface then at least in part because he must answer the call of others when he does not wish to do so. Yet Carver points out that he does not immediately suspect Claudius and Polonius have chosen this time to hide in order to overhear his conversation with Ophelia. Not until he gets to line 130, where Hamlet asks Ophelia, "Where's your father?" does Carver's character realize that she has set him up, explains the actor. After having made that discovery, says Carver, he remembers his mother's presence in the room when the plot took shape. Is she behind the arras too, wonders Carver's Hamlet? At this point, he begins to act as well, chiding Ophelia and his mother for the inconstancy of woman. Peacock says that Ophelia knows her father and Claudius are hiding during the scene and that she must lie to Hamlet in front of this audience. The prime motive, says Peacock, comes from her desire to get him to say he loves her because then others can help him. Yet other emotions, such as the sexual dimension of the relationship, also come forward. While neither performer believes that the characters have shared a physical relationship, Peacock says that Ophelia experiences the surges of sexual awareness during the scene and that these frustrations come out in the mad scene.

The technical problem presented by the scene concerned the nature of the remembrances which Ophelia delivers to Hamlet. Neville laughed as he contemplated the issue one day and enumerated what the remembrance might be: "the car, the stereo, the condo...." But because he did not want a Santa Claus approach to the gifts, the stage littered with presents, he referred the problem to LePage with the instructions that they should be small and authentic to the period. LePage came up with a small packet of letters attached with lace and flowers.

Once Hamlet leaves the scene, Ophelia lies devastated on the floor, and Polonius and Claudius emerge from behind the arras, "We Heard" begins. Blendick says Claudius hears something from Hamlet which he can not quite identify but which makes him suspect that Hamlet does not suffer from madness or love, rather from something unsettled within his soul. Blendick explains that Claudius can take no more time from his state duties to run around the castle hiding behind doors or arras to find out what his stepson is doing, so sends him away. "I have to get on with the business at hand, running a country," says Blendick of his Claudius. During this scene Polonius again tries to convince Claudius of Hamlet's love for Ophelia yet hardly notices her on the floor beside him, addressing her only perfunctorily. The director explored several ways of getting Ophelia offstage during the scene between Claudius and Polonius before settling on leaving her onstage throughout it. After the two actors exit, she sits alone on the floor before very slowly getting up and making her own way out the opposite side of the stage in what Neville found a very moving moment.

Guinand says the setting returned to the original throne room with the three red drapes for this series of scenes, although the lighting looks more neutral to signify that things have not gone so well. For the soliloquy the lights come down to highlight Hamlet, who crosses the stage. Guinand says that a followspot would have been ideal but would have meant adding a person to the running crew, so she designed a sequence of lights which picked up Hamlet and isolated him in the light as he crossed through different areas. She declares herself very happy with the way that sequence worked out although she acknowledges that it turned out as a rather tricky call for the stage manager, who must guess exactly when Carver would move his foot from the stage area lighted by one instrument to an area lighted by another. During the soliloquy, Ophelia kneels on the prie-dieu upstage right near a window whose light is fully visible only from a vantage point in the balcony, says Guinand. But once the "Nunnery" scene begins, the window provides the visible light source for the scene. She explains that she cooled down the light because she wanted to convey the image of the cold edge of rage for this scene. At the same time, she wanted to be very subtle in so doing so as not to take the focus away from the two performers.

Act III, Scene 2

This scene was divided into three parts: Scene 17, "Speak the Speech" (pp. 128-131), Scene 18," The Play" (pp. 131-138), and Scene 19, "Pickers and Stealers" (pp. 138-142). In "Speak the Speech," Neville says, Hamlet stands on the edge of discovering whether the ghost has spoken the truth.

In this production not only has Hamlet written a portion of the script for the actor to speak, but he has arranged the stage as well. In place of the thrones for Claudius and Gertrude, he and Horatio set up the same folding wooden chairs for the monarchs that the other members of their court will use because he knows he can throw Claudius off balance for a moment by making no distinction for him in the seating arrangements. Of the use of the wooden chairs, Neville joked that Hamlet had been to $1.44 day at Woolco, the downtown store visible from the rehearsal hall window.

Because Hamlet knows the players, Neville and Carver decided to play Hamlet's advice as criticism of previous performances which the young prince had witnessed. While Hamlet lectured the player who portrayed Lucianus (Peter Donaldson) and who reacted most indignantly at having his acting style criticized, some of the other players led by player prologue (Nolan Jennings) laughed and elbowed one another as if in argeement with Hamlet's opinion of their fellow actor.

During "The Play" scene Hamlet moves unpredictably about the throne room, first lying in Ophelia's lap and then stopping the play by his physical presence on the stage or with his vocal interruptions. The players display growing disgust at having their scene interrupted by each new antic of the prince. Neville staged the play scene on the down right portion of the stage, so Claudius, Gertrude, and the members of the court seated in an arc from up center to down right, as well as the members of the audience, could see the "actors." Neville blocked the play with circular movements, leaving the player king and queen alternately open. When Donaldson approaches to give Lucianus' speech, he disregards Hamlet's advice and delivers the speech in his best melodramatic fashion. Even so, the speech, combined with Hamlet's explanation of the rest of the play's plot, still strikes hard at Claudius' guilty conscience, and he rushes down off the top platform to within a few meters of Hamlet, having thrown aside his wine glass to stare hard at the young prince before crying for light. Polonius' line "Give o'er the play" comes immediately after the king's cry for light, rather than coming before it as the script indicates. By rearranging the lines, the horror of Claudius's realization that Hamlet knows what he has done, dramatized in the long gaze the actor directs at him, remains uninterrupted until the guilty Claudius exits clumsily from the other side of the stage.

During rehearsals Neville stressed that as this scene progresses the members of the court must become increasingly uncomfortable with the player queen's negative attitude toward a second marriage when they consider that Gertrude has just married for the second time. The king and queen, Neville explained, want to humour Hamlet as long as possible, so for a while they choose not to take the remarks adversely. Thus the members of the court must show how embarrassing the situation has become, he told the actors. As the scene goes on, the tension builds while the players hammer in the idea of a second marriage. Neville also cut the dumb show directly before the play and made extensive cuts within the text of the play scene. And Peacock explains that because Ophelia leaves the nunnery scene in such torment, she handles Ophelia calmly in this scene, the character's next appearance, by believing it takes place the next day. Throughout the scene, she says, Ophelia believes that the calmer she can keep Hamlet, the more she can help him shake off the madness for which she blames herself. Trying to help him, she concludes, also provides a strong positive motivation for her in the scene.

After Claudius sees his crime enacted on stage, he realizes that Hamlet knows, says Blendick, but he does not know how many other people do. For example, asks Blendick, "Have the players gotten a whiff of this thing?" Claudius decides he must get rid of Hamlet before he tells others. If the players do not figure out the implications of the production they have staged, Kennedy's Horatio does. Having decided that Hamlet has told him everything the ghost reported, Horatio knows at once not only that Claudius has reacted guiltily but why. But, Kennedy relates, Horatio now fears that they have rattled the king, thereby placing themselves at his mercy. Playing Horatio as fully knowing, as Kennedy did, also invalidates all of Claudius' moves to kill Hamlet because knowledge of the crime would not die with Hamlet.

"Pickers and Stealers" begins as Hamlet rushes about the stage celebrating this vindication of the ghost and of his story. At the players' gramophone, he sings the lines from III.2.301-315, which contain his speeches, in time to the music. Rosencrantz turns off the music, while Guildenstern pleads with Hamlet to calm himself. Neville says this scene reinforces Hamlet's hostility toward the pair, so the actors tried several different interpretations to show that idea. They eventually divided duties so that Dinicol's Rosencrantz would "try to jolly up Hamlet" while Dunlop's Guildenstern probes. The end of the scene contains the soliloquy beginning, "Tis now the very watching time of night," in which, in contrast to the last soliloquy, Hamlet believes himself ready to revenge his father, explains Carver.

Guinand had originally seen this sequence, beginning with Hamlet setting up the chairs, as cool, while LePage had seen it as warmer because of the texture added by the members of the court. They decided to begin the scene "cool" while Hamlet and Horatio quite literally set the stage and "warm" it for the entrance of the court. Side and top lighting gave a sculptured look to the characters that LePage and Guinand liked. The cyclorama behind the actors played in a lush shade of blue and a member of the court brought on a large floor candelabrum. After the king cries, "Give me some light," the candelabrum goes off with him and the scene grows decidedly colder, building to an even colder ending for Part l. When Hamlet starts the soliloquy, Guinand explains, she pulled down the full-stage lighting to highlight Hamlet in his own colour, light from a sharp angle from the front with back lighting the colour of the ghost. The front light went out a full second before the back light, a technique that Guinand says ''lost Hamlet in the void'' at the end of the act.''

Act III, Scene 3

This scene played as one unit called Scene 20, ''Up Sword'' (pp. l42-l45). Neville points to the scene as that most often cited by those who emphasize Hamlet's indecision. Neville says that, according to the theology of Shakespeare's day, if a person died repentant his soul went to heaven. Hamlet does make a decision here, not to kill Claudius. Actor and director saw the scene in the same way: Carver used the last line of the soliloquy, ''This physic but prolongs thy sickly days,'' to show his resolve to kill him at a different time.

Blendick says that during the play scene, which Claudius regards as a horror show, guilt and confusion drive him to make this prayer. For Blendick, the attempt rings hollow, for his Claudius wants to hold onto the crown and the queen and repent at the same time. Recognizing the difficulty in contrition, the character carries through with this gesture in hopes of something positive. Guinand lit this scene through a window at the front of the stage, casting shadows across the kneeling Claudius.

Act III, Scene 4

This scene was divided into two parts: Scene 21, ''The Closet'' (pp. 145-149) and Scene 22, ''Visitation'' (pp. 149-154). ''The Closet,'' says Neville, shows Hamlet taking decisive action, but killing the wrong man, Polonius. Of his lack of remorse, Neville says that Hamlet has caught Polonius spying on him a number of times, and Curnock points to Polonius' meddling in everyone else's affairs. He explains the character's desire to help Claudius deal with this domestic situation as a means of continuing to ensure Polonius' own place at court.

But the importance of this scene for the director centers on Hamlet's decision to trust his mother with the knowledge that he has only pretended madness and his success in driving a wedge between Gertrude and Claudius. The entrance of the ghost pulls Hamlet back to the business at hand. Schurmann says that he strove to keep the same horrible, pain-ridden essence of his ghost, and Shepherd believes the ghost's entrance comes as Hamlet stands on the verge of telling her what crimes Claudius has committed. In the "Closet" and "Visitation" scenes, she explains, Hamlet helps her to see inside herself and understand what she has done. This production demonstrates that Gertrude takes Hamlet seriously and does indeed change her allegiance; Shepherd says Hamlet has saved his mother's soul. Unlike Claudius, she can repent, and Shepherd believes that both mother and son find joy in healing the breach. According to her account, Gertrude does not discover that Claudius had murdered her first husband until the very end of the play, but by that time she has made her own self-discoveries, which might have proved impossible had she had to deal with his guilt before she discovered her own.

Guinand placed a window on the opposite side of the stage from the one she used with Claudius at prayer, a larger window to make the actual floor space seem smaller. She used more blue light to show night has progressed further, with a bit of warm light to give the room the appearance of shimmering candles.

As Hamlet drags Polonius' body off stage, the scene is cleared of furniture; then Hamlet reappears dragging the body on up left to down left. Ophelia enters from up right in time to see her father's body being dragged off stage and lets out a shriek of horror. Peacock says this discovery scene launched her into the mad scene she would shortly have to play. Guinand put greenish-blue tint on this scene to show how sickly things have turned, but kept Ophelia in a warm white area. The briefness of the scene works against the colours making their statements, she admits.

Act IV, Scene 1

This scene contained one part, Scene 23, "Heavy Deed" (pp. 154-155). Once Claudius leaves his prayers and walks into Gertrude's chamber, Blendick says, no doubt exists in his mind that he will have Hamlet killed. Blendick played the scene as if realizing that he would have died had he hidden behind the drape instead of Polonius. The most dramatic moment in the scene came on a line addressed to Gertrude, "O Come Away!" when Blendick starts out stage left while Shepherd wheels around to exit stage right. In rehearsal, Blendick did not know she would leave in the opposite direction and was stunned.

Act IV, Scene 2

This scene, Scene 24, "Hide Fox" (pp. 155-156), is where, Neville believes, Hamlet must begin to convince others that he suffers from madness, so he plays a game with the court members by running away from his guards, one of whom raises his rifle and brings the young prince into his sights before lowering it and rejoining the chase.

Act IV, Scene 3

The entire scene was used as Scene 25, "Politic Worms" (pp. 157-159). Blendick asserts that by this point Claudius no longer quibbles over a nice way to say that he wants Hamlet killed. He points to the line, "Do it, England," as an expression of his character's growing frustrations with the prince.

Act IV, Scene 4

This scene was divided into two sections, Scene 25, "The Captain" (pp. 159-160) and Scene 26A, untitled but containing Hamlet's soliloquy beginning, "How all occasions do inform against me." Neville acknowledges that in this scene the introduction of Fortinbras' army creates the contrast for Hamlet that highlights his own inactivity. In choosing to play Hamlet on the cusp of the old and new worlds, in LePage's view, Fortinbras is the symbol of World War I soon to come. In this world, this Hamlet, had he lived to see it, would have been as out of place as in the graceful Nineteenth Century Danish court. Leon Pownall, who played the captain, describes Hamlet's seeming unreality: "He's crazy! All you can say is, 'God by you, sir.' " The element of Twentieth Century militarism represented by this Fortinbras, Peter Donaldson, spoiling for the carnage of battle, provides an explosive backdrop for Hamlet's last soliloquy, ending:

> *Oh from this time forth, My thoughts be bloody or be nothing worth!* IV.4.65-66.

Here the cyclorama had nothing standing in front of it, to create the impression of a bright, windy day, but storm clouds gather about Fortinbras. Guinand pulled in to a single light on Hamlet, pulling him into himself for his soliloquy.

Act IV, Scene 5

This scene played in three parts: Scene 27, "Beauteous Majesty" (pp. 162-164), Scene 28, "Riotous Laertes" (pp. 164-168), and Scene 29, "Rose of May" (pp. 168-170). Neville began rehearsing the series of scenes by working privately with Peacock, trying to take the tension out of the scene for her by sliding into it easily, rather than focusing on the emphasis that this is THE MAD SCENE. Peacock laughingly asserts that Neville sent everyone else home to work and concentrated on her for a week. She appreciated Neville's sensitivity to her apprehension, and he helped her extensively by getting her on her feet and moving from the very beginning. In this production Opehlia's mood swings wildly from the sweetness of innocence to the bawdiness of a Tina Turner. During the St. Valentine's Day song, she embraces Claudius and rubs her leg against his thigh. Neville and Peacock admit that she could get too carried away here; he said to her, "Don't come out and save the play." When Ophelia sees Hamlet dragging her father's body, says Peacock, she knows he has killed him. Peacock says Ophelia cannot sleep because each time she closes her eyes she sees her love dragging her father's body. But with madness comes freedom from guilt and grief.

Blendick says of the moment when Claudius contronts her and realizes she has gone mad that his character first considers the political consequences when Laertes returns. Ophelia's madness adds to Claudius' burdens, he asserts. While Blendick's character still believes himself master of the situation, he says, now the stakes have gotten higher and his manoeuvring room smaller.

When Laertes does arrive, signalling the beginning of "Riotous Laertes," the intensity of his anger burns brightly. Wentworth explains that Laertes does not yet understand the cause of his father's death and wants an explanation of the hasty burial without state honours. Laertes' unchecked anger, he says, shows the degree to which his emotions now rule him. Unlike Hamlet, says Wentworth, Laertes has no practice in dealing with his emotions and gets himself into uncharted waters fairly quickly. Through sheer force of will Blendick's Claudius subdues Laertes' anger. Then Ophelia enters in the "Rose of May" scene. When Laertes sees that she has gone mad, Blendick says, Claudius must re-fight the battle he has just won. With all collapsing around him, his Claudius must contain the political damage. Neville chose to highlight the madness by giving the actress neither a real basket nor real flowers for this scene. She did practise for the first few weeks with a real basket, but she quickly moved into miming the business of distributing the flowers to the others present, including one of the guards (Christopher Thomas, her real-life husband) on her way out of the scene. Lighting designer, scene designer, and director decided to place this scene in a windowless, uninviting room.

Act IV, Scene 6

This scene played as one complete unit, Scene 30, "Letter" (pp. 170-171). As Horatio comes on to read the letter, the king and Laertes withdraw to stage left. Wentworth says they decided in conversations there that Claudius would explain all that has happened in Laertes' absence, including a description of Hamlet's madness.

Act IV, Scene 7

This scene was divided into two units, Scene 31, "Naked Kingdom" (pp.

171-177) and Scene 32, "One Woe" (pp. 177-178). Neville describes the of the scene, explaining that it develops from the irrationality Laertes brings to it. Underneath the scene lies Laertes' unstated charge against Claudius, which Neville verbalized in rehearsal to the company as "Hey, you're in charge here, and your nephew killed my father and drove my sister nuts. Now what are you going to do about it?" Neville explained that to make the scene work Laertes must taunt Claudius openly while Claudius craftily listens but turns Laertes' statements around to use them for his own purposes. This idea pleased both actors because the director's plan rescued the scene from simply picturing two men talking in a hall. Blendick says that this interpretation made his job easier because when he tosses out the idea of killing Hamlet, Laertes volunteers to be the instrument, as Claudius has suspected he would. Neville asked Blendick to chuckle occasionally during the scene as Laertes snatches up each new idea. In deciding to use the fencing match as the time to spring this plot, Blendick says, Claudius knows Laertes' reputation as a better fencer than Hamlet. He has no way of knowing that Hamlet has practised much more than usual, while Laertes has grown rusty in Paris, says Blendick; even so, Claudius has arranged the poison as a backup, now that he is obsessed with the idea of killing Hamlet. Wentworth sees Laertes as willing to aid Claudius because he has lost that tight grip on his emotions, becoming tainted by Claudius and so earning death as a result of the alliance.

When Gertrude announces Ophelia's death at the beginning of "One Woe," Neville wanted her to lay the guilt for the death at Claudius' feet because he and Polonius set her up for Hamlet's rejection. The director also warned Wentworth that the line, "Drowned! O, where?" (line 165) can sometimes get a laugh and suggested drawing out the word "O" and throwing away the word "where." After Laertes learns of his sister's death, Wentworth says, he leaves the stage because he does not want anyone to see him having lost control of himself. Blendick says Claudius again has to follow him because no one can predict how his sister's death will affect him, and he may make a fresh attempt at rebellion. As Claudius leaves the scene, his lines say, "Let's follow, Gertrude." But at the end of the speech, this Gertrude walks off in the opposite direction and no officer appears to assist the king, standing alone.

Act V, Scene 1

This scene was divided into three parts, Scene 33, "Lunch Break" (pp. 178-180), Scene 34, "Yorick" (pp. 180-185), and Scene 35, "The Funeral) pp. 185-188. Neville used Laing's soundscape of a summer day for the gravediggers' lunch as Hamlet and Horatio arrive, bringing storm clouds and thunder that build to an absolute downpour for the funeral. Asked about giving the royal party umbrellas, Neville acknowledges that a 1930s production did so and he was wary of copying. By the time the production opened, however, a few umbrellas had made their way onstage.

The first gravedigger, Eric House, looked at the location of the grave on the up left portion of the highest platform in rehearsal and asked Neville if the distance between the grave and the audience bothered him. No platform located further down stage had the necessary depth for the grave, so Neville solved the problem by having the grave diggers almost through with the work as the scene starts. They soon emerge from the grave and cross down stage on their lunch break. Neville asked House after a fitting how he liked his costume. "Are gum boots funny?" shot back House. The director stresses that House did not play the humour of the scene, but rather created a very real person--older, more philosophical--which to Neville's mind made the comic elements even stronger--in contrast to Ian Watson's second grave digger, played as a dim-witted youth.

After a brief conversation with Hamlet and Horatio, the first gravedigger makes his way back to tidy up the grave so that the focus shifts back to the two. Hamlet lifts Yorick's skull and holds it next to his own head as the scene progresses. As the funeral party makes its entrance into the scene from up right, Hamlet and Horatio hold the down right stage position. The king, queen, and Laertes take the top platform. The coffin, held by ropes, slides roughly into the grave, where first Laertes and then Hamlet jump in for the confrontation that follows. Carver explains that at this point the character finally knows who he is, saying, "This is I, Hamlet the Dane." The lighting, following the soundscape, began brightly on a bright cyclorama; Guinand says the audience had a visceral reaction to all that lighting pouring onto the scene, in contrast to the dimness for Claudius and Laertes in the previous scene. By the time "The Funeral" scene begins, she says, she turned motion wheels over certain lighting instruments, an effect that does not register on the conscious mind but comes across subliminally as motion.

Act V, Scene 2

This scene played as one unit called Scene 36, "Waterfly" (pp. 188-195). In the production of *Hamlet* Neville directed for the Grand Theatre, the scene began with Horatio's line (56) "So Rosencrantz and Guildenstern go to't." The scene follows nicely into the "waterfly" sequence without the lines which explain what happened to this pair, says Neville. He would have preferred to cut the lines again, but John Wood asked for them to play off the companion production of *Rosencrantz and Guildenstern Are Dead*. Assistant director Meg Westley, over a lunch break one day, cut the beginning of the scene to include the story line concerning their fate. Neville instructed David Brown as Osrick to begin his portion of the scene very calmly, increasing his agitation as Hamlet bates him. Osrick, Claudius' right-hand man, wore a black military uniform trimmed in gold braid and a hat fashioned in the style of Napoleon. Hamlet removes the hat, twirls it several times, and puts it back on his head sideways on lines 176-177 "...after what flourish your nature will." Neville brought Osrick back on stange as the lord who spoke lines 200-201, "The Queen desires you to use some gentle entertainment to Laertes before you fall to play." So the teasing of this "waterfly" continued beyond the usual limits the playwright set for it in the lines. Brown says Neville saw the character as the "shadow of the king," a position achieved through wealth rather than brains. Brown points to the energy and malevolence of his creation, and says that Neville did not choose to play the scene comically, as others sometimes play it, because he did not want to throw off the balance of the last scene with a large dose of comedy here. Kennedy also notes that Carver's Hamlet has returned a changed man: His resolution to kill Claudius has taken firm root and he no longer worries about the consequences of such an action.

Guinand says that the progression of the show calls for the lighting to get colder and colder, with some warm hues used as contrasts for the cooler colours, because this scene takes place in a small, cold hallway and because Hamlet himself has gotten so wrapped up in his own problems that very little warmth comes from him.

Act V, Scene 2

The scene was divided into two parts, Scene 37, "The Duel" (pp. 195-202) and Scene 38, "Proud Death" (pp. 202-204). Wentworth concludes that Laertes does not lie well, and when Hamlet asks for his forgiveness he must say he gives it when in fact he does not. Both Carver and Wentworth proved skillful fencers, so Fournier could structure an exciting fight. The duel sequence starts in a controlled manner, but once Laertes loses the first two bouts, he lunges at Hamlet and wounds him slightly on the arm in the interval before the third bout begins. At that point the tempo of this carefully staged bout increases markedly. Fournier told the duelers and spectators in rehearsal which moves went beyond the bounds of accepted practice so that when the crowd reacts they can add authenticity to Claudius' line, "Part them. They are incensed" (96). At one place Laertes stumbles backward inadvertently into Claudius' throne before Hamlet's foil smashes into the back of it. Up stage of the action Claudius crouches for cover. But when the fighters have spent their rage and the fight ends, Neville says, the exchange of forgiveness which follows rings with special poignancy. Wentworth too believes the last exchange of pardon an important action, for Laertes honestly desires it to rid himself of the contamination by Claudius' machinations.

Blendick says that Claudius goes into the last scene with two plans to kill Hamlet, both of them working against the king. In consultation with Neville and Shepherd, Blendick asked not to see Gertrude take the poisoned cup and start to drink, since he loves her too much to allow her to die if he had any possibility of stopping her. As the production was staged, Claudius sees her just after she has drunk or at the last possible moment before she sips the drink. At that point, says Blendick, the character's house built on sand swirls away from him; for all his dreams of glory, he turns out to be a very weak man. This actor liked the three-piece suit he wore for the last scene because he likens the stripping away of his kingly adornments to General George Patton's appearance out of uniform: "a little old man in a robe," according to an aide. Kennedy says that for Horatio the ending proves the disastrous finale he has worked so far to prevent.

The entrance of Fortinbras signals the beginning of "Proud Death." Neville says that in many productions Fortinbras conveys "the hope of the future." The director wanted a different look at the character, and he points to Fortinbras' line about Hamlet (391-392), "For he was likely, had he been put on, to have proved most royal." Neville wanted the audience to look at this man, openly spoiling for war, and ask "Is this alternative any better?" In so doing he sought to end the production on a note of uncertainty.

The last scene was full of warmth at its opening, lit with what Guinand describes as the brightness of power. in the duel, cross-fading of lights made the room grow colder, and colder still when Gertrude dies. By the time Hamlet kills Claudius, says Guinand, not a warm light still shines in the scene. Dead Hamlet, carried out by the four soldiers, was top-lighted and carried off stage across the path that the ghost took, so she used that light on him. To complete the reversal of fortune, Fortinbras stood in the middle of the stage in the special Hamlet theme colour.

Carver says his second portrayal of the Danish prince led him on two journeys, the one his title character undertook and the one he took as an actor for each performance in order to tell Hamlet's story. Just as he felt he came to understand the character, he discovered a new piece of the puzzle that made him rethink the whole. Hamlet chides Rosencrantz and Guildenstern for trying to pluck out the heart of his mystery, but Carver cautions that no actor in discussion about the role can fully disclose it either. Speaking the day before his last performance, he said that the tragedy pictures in its fifth act a man who has struggled to know life and his place in it and in so doing discovers that the "final acceptance lies in accepting death as well." As he watched Ophelia's funeral toward the end of the run, he felt strongly that all these people too were engaged in their own struggles. He also saw Hamlet finally reach the point of trying to take the responsibility for his own decisions for his "living moment by moment." He expands the point by explaining that the play takes place within a very short time period--perhaps no more than six days from the time he first puts on the mask of madness. At the beginning Hamlet "sees both sides of every question," says the actor, coping by resolving to revenge his father one moment and coping later by separating himself from the situation and seeing reasons not to take revenge. Yet when he comes back from the fated voyage to England, he has aged, explains Carver. He comes to accept the possibility of death in the graveyard scene and resolves to do the deed in his speech to Horatio about the fall of the sparrow (213-214). In the end "he becomes complete by living from the inside and accepting rather than by letting outside elements dominate."

Carver also stresses that the other important element focuses on the performer. The journey he takes must start with himself, and the performance will differ accordingly from day to day. Quite a discussion developed during the middle of the summer about how much Carver's performance varied from night to night. The actor acknowledges having heard those reports but says he was not aware of major differences until he noticed how intently Peacock and Wentworth stared at him the first time they shared the stage for each performance. Peacock and Wentworth agree that Carver's performance never fell below a certain level but both reported seeing differences. Wentworth saw Carver play the Pirate King in *The Pirates of Penzance* in 1985 and admired him then as an actor who fully understood how to use technique as a tool to help performance. But in this role, says Wentworth, it seemed as if he had discarded the safety net of technique and played the role from inside himself each night, a feat he praised as bold and courageous. Carver says that if by technique Wentworth meant an emotional restructuring of the lines or character, he agreed that he had discarded such a system for this role.

Although not everyone wants to play King Lear, Othello, or Macbeth, Carver says, almost everyone wants to play or can see himself playing Hamlet. Each person, he says, must placate his own private ghost clamouring for action. He compares the play to a Rubic's Cube: Few of us have the background to grasp the answer immediately, but few can resist the temptation to have a go at it nevertheless.

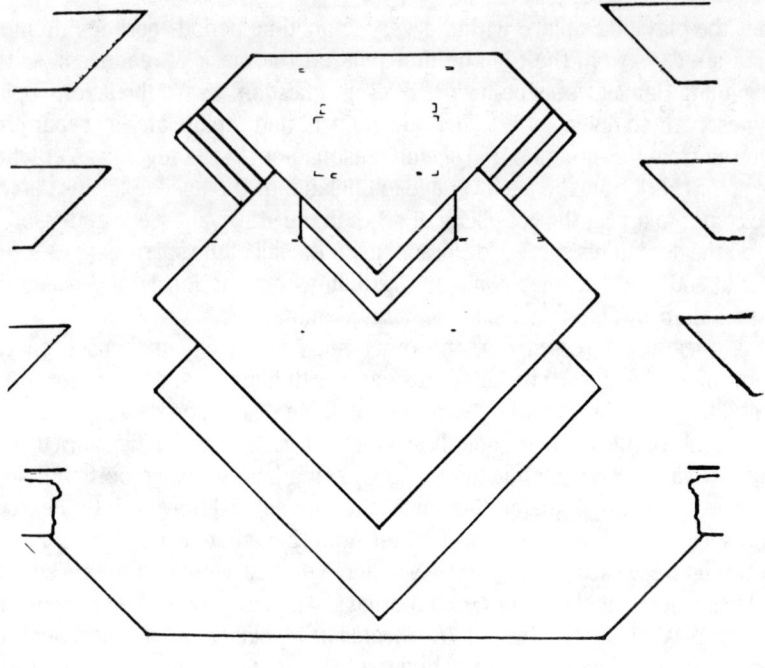

Illustration 4

Designer Sue LePage's ground plan for the 1986 Stratford production of *Hamlet* at the Avon Theatre. Side units at the front of the stage represent the proscenium arches; the others going up stage are the towers.

Rosencrantz and Guildenstern Are Dead

BY TOM STOPPARD

DIRECTED BY	JOHN WOOD
DESIGNED BY	SUE LEPAGE
MUSIC BY	ALAN LAING
LIGHTING DESIGNED BY	MICHAEL J. WHITFIELD

THE CAST
in order of appearance

Rosencrantz	WILLIAM DUNLOP
Guildenstern	KEITH DINICOL
The Player	RON HASTINGS
Tragedians	PETER DONALDSON, JEAN-PIERRE FOURNIER, ERIC HOUSE, NOLAN JENNINGS, IAN WATSON
Hamlet	BRENT CARVER
Ophelia	LUCY PEACOCK
Claudius	JAMES BLENDICK
Gertrude	ELIZABETH SHEPHERD
Polonius	RICHARD CURNOCK
Horatio	LORNE KENNEDY
Soldier/English Ambassador	DANIEL BUCCOS
Fortinbras	ERIC TRASK
Courtiers and Attendants	KEVIN CORK, CHRISTOPHER GIROTTI, DOLORA HARVEY, JOHN NELLES, ERIC TRASK
Stage Manager	MICHAEL BENOIT
Assistant Stage Managers	SUSAN KONYNENBURG MARYLU MOYER
Assistant Director	WILLIAM MERTON MALMO
Assistant Designer	JULIA TRIBE

This play takes place en route to, inside, out of, nearby, round about, and far away from ELSINORE.

Chapter Five: *Rosencrantz And Guildenstern Are Dead*

Rehearsals for *Rosencrantz and Guildenstern Are Dead* officially started on Monday, 24 February, 1986, in Rehearsal Hall 2 of the Avon Theatre, under the direction of John Wood, a graduate of Bishop's University. Wood began his career as a producer for Canadian Broadcasting Corporation radio in Toronto before moving to Winnipeg to direct both children's and mainstage productions at the Manitoba Theatre Centre. Wood, who studied as both a dancer and a pianist, says his CBC radio job demonstrated the effect and value that sound can have in the theatre. His long professional association with musician Alan Laing, who describes himself as a sound man first and a composer second, began soon after he left the CBC.

Wood first came to Stratford in 1972 when he and Laing, then music director for drama at the Festival, brought their production of *Pinocchio* from the MTC for a production at the Third Stage. Wood had adapted the play from Collodi's work, while Laing provided the music. The production had come about in Winnipeg when Wood was handed what he describes as some awful children's theatre play about a robot that he rejected in favour of returning to his own childhood memories--his mother's reading of *Pinocchio*. He and Laing wrote their own version of the play first for the MTC and then on the CBC, before the Stratford production. Wood developed his philosophy about children's theatre while staging productions for school audiences at the MTC. He opposes the concept of children's theatre as such because he believes so many plays in that genre talk down to children. Kids immediately understand their relationship to that kind of script, he says, and they close their minds to the production. He tries to be aware of the age group for which a show will play and avoid letting the production take on a patronizing tone toward its audience. The production "pleased children of all ages and played to 111 percent of capacity for three weeks." (Pettigrew, John, and Portman, Jamie. *Stratford: The First Thirty Years*, Macmillan of Canada, Toronto, 1985, Vol. II, p. 32) The older people got as much out of it as the younger ones but on a different level, Wood concludes.

He and Laing teamed up again in 1973 to do Michael Ondaatje's *The Collected Works of Billy the Kid* and again at the Third Stage to do Sharon Pollock's *Walsh*, the story of Major James Walsh of the Northwest Mounted Police. He still fondly remembers the excitement of working with new Canadian plays in the early Seventies. During the 1976 season artistic director Robin Phillips assigned Wood the direction of the first full-scale production of an American play ever scheduled at the Festival, *The Crucible*. Miller was not Wood's favourite American playwright, but he says he liked *The Crucible* better than any of Miller's others. The production played as a late-season opener at the Avon. During this time Wood also served as artistic director for the Neptune Theatre in Halifax.

His next visit to Stratford came in 1978, again at Phillips' invitation, to direct *Julius Caesar* on the Festival stage, again as a late opener. By this time Wood had moved to Ottawa as artistic director of the English Theatre at the National Arts Centre. In Ottawa, Wood scheduled the premiere performance of Edward Atienza's one-man show *When That I Was....* When that show received a slot in the 1983 Festival season, Wood accepted the directing responsibilities and again formed an alliance with composer Laing, with whom he would work on the 1986 production of *Rosencrantz and Guildenstern Are Dead*. The costume and set designer for the 1986 paired productions of that play and *Hamlet*, Sue LePage, also designed that 1983 production.

Wood, who has worked extensively as a guest director in addition to having run his own theatres, says that the interesting facet of working as a guest director is being asked to direct plays he would not have chosen to direct himself. Yet, he explains, someone else sees a match between a play and his personality in asking him to direct. He got such an unexpected pairing with all three of his major Stratford productions, he says.

Wood remembers that his 1986 venture with the Festival began in a rather large gathering at the Queen's Hotel in the late spring of 1985, where Neville looked down the table at him while cupping his hands around his lips and mouthing the words *Rosencrantz and Guildenstern Are Dead*--to his astonishment. He says he went home to read the play quickly, and said to himself, "I don't understand what this means." He remembers having seen two productions he recalls as "dark but clever" and both of which intimidated him. Reading the play very slowly then helped ideas fall into place, and once he had an understanding of the piece he determined he would not stage an Elizabethan or dark production or produce it as an example of pseudo-Oxford cleverness. In working on the play early, he knew he wanted to look for places to insert North American references to break the play out of its English-locale straightjacket. For example, the band the two title characters hear in the first scene plays a New Orleans jazz sound.

Wood says he finds the clothing of the Elizabethan era too constricting, although he does not object to doing period plays. His production of *Richard III*, set in its proper time, he enjoyed doing because the clothing styles had not yet changed over to those of the Elizabethan era; *When That I Was...* was done in the Elizabethan mode. When Neville asked him about sliding these paired productions closer to the modern era, Wood says he was delighted.

Wood shared Neville's excitement in examining how much of the same world these two plays, *Hamlet* and *Rosencrantz and Guildenstern Are Dead*, could share. In a meeting with Neville and the two actors who played the title roles on Friday, 6, February, Wood sketched out a background he had put together to use as the starting point for the characters in both productions. He stressed that all the clues he had collected about the essence of these two shadowy characters came from *Hamlet*, although Wood and Neville agreed that very little hard information exists in the text to suggest the nature of the characters' relationship to Hamlet. Wood surmises that Rosencrantz and Hamlet formed a friendship at the Wittenberg University gym, where they fenced together. Guildenstern and Hamlet became friends at the university library, where they studied together. But something a little strange hangs about both Rosencrantz and Guildenstern. In Wood's view they do not know one another well or even like each other very much--one being a jock and the other a scholar--but they room together because nobody else would room with either one of them. Rosencrantz feels fear but will not admit it. He adheres more to the practical side of life and approaches each day in terms of getting that day's jobs done, while Guildenstern seeks the bigger picture, wanting to know why things happen as they do, explains Wood. In this way, Guildenstern has made Rosencrantz more aware of the events that go on about him and has even raised his IQ a couple of points, Wood says. He also thinks Guildenstern the more sinister of the two because he thinks, admits fear, and gets physically violent with the players.

Neville liked Wood's conjectures and agreed that they would serve as a beginning from which the characters could easily approach both plays, but he stated a proviso. He did not want Rosencrantz and Guildenstern to develop to the point where they justified their own existence within the world of *Hamlet*. The whole point of the Stoppard play, he pointed out, lies in their appearance remaining an enigma in *Hamlet*.

Neville put rehearsals for the two title characters ahead of the 24 February official starting date because he believed that until they had established the characters they would play in *Rosencrantz and Guildenstern Are Dead*, setting the direction they would travel in *Hamlet* would prove problematical.

This extra time with the two actors was valuable to Wood. He says that a director struggles to make sense of the text in advance of rehearsals by becoming as familiar as possible with it. But despite reading it a number of times, he says, when he directs he has to hear the words spoken before he can appreciate their full value. The real work he does on a script occurs during rehearsals. These two extra weeks gave him the benefit of hearing large parts of the script spoken aloud for the first time.

Wood says he explained the structure of the play to the actors in this manner: Two men stand alone in a field beside a railroad track discussing their lives. Suddenly a train arrives and the two men board it. Once on board they find a completely different life in progress; a party atmosphere fills the compartments, but nobody speaks to the two men and nobody offers them a drink. They wander about the train unable to enter into the world of the party. Then they must disembark before the train pulls out again, leaving them to their own devices as they try to make some sense out of the experience. They stand alone for a long time until the next train pulls in and stops. A completely different world exists on this train, too. So Rosencrantz and Guildenstern spend the entire play waiting for occasional bits of information but ultimately cannot relate them to anything that has meaning. While Wood worked with the two actors, he checked frequently with the designer, Sue LePage, with whom he had worked on as many as fifteen different productions. They have even developed a system of shorthand that they use in talking to one another, he says. LePage says that she had never seen a production of *Rosencrantz and Guildenssern Are Dead*, but found it intriguing when she read the script. She began early to do text work but to meet the design schedule had to take her cue from *Hamlet* and let *Rosencrantz and Guildenstern* live in the world of *Hamlet*.

LePage says that she feared Rosencrantz and Guildenstern might look ahead of their time because they wound up "so casual and so American," even though their costumes actually came out of pictures of college boys from about 1905 to 1910. She calls it an earlier version of "the 23 skiddoo fashion, which featured the slightly rah-rah look of baggy pants and pork pie hats." Another concern, she explains, was that two guys standing around in street wear might not make the most visually interesting beginning, especially once the audience realizes that they are the center of the show. So she went for a slightly theatrical look which featured motoring coats, hats, and goggles to make them look enigmatic rather than ordinary. She points out that Stoppard calls for two Elizabethans in full regalia--hats, cloaks, sticks, and money bags--to begin the play. And since as she says her first reaction to that stage direction raised the question "Why?", she continually sought ways to avoid the opposite extreme, which would make them too ordinary.

After beginning with the idea of military flavour in the costumes, her ideas evolved to three-piece brown and gray tweed suits to which she added the accoutrements described above. LePage came up with five costume designs; of those discarded, LePage says, each represented a possible Rosencrantz or Guildenstern, but none of them worked for this pair. She says that designers acknowledge the difficulty of working on a costume before knowing what actor will wear it.

Exploring the continuity between *Hamlet* and *Rosencrantz and Guildenstern Are Dead*, she found the most difficulty in making the band of players similar because the players themselves bring life into the world of *Hamlet* and death into the world of *Rosencrantz and Guildenstern Are Dead*. To make as many of the costumes work for both plays as she could, she explains, they started out dark and devoid of decoration for *Rosencrantz and Guildenstern* and bits of ribbon and trim were pinned on for *Hamlet*. Other individual costumes changed between the two shows but maintained the same silhouette, says LePage. While Neville, Wood, and LePage decided most events and characters in the two plays could benefit from mutually shared surroundings, some exceptions pushed themselves into the process, as a look at the rehearsal period will demonstrate.

Lighting designer Michael J. Whitfield received his M.A. in theatre from Villanova University and did design work at the University of Illinois before coming to Stratford in 1974 as assistant technical director and assistant lighting designer to Gil Wechsler. He designed the Third Stage productions that year, working with Wood on *Walsh*. His work with the Festival took him exclusively into lighting; the first production for which he designed the lights was *A Midsummer Night's Dream* in 1976. He took over as resident lighting designer in 1979, lighting that year a record twelve productions. He lit *The Mikado* that has toured internationally and *Virginia*, which played at the Haymarket Theatre in London after its Stratford run. He has worked at regional theatres, including the Neptune, Manitoba Theatre Centre, the St. Lawrence Centre, the Canadian Opera Company, the National Ballet of Canada, the Houston Grand Opera, the Michigan Opera, and the Amsterdam De Nederlandse Operastichting.

He and John Wood decided on a strong, dynamic quality in the lighting for the play, isolating Rosencrantz and Guildenstern and their world by bright light coming in from the wings that symbolizes the offstage party to which they're not invited. When the *Hamlet* characters come on stage, they bring the strong light with them, disorienting the audience and Rosencrantz and Guildenstern. The lighting was intended to demonstrate the characters' world as off center or on edge, Whitfield says.

Both Keith Dinicol (Guildenstern) and William Dunlop (Rosencrantz) went on the 1985 American tour, and naturally they wanted to get together soon to begin working on the play. But, according to Dunlop, Wood had instructed the pair to do no more than read the script once. As the tour drew to a close, Dunlop and Dinicol noticed that they had begun to spend more and more time together, and the rest of the company gave them some ribbing about it.

When rehearsals formally opened for this play--which had never received a Festival production--Wood dispensed with an opening discussion and spent the morning session in a read-through and the afternoon session beginning to block. At the time he described his plan as:

> Whatever happens, happens. It's a real team effort and you make certain choices. You've chosen the actors, you've chosen the designer, the composer. You have read the script five or six times.

Wood works best when he hears the script come alive and does not block in advance. "You have an impression. You've got the right actors. You go with them and they will tell you what comes next." Wood likes to postpone working on text until the actors have developed some sense of the playwright. Then he builds a base in physical movement, changing nearly until the last preview. He imposes it without much input from the actors at first because he wants to establish that starting point for the movement quickly and because the actors will have time in the weeks ahead to consult him about making alterations.

Once the play takes on definite shape, he explains, he can sit back and watch while deciding how to pull it apart to look at new ways to do it, what he calls a forward step even if that piece goes back together as it had started. Wood took as an example adding the window used for the last scene in *Hamlet* to the last scene in his play, a change which he says took an hour and a half to complete. During that time they tried the scene a number of different ways until Wood got it the way he wanted it. He explains:

> I have a reputation for changing my mind. I don't change my mind, ever; I reject something and go on to the next, and it may take twelve steps to get there, but I think that's what you have to do.

After two weeks of rehearsals, Wood had his two title characters switch roles, to work against type casting: He came to see he had cast the actors in the wrong roles. LePage says the play became more interesting when the actors said opposite lines. The switch of roles created a choice for Neville, who by this time had progressed some five weeks into *Hamlet* rehearsals, and he chose not to have the actors switch roles for his production. Consequently Dunlop played Guildenstern in *Hamlet* and Rosencrantz in

Rosencrantz and Guildenstern Are Dead, and Dinicol played Rosencrantz in the former and Guildenstern in the latter. At this point, too, Wood quit attending the rehearsals for *Hamlet*, and the plan to rehearse the two plays together by interspersing scenes was scrapped, since with the change in casting the plan no longer was valid. While the directors, actors, and designer date the point at which Wood began to take the play in its separate direction as the time at which the actors switched roles, Dunlop believes such an uncoupling would have occurred at some point when it was common sense to do so.

Dinicol explains that Dunlop had looked up meanings for words that Guildenstern uses in Stoppard's play, so he benefited from Dunlop's preparations as well as his dictionary. Wood recalls that the basic characterizations he had envisioned for each role did not change when the actors turned the roles around because each had heard the conversations with the other one about character and each remembered the remarks addressed to the other.

Wood believes in trusting his instincts, that being prepared for a scene means being open to it. He makes a mistake, he says, when he backs an actor into specifics too early. The director will not be playing the part, he says; the actor will. The director's job is sparking an actor's imagination. He also stresses that the process works best when the rehearsals remain fun for director and company. He does say that lack of prior planning ensures problems at the end of the rehearsal period just as the production prepares to go into preview performances, when additional pressures can hurt a production. At Stratford, he relates, planning eliminates problems and pressures, allowing the sense of fun to prevail. If problems arise, the whole support system exists to assist in solving them, he says, which leaves the director free to work on the production.

Wood says that profitably using the time between the primary days scheduled for the play became a problem for him personally because he had not rehearsed on such a schedule when directing a late-opening show. (Generally the schedule called for each of the three plays rehearsed at each theatre to get two primary days a week in which it could call whatever actors the director wanted; two secondary days during which the availability of actors depended on the schedule posted by the director with primary rehearsal that day; and two tertiary rehearsals for which availability of actors depended on schedules for the other two shows.) But as he learned to use those days off to let the production work on his subconscious, he came to enjoy not having to make choices overnight between the end of one day's rehearsal and the beginning of the next day's. As one example, Ophelia must return Hamlet's remembrances. Because Wood had decided to do the scenes that come from *Hamlet* in a highly stylized, comic manner, he asked for shopping bags filled with such items as a teddy bear and a pennant from Wittenberg U., the kind of idea that comes of trusting one's instincts to work at the right time. Know the play well, he summarizes; get the right cast and don't decide anything in advance. Rather, go to rehearsals open and, as things begin to happen, say ''yes'' or ''no'' but until that point, just float, he recalls advising a young director. Wood and Laing went into a rehearsal of part of the second act with a tape recorder for backup, and Wood asked Laing to improvise some music and play it under the scene then in rehearsal. Laing played ''There's No Place Like Home,'' the company responded with laughter, and Wood accepted Laing's choice at once.

Laing says that the more the two shows began to grow apart during the rehearsal period, the more he believed that he and LePage had to make as many links between the two as possible, and Wood agreed. The score for the two shows remained pretty much the same except for additions for *Rosencrantz and Guildenstern Are Dead* composed in New Orleans jazz for the players. Wood also asked Laing to use the music to disorientate the audience, and Laing says he did so in two ways. First, he used a sound he describes as an isolated ''electronic shimmer'' to provide a single, glaring note at times when Rosencrantz and Guildenstern ask a particularly pertinent question or just before someone makes an entrance. By putting in this note unpredictably, he kept the audience off balance, says Laing. Also, he used music from *Hamlet* suddenly and only once in this show, and at a different spot. Laing says, ''It heightens the discontinuity of what Stoppard wrote. In the middle of all the powerless, posturing dialogue of this pair, all of a sudden, wham! Something from another world intrudes itself.'' Most of the actors cast as players could not play musical instruments, so they carried a Victrola with them. Laing had intended to write Northern European gypsy music for the players, but the jazz music, which Wood preferred, enabled the players to make their entrance like New Orleans musicians on their way to a funeral. In the second act, more jazz sounds of an offstage party play under most of the scenes. At the end of Wood's production the players make their way back onto the stage to get Hamlet's body, as do Fortinbras' soldiers in *Hamlet*: Laing explains that he sneaked the jazz music back in here, but this time the rendition played in the style of Hamlet's theme music. One note of constancy between the two shows was the use of the Danish National Anthem, which played before the first court scene in *Hamlet* and before Rosencrantz and Guildenstern meet Hamlet in their play. Finally, Wood recalls that he first heard Laing's theme for Ophelia in *Hamlet* when he was on a ladder painting and admired the music so much he nearly fell off. He worked it into this show by playing it on different instruments at the spot in the second act where the two title characters fail to recognize themselves being put to death in the dumb show, what Wood calls "an ominous turn."

Because other characters from *Hamlet* are visitors to the world of *Rosencrantz and Guildenstern Are Dead*, they appear here as "enlarged, oblique angles of the people we see in the other play," according to Lorne Kennedy (Horatio). Elizabeth Shepherd (Gertrude) says this decision was made while the show was "on its feet" during the rehearsal process, and that Gertrude and Claudius begin as a proper king and queen and "from there they begin to slide downhill." At one point in rehearsals, she says, Claudius (James Blendick) had a weakness for Ophelia (as pictured on the last page devoted to this production in the Festival programme), and Gertrude responded by taking Horatio's arm. That made Claudius raise his eyebrows at her, she says. Of his Horatio, Kennedy notes, "Bond is the name. Horatio Bond." He wears an "elegant tuxedo," sports the queen on his arm, and smokes a cigarette. Kennedy calls this character "Horatio through the looking glass." Also, Richard Curnock's Polonius, in reciting kinds of plays that the players could perform, smashes into one of Silver's black towers on his way out of a scene. Peacock asked Wood why he directed her as if she were always crying, but she found in *Hamlet* that the character is always close to tears. This production takes the character to the most logical extreme, she concludes. Ophelia winks at Rosencrantz, slips a glass of wine off a tray, and drinks it before Polonius can grab it. In sum, says Shepherd, the court has its own intrigues to occupy its time, and no one concerns himself with Rosencrantz and Guildenstern.

The production that opened on Thursday, 21 May, 1986, contained thirty-one scenes into which Wood had divided Stoppard's script. The director also provided the titles for each scene. The page numbers refer to the faber and faber edition (publisher's lowercase letters) used for this production.

Act I

Act I contained eight scenes: Scene One, "Syllogisms" (pp. 7-16); Scene 2, "Times Being What They Are" (pp. 16-25); Scene 3, "Without Their Helps" (p. 25); Scene 4, "Full Bent At Your Feet" (pp. 25-28); Scene 5, "I Want To Go Home" (pp. 28-33); Scene 5A, "Hamlet's Behind" (p. 33); Scene 6, "Question and Answer" (pp. 33-38); and Scene 7, "Method Madness" (pp. 38-39). In Scene 4 of Wood's divison, Stoppard included a portion of Act II, Scene 2, of Shakespeare's *Hamlet*, another portion of which Stoppard included later in Act I in what Wood called "Scene 7."

The play opens with both actors in motoring coats, goggles, and hats, standing in the first of a series of three positions so that as the light came up they seemed frozen for just a few seconds. The overhead light created a

95

single pool of light that imprisoned the two startled characters each time the light showed them. A single large platform of the *Hamlet* set remained in place: Set against the black box interior of the Avon stage, it appeared pointedly austere, bleak, and isolated. (See Illustration 5-1.)

As the lights come up for "Syllogisms," the characters of Rosencrantz and Guildenstern ("If characters is what they are," muses Dinicol, weighing the alternatives) take positions on opposite sides of the platform, one sitting, one standing, to be off balance. Rosencrantz's traveling bag masks the piles of coins that he has won at tossing. From the time the scene begins with seven coin tosses, all of which come down heads, and after which Rosencrantz announces the total score as "seventy-six--love," both characters react to demonstrate their awareness of having entered a world that they can neither explain nor understand. Dunlop says Rosencrantz is embarrassed at having taken all of his friend's money but does not realize that he's had any extraordinary luck. Dunlop says Dinicol's Guildenstern increasingly recognizes and mistrusts their situation, but his character does not fully discover fear until much later in the act. Dinicol agrees that the run of heads during the coin toss scene frightens the introspective Guildenstern, but the character cannot use this insight to any advantage.

"Times Being What They Are" begins as the players enter. Wood and LePage, figuring out what kind of cart the actors would use, initially considered using a bicycle. They came across a picture of an ambulance hooked to a bicycle from the right era. Together they came up with the plan to combine a bicycle with a hearse, an approach Wood liked because he wanted to use the players to be a band of angels who stumble across Rosencrantz and Guildenstern on their way to pick up Hamlet. The Player (Ron Hastings) lies hidden inside the hearse but suddenly sits up in time to see the pair through the window. Hastings says the character is showing members of the troupe how to perform a death scene and gets carried away.

Hastings says that he and Wood began rehearsals envisioning his character as the Angel of Death, but the angel so enjoys his new-found persona as the Player that he is frequently led off into the make-believe of the real players; sometimes he is diverted from his appointed task. Hastings creates a character from elements within himself and needs to find some admirable qualities in a character he creates, so for this role he approached the Angel of Death by looking for positive qualities and found help in the work of Dr. Elizabeth Kubler-Ross on death and dying. Hastings thus saw himself as a teacher who would lead Rosencrantz and Guildenstern through stages to deal with the actuality of their own deaths.

As the Player walks offstage, Rosencrantz and Guildenstern turn away from a bright light and freeze as Ophelia and Hamlet run onto the stage to play "Without Their Helps." Rosencrantz and Guildenstern thus do not see Hamlet and Ophelia play this scene of his appearance to her in *Hamlet* that is told by Ophelia to her father (II.1.74-100). Dinicol says the key to understanding the play lies in Rosencrantz's line from Act II, "We're out of our depth here." Wood and Laing decided to add some of that dialogue to the musical sound track, which then played over the scene so that the audience would have no trouble understanding the context of what they witnessed. Ophelia comes on stage with a huge embroidery hoop covered with bright yellow material with stitching. She wears exaggerated makeup, and when Hamlet follows, he comes dancing. Wood received some criticism for the comic treatment he chose for the *Hamlet* characters in this production and defends his choice by pointing to Stoppard's use of Shakespeare's description of Hamlet in this scene:

> Lord Hamlet, with his doublet all unbraced, Nor hat upon his head, his stockings fouled, Ungartered, and down-gyved to his ankle, Pale as his shirt, his knees knocking each other, II.1. 78-81.

"How can one do the scene without making Hamlet look like an old man with his knees knocking together?" asks Wood. This scene served as a starting point for Wood's treatment of the other *Hamlet* characters. As Ophelia and Hamlet exit in opposite directions, the red drapes used in the first court scene in *Hamlet* drop unevenly and stop six to eight feet from the stage, as the Danish National Anthem plays, giving the idea of imbalance and tension.

"Full Bent At Your Feet," the title of which accents the title characters' bobbing up and down in response to being called by wrong names, also features Gertrude reading her opening speech off little pink note cards, Shepherd's idea put in only a few previews before opening. Because Stoppard's premise in writing the play is based on an offstage performance of *Hamlet* which occasionally coincides with scenes on stage, another character from *Hamlet* also appears in this scene. Claudius, who has had several glasses of wine in the first court scene in *Hamlet*, looks intoxicated. Dunlop explains that what the audience saw in the highly stylized comic characters from *Hamlet* resembles the view that Rosencrantz and Guildenstern must have had of the people and events in *Hamlet*, which Dunlop describes as "a heightened version of what's going on almost to the point of being absurd or ridiculous....It's almost as if they [the audience] are seeing the play through our eyes."

Curnock's Polonius follows Claudius offstage, proclaiming, as that character does in *Hamlet*, that he has found "the very cause of Hamlet's lunacy...." The assertion that Hamlet has gone mad immediately elicits a response from Rosencrantz, "I want to go home," the title of the scene which begins as the *Hamlet* characters leave the stage. The drapes rise, leaving Rosencrantz and Guildenstern to their own devices. Dunlop says that if Hamlet is mad, they have no hope of "gleaning what affects him," as the king has charged them. They feel the terror, says Dunlop, that Guildenstern expresses over the coins in the first scene. The task-oriented Guildenstern now focuses his ideas and energy, explains Dunlop. Dinicol agrees but relates that he searched for a cause for Guildenstern's first comment, "Don't let them confuse you," in a line of illogical developments ending with the assertion of Hamlet's madness:

> *If something like that happened to us right now, we wouldn't sit around and say, "Don't let them confuse you." But that's the humour of the situation, so obviously it's done for the humour, to get the laughs, and that's why it's there, and anything other than that I think it is dangerous to start to get into.*

The scene also contains the word game, which an audience does not immediately understand and which the two characters must thus play with an ease that bespeaks familiarity. For Dinicol, the word game symbolizes all the twists these characters put on words throughout the play; they are momentarily amusing but do not in the end help them. In explaining the difficulty of working on this text, he says he and Dunlop worked to discover the meaning behind some of these lines. They were left to conclude that Stoppard's purpose lay solely in setting up the next joke. Dinicol explains that because the play belongs to the comic genre, their sharp-witted questions lead to little understanding in this game of intellectual blind man's bluff, which symbolizes the world of this play. Wood says that during rehearsals for a particular scene he and the cast spent as much as an hour on some of the more difficult passages of text, looking for the right meaning, and finally stopping in order to keep up the pace. Wood believes that Stoppard wrote the play as a comedy and intended groups that performed it to have fun with it. He admits that telling an actor "I don't know" about an interpretation is difficult for a director, but he had to do it sometimes when work with the text did not offer a given interpretation. Dunlop credits Wood with asking him repeatedly for the meaning of a word, the nature of one of his character's referents, or the reason for a piece of business he performed: Back to the dictionary and the script. Unfortunately, he says, not all directors stress text to the extent that Wood did.

"Hamlet's Behind" was Hamlet's cross up stage while reading a book so that Guildenstern catches only a glimpse of his back. Stoppard uses the scene to set up the one from *Hamlet*, II.1.171-220, in which Polonius questions Hamlet. Stoppard's version of that scene, which Wood rehearsed as Scene 7, "Method Madness," closes the first act.

"Questions" results from Guildenstern's momentary shock at seeing Hamlet, putting him back on the job of probing his behaviour. The two practise their inquiries by role playing with each other before trying it out on the prince. Rosencrantz is slow to understand, and Dinicol explains that during rehearsals he had to fight his tendency to get angry at the plodding Rosencrantz, which would have made the relationship ugly and cost the play some humour. The friendship must show through, he stresses: The real fault lies in Guildenstern's lack of clarity about his proposal and not in Rosencrantz's subsequent muddleheaded response to it. Dinicol also uses this scene to make another point about the relationship between the two. Roles have been reversed, he says, so that whenever one of them has had enough and wants to turn back the other takes charge and decides to stay the course, setting up the end of the play in which Guildenstern says, "...there must have been a moment, at the beginning, where we could have said...no. But somehow we missed it." Both characters say "no" during this play but, as Dinicol says, never at the same time. The one saying "yes" always manages to carry the day.

In "Method Madness" Hamlet does not recognize the pair until an elaborate charade of head and hand gestures signals them to move all around at his will. Throughout the time Hamlet gives the signals, he stares at them and studies them intently, and for comedy the script dictates that, even so, he get their names backwards. In this production, Hamlet walks between them, turns his back to the audience, and sticks out his elbows for a very perplexed Rosencrantz and Guildenstern to take as he leads them offstage while house lights come up. Brent Carver as Hamlet moved in the same oddly stylized manner he had used since his first entrance with Ophelia. Thus the scene supports LePage's contention that the production style reveals more about the characters and their situation than does Shakespeare's familiar text.

Act II

Act II contained sixteen scenes: Scene 8, "Buzz, Buzz" (p. 40); Scene 9, "He Murdered Us" (pp. 41-45); Scene 10, "Can You Play?" (p. 45); Scene 11, "I Saw You Do It" (pp. 45-51); Scene 12, "Stuffed In A Box (pp. 51-53); Scene 13, "Sweet Gertrude" (pp. 53-54); Scene 14, "Toffee Apples" (pp. 54-55); Scene 15, "Well, Well, Well" (pp. 55-56); Scene 16, "Dress Rehearsal" (pp. 56-58); Scene 17, "No More Marriage" (pp. 58-59); Scene 18, "Chaos On The Night" (pp. 59-64); "Scene 19, False Fire" (p. 64); Scene 20, "Sun Rise" (pp 64- 65); "Scene 21, Wisest Friends" (p.65); Scene 22, "Wheels and Marches" (pp. 65-67); and Scene 23, "How All

Occasions'' (pp. 67-72). The following scenes contained portions of dialogue from Shakespeare's *Hamlet*: Scene 8, II.2; Scene 10,II.2; Scene 15, III.1; Scene 21, IV.1; and Scene 23, IV.2-IV.4.

During the intermission, a second large platform was positioned on top of the one which played throughout the first act, and two stairs formed a V-shape above the top platform, to alter the appearance of the stage as if the characters did not enter during the second act the world they had left behind at intermission. (See Illustration 5-2.) As Hamlet leads the pair back onto the stage for ''Buzz, Buzz,'' they stumble over the step units that Hamlet skilfully avoids. Some ten lines later, Hamlet is ''about to leave,'' but Wood had Carver already offstage there and slipped him back to listen to them and then interrupt them with, ''But my uncle-father and aunt-mother are deceived.'' II.2. 374-375, coming up behind them as they sit on the stairs. Dinicol says that just enough of Shakespeare's scene was transferred to this one to get the laughs. He cites Hamlet's line ''I am but mad north north-west; when the wind is southerly I know a hawk from a handsaw'' (II.2.377-378).

As Hamlet leaves them alone for the second time, ''He Murdered Us'' begins. Dinicol notes that Guildenstern sees progress in their interview with Hamlet, which in Stoppard's play takes place during intermission. Rosencrantz quickly explodes that fiction, says Dinicol, by announcing the score from their encounter with the prince as ''Twenty-seven--three, and you think he might have had the edge?! He *murdered us*.'' This scene is a kind of foreshadowing of the play's ending, where Guildenstern's philosophical bent serves this pair no better than Rosencrantz's practical approach, a conclusion borne out during the rest of the scene by their inability either by theoretical or pragmatic methods to determine the answer to so simple a question as which direction is south.

Rescue from this dilemma comes with the arrival of the players in the ''Can you Play?'' scene, parading across the upstage portion of the set from stage left to right, some pantomiming playing musical instruments to Laing's jazz. Hamlet and some of the lesser nobles of the Danish court join in the festivities as the group makes its way across the stage to give the prince time to strike the deal with the Player to insert some lines into the play.

''I Saw You Do It'' begins as Guildenstern approaches the Player with the line,'' So you've caught up,'' words from the Player's speech in *Hamlet*, where, in describing the ''mobled'' queen in the scene Hamlet has asked him to recite, he pictures her robe as ''A blanket in the alarm of fear caught up.... (II.2.507). During each performance of *Hamlet* Hastings' Player addresses the words ''caught up'' directly to Dunlop's Guildenstern, who says that although playing in *Hamlet* at the moment the line provides him with a direct transition to *Rosencrantz and Guildenstern Are Dead*. The actors acknowledge an audience may not follow these complicated connecting links. In another of them, Hastings recites the speech (p. 47) in which he describes the troupe's play for the pair in words that rework the Hecuba portions of Hamlet's soliloquy, beginning, "Oh what a rogue and peasant slave am I!" (II.2.547-603).

Dinicol says Guildenstern has been cocky with the Player but now needs his help, and the Player overlooks their behaviour to get on with the business of teaching them. His injunction, "I should concentrate on not losing your heads," is from his character of the Angel of Death, again so caught up in his impersonation of the Player that the warnings simply slip out at times. But for whatever purpose, says Hastings, he puts Rosencrantz and Guildenstern back on track with the information that Hamlet loves Ophelia.

Dunlop says the next scene, "Stuffed in a Box," beginning with the line, "Do you ever think of yourself as actually *dead*, lying in a box?" and containing the line, "I'm going to stuff you in this box now, would you rather be alive or dead?" (p. 54) concerns itself with the same matters Hamlet considers in "To be or not to be" (III.1.56-89) and provides still another link between the two plays. Now, says Dinicol of this scene, Rosencrantz begins to question the situation and furthers the plot, setting up all the laughs he gets in thinking that sequence through. Dinicol keeps pointing to Stoppard's comic purposes and to the way that seemingly serious situations come to a halt for the purpose of making a joke before proceeding again. A number of points connect the two plays, but Dinicol believes that Rosencrantz's look at the "To be or not to be" soliloquy, like many others, first serves the comic purposes of the playwright and only secondarily serves to further his plot.

The red drapes partly descend again, and Claudius and Gertrude rush back onto the stage for "Sweet Gertrude." In this production Rosencrantz sees the queen and king and immediately bows, then snaps his fingers in the direction of Guildenstern, who has relaxed into a peaceful reverie at the moment as he works on solving a problem. This particular problem is the contemplation of "death followed by eternity...the worst of both worlds. It is a terrible thought." Despite what he says, it brings him a certain amount of satisfaction to contemplate, says Dinicol. No sooner has Guildenstern seen the royal party and jumped to his feet than they just as quickly rush offstage with drapes ascending, but more importantly to Dinicol, without imparting any information.

The "Toffee Apples" scene begins with them alone, still without information. Rosencrantz spots Hamlet, and their expectancy takes over. Again it is undercut by the comedy of Guildenstern's inquiry, asking if Hamlet approaches selling toffee apples, says Dinicol.

During "Well, Well, Well," Hamlet enters with a book and sits on the staircase with his back to them, reading, eventually leaning backward far enough for his head almost to touch the stage floor. Ophelia's entrance diverts his attention, and he runs off in pursuit, taking no notice of Rosencrantz and Guildenstern. Several times the two resolve to approach him but never muster the nerve. Only after Hamlet has spotted Ophelia and pursued her on the line, "Nymph, in thy orisons be all my sins remembered," does an audience familiar with *Hamlet* realize that Rosencrantz debated interrupting him while he silently says, "To be or not to be."

"Dress rehearsal" begins to the sounds of the party offstage in the wings, a party to which no one invites Rosencrantz and Guildenstern, says Wood. Horatio strolls in with the queen on his arm. Kennedy, who played Horatio in both productions, says he used the Player's speech, "Look on every exit being an entrance somewhere else," as the basis for his action. Because he brings on the chairs for the performance of the play in *Hamlet*, he asked Wood about carrying the chairs out of this scene depicting the rehearsal as if he were on his way with them into the other scene. But because Wood needed chairs for this scene as well, says Kennedy, Horatio brings on chairs for this scene. Kennedy says Horatio must, in the style of the sorcerer's apprentice, provide chairs for both, and he finally falls exhausted into one of them, only to have the Player propel him up and on his way again with the line, "Off we go." Hastings says that while the line could refer to beginning the rehearsal, he uses it to get rid of Horatio because he wants to stage this version of the drama privately for Rosencrantz and Guildenstern to teach them something meaningful before time runs out.

No sooner has the dumb show concluded and the play started than Hamlet and Ophelia interrupt the rehearsal with the ending lines of the *Hamlet* nunnery scene. Peacock says she cannot think of it as the same scene she plays in *Hamlet*, preferring to think of herself as "the little girl" who pursued Hamlet with two shopping bags full of remembrances to deliver. As Hamlet exits, Ophelia remains on stage crying, and watches wide-eyed there. The rehearsal picks up momentum; Claudius and Polonius enter from behind the arras (the same burgundy drapes) as they do in *Hamlet* III.1.l163-189, for the "No More Marriage" scene in this play. The humour springs in part from this private conversation being held here within the hearing of everyone on stage and the pair reacting as if they do not choose to notice the others. Blendick snatches the crown from the player king and places it on his own head as he plays his brief scene with Polonius, tossing it from the wings as he exits to an astonished player king (Peter Donaldson).

Now left alone with Rosencrantz and Guildenstern for an extended time during "Chaos on the Night," the Player can help them understand what will happen to them by presenting this full-dress rehearsal of their own deaths. Later he confronts them with two spies, actors who have the same body types and dress as Dunlop and Dinicol. Rosencrantz crosses the stage to stare at them before deciding that he does not know them after all. The spy dressed like Guildenstern (Eric House) pulls a coin from his pocket and tosses it in the air several times, but not even this device produces a glimmer of self-identification for which the Player has so fervently hoped. Dinicol says that here Guildenstern moves from the security of having a problem to solve to uncertainty and suspicion at the point where, Hastings says, the Player has begun moving more pointedly to the subject of death. Since Guildenstern wants to talk intellectually rather than existentially about death, he has not grasped the personal significance of death at all. Dinicol also says the scene is meaningful in setting up the end of the play during which Rosencrantz and Guildenstern die in exactly the manner Guildenstern has described to the Player--that is, they quite simply fail to reappear.

The lights come down as "False Fire" begins. Here Wood decided to add to Laing's musical soundtrack more lines from the end of the play scene in *Hamlet* III.2.274-279 than Stoppard originally used, so that an audience would have no doubt that during the blackout the king and queen saw the play and that the king has broken off the performance as he did in *Hamlet*.

As the lights come up on the "Sun Rise" scene, Rosencrantz and Guildenstern lie under their motoring coats, which had been stripped off the spies and used to cover their "dead" bodies as the lights come down. By this time, explains Dinicol, both the title characters as well as the audience have no idea what will happen next, and so when they wake up onstage alone, that situation gains immediate acceptance.

The entrance of Claudius begins the "Wisest Friends" scene, during which he charges the pair with finding Hamlet and the body of Polonius. Wood made a small textual change in Shakespeare which made a large difference in meaning for the scene: In *Hamlet* Claudius says:

Come, Gertrude, we'll call up our wisest friends And let them know both what we mean to do And what's untimely done. IV.1.38-40.

Wood changed the line to read:

Come, Gertrude, we'll call up our wisest friends And let them both know what we mean to do.

While Claudius and Gertrude rush out, "Wheels and Marches" begins. Dinicol says the king's command drives Rosencrantz and Guildenstern to the next sequence, figuring out how to accomplish his purposes. Dinicol says Stoppard jokes even here when they stretch Rosencrantz's belt across

Hamlet's path, succeeding only in losing Rosencrantz's pants, a sight gag that speaks volumes about the effectiveness of these characters.

The entrance of Hamlet begins the "How All Occasions" scene. Neither Rosencrantz nor Guildenstern has succeeded in getting the information Claudius wants, so they fear the king might have them killed. When Claudius asks for Hamlet, Dunlop's Rosencrantz passes the buck by saying to Guildenstern, "Ho. Bring in the lord...." when neither of them has any idea where to find Hamlet. Salvation comes quickly and unexpectedly as Hamlet, under guard, is marched in, setting off another vague alarm bell in Guildenstern's head. Rosencrantz believes that whatever happens cannot be any worse than what has already happened--and might even be better--but Guildenstern cannot adopt that optimism. Dinicol says he has had an almost mystical experience wherein he knew in advance that they would draw the assignment of taking Hamlet to England. He is unsettled, and Dinicol believes that the audience experiences this show through his eyes because he comes so close to the truth. But just as importantly, the actor stresses, here the pair has missed another opportunity to say "no."

After the second intermission, Act III begins, containing eight scenes: Scene 24, "We're on a Boat" (pp.73-84); Scene 25, "Black Resolve" (p. 84); Scene 26, "Gay Sight" (pp. 84-86); Scene 27, "Banging on Barrels" (pp.86-89); Scene 28, "General Panic" (pp. 89-90); Scene 29, "The Barrel is Missing" (pp. 90-96); Scene 30, "Court and Corpses" (p. 96); and Scene 31, "Tableau" which contained Wood's addition to the ending. The step units added for Act II were shifted to the right and left sides on a triangular piece added to give this set the same small shape as the *Hamlet* set. Three barrels were added on a diagonal from down right to up left. (See Illustration 5-3.) Laing laughingly says that Wood had entirely too much time on his hands, and so as he read the opening of the third act one day came across Stoppard's direction for "snatches of a sea shanty maybe." Wood then told him, "There ought to be a sea shanty maybe," and Laing offered to write the music after Wood had written the lyrics. In the word game spirit of Stoppard's play, Wood wrote the words around the key word "maybe." One line from his lyrics makes the point over and over again: "Maybe there's a girl in Portsmouth Harbour."

During "We're on a Boat," Stoppard again begins with Rosencrantz and Guildenstern, plunging them literally and figuratively into the dark. When the lights do come up, on Hamlet, he sits in a deck chair on the top level, partly shielded by a large patio umbrella. Rosencrantz and Guildenstern sit on opposite sides of the down stage area. Both actors point to the changing nature of their relationship during this scene. Guildenstern begins the act peacefully because he rather enjoys the boat ride, says Dinicol. But now

Rosencrantz grows uncomfortable and begins to ask questions that sound like Guildenstern's, such as "What now?" in response to no direct stimulus. While Guildentern has a purpose which orders his thinking, taking Hamlet to England, Rosencrantz questions even that. "What for?" He begins to disturb Guildenstern, but Dinicol finds the high point of the scene in learning that they must transport Hamlet to his death. Their letter to the English king requests that he cut off Hamlet's head. Dinicol says that for a moment Guildenstern stands stunned because he has thought of Hamlet as his friend. Slowly, the actor says, Guildenstern begins to find logical reasons why they must not interfere with the will of fate, much less the will of kings. Dinicol finds that once he has worked out the rationale, Guildenstern concludes the debate by saying, "It could have been worse." He meant, "It could have been us."

During "Black Resolve," Hamlet exchanges the letter calling for his death for one calling for the deaths of Rosencrantz and Guildenstern. Wood and Carver spent a long time over the question of Hamlet's guilt, because Carver did not see Hamlet as the villain of the piece, as Wood wanted to play him. Wood explained that Hamlet treats this pair quite badly--ignoring them, retreating from them. While Hamlet performs the same actions in this play that the text of *Hamlet* describes him as performing, the difference between the two plays, Wood explained to Carver, lies in Hamlet's having no emotional basis in this play to perform those actions. Consequently, Wood says, he must simply discharge them and thereby becomes a blackguard. Carver argued that just as Hamlet has a choice, so do Rosencrantz and Guildenstern, who choose to be toadies. Wood saw them as pawns caught up in a larger power struggle; Hamlet could have recognized their powerlessness and helped them out, and does not.

As Rosencrantz and Guildenstern awake, "Gay Sight" begins. This scene's flute-like music represents something new and gives Guildenstern a chance to put his logic to work: The source of the music is discovered as the players climb out of the three barrels to begin "Banging on the Barrels." Dinicol says Guildenstern has a chink in his logical armour. He cannot make sense of their presence on board the ship to England. The usual gags are traded, centering on travel, like those built into the beginning of the play. Just before the pirates attack this pair recounts their exploits for the players, ending with the line, "Incidents! All we get is incidents! Dear God, is it too much to expect a little sustained action?!"

During the pirates' attack, "General Panic," the pirate king's theme from *The Pirates of Penzance* emerged clearly through the sounds of battle. The Festival staged this Gilbert and Sullivan operetta in the Avon in 1985 with Carver as the Pirate King in the production. The music had a familiar ring for many in the audience. The Player, Hamlet, and Rosencrantz and Guildenstern madly dash around the stage looking for a hiding place before diving into the barrels just before the entrance of the rest of the players, now dressed as pirates, which occasions the blackout ending the scene.

As the lights rise, "The Barrel is Missing" begins. Once they discover that they have lost Hamlet, Dinicol explains, "It's panic time from then on." A double death scene ensues, involving at first just the death of the Player and eventually all the players, giving the Player a second death scene. Hastings recounts that in early September, with only seven performances to go, Wood sent him a note that the speech provided the Player with his last chance to teach Rosencrantz and Guildenstern something. So, Hastings says, he played a portion of the last line to each of the two characters: "So there's an end to that--it's commonplace (to Rosencrantz), light goes with life (to Guildenstern), and in the winter of your years (upward rather than to either of them) the dark comes early...." Now that they have no reason to live, death comes to them as Guildenstern always said it would. First Rosencrantz walks away and fails to reappear, and then the light fades out on Guildenstern, leaving the stage in blackness.

As the lights rise for "Court and Corpses," the actors take their places as in the final scene of *Hamlet*, which, as Stoppard indicates, resemble the dying players' positions. At the conclusion of Horatio's speech ("Tableaux") the players enter and look at the dead bodies before selecting Hamlet's as the one they want. They carry him out in front of an intense orange glow lighting the cyclorama that reveals the hearse. On top Rosencrantz and Guildenstern sit in silhouette; as the cart begins to move off, supposedly to meet the players carrying Hamlet's body, the two title characters from this play begin to flip coins. Of the final image, Wood says he doesn't know how he got the idea but he does know that he wanted to see both the characters and the hearse again.

In summary, Wood emphasizes two points about the play. The first concerns the way Rosencrantz and Guildenstern are used as victims throughout. Because they do not perceive themselvces as having an independent will from that of the king, they never see an alternative to doing his bidding. The other point he makes concerns the humour Stoppard uses. Born in Czechoslovakia, Stoppard came to England at about the age of nine. The word games he plays and the jokes he makes about having no faith in England, says Wood, reveal the sensitivities of someone who came to English as a second language. The resulting jibes he takes at the language give Anglophiles a glimpse at the workings of their language they might otherwise take for granted.

A postscript. Actor Ron Hastings accepted the role of Marley in *A Christmas Carol*, directed by Brian Rintoul (who directed Hastings at Stratford in *Henry VIII*), at the Manitoba Theatre Centre during the 1986 Christmas season. At the closing-night Stratford party, he said he did so at least partly because he viewed the role as a chance to play another ghost who wanted to teach someone something helpful.

Illustration 5-1

Designer Sue LePage's ground plan for Act I of *Rosencrantz and Guildenstern Are Dead*, with the diamond-shaped platforms.

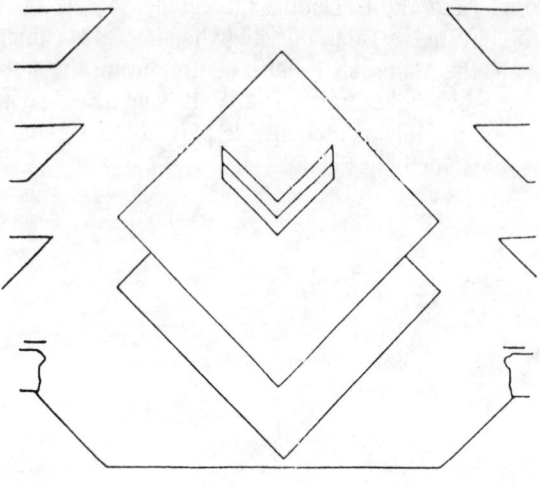

Illustration 5-2

Designer Sue LePage's ground plan for Act II of *Rosencrantz and Guildenstern Are Dead*. A second platform and two step units have been added.

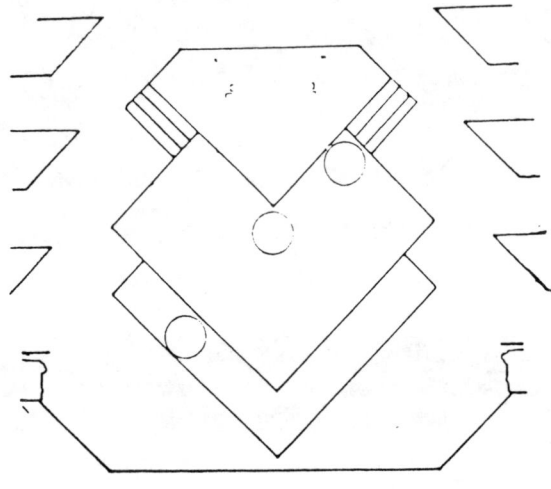

Illustration 5-3

Designer Sue LePdage's ground plan for Act III of *Rosencrantz and Guildenstern Are Dead*. The step units have been moved off to the side, and a third , triangular, platform has been added, along with the three barrels.

HENRY VIII

BY WILLIAM SHAKESPEARE

DIRECTED BY	BRIAN RINTOUL
COSTUMES DESIGNED BY	DEBRA HANSON
SET DESIGNED BY	PHILLIP SILVER
MUSIC BY	GARY KULESHA
LIGHTING DESIGNED BY	MICHAEL J. WHITFIELD
DANCES CHOREOGRAPHED BY	JOHN BROOME

THE CAST

in order of appearance

Gentleman	BRENT CARVER
Gentleman	IAN WATSON
Thomas Cranmer, Ambassador to the Papal Court, later Archbishop of Canterbury	DAVID BROWN
Anne Bullen, Maid of Honour to Queen Katherine, later Marchioness of Pembroke, later Queen of England	CAMILLE MITCHELL
Duke of Buckingham, Lord High Constable	JAMES BLENDICK
Earl of Surrey, Deputy of Ireland	LORNE KENNEDY
Duke of Norfolk, later Earl Marshal of England	DAVID SCHURMANN
Wolsey, Cardinal of York and Lord Chancellor of England	WILLIAM HUTT
Gardiner, Secretary to Cardinal Wolsey, later Bishop of Winchester	SCOTT WENTWORTH
Thomas Cromwell, Secretary to Wolsey, later Secretary to Henry	MICHAEL FAWKES
Duke of Suffolk, later High Steward	DANIEL BUCCOS
Sergeant at Arms	MAX HELPMANN
King Henry VIII	LEON POWNALL
Katherine of Aragon, Queen of England, later The Princess Dowager	ELIZABETH SHEPHERD
Marquis of Dorset	KENNETH WICKES
Surveyor to Buckingham	KEITH DINICOL
Lord Chamberlain	ERIC HOUSE
Lord Walter Sands	WILLIAM DUNLOP
Sir Thomas Lovell, Chancellor of the Exchequer	DAVID GARDNER
Gentlewoman to Queen Katherine, later Lady-in-Waiting to Queen Anne Bullen	CAROLYN HETHERINGTON
Servant to Wolsey	CHRISTOPHER THOMAS
Cardinal Campeius, Legate from Pope Clement VII	RICHARD CURNOCK
Griffith, Gentleman Usher to Queen Katherine	RON HASTINGS
Priest	CHRISTOPHER THOMAS
Bishop of Lincoln	NOLAN JENNINGS
Archbishop of Canterbury, Warham	KEITH DINICOL
Singing Gentlewoman	LUCY PEACOCK
Patience, Gentlewoman to Queen Katherine	HAZEL DESBARATS
Messenger	JEAN-PIERRE FOURNIER
Chapuys, Ambassador from Charles V	KENNETH WICKES
Lord Chancellor, Sir Thomas Audley	KEITH DINICOL
Door-Keeper of the Council Chamber	MAX HELPMANN
Garter, King at Arms	JEAN-PIERRE FOURNIER

Priests, Guards, Executioner, Standard Bearers, Commoners, Bishops, Pages, Ladies-in-Waiting:
KEVIN CORK, HAZEL DESBARATS, WILLIAM DUNLOP, JEAN-PIERRE FOURNIER, CHRISTOPHER
GIROTTI, DOLORA HARVEY, RON HASTINGS, CAROLYN HETHERINGTON,
NOLAN JENNINGS, JOHN NELLES, CHRISTOPHER THOMAS, ERIC TRASK,
IAN WATSON, KENNETH WICKES

Stage Manager	JANINE RALPH
Assistant Director	KELLY ROBINSON
Assistant Designers	ANNE DIXON
	ANDREW MURRAY
Assistant Lighting Designer	ELIZABETH ASSELSTINE

"Cromwell, I charge thee, fling away ambition:
By that sin fell the angels. How can man then,
the image of his maker, hope to win by it?"
Henry VIII III.2.440-442

Chapter Six: *Henry VIII*

Rehearsals for *Henry VIII* began on 3 March, 1986, in Rehearsal Hall 1 of the Avon Theatre, the same space where four weeks earlier the 1986 season had begun for the acting company with the start of rehearsals for *Hamlet*. Director Brian Rintoul was staging his first Stratford production after an association which began with serving as assistant stage manager for a 1969 production of *Hamlet* directed by the then associate artistic director of the Festival, John Hirsch. Hirsch also provided Rintoul with his more recent Festival experience by using him as his assistant director for both the 1984 productions of *A Midsummer Night's Dream* and *A Streetcar Named Desire* and the 1985 productions of *King Lear* and *The Glass Menagerie*.

Rintoul's background includes having directed productions for leading theatres all across Canada, from the Charlottetown Festival to Theatre Calgary, as well as having taught acting and directing at professional studios. In addition he is founding artistic director of the Gryphon Theatre and a past associate director of Alberta Theatre Projects. Neville knew Rintoul's work and had tried to get him to direct at the Neptune while he was artistic director there, but Rintoul had a previous commitment. In October of 1985, just before *Twelfth Night* and *King Lear* left on the American tour, Neville telephoned Rintoul with an offer to direct *Henry VIII* at the Avon Theatre during the 1986 season.

Rintoul, himself a Stratford native "born in the local hospital," had always wanted to direct in his hometown for the Festival, so he accepted the offer, admitting, however to having had a long list of plays that he would rather have directed. He says he had only read the play once--"if skimming counts"--and even that some time ago. But as he reread the script he began to see a modern context emerge that he decided to play instead of surrendering the piece to those critics who condemn it as costume drama. The modern struggles for power and influence are as real for North Americans in 1986 as they were for Englishman 450 years ago, he holds. Furthermore, the power struggles of today are not limited to the world of politics but pervade the norms and customs of the North American pop culture, as television shows such as *Dallas* and *Dynasty* and the numerous imitations they have spawned eloquently testify, he says. What attracted Rintoul to the play, he explains, was the idea that struck him upon reading it:

> How little has changed between our society and their society.... It's still essentially the same moral dilemma: whether or not man should drive himself, his family, and his country forward and sacrifice everything to that end or whether man should behave as God wants him to behave, or more to the point as Christian doctrine wants him to behave...and lead a more spiritually and morally based existence. That's exactly what's in the middle of Henry VIII and exactly what we are talking about today all the time.

Rintoul also explains that because it is one of the longest plays in the canon, one needs to find a way to cut it so that it retains a specific shape. Once he found the "Dallas in funny clothes" through line of the action that he wanted to emphasize, he understood where to go about cutting away some of the text that did not enhance this aspect of the play. The other guideline he used in cutting related to the nature of the play. "It's not a character play: It's a personality play." At the center of this world sits Henry, who is the one personality remaining constant throughout the play, Rintoul says. "Everybody else is either rising, falling or regrouping."

Another aspect of the play to which the director paid special attention pertained to the relative goodness of the characters. He believes that the only truly good character in the play, Queen Katherine, must be balanced against the rest of the characters because "everybody else," he stresses, with the possible exception of Cranmer, "is deeply pock-marked."

When Rintoul accepted the show, he did not realize that the Avon had been redone into a "black box" and that he would be sharing the space with director Walter Learning's production of *A Man for All Seasons*, in sets designed by Phillip Silver. Rintoul explains how well Silver's set served the play by avoiding all the traps of the black box environment that he felt would have killed *Henry VIII* before it started: lack of height, lack of colour, and lack of traffic patterns that simulated those of the Elizabethan theatre. Thus while a basic black box set can appear very sparse and forbidding when used by itself, the kind of environment that Rintoul wanted to avoid, a set for each of the two groups of paired shows at the Avon Theatre was enhanced by the neutral black colour against which it was contrasted.

After redesigning the Avon, Silver was asked to design the sets for both *Henry VIII* and *A Man for All Seasons* in August shortly after the

1986 season had been announced. Then Debra Hanson was asked to do the costumes for both shows. Both Silver and Hanson had extensive experience with the Festival, recently working together as designers on the 1982 Avon production of *Translations* for which he designed the sets and she the costumes. This production, directed by Guy Sprung, later moved to the Toronto Free Theatre, where Sprung is artistic director, following its Festival run. Because Silver also designs costumes and Hanson also designs sets, they enjoy working together because each anticipates the problems of the other.

Silver had another design decision to make. A director who would be working at the Festival Theatre had asked for Silver to design his show as well, and Silver was tempted because he wanted to work with that director. The shows he had been offered at the Avon did not yet have directors. But in thinking over his offers he decided that both *Henry VIII* and his newly designed Avon space would offer special challenges.

Once Rintoul accepted *Henry VIII* he and Silver began work at once. Although they had known each other's work for a long while, since they had met in passing in their work as freelance artists, they had never worked together. Silver remembers that because time was getting tight, he and Rintoul had to begin making decisions about the set both plays would share despite the fact that *A Man for All Seasons* did not yet have a director. Silver says that he was the man in the middle. Once Learning was appointed, he says smiling, "luckily there were no major disagreements." Rintoul and Silver agreed to cover the black floor; Rintoul originally wanted English Medieval tiles, but Silver notes that because so little of that tile still exists, few people are aware of its popularity in that period. A period floor, perhaps with a family coat of arms worked in tile, could be both stunning and appropriate to the period, Silver agreed; but labour costs to use pieces of masonite cut and silk screened were alarming. Silver then thought of Hampton Court with its brick floor, also an appropriate choice for Sir Thomas More's home. The actual material used was masonite prefabricated "rumpus room paneling," explains Silver. "Cut into different panels, delineated with a design, and then very carefully painted and shellacked, it looks quite glorious and was relatively inexpensive." Both directors accepted the amount of floor space, and by "shuttle diplomacy" Silver got an accord on having three steps lead off stage left.

The major scenes were defined in *Henry VIII* by a series of screens which flew in or out to allow the amount of floor space to be used for a scene and/or to create a particular setting for a scene. Originally Silver and Rintoul had considered using a series of Gothic arches to frame the stairs--fine for *Henry VIII*, but probably too imposing for *A Man for All Seasons*. In considering windows, Silver did some preliminary research on Hampton Court, built by Wolsey in 1516 and taken over by Henry VIII in 1518. Starting with windowpane shapes, Silver relates, he went to "griddles, cages, and doorways." Silver and Rintoul also wanted to position Henry apart from the other characters (in what they believe must have been the inner above stage at the Globe), keeping an eye on the people speaking on the main stage. To solve some of these problems Silver suggested the use of a giant rectangular screen, short side parallel to the stage floor, framed in wood and divided into individual squares for panes of glass by strands of thin material. Silver described the moment when the show fell into place for him as being the point where Rintoul asked him how they would handle the Buckingham scene. Silver thought for a moment and, using their model, raised one of the screens about eight feet off the floor so that it resembled a portcullis. Rintoul was delighted. From there they moved through a series of enthusiastic discussions about how the screens could be moved in order to create different environments for the scenes, and the number of screens (the dominant look for the scenery) grew. Learning too approved the set idea early in the design process.

Rintoul also liked the design of the screens because they had a slightly contemporary look that Silver says he learned from Polish designer Josef Svoboda, who had told a class, "The reason I design this way is that, even when I am doing a period play, my audience is coming to the theatre in cars." Silver adds, "Even when you are doing a Seventeenth Century play, you are doing it for people who are conditioned by the world in which they live," and he cites two methods of adding modernity. The play can be set in a time different from the one in which it was written--e.g., Neville, Wood, and LePage's *Hamlet*, and *Rosencrantz and Guildenstern Are Dead*, moved to 1905--or a classical play set in its proper time and place can be given modern accents. He and Rintoul doubted that *Henry VIII* could profitably be updated, yet certain scenic elements are correct for the period: line, texture and detail, but with what Silver calls an exciting modern silhouette.

But eventually as he looked at the two plays, Silver had to create some method whereby, using that common set, he could differentiate between them. The point he chose which, he says, was acceptable to both directors, placed *Henry VIII* in the very urban world of the king and his court--a visual show of luxury and splendour, primarily interiors. *A Man for All Seasons*, on the other hand, was set at the "middle class" house of Sir Thomas More on his river bank. So, Silver explains, the black rear wall could be used for *Henry VIII* and a cyclorama painted with light and enlarged by opening offstage areas for *A Man for All Seasons*. The screens take on a different appearance against the lighted cyclorama because they are seen in silhouette; whereas in *Henry VIII* they "read as highlight against the black," comments Silver.

Set pieces or furniture used in each show had to be distinct as well, with some of the benches and one chair the only pieces used in both. To cut down on the amount of furniture required, some pieces are used more than once: For example, the thrones in *Henry VIII* used at Whitehall are the same ones used at Blackfriars or Hampton Court, all from Silver's stock of "no name, generic Tudor furniture." That device is a part of the conception in *A Man for All Seasons*, where the common man changes the props but much of the furniture stays on stage from scene to scene, says Silver. The other major difference between the two shows, which Silver says he appreciated, was the different looks brought to basically the same set by lighting designers Michael Whitfield for *Henry VIII* and Larry Frehner for *A Man for All Seasons*-- seeing elements to the sets under lights which he had not at first envisioned.

Rintoul and Silver began their discussions by talking about characters. Rintoul was concerned that a modern audience get all the help possible in understanding who these people were and what life in this palace was like. The screens aided in this process because they allowed the director to emphasize the sense of intrigue, as guards come out from behind screens to interrupt conversations or Henry stands up stage watching others. Whitfield put brilliant light across the back of the stage in the coronation scene, leaving Lord Sands and his party in the shadows as if hidden behind a column at Westminister Abbey. From the beginning then, even before the decision to use the screens, director and designer wanted to create an atmosphere of light and darkness in which people are not always able to tell who their friends are in the "dangerously charged atmosphere of the Tudor court," says Silver. Shakespeare's audience would have known exactly who each person on stage was; audiences today need visual clues.

The conflict between the Bishop of Winchester and Archbishop Cranmer in the closing scenes of the play presents another difficulty for a modern audience. An Elizabethan audience would have understood that in that conflict stir the winds of the Reformation that had swept through Europe a short time earlier. But for a modern audience to recognize that split in the very few lines given it in the text requires understanding of the highly charged atmosphere of shifting allegiances, crumbling alliances, and unstable affiliations with which director and designers had begun the building of this production.

The director decided to alter traffic patterns for the play by using the doors on each side of the proscenium arch in the manner of the vomitoriums in the Festival Theatre, so that, as in the Festival Theatre, the director could bring an actor on from the up left stair case and take that actor out through the down right proscenium door. These strong diagonal lines recreate the theatre of Shakespeare's time, Rintoul believes, and Shakespeare was thoroughly familiar with the theatrical production of his day. Placement of the exits and entrances would have been part of the formalized architecture of Shakespeare's theatre and would have remained the same from production to production. Although Shakespeare's stage had a door up center, this production had to be fitted for touring, and a soft black drape was dressed with actors--for example, a set of guards with banners on each side of this center "door." By the time the play opened Rintoul and Silver had come to believe this actor-created door was more effective than an actual one. Also, even though the director and the set designer wanted to make the play more than just a costume drama, that aspect had to play a large role in their concept of the space needed. The pageantry of such scenes as the masque, the trial, the coronation, and the baptism demanded moving around numbers of people with enough space to show off each costume to best advantage. The stage area is larger than designer Silver would have liked for intimate scenes, but the large down stage and the different levels for actors help the larger scenes. (See Illustration 6-1.)

Costume designer Hanson stopped by the Dalhouse University theatre as an undergraduate on her way to law school and hasn't made it to law school yet, she relates. When working at the Neptune Theatre, she caught the eye of several designers who encouraged her and provided her with a job as assistant cutter. She moved on to the National Theatre School, whose design program, she points out, is the only section of the school integrated with French- and English-speaking students, with classes taught by French, Swiss, Italian, American, English, and Canadian authorities. She first came to Stratford as design assistant to both David Walker for *The Rivals* and Susan Benson for *The Comedy of Errors* in 1981. Benson was head of design that year, and she decided to develop young designers willing to learn how the complex "Stratford machine" worked and more specifically how to make it work to advantage. The production of *Translations* for which she did costume designs in 1982 was the first time Hanson had not designed both sets and costumes for a show. Since then she has designed costumes for the 1983 Avon production of *Death of a Salesman* and the 1984 productions of *Waiting for Godot* at the Third Stage and *A Streetcar Named Desire* at the Avon. She received a call in October inquiring if she were interested in costuming *Henry VIII* and *A Man for All Seasons* but was busy at the Theatre Plus; as it worked out, by the time her Stratford shows got into full swing she was available full time. Designing costumes in conjunction with Silver's set designs for *Henry VIII* and *A Man for All Seasons* is the first time Silver and Hanson have worked together since their *Translations* partnership; she says, "Phil and I spent a lot of time talking colour before we started."

As soon as the contract was worked out Hanson and Rintoul began work on *Henry VIII* in Hanson's Toronto studio because Rintoul was in Toronto at that time. Rintoul also expressed his concern to Hanson that the play be modern, not merely "a history play." Hanson said she believed that she knew the period quite well but nonetheless hit the research libraries and bookshops collecting source material. She spent an especially long time studying the paintings of Hans Holbein, the official court painter. Different books on Holbein highlighted a single painting; the value to her was the different portions of the paintings that each book chose to highlight. Yet as striking as those portraits are, Hanson did not want to lift them off the page of the books but rather to fit them into the context of the play. Director and costume designer wanted these actors to look like real people wearing real clothing, and so strove for clothes which looked domestic and suggested personalities for those who waged power struggles in the back palace corridors. Intermixed with these everyday scenes were those of pageantry: the masque, the trial, the coronation, and the baptism--which Rintoul saw as full displays of wealth. In this way the scenes showed the people alternating between their everyday clothing and dress-up finery.

Written into their contracts designers have their budgets and a rough estimate of the number of costumes needed to do the show. As soon as Rintoul and Hanson began discussing the show, they were calling Stratford to say that there were more costumes in the show than the contract had specified. But neither of them could come up with an exact number because they did not know how many people were going to be in the company. As Hanson relates the story, the Festival wanted to start construction in January. She decided to "storybook" the whole show, a process that involved working out what people would wear in each scene rather than plotting each character's progress through the show. Director and designer knew what principals they needed for each scene but not how many non-speaking characters; that decision hinged on the size of the company. Hanson says the storybooking showed director Rintoul all the costumes for a particular scene, side by side, generously allotting actors to scenes for a total of 168 costumes. When she and Rintoul began to talk through what she had done, they started adding even more costumes. Then when the company turned out to be a great deal smaller than either Rintoul or Hanson had guessed, the necessity for many of the costumes was eliminated. Telephone calls went back and forth from Hanson to the Festival, negotiating the number of costumes. Finally Hanson and Rintoul came to Stratford to meet with Bob Beard, and the number was fixed closer to the 124 costumes that eventually ended up in the show; Hanson believes that while she made compromises she never had to make concessions. For example, the two pages who moved the furniture to signify the change of location were dressed in the same black costumes throughout the play, although Hanson admits that she would have liked to have had the pages dressed in the scenes' dominant colours. The saving made the cutbacks reasonable, she says.

After director and designer talked through the major characters and the emotional colouring of each scene, Hanson says, she achieved a scale large enough to communicate the king's power visually. She suggested to Rintoul that they handle it like an opera; so to simplify work for herself and the wardrobe crew, she designed serially. The three costumes they had discussed for Norfolk, for instance, all had the same outline so that the cutters had to cut one kind of sleeve for Norfolk three times, one kind of undertunic, and one kind of cloak. Once these were sized out and proportioned properly in the fitting room, she cut them from different fabrics and decorated them differently. Also, ladies in waiting all wear the same basic costume, each coloured and trimmed in a different fashion. Hanson cites the advantage of designing big shapes, commanding in appearance and yet repeated often enough to make building everything on that scale practical.

All costume designers' contracts called for twenty-five percent of all costumes to be pulled from stock, but Hanson says there was no Tudor stock. *Henry VIII* had been done in 1961, but Hanson reported that those costumes were either in tatters or gone, leaving only the clerical costumes. She remembered that the masque scene caused her the most difficulty because of the dearth of visual research material and the translation of written material into a visual style. Because Rintoul had confidence in her work, she says that he could look at some of those early sketches for the court masque and break out in laughter as he told her they would not work. Rintoul finally asked her to "make the men look really sexy," so from then on she gave designs the look of ritual, youthful zest, and sensuality. Out of these ideas came the one presenting the king and his party as Greek gods, complete with golden masks. Because the scene would be lit by candlelight, the masque would shimmer.

Composer Gary Kulesha was asked in December by music administrator Art Lang to provide the score for *Henry VIII*. Kulesha and Rintoul had worked together on *A Streetcar Named Desire* in 1984 and *The Glass Menagerie* in 1985, when Kulesha had composed the score and Rintoul had worked as assistant director to John Hirsch. Kulesha had also composed scores for a 1984 Mark Lamos production of *A Merchant of Venice* and the 1985 Michael Bogdanov production of *Measure for Measure*. His association with the Festival began when he came to conduct the chamber music programme, from which he progressed to composing the music for the 1982 Third Stage season of *A Midsummer Night's Dream* and *All's Well That Ends Well*. He also served as the loft conductor for the Festival Theatre in 1983.

He began thinking intently about the script for a time and he met Rintoul in February to discuss the shape of the show, which means determining a climax and the placement of multiple focuses. He says, "There will be a piece of music which is the single most important piece of music....There may be other cues which are also very important." This form guides him in laying out the instrumentation, since he usually likes to build the score from a spare beginning into a somewhat richer fabric as the play approaches one of the moments of focus; from there a much more textured sound emerges as the climax is reached; then the music is wrapped up.

In looking at the decisions made according to structure, Kulesha and Rintoul focused their attention on what they called the double-wave effect of the show. Rintoul decided to take the interval after the trial scene, Act II, Scene 4, so the first half builds to the trial as a first wave. The second half, beginning with Katherine's demise to Elizabeth's baptism, constitutes the second wave. The logical event toward which to point the music was the baptismal scene, even though it is not the climax of the play. Director and composer asked themselves if this music should suggest the repetition of marriages or end on a happier and more reassuring note. Rintoul and Kulesha debated but eventually agreed on the latter course.

Both Kulesha and Rintoul wanted to use the musical score to provide moments for reflection rather than using it to manipulate or comment. Kulesha admits there is a fine line between the two but explains that he attended rehearsals and responded to the mood of the scene, rather than trying to reinforce the dominant emotions. He also favoured the use of counterpoint or reverse commentary, especially during the musical covering for a scene change. Another decision concerns whether to use the change to end a scene, build a base for the next scene, or do both by cross-fading the music. This process also requires that the director declare his choice for each interlude between scenes so that the composer can begin his work.

After the initial meeting between composer and director, Kulesha began work on the set pieces of music to be played entirely within one scene. He could not do more than sketch in the dance during the masque scene because he had not yet met choreographer John Broome. Once into rehearsal, Kulesha played the set pieces for Rintoul and Broome, who wanted to emphasize the sensuality and tremendous energy of the dance, and "finally, Henry's showing off in the last eight bars." Broome and Rintoul liked an existing piece of music for the dance, and Kulesha, who prides himself on never using something he has not written, wrote a new piece of music that captured much of the flavour of the existing piece. Rintoul and Broome both agreed to use the new piece, finally recorded with the composer backing the tempo by recording one version at a slower pace, the next at the tempo he expected to be correct, and the final version at a faster tempo. He says that the faster version wound up being the one used in the show, which is interesting in that his experience has taught him that in most cases the slower version is the one that gets placed into the show tape for use in production.

Once the set pieces were in place, the whole process started to speed up, says the composer. He was looking at a recording date in the studio far in advance of dress rehearsals to give time to select the piece from the recording session for the show, so the sound engineer could familiarize himself with the tape before rehearsals. (Because extra recording sessions are expensive, Kulesha recorded more music than he wound up using.) Yet with that recording date looming on the horizon, the show had had little time on the main stage. Timing for the music cues, at scene changes, for example, was only roughly approximate. Nonetheless he wrote music for each of the cues and played the score for Rintoul. The recording session took place in the town of St. Joseph's, about fifty kilometres from Stratford. Then sound levels had to be set and checked, in one fourteen-hour day. The following day the cue-to-cue rehearsals took place, and from there on, when a sound cue did not work as expected, Kulesha was cutting and splicing tape or providing some of the extra music he had recorded for Rintoul for just such cases. Because Rintoul was present with Kulesha in the recording studio making decisions, the composer believes, he was asked to make far fewer changes in technical and dress rehearsals, what he calls a "luxury." This was not the end, really only the beginning of a process of fine tuning the sound tape and sound levels right up to opening night, because actors have to change the scenery with sufficient cover, and audience members fill up the theatre, necessitating changes in sound levels.

Lighting designer Michael Whitfield says that he and Rintoul decided on several overall looks for the lighting. One, owing to their shared belief that Hanson's dark, luxurious costumes would take light very well, was a choice of side and back light wherever possible. In this way the actors stood etched against a background of brightness. Rintoul wanted some scenes played in shadows, in a conspiratorial darkness, to contrast against those with figures standing out against brightness. Several scenes dominated the early planning. For the party scene at Hampton Court, Whitfield selected low angles and some torches to give off shimmering light so that the faces of the crowd looked like a Rembrandt painting of light and shadow. For the trial scene he set in a high diagonal back light, as if it came from a rear window. He and Rintoul played shadow against its dimension. In addition, Whitfield says, he tried at times to rim the diagonal screens with light to give them different looks. Because he and Rintoul had such a strong concept for the play, he says, he could set cues and call his lights during a run-through, usually a practice in opera production that allowed for tidying up and work on transitions later.

Critics who do not always treat this play favourably usually point approvingly to the three great roles: Henry, Katherine, and Wolsey. Actor Leon Pownall, who played the title role, began his research before coming to Stratford. He discovered the dichotomy of his character's charm and vengeance, "marking Henry as a genius." He has worked with some geniuses during his career, he says, and things can get "pretty helter skelter." Despite Henry's flawed nature, Pownall believes him a likeable man who sincerely believes in the divine right of kings that makes him answerable only to God. Also, Pownall was fascinated by Henry's stature as a Renaissance man-- athlete, dancer, composer, writer. The one quality that Rintoul and Pownall used as a starting point for Henry was his knowledge of and use of power. The Jasper Riddley biography of Henry VIII helped considerably in spelling out Henry's ability to use power to advance his causes as well as to shield himself from pitfalls, Pownall says; yet he admits when it came time to block the play he promptly forgot it all.

Actress Elizabeth Shepherd says Rintoul first spoke with her about playing Katherine at a party in Los Angeles in November 1985, following the opening of the Stratford company tour there. Shepherd, who did not know the play, nonetheless found Rintoul's description of the character captivating. By the time she had arrived in Stratford, three months later, she knew a great deal about the historical Katherine, who had married Henry's brother Arthur when she was about sixteen. Katherine told the representatives of the papal court much later that she and Arthur had attempted to have intimate relations seven times in five months but had never succeeded, says Shepherd, who attributes Arthur's boast after the wedding night that he had dwelt that night in Spain to the romantic notions of a young man already ill and fated to die five months later. Then Katherine held a most unenviable position, she says. Her father stopped making her dowry payments until Henry VII announced her betrothal to Henry VIII, and Henry VII refused to do so until her father finished the payments. So, Shepherd continues, Katherine sat in England for seven years, living a very meagre existence. She also watched Henry VIII grow from a ten-year-old boy into the "golden prince of Christendom," handsome, intelligent, devout, and athletic. He married her as soon as his father died and from all accounts they had a wonderful life together, Shepherd explains. Katherine loved Henry passionately and was pregnant ten times by him. Only one child lived--Mary. The tragedy of her life, sighs Shepherd, is that those boys died. If they had not, she speculates, England might still be Catholic.

William Hutt, who played Cardinal Wolsey, returned to the Festival for this production after a five-year absence. He says that he did not do a great deal of research on the role because of the difficulty of playing the footnotes from a history textbook and credits Rintoul with feeding him the history he needed. He preferred to work from the script. He does not like the play, he says, but he very much liked the part. After reading the play, he describes wanting to establish a "watershed" for the character. He says that he believes Wolsey had to have had a conscience to go originally into the line of work he did, but obviously he buried it and has not much touched it at the point Wolsey begins the play. Hutt says that after much experience playing Shakespeare, the question for him in tackling a new role centres on what variation of the theme he wants to play. In searching for that variation, he begins by stressing the word or words which make the most interesting choices. He says that while those accented word choices may change during the rehearsal, he tries to head for a particular set from the beginning of the process.

On 3 March, when Rintoul began rehearsals, the stage management team, led by Janine Ralph, set up tables to form a rectangle around which the actors gathered for the first day. Most of the cast members also played in *Hamlet* and some in *Rosencrantz and Guildenstern Are Dead*; to this group were added four new actors: William Hutt, Kenneth Wickes, David Gardner, and Carolyn Hetherington. Hutt moved around the table greeting everyone in turn. Rintoul welcomed the company to "Shakespeare's version of *Ben Hur*." Because the play is so seldom performed, he advised the cast to enjoy this rare opportunity. Indeed, only Max Helpmann, who played the sergeant-at-arms and the doorkeeper of the Council Chamber, had been in the 1961 version, where he played Gardiner for director George McCowan.

Considering that Rintoul knew little about the play when he accepted the assignment to direct it just over four months earlier, his opening-day explication to the company testified to his intensive study in a short period. "As opposed to Shakespeare's other history plays, this one deals with spiritual, rather than political chaos," he explained, adding that the Christian ethic holds the play together despite tension between spiritual and earthly concerns. He used Buckingham's line:

> And if he speak of Buckingham, pray tell him You met him half
> in heaven. II.1.87-88.

The half of Buckingham in heaven is beyond earthly care; the half on earth expresses concern about those he knows have been false to him. This tension, explained Rintoul, occurs over and over again in the play. He asked the company to pay special attention to what those who are headed downward toward death have to say as compared to those who are forging ahead in this world.

The play was very hard to cut, he said, because every scene makes a strong visual and thematic statement that is then surpassed by the next scene.

The cuts he and literary manager Elliott Hayes worked out would serve as a starting place and could be changed, he concluded.

Phillip Silver made the set design presentation, explaining the seventeen different locations in the play, an adaptation of the *A Man for All Seasons* set. Along with staircases on each side and screens coming in at different locations to define spaces, large replicas of the seal of England for different locations on stage would fly in. Costume designs were taped to the wall for weeks thereafter so that everyone could view them and ask questions.

Rintoul embarked then on an explanation of the history in the play, in which he covered all of the major characters, explaining how he or she differed from Shakespeare's character. He cited an impressive list of names, dates, and places; from among the fulsome biographies, he noted: 1.)The Tudor reign began on Bosworth field as Richmond, soon to be Henry VII, defeated Richard III. 2.) The Duke of Buckingham in this play is the son of Richard III's Duke of Buckingham. 3.) Wolsey rose from his position as Henry VII's chaplain to that of Lord Chancellor of England.

But before the read-through for *Henry VIII*, Rintoul, as did Neville with his *Hamlet* cast, asked the actors to read the text very slowly. Because Wolsey appears in the first scene, very early in the read-through Hutt went for the word he wanted to accent, slowing down the pace to explore the weight he wanted for each word. Once Hutt had read his lines in this fashion, many of the other actors followed suit, giving Rintoul the kind of read-through he had asked for. "What a marvellous reading," he said. "What a great story. Let's not lose track of what a marvellous story it is in the weeks ahead."

As he blocked the individual scenes, cast members involved sat around a table both to read and discuss thoroughly the implications of a scene before he put them on their feet to block it; he made more use of this technique than did any other director. Many questions of interpretation were settled in those sessions around the table, as Rintoul called for silence after a scene had been read, looking about for actors to make contributions aimed at answering a question. One example of this process was Act I, Scene 4, the court masque staged by Wolsey to which the king comes disguised as a shepherd. Rintoul and Hanson had agreed months before that Wolsey knows the king is there in disguise, but when the actors began to explore the subject, Rintoul let them talk it through. Hutt summarized their agreement by saying that either Wolsey knows or one is forced to believe that Wolsey would accept the notion of four shepherds floating down the Thames looking for a party! If a long time passed between workings of a particular scene, Rintoul began at the table again and had the actors discuss and review the important issues at stake.

After rehearsing a scene, he generally moved around the rehearsal hall floor speaking with individual actors for whom he had notes. He began by working on individual scenes, then on larger chunks, until he was ready to run each act. Thereafter the normal rehearsal pattern consisted of running several scenes with individual scene work only on the problems.

While all of the shows mounted during the 1986 season placed heavy demands on the costume shops, none was as difficult to mount as *Henry VIII*, with more costumes than any other show. Most of the costumes were for the nobility of the court, while some represented the very finest clothing of those in the upper echelons of power. The actors had seen some of the costumes during the photo call on 11 April, but the technical dress rehearsal planned for 28 April was the first time they had seen most of the costumes on stage. Getting used to the extra weight for the first time caused delays, as did work on quick changes between actors and dressers. At the end Leon Pownall stepped forward to make a curtain speech expressing the actors' appreciation to the ladies and gentlemen of the wardrobe. Although some who had come to see the results of their handiwork on stage had left before the reheasal was ended, word of his speech passed rapidly through the costume shops the next day.

The production which opened on 24 May, 1986, contained forty-one scenes into which stage manager Janine Ralph had divided the script, with titles for each scene. All pages numbers refer to the New Penguin edition of the script used for this production.

Prologue

"Scene 1, Procession to the Block," contained what the New Penguin edition calls the prologue. The director divided the lines in the scene between two Gentlemen, Brent Carver and Ian Watson. Rintoul recalls his attraction to the scene from the first time that he read it, leading him to keep it when others advised him to cut it. He jumps to the end of the play to explain his reasoning: In the last scene, Henry forgives his wife for having given birth to a girl and is reconciled to his daughter, Elizabeth. "But things don't stay that way. Queen Anne is executed "some 1,000 days later." Camille Mitchell, who played Anne Bullen, says Rintoul flirted with the idea of beginning and ending the play with Anne on her way to her beheading. But having decided not to undercut the joy of that final scene, the baptism of Elizabeth I, musically or scenically, Rintoul used only the prologue. He says he sought to underscore the serious nature of the play by staging the procession leading Anne Bullen to the block as the two Gentlemen speak the prologue during which Shakespeare invited the audience to picture again these persons as if they were alive. This added pantomime served as a reminder, says Rintoul, that in the Tudor Court the stakes of playing for power were much higher than in today's world. The opening procession also brings the production full circle from the horror of Anne's beheading to the unbridled joy of the play's last scene. The director used the same blocking for the opening procession that he would repeat later in the play for the coronation of Queen Anne. Mitchell says as the character opened the play on her way to her death, she had an eerie feeling about walking the same path that had taken her to power and encountering the same two men she met before; this time they do not bow. She also stresses Anne fought for her dignity and against the sheer terror that welled up inside her. By setting up the opening scene as he did the director also wished to make a point about Henry; Rintoul hopes audiences will find great charm in the man, will detect something in his demeanor that might make them uncomfortable purchasing "swamp land in Florida" from him.

Rintoul believes that, instead of characters, Shakespeare wrote about people in this play: The people onstage would have been related to many of the people who saw this play. Many members of the audience could have supplied much information about the well-known people in the play from either their own knowledge or from information which had been passed down. Rintoul contends that he and the actors have had to supply much of the subtext for the play that would have been common knowledge in Shakespeare's day. The scene-by-scene discussion which follows, then, emphasizes the historical actions of the play as a framework for discussing this production's approach.

Act I, Scene 1

Act I, Scene 1, is subdivided into four scenes: Scene 2, "Vale of Andren" (pp. 65-69); Scene 3, "Wolsey's Crossover" (p. 69); Scene 4, "Butcher's Cur" (pp. 69-72); and Scene 5, "Arrest Thee" (pp. 72-73); it was set outside the court. "Vale of Andren" supplies an excellent example of how Shakespeare's play assumes some knowledge of the history of that period. The Duke of Buckingham has not attended the meetings between Henry and the French King at the so-called Field of the Cloth of Gold (which historically took place between 7 and 24 June, 1520, and which the Duke did not attend.) The name refers to the clothing worn by the monarchs, whose dress each day exceeded that of the previous day in splendour. "If I had a chance to go to an event of this size, it would take one hell of a cold to stop me," says the director, referring to Buckingham's excuse:

An untimely ague Stayed me a prisoner in my chamber... I.1.4-5

Actor James Blendick decided to interpret the word "chamber" to mean that Buckingham stayed in England rather than that an illness confined him to his tent in France. Rintoul says that Buckingham has in fact boycotted the

125

meetings. Blendick explains his character's reasons for this extreme action. Henry and Buckingham have grown up together and for a time Buckingham served as his chief counsel and unofficial second-in-command. But Cardinal Wolsey, Lord Chancellor, has taken Buckingham's place. Buckingham sees how proud and haughty Wolsey has become and openly rails against the dangers Wolsey represents to the king. The clear message here, says the director, is how trivial Buckingham thinks all of Wolsey's trappings are, implied in the very name, the Field of the Cloth of Gold.

"Wolsey's Crossover" introduces the Machiavellian hero of the piece, explains the director. "He has read *The Prince* from cover to cover, even though it's not been written yet," and he understands that both Buckingham and the queen must go, for the good of the state. Hutt's Wolsey saw Buckingham as a threat to his influence with the king and he knew Buckingham's vulnerability. But, says the actor, all one can play in the two lines here given Wolsey comes from his decision to topple Buckingham, a choice he makes because Buckingham refuses to pay him obeisance. When the "Butcher's Cur" scene between Buckingham and Norfolk works at its best, the director says, it becomes a clash between romantic idealism and pragmatism. Blendick explains that the romantic Buckingham knows attacking Wolsey is dangerous but will not compromise his principles. Those around Buckingham see how Wolsey enjoys the king's favour, perhaps because he is so capable, and temper their criticism accordingly, advising Buckingham to do the same, says David Schurmann, who played the practical Norfolk.

Anything that happens in this play happens because there is a piece of paper to back it up, Rintoul continues. In the early scenes Buckingham calls Wolsey a traitor; when Wolsey strikes at Buckingham in "Arrest Thee," he has a warrant. Then even Buckingham begins to look toward his own death, since, as the director explains, Henry is the architect of everyone's downfall in this play. Each person who falls, while on that torturous downhill slide, nonetheless turns and praises Henry. Rintoul believes part of the answer lies in the Christian dogma of the day which held a person sinful if he died with a soul overcharged with spleen. The director offers the example of the condemned man publicly forgiving his executioner. While conceding how difficult the actor's task becomes in motivating an act of deeply felt forgiveness in such a short time, Rintoul contends it must ring true. There are many other good plays about political power struggles, some of them better than this one, "and Shakespeare even wrote them," he says whimsically. "But what is unique about this is that whole process of forgiveness and accepting one's position as being a tiny speck on the face of an enormous canvas."

126

In history Buckingham's son-in-law Abergavenny was also arrested, a fact Shakespeare retains in this scene. But because the character never appears again, the director and actor Lorne Kennedy, who played the Earl of Surrey, incorporated both characters into Surrey because he also married one of Buckingham's daughters and, like Abergavenny (later released from prison), never progressed to the rank in Henry's court he might have achieved had he not had the relationship with Buckingham. Kennedy also points to the impossiblity of showing an audience all of the history that the scene contains. What he chose to show, his support of Buckingham and dislike of Wolsey, provided the basis for his later actions, says Kennedy.

Act I, Scene 2

Act I, Scene 2, contained two scenes: Scene 6, "Full Charged Confederacy" (pp. 73-77) and Scene 7, "Buckingham's Corruption" (pp. 77-81), in the Council Chamber. This scene introduces the title character. Leon Pownall's king combines the street fighter and the charmer. Rintoul says that these were qualities he knew Pownall brought with him as an actor, qualities that Rintoul wanted this Henry to possess. The director explains that Henry's court has not yet reached the zenith of English power, which it will do under Elizabeth I, but is ascending. "If Henry even smells a little bit like Richard II, the game is over," says the director in explaining that the regime has to work hard for everything it gets and recognizes the value of public relations, with Henry out front. Rintoul's research showed him that Henry sought to inspire and left the follow-through to others. Laying Henry's vision of this role against the backdrop of unstable governments and mounting insurrections in Europe, Rintoul continues, one begins to understand the large expectations he had for those in his inner circle. Pownall explains Henry's leadership style: "My Henry finds as many different ways to exercise power as he possibly can, not just bullying, not just threatening, but by some wit, by some double entendre, by keeping people off balance, by cat and mouse...by intellectual seduction."

As the "Full Charged Confederacy" scene begins, Queen Katherine asks Henry for relief from a new and heavy tax on behalf of the common people. Henry proclaims he knew nothing of the tax and chides the Cardinal, whom Katherine blames for it. The scene provoked interest, Rintoul says, because Hutt suggested early in rehearsals that the king not only knows about the tax but has approved the levying of it. Pownall and Hutt exchange a knowing wink, but, as Pownall points out, Henry uses power to shield himself; Wolsey thus takes the blame. Furthermore Pownall says, a memo exists somewhere proving the king knew, but the monarch rests secure in the knowledge that he can use power to protect himself. As for Katherine, Pownall says,

Henry yields to her on this issue because she has always been popular with the people. Pownall also explains that at this point Henry and Katherine still have a genuine love and a healthy respect for one another. As for Wolsey, Pownall says, he continues useful to Henry as long as he serves, but the king has him watched and keeps him out of foreign affairs, except for handling the connection with the Pope. "Anybody who is that good at his job...you are very careful to watch," says Pownall's Henry of Hutt's Wolsey.

Shepherd explains that Shakespeare uses Katherine's popularity with the common people, a fact well known to Elizabethan audiences, to have her intercede between Henry and Wolsey on this issue. She also concludes that her Katherine, having learned the necessity of shrewdness from her years of observation at the English court, understands full well Henry's role in issuing the new tax. But she points out that same shrewdness keeps her from openly attacking Henry but sends her instead after her natural nemesis, Wolsey. The historical Henry devoted much of his time in the first part of his reign to pursuing his own pleasures and left Wolsey to run the domestic affairs of the country, says Shepherd. Pownall, Shepherd, Hutt, and Rintoul see the play in part as Henry's taking back the full power of the government to himself. Shepherd says that in this scene Katherine makes just such an appeal to Henry, for she does not trust Wolsey's handling of domestic affairs any more than do the lords of the realm who also oppose Wolsey.

Hutt says that Katherine proves an irritant to him in this scene, but then she has done so for years, he adds laughing, and Wolsey can hardly say anything about what he regards as her impertinent intrusion into affairs of state because the king sits across from him during the scene and makes no move to restrain the queen. But if Wolsey loses this opening round, he wins the confrontation in the latter half of the scene.

"Buckingham's Corruption" deals with Katherine's distress over Buckingham's fall. Again Shepherd points to the historical queen who interceded occasionally with her husband on behalf of those at court who had fallen into the king's displeasure. Here, as with the ploy for the tax, she knows the charges repeated against Buckingham by his household overseer ring false. But this time because she cannot challenge the men openly, she cannot get at what she regards as the real issues. Those issues prove complex, depending upon the viewpoint of the observer. Blendick's Buckingham does not believe that Henry thinks him a traitor, but rather sees Henry's acquiescence to Wolsey as caused by the Cardinal's importance to the king as both statesman and churchman. Therefore, he says, Henry lets Wolsey have his way with Buckingham, who is popular with the common people, because, after all, they are easy to control. Once Buckingham has been executed, Wolsey believes, the duke will be quickly forgotten.

Since in this production all power springs from the king, Henry's attitude toward Buckingham becomes the main issue. "Buckingham, like anybody else, is fine so long as he serves the Tudor goal, the perpetuation of the line, and building up the country," says Pownall. All the warlords of England-- Norfolk, Suffolk, Surrey, Buckingham, and the rest--are described by Pownall as "the tanks of England." Henry wanted "all the tanks" with him at the Field of the Cloth of Gold; Buckingham failed him by his absence. Buckingham has popularity and power and perhaps a better right to the throne than Henry, who is the second son of a usurper, says Pownall. "If that tank turret [Buckingham] starts to turn, the others just might come around," Pownall reasons. He sees a possible swerving of that turret in the charge Buckingham's overseer says he levelled against Henry--that he had no male heir. Henry, who feels vulnerable on the succession issue, says Pownall, begins to grow impatient with Katherine's defense of a man who also has a claim to the throne. As a result, for Pownall this scene, which begins by featuring a warm and loving relationship between Katherine and Henry, ends with the sowing of the seeds of alienation as a result of Katherine's defense of Buckingham.

Act I, Scene 3

Act I, Scene 3, contained Scene 8, "Spells of France" (pp. 81-84), and was set on a river bank. Rintoul wanted to play the scene in a pub where gentlemen dressed in the current French fashion described in the scene would make an entrance. But for a number of reasons, including budgetary ones, he chose the river bank for the scene, which he describes as "the Brits at their xenophobic best." A bill has been passed outlawing the French fashions and presumably Frenchmen at court, says Rintoul, but what delights the English is that their love lives will improve without the French competition. These nobles--Lord Sands, William Dunlop; Lord Lovell, David Gardner; and the Lord Chamberlain, Eric House, as well as countless others--are "always sending feelers out" trying to determine where they stand in relation to others in the shifting eddies and currents of life in Henry's court.

Act I, Scene 4

Act I, Scene 4, was divided into two scenes, Scene 9, "General Welcome" (pp. 84-87) and Scene 10, "Broken Banquet" (pp 87-90). The discussion of sex in the previous scene sets the flavouring for the Cardinal's having gathered all the young ladies and influential members of Henry's court together for the purpose of pairing them off later. Most marriages in that day having been arranged, everyone accepted a certain amount of mistressing going on, says Rintoul. Young women offered themselves hoping for advancement; when they bore illegitimate children, Rintoul points out, the nobles responsible were expected to provide.

Hutt sees Shakespeare's purpose as giving an opportunity to get Henry and Anne together, using the historical Wolsey's lavish parties as a means to do so. Hutt points out that Wolsey provided the king with the guest list in advance so he could make whatever changes he desired in it before the party took place. He believes Anne Bullen, who served Queen Katherine as one of her ladies-in-waiting, was one of the king's additions to his guest list for this party.

As much as Shepherd believes Henry and Katherine had a full and passionate relationship prior to the break, she acknowledges that Katherine has had to turn a blind eye to his large appetite for other women throughout their marriage. But the practice of kept women extended to European royalty and nobility as well, Shepherd declares. She recalls reading that the French king visited Henry with his wife and mistresses; he and Henry paraded their stables of women in front of one another.

Into the scene come four men disguised as shepherds, one of whom is the king. While Wolsey pretends not to know the identity of these "shepherds," Pownall and Hutt agree that Wolsey expects the king at the party. That Wolsey would allow himself too much to drink when expecting the king, as he did in this production, spoke "volumes" to Pownall of the relationship between the two men. But if Wolsey expected this royal visit, he does not immediately know behind which of the four masks hides his king. Hutt says his Wolsey ultimately identifies the king successfully because he goes for the prettiest woman in the room. (Hanson and Rintoul had decided not to make the king's costume or mask different from the others.) Rintoul explains the "Broken Banquet" scene by saying that Henry VIII loved to dress up in disguise, having thereby the freedom to watch others who did not then react to him as they did to their king. The director asserts that Anne Bullen, for example, sees only Henry's eyes and does not know who is behind the mask, while Henry checks out the chemistry between the two. Rintoul looks at the competitive nature of the relationship between Henry and Anne, an alliance that "had doom sniffing around it from the beginning." He notes that when Henry attempts to kiss her she plays a trick on him by substituting her hand for her lips. Rintoul believes that Henry sees in Anne:

someone very much like himself, which is what...he finds overwhelmingly attractive....She is the exact opposite of everything Katherine was or wanted to be for that matter....But...he sees someone whose sense of life is much more like his, which is why he believes fully that she will give him a son, which is terribly important to him, conscience aside.

Mitchell explains that in order to show some of the reasons that the relationship between the two eventually disintegrated she wanted to build some of Anne's "hyperness, mischief, and hysteria" into this scene--thus the business of the rejected kiss. To continue to demonstrate Anne's independence she allowed Lord Sands to "nuzzle my neck" in view of the king. Pownall describes the difficulty of communicating the reasons for or even the steps in Henry's journey from Katherine to Anne because the playwright gives him no speech that expresses it until the end of Act II, Scene 4. As a result, explains Pownall, Henry has moved here as he does in other places in the play in "quantum leaps" and with little or no explanation of why he has done so. According to Pownall, Henry sees in Anne an attractive and younger woman capable of bearing him children; Katherine was six years older than Henry. Henry had made her older sister his mistress, and Anne had played very coy to his advances for almost a year and a half, so he wanted her all the more. Saying no to Henry, Pownall postulates, must have been like saying no to Joseph Stalin. The actor believes that while a case can be built for the incompatibilty of the two, as demonstrated in this production by the "not on the lips, Hank," kiss, the real problem lay in the birth of the daughter--Elizabeth I. If they had had a son, says Pownall, they would have stayed together.

Act II, Scene 1

Act II, Scene 1, was divided into three scenes: Scene 11, "Buckingham Condemned" (pp. 90-92); Scene 12, "Come Pity Me" (pp. 92-95); and Scene 13, "Stop the Rumour," and was set at Traitor's Gate. Rintoul calls the juxtaposition of scenes from the banquet at Wolsey's to the procession of Buckingham to the block one of the strongest in the play. Scene 11 establishes that the two Gentlemen who serve as spokesmen or chorus for the play place blame for Buckingham's death sentence on Wolsey. In Scene 12 Buckingham makes his last speech to the common people. Blendick acknowledges that the transition from his first scene of plotting and scheming against the Cardinal to this concern for a spiritual peace requires a complete shift in priorities. He says that he looked up the word "politician" and discovered that one meaning of the word was "one who manipulates," nicely describing the world that Buckingham has left behind. As Lord Lovell comes forward to ask his forgiveness, Blendick explains, Buckingham realizes that if more people had been willing to stand up with him Wolsey might have been stopped. But as he knowingly moves toward his death, none of those old power ploys matters any longer. Buckingham has his eyes firmly fixed on that next world, says Blendick.

During Scene 13 the rumours about a split between the king and queen have again broken out. Rintoul says that as opposed to old rumours on the same subject these are the brand new, hot-off-the-press rumours that Henry has denied as long has he could. Rintoul also explains that the scene sets up Cardinal Campeius, just arrived from Rome, as the planner for the divorce rather than an impartial judge.

Act II, Scene 2

Act II, Scene 2, was composed of four scenes: Scene 14, "Sad Thoughts and Troubles" (pp. 96-99); Scene 15, "How Sad He Looks" (pp. 99-l00); Scene 16, "Precedent of Wisdom" (pp. 100-101); and Scene 17, "Give Me Your Hand" (pp. 101-102), and was set in a palace corridor. Scene 14 gives the first taste of Norfolk, Suffolk, and the Lord Chamberlain's disapproval of Wolsey, perceiving that he stands behind the king's displeasure with the queen. Rintoul explains that the scene establishes several important ideas. First, Norfolk's line:

a loss of her That like a jewel has hung twenty years About his neck, yet never lost her lustre. II.2.29-31

shows how much the people respect the queen. Second, it is the first time that the king has been criticized, as in Suffolk's aside, "No, his conscience has crept too near another lady," (II.2.16-17) followed immediately by Norfolk's line: "Tis so; This is the Cardinal's doing," II.2.17-18. Schurmann points to the lords' growing discontent with Wolsey because he has the power the lords desire. But Kennedy quickly notes that even though they are anxious for a fight, they will not attack Wolsey until a more opportune time. Scene 15 contrasts the weakness of the lords, in this case Norfolk and Suffolk, with Wolsey's great power, says Rintoul. This is the scene that pictures the ill-timed entrance of Norfolk and Suffolk into Henry's private chamber while he waits upon Wolsey to usher in Cardinal Campeius, newly arrived from Rome, to judge the divorce case with Wolsey. Scenes 16 and 17, showing the arrival of Cardinal Campeius, give the "first sniff that something's rotten in the State of England," Rintoul says with a chuckle; the king is determined to leave the queen before the case has even been tried. Scene 17 concludes with Henry's line:

Would it not grieve an able man to leave So sweet a bedfellow? But conscience, conscience! O, "tis a tender place, and I must leave her.
II.2.140

Of Scene 16, Hutt says Wolsey introduces Cardinal Campeius. But the actor finds Wolsey's labelling of his fellow Cardinal as a "priest," rather than using any of the grander titles he could have given him, of special interest. For if part of Wolsey's job lies in reassuring the king and thereby an audience, he says, "You must first show them what they should have worried about." Richard Curnock, who played Cardinal Campeius, agrees that under most circumstances his character provided little resistance to the powerful wills of Henry and Wolsey. Yet Campeius fears the pope's displeasure above all else, a factor important in the trial scene. Rintoul describes Campeius as "a poor little out-of-his depth Italian," and Pownall calls him "a rowboat between two battleships," noting the enormous victory Wolsey has won in Rome, which at first insisted on a more impartial judge than Wolsey. Also of interest, Wolsey presents his secretary Gardiner to Henry; actor Scott Wentworth says that he accepts advancement into Henry's service to spy on him for Wolsey. That in the moment of his victory over Rome, Wolsey should attend to extending his spy network into the palace confirms the presence of highly charged political tensions within this court.

Act II, Scene 3

Act II, Scene 3, comprises three scenes: Scene 18, "Cruel Fortune" (pp. 103-106); Scene 19, "Secret of Your Conscience" (pp. 104-105); and Scene 20, "Begging Sixteen Years" (pp. 105-106), and was set at a garden at Hever. In the first of these scenes, the Old Lady (Carolyn Hetherington) jokes with Anne about being Queen of England, presumably because she too wants to advance if Anne rises higher. But, as the director points out, Anne is in a very tough spot. If she admits she wants to be queen and Henry changes his mind, then she might very well lose her head, so she has to joke about it. Mitchell agrees and adds that by this point in this production Henry and Anne were sleeping together and Anne was pregnant at the time of their marriage. Once the Lord Chamberlain arrives in "Secret of Your Conscience" and awards her both title and pension, Mitchell says she decides to send Henry a rose, a token which neither the Lord Chamberlain nor the Old Lady can believe an improper gift. Mitchell also points to the special thrill Anne receives when the Lord Chamberlain bows to her because it gives her for the first time a tangible sign of her ascendancy. But once the Lord Chamberlain leaves, the Old Lady turns bitterly on Anne, who has started up that ladder of power and influence on which the Old lady has never succeeded in catching the bottom rung.

Act II, Scene 4

Act II, Scene 4, was composed of two scenes, Scene 21, "Commission from Rome" (pp. 107-112) and Scene 22, "Queen of Earthly Queens" (pp. 112-115), set at Blackfriars. These two scenes were the trial and were divided after the queen's exit following her appeal to Rome. Costume designer Hanson says a number of churchman wear liturgical vestments, highlighted by Wolsey, whose vestments as Cardinal appear more intense and vibrant than those of Campeius. In order to give Katherine a full measure of nobility and a bit of a foreign look, Hanson put her in a black dress trimmed in gold, elegant in its own right and suggesting the Spanish court. Hanson also costumed the Spanish ambassador, Chapuys (not in this scene), in those colours for both *Henry VIII and A Man for All Seasons*. Having used black for Katherine, Hanson then could not use it for Henry. By putting the wronged queen in black and the offending king in white, she has reversed the roles normally associated with these colours and thereby created a strong tension within the scene.

Rintoul says of the trial scene that in spite of all of the elegant visual trappings, he suspects an audience can quickly sense what takes place beneath the surface. For example, Rintoul says, Katherine has crossed Wolsey on many occasions and has earned his enmity. But whatever the cardinal's motivation and despite the appearance of a fair trial, Katherine knows she will not get justice from Wolsey, so she appeals directly to Henry. Rintoul explains that Katherine understands precisely what politics come into play here: If she cannot win Henry's support, she is probably gone. The director points out that her speech shows she knows both his good and his bad sides; consequently the speech both appeals to his better nature and hints at his shortcomings. The cardinals must take over when she has finished, the director points out, because what she says would not look good on the public record. But Katherine understands that she cannot have her case heard by these cardinals and attacks Wolsey in part because she cannot attack the king.

In this production, the director and actors carefully built a close relationship between the king and the cardinal. At Wolsey's party, for example, the Cardinal encouraged the king's advances toward Anne Bullen. When Cardinal Campeius first arrives Wolsey fully enjoys extolling the king's virtues to Campeius. Indeed, explains Rintoul, one school of historical thought says that Wolsey's formula for rising to the heights lay in his ability to find out what the king wanted done, doing it for him, and praising him for having done it. That Katherine recognizes that closeness and chooses first to appeal to Henry and then to attack Wolsey as she had in the "Full Charged Confederacy" demonstrates the political savvy of the queen, says Rintoul. Katherine bases her appeal to Henry on her faithfulness to him throughout their marriage. Shepherd strove to achieve the indignity and majesty--and great love for Henry--that she believes Katherine would have placed in that appeal. Katherine never accepted the proceedings which resulted in the divorce and would never accept the Act of Succession, which declared the offspring of Henry and

Anne as the legitimate heirs to the throne; Shepherd says her Katherine continued to love Henry and would never do anything to harm him or cause him difficulties except on these issues.

Hutt believes that because Wolsey and Henry have that close relationship, they have not needed to do a great deal of talking beforehand about this trial. Hutt speculates Wolsey's motivation, apart from getting rid of this old adversary, comes from a desire to marry Henry to a French princess, thereby sealing an alliance with that country.

Once Katherine cannot carry the day, she leaves the court, appealing directly to Rome to hear her case. When she does leave, Wolsey denies that he has ever spoken to the king about the divorce. Rintoul explains the necessity of the appearance of a fair trial for acceptance of the verdict of the court. Therefore Henry must back Wolsey in denying collusion, he stresses. An interesting historical note used in this production concerned Cardinal Campeius, who, although Italian, had a bishopric in England that paid him revenue. Thus while he was a representative of the papal court, he also had some personal stake in England, explains the director. The production also assumes that Campeius was one of the people that Wolsey had chosen to pay in his attempt to secure the papacy, an assumption based on Wolsey's line in a later scene:

'Tis th' account Of all that world of wealth I have drawn together For mine own ends--indeed, to gain the popedom, And fee my friends in Rome. III.2.210-213.

The cardinals, says Rintoul, do not like Katherine's having taken the trial out of their hands; as a result, she might get "an objective trial, rather than a fair one." Because as queen she has the right to a papal trial if she insists on one, a strong effort must be made to talk her out of it.

Curnock says that because Campeius feared the displeasure of the pope he insists that the trial stop until Katherine can be talked into coming back to court. Pownall says he expects Wolsey to take Campeius into the back room for tea, show him the rack, and then get on with the trial. When Wolsey can not find a way to get the trial restarted, Pownall says in no uncertain terms, "He's gone!" From there on, he suggests, the question focuses on allowing Wolsey enough room to condemn himself and the king's attention goes to Thomas Cranmer and Gardiner, now in the Bishop of Lincoln's chair. Hutt too felt the deep displeasure of the king at not finding a way to proceed with the trial, but he cannot risk openly offending the pope either; for if his political ties to Rome vanish, so does his usefulness to this king. Hutt says the other surprise for Wolsey in this scene comes in Henry's line, "Prove but our marriage lawful." II.2.226. Nothing has prepared Wolsey for that line, says Hutt.

Rintoul decided to take the play's interval at this point, after Act II, Scene 4, because it concludes the first major build in the play ("We have now had our day in court"). Also, with Henry's expressed displeasure with the cardinals, several paths that the action might take have opened up. An interval after Act III, Scene 1, might have done a better job of breaking the play into more even halves, but Rintoul believes it provided a weaker ending.

Act III, Scene 1

Act III, Scene 1, was divided into two scenes, Scene 23, "Take Thy Lute" (pp. 115-116) and Scene 24, "Is This Your Comfort?" (pp. 116-122), and was set in the queen's chamber. The division between the two scenes occurred after the gentlewoman's song. That song (sung by Lucy Peacock) quite literally provides the calm before the storm, says Rintoul. The two cardinals come to visit because Wolsey knows very well that his stock took a downward turn when he did not provide the divorce Henry wanted, and, explains the director, he has come to try to get things turned around by cajoling Katherine into letting the cardinals mediate the dispute. Rintoul describes it as a classic good cop/bad cop routine, with Campeius playing the role of the heavy because Wolsey "is the sullied partner here. But Campeius lacks Wolsey's genius and subtlety. All he can do is bludgeon Katherine and in the end proves ineffective." Hutt sees an awkwardness in this scene. The cardinals come for the express purpose of getting the queen to disclose to them her state of mind. They argue with her for most of the scene and then proceed offstage to do what they came to do in the first place, he comments.

Campeius disappears from the play after this scene. Pownall says that Campeius fled the court and went into hiding, presumably for fear of his life, until escaping and returning to Rome. Pownall believes he wound up fearing two sets of henchman--those of the king or of Wolsey.

The next scene, 24A, was inserted into the play after the first couple of previews when audience members complained of not recognizing Cranmer when introduced in the last few scenes, as prescribed by the text. This scene comes from *Sir Thomas More*, a play for which Shakespeare may have written at least some scenes. This scene, "apparently the only scene that exists in [Shakespeare's] own handwriting," says Rintoul, contains the portion of the events where Henry gives More the Lord Chancellorship of England and for purposes of this production was slightly altered so that Henry makes Cranmer the Archbishop of Canterbury. The scene pictured Cranmer returning with opinions of various universities that grant Henry the divorce, and for this service Henry rewards him. Rintoul guesses that eighty percent of the lines in this very short scene are Shakespeare's and the remaining ones were a combined effort by literary manager Elliott Hayes, Pownall, Rintoul, and of course whichever of Shakespeare's contemporaries might be responsible for *Sir Thomas More*. Pownall says while the others wrote down the ideas for additions to the scene, he added the metre to make them fit with the rest of the scene. Hayes had shown Rintoul the scene before rehearsals started, but at the time Rintoul did not want to raise the Thomas More issue and not deal with it, especially since the play was being done in conjunction with *A Man for All Seasons*. But once the play went into previews and the Cranmer problem arose, both Pownall and resident director Robert Beard suggested "a scene" as the solution: Rintoul went back to this scene. Pownall also liked the scene for another reason. The play makes almost no mention of one of the seminal events of English history--the Reformation. The scene also shows the authority of the universities in the beginning of the Church of England.

Act III, Scene 2

Act III, Scene 2, was divided into five scenes: Scene 25, "Unite in Your Complaints" (pp. 122-125); Scene 26, "Wolsey's Holdings" (pp. 125-127); Scene 27, "Wolsey's Wealth" (pp. 127-130); Scene 28, "What Anger" (pp. 130-135); and Scene 29, "Wolsey's Nightmare" (pp. 136-139), and was set in the council room. "Unite Your Complaints" played until the entrance of Wolsey and Cromwell. It shows Wolsey's opponents on the council, usually so guarded in their criticism, now openly reveling in his slipping fortunes. Rintoul explains that the cardinal's influence has been waning since the trial, more specifically since the moment that Wolsey had no counter to Campeius' decision to stop the trial. Now the nobles to whom Wolsey has denied power for so long, including Buckingham's son-in-law Surrey and his friend Norfolk, have gathered to watch the cardinal's demise because, as Rintoul says of the earlier scene, they have the official papers to back them up.

"Wolsey's Holdings" played until the entrance of the king. The scene depicts a moody, preoccupied cardinal brooding on the rise of Cranmer. Rintoul changed line 102 (Wolsey's line) from "An heretic, an arch-one, Cranmer...." to "An heretic, a protestant, Cranmer...." to point up the growing impact of the Protestant Reformation, which Wolsey now faces, and Anne Bullen, whose Lutheranism he fears. But Rintoul also believes that Wolsey opposes Henry's marriage to Anne because the Bullens were minor nobility.

"Wolsey's Wealth" played from the entrance until the exit of the king. The inventory of Wolsey's personal possessions and his letter to the pope opposing the divorce have mistakenly been included in a packet sent to the king, and in this scene Henry gives him both documents:

> ...*Read o'er this, And after, this; and then to breakfast with What appetite you have.* III.2.201-203.

Rintoul says Henry always understood Wolsey, for as early as the party scene he says:

> *You hold a fair assembly; you do well, lord. You are a churchman,*
> *or I'll tell you, Cardinal I should judge now unhappily.* I.4.87-89.

Pownall says that what makes this scene "so delicious" for Henry is Wolsey's having been the architect of his own downfall. The actor explains that his Henry has everybody from the FBI to the Royal Canadian Mounted Police out looking for something to use against Wolsey. Pownall uses the following fictitious example to illustrate the kind of evidence Henry has obtained from his spies. The cardinal has a woman down at Turnbridge Wells to whom he has given some of Henry's property, say the king's agents. "Not good enough," says Henry. "Come up with something else." Then one day in the midst of his morning mail, Henry discovers the evidence--and Wolsey has put it there himself. Pownall explains: "I don't believe it. He's made not one but two mistakes....All I have to do is walk in there....I don't need witnesses. I can go in there and say, "How the hell are you today? Why don't you read this...and this? You're cooked.'" Pownall also says that it is a very demonic kind of evil to revel in destroying someone, and he recoils at the applause this scene sometimes gets. Pownall also points out Henry's vulnerability in this scene, expressed in telling Wolsey that he has loved him and that his father had also loved him. As king, he expected that the friendship would be returned in equal measure. But as strong as those sentiments can be, Pownall says, it's important that they not take over the scene, but rather bubble up from underneath In "What Anger," perhaps Wolsey can talk his way out of the inventory listing his extensive holdings but the letter to the pope opposing the divorce, said Rintoul in an interview before rehearsals had started, proves the "smoking gun" in this Tudor version of the Watergate scandal.

While Pownall's Henry takes such joy in Wolsey's having undone himself, Hutt had originally come to the same conclusion. After he reads the inventory, Wolsey blames himself, says Hutt. But during the rehearsal of the previous scene one day, while Wolsey stood lost in contemplation, Hutt heard Schurmann's Norfolk read the lines, "Some spirit put this paper in the packet...." (III.2.129-130) in such a way as to imply that he (Norfolk) was that spirit. So, concluded Hutt, if that's the way "the pennies were going to fall for Schurmann's Norfolk," then Wolsey picked up on that implication.

When the Lord Chamberlain, the Dukes of Norfolk and Suffolk, and the Earl of Surrey came to humiliate him in the process of asking for the return of the Lord Chancellor's seal, Hutt shot Schurmann a dirty look.

Schurmann asked himself why Hutt had done so before realizing that he was the one responsible for the intercepted packet. Wolsey's refusal to yield the chain of office Rintoul explains as the character's last hurrah. "This is the final great expression of self, of who I am. Seal or no seal, I am the same person," says Rintoul, paraphrasing Wolsey, to which Hutt adds that Wolsey has his back to the wall and in that position cannot chose but to fight. But Hutt also wanted a way to take the character from all of the corruption in which he has engaged to an act of repentence for which the script calls, and so he looked for a way to achieve that watershed movement, he explains. He solved the problem by deciding to be ill when the lords come, as if this act of physical regurgitation rid him of all the horrors in which he had engaged and left him again with that religious inner core, long buried.

"Wolsey's Nightmare" took place between the exit of the nobles and the end of the scene. Here Rintoul points out, Wolsey begins divesting himself of all the things that have defined him, all his material possessions. His thoughts, like those of Buckingham before him, turn toward spiritual matters in a truly repentant fashion. During the first read-through of the scene, following Wolsey's exit line, "My hopes in heaven do well," Hutt looked up from his script and muttered, "That son of a bitch." But that judgment represented the opinion of the actor, says Hutt; Wolsey does not see himself in those terms. No one sees himself as a villain, he adds; even Al Capone most probably saw himself as an opportunist. But in a more serious vein, Wolsey's repentance continued to provide Hutt grist for thought throughout the run of the play. The one question that he says he steadfastly refused to answer all summer hinged on the genuineness of Wolsey's contrition. For him the act was real, but he wanted audience members to decide for themselves how to evaluate his character's final scene.

As Wolsey goes down he helps his new secretary, Cromwell, Michael Fawkes, advance by giving him the advice cited in the chapter heading, urging him to serve God first. Rintoul points out that if Wolsey had followed his own advice he would not have been speaking as a former Lord Chancellor; "I think if someone lives to die a martyr it's a very different life from that of someone who lives to succeed in business or politics," concludes Rintoul.

Act IV, Scene 1

Act IV, Scene 1, was composed of three scenes: Scene 30, "Coronation List" (pp. 140-141); Scene 31, "Procession" (pp. 141-145); and Scene 32, "She's an Angel" (pp. 141-145), set at Westminister Abbey. In "Coronation List," the two Gentlemen discuss nobles who claimed their offices for the coronation, demonstrating that others rose at least momentarily with Anne. "Procession" and "She's An Angel" were spliced together so that Anne enters and runs up the stairs stage left, pausing only to have her train properly arranged before entering the church. The Gentlemen bow to her. While that business lasted only a moment, the blocking pattern was exactly the same one Rintoul had used to open the production, with Anne on her way to the block. The two Gentlemen are joined by Lord Sands. They comment on the split between Cranmer and the Bishop of Winchester, and then fall to repeating the latest rumours about Katherine. By playing the two gentlemen and Lord Sands' discussion of Katherine over the procession of the coronation scene, Rintoul wanted to contrast Anne's rise with Katherine's fall, in this scene splashed with coronation gold. The director explains that the first gentleman takes Katherine's part but goes to the coronation banquet because "life goes on."

Mitchell says her Anne felt as if she had won a beauty contest in this procession and so walked down the ramp in triumph. She describes Anne's reaction by discussing a wardrobe call she had to fit her crown. After the fitting she and actress Goldie Semple compared notes, she recalled. Semple thought her own crown as Queen Hermione in *The Winter's Tale* much more subtle and refined than Anne Bullen's crown, which Mitchell describes as a "bit garish." Michell explains that for a woman who came from the lesser nobility and lacked refinement or dignity, Anne would also play this moment for everything she could get out of it and perhaps appear garish to the more sophisticated court audience.

Act IV, Scene 2

Act IV, Scene 2, was composed of three scenes: Scene 33, "Loaden Branches" (pp. 145-150); Scene 34, "Saucy Fellow" (p. 150); and Scene 35, "Take Comfort," and was set at Kimbolton. Griffith, informing Katherine that Wolsey has died, urges that they think upon the good he has accomplished. Rintoul sees that good written in a bold hand, since Wolsey was a statesman of the highest order and may be the only character in the play who could by virtue of his gift for diplomacy thrive in today's world. But Rintoul also points to his highly developed aesthetic taste. Wolsey built Hampton Court at the same time Henry VIII built St. James, he says. Hampton Court still speaks of the creative genius of Wolsey, while St. James looks like a public building, concludes Rintoul.

During "Loaden Branches," Katherine takes offense at the impertinent messenger who announces the arrival of her nephew, the Spanish ambassador, Signor Chapuys, who enters in "Saucy Fellow." The name is "Capuchius" in Shakespeare's play but was changed in this production to conform to the name Bolt gives the character in *A Man for All Seasons*; he has come to bear Katherine's petitions to Henry. For this scene, Rintoul gave

Katherine a hard edge, avoiding the sentimentality that would hurt her effectiveness for viewers from our age. Shepherd explains that Katherine never accepted the change in her station that the new title "princess dowager" conveyed. Consequently she insists that the messenger who arrives to announce Chapuys kneel to her. Once the Spanish ambassador arrives she asks favours for others, such as her ladies in waiting. She says in this regard the Katherine of this play is a remarkable woman seen through the eyes of a remarkable man (Shakespeare) who had also reached the point in life where he faced a summing up of one's life and making a good end. Katherine's thoughts in this scene go back to Henry, whom she still loves very much and has not seen for nearly six years, says Shepherd. In speaking good of Henry, she believes this character, whom the audience respects, turns around and hands the play back to Henry; without her blessing they might well be wary of him. Such a generosity of spirit, she says, comes right out of the nature of Katherine of Aragon.

Act V, Scene 1

Act V, Scene 1, was made up of four scenes: Scene 36, "Queen's in Labour" (pp. 153-156); Scene 37, "An Heir" (pp. 155-156); Scene 38, "The Tower" (pp. 156-159); and Scene 38A, "'Tis a Girl" (pp. 156-159). In the first of these, Gardiner and Lovell discuss the queen's difficult labour. The birth of any baby to Henry and Anne also carries political and religious complications; Rintoul calls this scene "chaos on a stick." Into that chaos walks Henry as "An Heir" begins, dismissing the nobles so he can speak privately with Cranmer. Pownall says that the rigours of the Privy Council, Cranmer, and the birth of the baby are rigours indeed. "That is a very complicated little sequence of the play" for Henry, he says. "He's having to deal with spies, he's having to deal with encroachment of privacy, he's having to deal with 'the tanks' with Suffolk being there." Pownall adds that he has to deal with them by himself because Wolsey's not there and he will not allow any replacement to gain as much power as Wolsey held. The lords are trying to nullify Cranmer's power, so that the church will not slide into the power vacuum they fear Wolsey's demise created. But, says the actor, by taking on all the affairs of state, Henry weakens himself, turning uncertain at times. Pownall strove to create a character who has to "wing it."

"The Tower" depicts the meeting between Henry and Cranmer during which Henry tests Cranmer by telling him that the Privy Council will bring him to trial; but Cranmer surprises Henry by welcoming the chance to be tested. Pownall summarized Cranmer's priorities one day in rehearsal as "honesty, integrity, country, and lastly, 'Can you help me?' " Once he finds Cranmer as honest as he thought him to be, Henry gives his ring as his pledge to help him. Brown's Cranmer worked through several sets of choices to illuminate his goodness and strength of character. Pownall suggested that Brown come at him hard to defend his goodness; Brown felt more comfortable, since goodness was the question, maintaining a quiet dignity. The latter describes the qualities on which he found a hook for his interpretation as the Archbishop's narrowness of focus and his zeal for serving his king. "'Tis A Girl" began as the Old Lady announces the baby's birth. Immediately Henry says, "Say it's a boy," and she does, only to correct herself later. Pownall says:

> If it's a boy, I'm vindicated. If it's a boy, then Norfolk, Suffolk, all the "tanks" will shut up. The church can go away and make wine....I have the Tudor line established and I can go back to building up my navy and wiping out Spain.

Then it's all taken away from him, says the actor, slamming his hand on the dressing room counter, "and it's back to the Privy Council and the court."

Act V, Scene 2

Act V, Scene 2, was cut.

Act V, Scene 3

Act V, Scene 3, contained two scenes, Scene 39, "Why Are We Met?" (pp. 162-166), and Scene 40, "Play the Spaniel" (pp. 166-169), divided by the king's entrance. Rintoul says that the intention of the scene is to show Cranmer's accusers, all taking swipes at him because no one can hit him solidly. The basic problem here, he explains, is not enough depth of thought. The Privy Council members have not pursued him as slowly and carefully as they did Wolsey, jumping on him because they fear both his power and that of the Protestant Church. In "Play the Spaniel," Henry forces a reconciliation with the council; Cranmer has shown them the king's ring signifying his protection at the very moment they ordered him to the tower. At Henry's insistence, all make up with Cranmer except for the Bishop of Winchester. Henry moves on to another topic, but turns later to insist that Winchester, too, embrace Cranmer. Rintoul says he took Wentworth aside in rehearsal and told him that having held out against the king's first order to be reconciled, he must somehow top the others in making up with Cranmer. The next time they ran the scene, Winchester kissed Cranmer squarely on the lips, which almost always produced the same absolute shock in the audience as it did that day in rehearsal. Both Rintoul and Pownall stress that Henry knows this accord will not last but that Henry forces it in order to remind the council members that they have to play the game his way. But he has also told them, Pownall says, that Cranmer is "not just a guy from college; he's as good as we say he is." His strength comes from his role as servant, an example which Henry wishes his other counselors would emulate. Pownall believes that by the end of the scene the council understands that Henry could not operate independently under Wolsey but will do so with Cranmer because, while the stated issue stemmed from protecting Cranmer, Pownall says, the real isuue lay in establishing the independent power of the king.

Act V, Scene 5

Act V, Scene 5, contained one scene, Scene 41, "Christening" (pp. 172-175). "And then miraculously the play ends," says Pownall, smiling. For the ending Hanson dressed everyone but the two pages in gold and ivory, and Silver provided two golden fonts to receive the baptismal gifts. Pownall says he felt some incredulity when the play builds to such a moment of intensity without then going on to resolve any of the difficulties. There is no resolution either to the character or the plot of the politics of power, about which the show has had much to say. The Archbishop of Canterbury comes forward, explains Pownall, and says of the baby Elizabeth, "Hey, Hank, this one might have a boy." He adds, "Well, that's a bit Walt Disney, but I'll go for it. I've got a nice closing speech, and you should see the curtain call." Pownall concludes that the ending shows things are rough, but there is hope they will get better, "so there is some forgiving there." Rintoul says the scene belongs to Henry. He has discovered the joys of being reconciled to his wife and daughter. "We all know it isn't going to last, but wouldn't it be nice if it did?" he asks, confessing that "If anyone knows Henry, he knows it's all downhill from here....He goes through great moral and physical degeneration....He becomes Al Capone and Cromwell becomes Heinrich Himmler. Mitchell tried in this scene to show that Anne understands that things will not go well. She "paled Anne down a lot," trying to give the impression with dark makeup under the eyes that Anne has suffered sleepless nights.

Two footnotes of interest involve actors Scott Wentworth and David Brown. Wentworth explains that because Shakespeare could rely on people's knowledge of recent events he left out facts or events needed for a complete understanding of the text; these had to be supplied by the director and actors. Rintoul had worked to learn his history and to provide as much of what was left out as possible in stamping a form on the play. For that reason, Brown continues, he believed it was the show that remained the most constant throughout its run. Several other performers agreed.

David Brown says he was fascinated by a piece of research by assistant director Kelly Robinson that revealed Cranmer had once been married to Black Joan of The Dolphin Inn, for which he lost his university scholarship. But because Black Joan had died nine months after the marriage, his scholarship was reinstated. The church at that time did not recognize a marriage of less than one year as legitimate. The play did not allow any way to play this bit of information, but Brown enjoyed the idea of the good and dignified archbishop once married to this questionable character. When asked if he wore a black dolphin tattooed on his arm under his clerical garb, Brown laughs and replies, ''Oh yes, but not on my arm.''

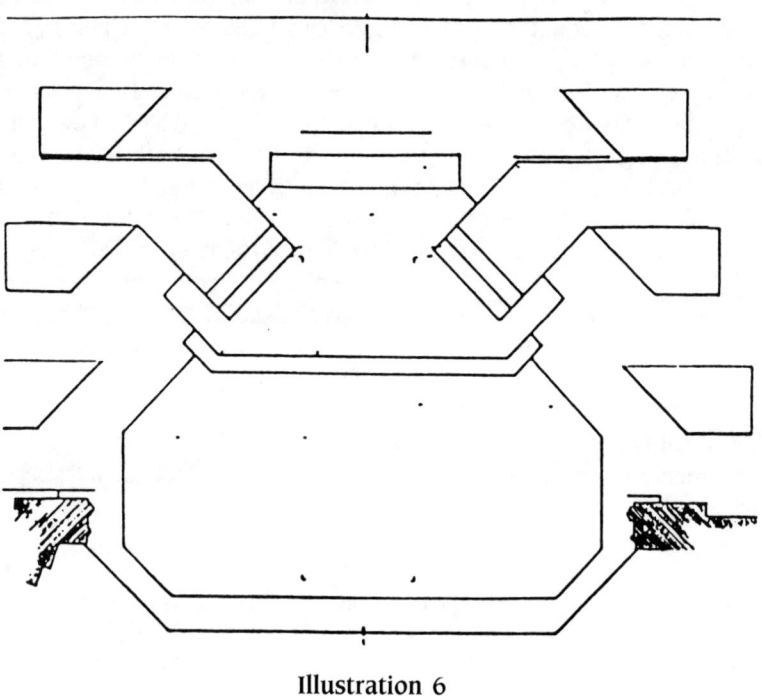

Illustration 6

Designer Phillip Silver's ground plan for *Henry VIII*.

A Man For All Seasons

BY ROBERT BOLT

DIRECTED BY	WALTER LEARNING
SET DESIGNED BY	PHILLIP SILVER
COSTUMES DESIGNED BY	DEBRA HANSON
MUSIC BY	BRUCE RUDDELL
LIGHTING DESIGNED BY	HARRY FREHNER

THE CAST

in order of appearance

The Common Man	DOUGLAS CAMPBELL
Sir Thomas More	WILLIAM HUTT
Master Richard Rich	PETER DONALDSON
The Duke of Norfolk	DAVID SCHURMANN
Lady Alice More	PAT GALLOWAY
Lady Margaret More	CAMILLE MITCHELL
Cardinal Wolsey	DAVID GARDNER
Thomas Cromwell	MICHAEL FAWKES
Signor Chapuys	KENNETH WICKES
Chapuys' Attendant	CHRISTOPHER THOMAS
William Roper	SCOTT WENTWORTH
King Henry The Eighth	LEON POWNALL
A Woman	HAZEL DESBARATS
Thomas Cranmer	DAVID BROWN
Stage Manager	MARGARET PALMER
Assistant Stage Managers	SUSAN KONYNENBURG
	JANINE RALPH
Assistant Director	WINSTON SUTTON
Assistant Designer	ANDREW MURRAY
Assistant Lighting Designer	KEVIN FRASER

"The King in Parliament cannot bestow
the Supremacy of the Church because
it is a Spiritual Supremacy. And
more to this, the immunity of the
Church is promised both in Magna
Carta and the King's own Coronation
Oath." Sir Thomas More
A Man for All Seasons II.8

Chapter Seven: *A Man for All Seasons*

Rehearsals for *A Man for All Seasons* began on 3 June, 1986, in Rehearsal Hall 1 of the Avon Theatre under the direction of Walter Learning. Learning came to directing through two degrees from the University of New Brunswick before taking his Ph.D. at Cambria in Australia. He studied theatre from a number of perspectives, from stripping the paint off of old flats to theatre scholarship and acting. On his return to Canada, he founded Theatre New Brunswick, where he served as artistic director for ten years. He was head of the Canada Council's Theatre Division for the next four years, during which he directly supervised the Stratford Festival's federal funding. "I was not always a popular visitor," Learning laughingly recounts, "then or now." He next went to Vancouver Playhouse as artistic director, where he served for five seasons, until December 1986. Immediately after the opening of the first play of the 1986-87 season there in late September, Learning returned to Australia for a directing assignment in Cambria. He had directed or acted in *A Man for All Seasons* three times before this Stratford assignment; he directed the 1984 Vancouver Playhouse production in which William Hutt played Sir Thomas More and Leon Pownall Henry VIII, roles they played in this production. Learning credits his engagement as director for this piece to Hutt. He also played the Common Man in an Australian production in 1963-64 and directed the play while appearing as Henry VIII for Theatre New Brunswick in 1969.

Because Hutt and Pownall repeated their roles and Michael Fawkes had played in the Vancouver Playhouse production, Learning sensed an attitude early in rehearsals that the cast thought of this as "a remount" of that production. Consequently, the director says, he made a conscious effort never to mention the previous production in order to take a fresh look at the play, beginning with the new set. He says he liked the set that he, Brian Rintoul (director for *Henry VIII*), and designer Phillip Silver negotiated and believed that in the main it worked for his production. However, both directors and the designer admit to having to talk through desired changes. Learning wanted more elevations on which to stage the action and less stage space. In *Henry VIII*, a play produced with lots of costumes and spectacle, stage space gets a high priority, says Learning, but this paired production of *A Man for All Seasons* must play in a much more intimate atmosphere because it is for the most part a "two hander"--a two-actor play. The two characters on stage change from scene to scene, giving the impression of a more complex structure; Learning says that keeping that sense of familiarity in the larger space proved challenging. By the time Learning accepted this play, Silver and Rintoul, working under the strictures of time, had already made some basic decisions about the set that eventually influenced his production. He did his negotiating in the later discussions, Learning says.

Learning began with the idea that the play could not successfully move outside its historical period but, he says, "You can frame it, and that's what I've done with the music." To composer Bruce Riddle, with whom Learning has worked on numerous occasions, he explained that he saw the production as different parts of a mass and asked Riddle to start by composing a mass in the style of the period for this play. His preliminary discussions with costume designer Debra Hanson centered on colours. The original concept for *Henry VIII* and *A Man for All Seasons* called for many of the costumes to double between the two shows, but since *Henry VIII* reflects the court and its splendour and *A Man for All Seasons* reflects the domestic life of More, the original idea had to change. Learning did not want to work against his historical period, so when new costumes came into the production concept he asked Hanson to stay with the colours and fabrics that her research showed him had formed the bulk of the clothing of that era.

Hutt and Learning collaborated here for the sixth time. When they had done the play in Vancouver, Learning says, they had placed considerable emphasis on reining in the emotional side of More, so that at times he seemed quite cool and uninvolved. Learning thinks such an approach bears up under a careful evaluation of text, but he and Hutt wanted to take a different tack by showing the wit and passion within the man, even if he did have to "sit on" that passion at some points. In that way, More has some eruptions earlier in the piece rather than holding back for the trial scene. Learning believes that they have achieved a fuller and more interesting stage character. Hutt agrees, saying that he much admired Paul Scofield's performance in the film version of this piece, a performance that has remained vivid over the years in his mind. Since the Vancouver performance, he has come to see it as William Hutt imitating Paul Scofield playing Sir Thomas More; much of the laid-back quality of that performance came from Scofield's character. Hutt adds that when Stratford offered him the role, he wanted to make sure he created his own More by making some very different initial decisions. For him these centered on stripping away the uninvolved manner of his previous portrayal.

Riddle says that because Learning requested him the Festival appointed him and he was in place by November 1985. Learning asked him to read the play, and then they got together to discuss it after their appointments, since both live in Vancouver. They had a lot to talk about, Riddle says; they had similar impressions that the script lacked an exploration of More's spiritual nature, although that very quality guides More through the entire play. Using a modern worship service as a basis of comparison, Riddle explains that the music that evolved for this production spiritually transports the congregation/audience. In his abbreviated mass, Riddle began with a *Kyrie*, *Benedictus*, *Credo*, *Sanctus*, and three versions of the *Agnus Dei*. Then he composed fanfares and drum flourishes for a number of occasions, such as the ones used for the king's entrance to More's house and More's own entrance to Hampton Court. Finally he constructed a third level of music, single lines for the recorder which underlay much of what the Common Man says. He chose the recorder both for its historical correctness and its haunting or melancholy sound.

He purposely did not attempt to tie particular scenes in the play to particular parts of the mass. That film device, he says, rarely works in a play, and he did not want to force particular pieces under specific speeches. The first piece begins even before the opening by the Common Man, and the movement through, in the form of a worship service, takes place very subtly. In so doing, he notes, he has also taken the audience out of one scene and into the next in an emotionally accurate manner.

In designing the set, Silver says, he wound up in a curious position because when the two directors sharing it started to head in opposite directions on any particular he had to come up with a compromise. His initial discussions with Learning focused on the play's openness, simplicity, and modernity; then Learning "allowed me to go away and do *Henry VIII*," says Silver. When Learning came to Stratford, Silver had all the sets worked out in models. He had also done *A Man for All Seasons*, and as he designed *Henry VIII* he built himself "lots of toys" for the play so that he could say, "The Henry set functions like this," using the model to present Learning with suggestions for the way to use the set in his play. They agreed to the basic look of the set, including the cyclorama and the brick or tile surface to cover the stage floor. Silver says that his two directors accepted compromise gracefully.

Learning told him after rehearsals had started that in prior productions he had employed the Common Man to do a great deal of furniture rearranging, but in this production very little rearrangement proved necessary. Certain scenic elements play only in *A Man for All Seasons*, such as the drape behind the scenes in More's home, because director and designer thought a screen inappropriate for domestic scenes. In addition to the two large coats of arms which play in *Henry VIII*, a third one plays in this production. (For specific details of set design and construction, see the chapter on *Henry VIII*.)

The scenery in *A Man for All Seasons* goes from several tables, which always play on stage--lit and visible, or unlit and invisible--to a bare stage at the end. It somehow seems quite proper to him, says Silver, that as More strips away layer after layer before achieving his goal, the stage does also. In rehearsal, the tables were taken off at different points in the last act until Learning and Silver decided that striking them too early destroyed this parallel movement between actor and scenery. Finally they settled on leaving them onstage until after the trial scene and then pulling them all off during the blackout, when adding the chopping block for the execution. The Common Man does the last speech on a totally bare stage, a visual effect that Silver calls hard to describe. No review or writing can capture on the page the power of a visual presentation on stage, and that problem sums up the joy and terror of the medium of theatre, says Silver.

During dress rehearsal, women with large skirts had difficulty sitting in what seemed to them narrow chairs. After a quick search of the Tudor chairs in stock turned up no possible replacements, Silver went back to his research materials, which told him that the size of the existing chairs was correct for the period. Armed with that information, Silver looked again at the Holbein painting of the More family and suddenly understood why Alice More had taken the pose that she had: to make her dress fit into the chair. The posture, he explains, resembled almost exactly the one that actress Pat Galloway as Alice finally took in rehearsal to make her dress fit, too.

Lighting designer Harry Frehner liked the set because Silver's design left him so many possibilities, and Silver explains that the set exists for a good lighting designer. In early conversations, the two talked about the time of day or dominant mood of each scene. Ideas changed over the course of the production meetings and the rehearsal period, Silver says, but he wanted Frehner to be a party to the discussions and arrangements. These discussions with Frehner, says Silver, included the idea of opening up the set by using the cyclorama both to give the set a different look from that in *Henry VIII* and to achieve the openness the director wanted. Frehner's job consisted of making modifications where possible. Resident lighting designer Michael

Whitfield and Louise Guinand (designer for *Hamlet*) had already done the basic rig at the Avon, and it provided seventy-five percent of the available light. Once the technical rehearsals began, Silver says, he worked with Frehner, Learning, and stage management to determine the cues for lighting when scenic elements were to fly in or out. For example, he says that Learning might want a particular actor to provide the ending to a scene for which the scenery going out actually made a bigger statement. Silver says that when he does a design for a play with transitions from scene to scene, he always designs them as well, so he does not mind adding that information to the "pool of knowledge from which a director can select or invent his own solution."

Silver points out that in designing a show such as *A Man for All Seasons* --where one character serves as narrator, scene changer, and prop master, as does the Common Man--then the designer simplifies that job for the actor. In this case, he put cloth on the feet of the furniture pieces so that dragging them from place to place became easier; constructed props such as the sign for the inn and the axe for the execution out of lightweight materials such as styrofoam and plywood; and segmented the trunk so that the properties needed for each scene would readily come to hand. At university, Silver says, he used to tell his students that the actor walked a metaphorical tightrope each night, and if he fell off the design team would bear the responsibility for not having rigged that apparatus properly.

Costumer Debra Hanson says that of the thirty-two costumes in *A Man for All Seasons*, twelve came from *Henry VIII* and twenty were built, the reverse of the Festival's initial projection. When Hanson and Learning began to work on the costume concept, casting and cross-casting for the two plays were not complete. They did know that Lady Alice More did not appear in *Henry VIII*, that two different actors would play Cardinal Wolsey, and that the More family would progress from the middle class to poverty by the end of the play. She says that they knew enough to go to executive director Peter Roberts, resident director Bob Beard, and John Neville for clearance to build the extra costumes. This play, she says, offers opportunities to change costumes more frequently than she opted to do because clothes in that era cost a great deal of money, and people wore them out before getting new ones. In the production's scenes that take place two years apart, Lady Alice and Margaret wear the same day dresses.

The costume progression in *Henry VIII*, she says, moves away from individuality, but in *A Man for All Seasons* individuality of the characters must remain expressed in costumes throughout. Hanson, Learning, and Hutt wanted to costume More to show both the security of his position and his pride in such material things. His costume for the top of the second act Hanson took from the Holbein painting, but eliminating the hat; in that scene, he resigns the Lord Chancellorship. Hanson moved around the theatre during dress rehearsals, but on opening night her ticket put her in the far right balcony. As the second act began she noticed that Hutt sat in exactly the same position and manner she had put in the costume sketch. The sketch suddenly came alive for her, a very rare occasion for a designer.

Occasionally an actor or actress will help in individualizing a character, says Hanson, as when for Lady Alice she selected a plain house dress. Actress Pat Galloway pointed her to Bolt's script note that the character should look "overdone," so she gave Alice a few more braids and pieces of jewellry as accessories. The designer says that as soon as she saw the difference that those additions made, she knew what Galloway had wanted to achieve and that the character's enhanced look fit nicely into her concept of finding a way for the characters to retain a distinctive personal look. In a similar situation she designed short-sleeved costumes for the Common Man, played by Douglas Campbell, because Campbell had injured the ligaments in his right arm and she wanted to make costume changes comfortable. One costume changed as a result of seeing the production in rehearsals. The dress worn by the Woman, which came from *Henry VIII*, read like a party dress to Learning, Hanson says. Seeing that the dress would not work in the scene, she pulled wardrobe stock from the warehouse and found one of designer Susan Benson's black dresses from *A Midsummer Night's Dream* done in 1977-78 and stripped off all the trim. As she arrived at rehearsal, Learning called her over to him, pointed at the Woman, and asked the designer if she had anything black in which she could dress the character. In summary, Hanson says she relishes the opportunity to have her costumes created for the two plays on view side by side where in each case she has tried to serve the play and playwright faithfully.

Lighting designer Harry Frehner gave up a math major to begin his theatre career as a University of Waterloo drama graduate trained in all aspects of theatre arts, although he still has a cherished predilection for numbers. He accepted both technical and acting jobs before moving exclusively into technical theatre and got his first opportunity to light several shows in a small theatre in Thunder Bay. Michael Benoit, who this year served as stage manager for both *Hamlet* and *Rosencrantz and Guildenstern Are Dead*, suggested Frehner as an assistant to Stratford lighting designer Michael Whitfield. After going through an interview in the Calgary airport, Frehner says, he came to Stratford as an assistant lighting designer in 1977. During 1978, 1979, and 1980, he lit all the Third Stage productions, and when *Ned and Jack* moved from the Third Stage to the Avon in 1978, he lit that show in the larger house. *The Taming of the Shrew* in 1981 marked his debut as a designer on the Festival Stage, and since then he has lit two to three productions a year. Frehner sees the price tag for failure at Stratford as so high that ninety percent of what he puts on the stage he knows from his previous work will do the job. In the winter season he experiments with new ideas in the alternative theatres in Toronto.

Learning, having done the show before, had a definite idea about the specifics of each scene that he and Frehner discussed. Then Frehner watched rehearsals, set the cues for the shows, and showed them to Learning. Some of the cues looked very different from Learning's expectations, says Frehner, but the director liked some of his innovations and they stayed. Frehner says that he feels this kind of collaboration works best but will stick strictly to what a director wants if he prefers to work that way.

Learning wanted a very simple approach to the play because anything that smacked of theatricality seemed to betray the simple, honest nature of the play. And, Frehner notes, when a designer creates a set as open as this one, he obviously has a plan for lighting it. He and Silver discussed the designer's plan, which he by and large adopted, putting light on the cyclorama during the scenes in the play that called for openness and excluding the light to close off the environment.

During the first rehearsal on 3 June, Learning scheduled a read-through of the play, after which Hanson and Silver spoke about the design concept as described above. Because the play did not open until 24 July, Learning said, the company had plenty of time and would take an occasional day off. Rehearsals on those six days a week went from 7 to 10 p.m. Tuesday to Friday; between 10 a.m. and 1 p.m. on Wednesdays and Saturdays, matinee days; and Sunday afternoons from 1 to 5 p.m. In the first weeks in June extra student matinees freed the actors for evening rehearsals; Learning and stage manager Margaret Palmer had to work around actors performing in the other shows in the Avon repertory. For instance, Peter Donaldson, who played Richard Rich but also appeared in two other shows, spent time outside of scheduled rehearsals with Learning in sessions which Donaldson says allowed them to explore fully the dimensions of the character. Hutt played Wolsey in *Henry VIII*; Galloway, Campbell, and Camille Mitchell (Margaret) did not have other Festival responsibilities during the rehearsal period; Campbell directed *The Boys From Syracuse*, which had opened on 19 May; and Mitchell, who played Anne Bullen in *Henry VIII*, had dislocated her kneecap during the final preview and spent much of the rehearsal period for *A Man for All Seasons* in a wheelchair. She did not resume the role of Anne again until after this play had opened. As a result of these circumstances, Learning usually had enough actors available on a given day to put together a workable rehearsal schedule.

Silver remarks that the early rehearsals frequently looked out of proportion because his eye had adjusted to seeing these actors onstage in their elaborate *Henry VIII* costumes. When these performers moved back to the rehearsal hall in their own summer clothing, the designer's furniture and properties appeared much too large until the actors again wore costumes. His comment points up another oddity of the rehearsal period. Some of the actors played the same characters that they played in *Henry VIII*: David Schurmann as the Duke of Norfolk, Michael Fawkes as Cromwell, Leon Pownall as Henry VIII, David Brown as Thomas Cranmer, and Kenneth Wickes as Signor Chapuys. Others had roles without counterparts in the other play: Pat Galloway as Alice More, Camille Mitchell as Margaret More, Douglas Campbell as the Common Man, Peter Donaldson as Master Richard Rich, and Scott Wentworth as William Roper. In addition, David Gardner played Cardinal Wolsey for the first time and William Hutt played More for the second time, but after a two-year interval. Early rehearsals, then, combined actors with very clearly developed characters and character intentions with actors whose characters had not yet taken shape. All the actors who repeated roles between the two shows eventually came to modify their characters. For some, such as Pownall's Henry VIII, only a slight alteration proved necessary. For others, such as Fawkes' Cromwell, the adjustment between playing a younger man in *Henry VIII* and the older, more experienced version of that character in *A Man for All Seasons* called for a great deal of adjustment. Learning's job of getting the right characters into the dominant positions in the early rehearsal stages of a particular scene was tricky at times.

Learning usually worked a scene once and then moved around the rehearsal hall speaking quietly to individual actors about what he wanted them to do differently as they ran the scene again. He says he brought strong feelings about the piece to rehearsals but wanted this cast to have the opportunity to make their contributions before nailing down scenes in specifics. He talked with them individually to explore their ideas and feelings about their scenes. Frequently he incorporated those ideas into the scene for a period of time, refining them before deciding to accept or reject them.

As the play began to take shape, the director wanted to rehearse scene changes with the Common Man on the set as quickly as it became practical. As a general rule, before rehearsals begin, the stage management team equips the rehearsal hall with furniture and properties that resemble the size and shape of those needed; these substitute pieces are replaced by the actual items as soon as the various Festival shops turn them out. Nevertheless moving a piece of furniture on stage, under lights, and in costume can create a different experience for the actor from doing it in the rehearsal hall, so Learning shifted the location of the middle rehearsals between the rehearsal hall and the stage, depending upon the availability of the latter.

No previous performance of this play had been done at the Stratford Festival when this production opened on 24 July. Stage manager Margaret Palmer divided the play into 30 scenes and gave them titles, using the English Samuel French edition. The page numbers used refer to that edition. The New York edition of the Samuel French script contains some changes made in the New York production after the printing of the English edition; this company found the incorporation of some of these changes useful.

Act I, Scene 1

Act I, Scene 1, contained four scenes: Scene 1, "I Need a Costume" (pp. 1-2); Scene 2, "Entrance of More" (pp. 2-4); Scene 3, "Stooped From The Clouds" (pp. 4-9); and Scene 3A, "Common Sense" (pp. 9-10). Riddle says he began the show with a full-length version of the *Kyrie* written in the four- and five-part harmony typical during the period to set the spiritual mood. In the opening monologue by the Common Man, Douglas Campbell makes the whole of "I Need a Costume" sound like the words of a chorus or narrator more than like a character linking scenes. According to the actor, the character makes an excuse for everything, and he sees the Common Man as something of a coward, who does in every case what benefits him. He certainly does not qualify for the status of hero as he sometimes is played, says Campbell. Campbell compares the character with those in the National Film Board's production of *Return to Dresden*, in which Allied pilots who had bombed Dresden despite its status as an open city return there. Many of them showed real remorse at what they had done when younger just because someone had ordered them to do it. Campbell says:

> But I dare say if we go on in the world expecting that to be the truth we cannot exonerate ourselves by saying, "Well, I was ordered to do it." Surely we can disobey the orders.

As the character introduces More, the "Entrance of More" scene begins. As the lights come up, a table and three chairs played stage right, backed with the drape Silver used to describe More's house, and Frehner kept the lights muted on the cyclorama. Hutt says of this scene that the audience must immediately understand that Richard Rich has received an invitation to the dinner party given by the More family, with the Duke of Norfolk as the only other guest, because of his intellectual promise. Hutt believes More enjoys the mental workout that Rich provides, while his friend Norfolk talks only about falcons and water spaniels. But the relationship with Rich never gets started because More sees him as influenced by Thomas Cromwell and drawn to the pragmatic ideas of Machiavelli, explains Hutt. Hutt says that a little alarm goes off in More's head at the mention of Machiavelli and Cromwell that makes him begin to suspect Rich's intellectual honesty and leads him to point Rich out to Norfolk for employment, rather than recommend him, in the next scene. Donaldson, too, believes a great deal of the success of the piece rides on establishing the relationship between Rich and More in this scene because, he says, the growing breach begins here. If an audience misses the idea of a break in their friendship and sees them only as mistrustful of one another from the beginning, then Rich's eventual betrayal of More loses some of its punch, says Donaldson.

The arrival of the rest of the guests from the dinner party--Norfolk, Lady Alice, and Lady Margaret--starts "Stooped From the Clouds." The title refers to a falcon that Norfolk claims can "stoop from five hundred feet in the air to catch a heron." Schurmann admits he does not know how many audience members understand that in this play the falcon represents Henry VIII and the heron represents Thomas More, but he does all he can to make the point plain. He sees Norfolk as trapped by the stereotype of the English aristocracy --unread and interested only in hunting; his Norfolk, despite what he says, has read both Aristotle and Machiavelli but does not dare show it. More stimulates Norfolk by intellectual discussions, says Schurmann, but Norfolk does not let More see that he has succeeded in engaging his mind.

Galloway did historical research for her role as Lady Alice, carefully read the stage directions, and then threw both away. The historical character, she says, may not have played the traditional role of mistress within their marriage at all but may simply have managed More's large and complex household. Bolt obviously saw them as a warm and loving couple, she says; the stage directions in the script call for Alice to respond repeatedly in anger to More. For a time that paradox was difficult to incorporate into her performance, until she concluded that the anger came from her love of him. She threw out the idea that Alice simply delivers her words angrily and began to play the genuine caring in the anger.

Mitchell begins an explanation of her Lady Margaret with a technical concern. She calls the character "shy and retiring" but still maintained a high energy on the stage. She thinks that Margaret has an excellent mind and a wonderful relationship with her father. It served as the cornerstone of Mitchell's character, and she modelled much of the character on Hutt's More, believing that Margaret represented a feminine counterpart to her father.

During the "Common Sense" scene, the Common Man changes the set from More's house to Wolsey's apartment at Richmond. Because of the prop changes Silver and Learning had decided on very little rearrangement of the furniture. Removing a tablecloth to reveal the one underneath it was the major change engineered by the Common Man. The drape behind More's house flew out, and one of Silver's screens, developed for *Henry VIII*, descended for Wolsey's apartment. The scene took place at night, so Frehner used no light on the cyclorama and very little in the room itself.

Act I, Scene 2

Riddle used a very simple line of the *Benedictus*, written in a minor key as the bridge from "Common Sense" to "England Needs An Heir" in Scene 4 (pp. 10-13). Learning liked the irony of that music going into the scene with the worldly Wolsey, and the canticle as Riddle wrote it contained a hint of danger and foreboding. According to Gardner, Wolsey was a very cruel, manipulating, and world-weary man. The scene is very short, but Gardner stresses that it reverberates for the next fifteen minutes because the other characters keep mentioning Wolsey. Gardner used Cromwell's line in the next scene where, referring to Wolsey, he says, "You left him--in his laughing mood, I hope?" as an example. He looked for places in which he could show the character's potential for laughter but decided to subdue his laugh to sound cruel, for More tells Cromwell that he did not leave Wolsey in his laughing mood. Wolsey in this play, he says, is a meaner and less smooth character than the one he understudied for Hutt in *Henry VIII*. This scene offers a bold threat that lingers until Henry poses the next one some four scenes later. Gardner also says he believes that the actor playing Wolsey must dominate the actor playing More, and topping an actor of Hutt's stature proved no easy job. He credits Learning with pushing him to use his own voice and not overproject, in order to threaten More.

Hutt says More remains respectful because at that point Wolsey occupies the Lord Chancellor's chair, and More has no official position, but comes in answer to a summons to give advice. Even then he chooses to say very little. More's silence begins here, says Hutt. The actor quotes Wolsey's line, "Then come down to earth, Thomas! And until you do, bear in mind that you have an enemy!" More questions Wolsey, "Where, your grace?" and Wolsey replies, "Here, Thomas." Hutt looks at the persona behind the line; Wolsey does not simply mean that he opposes More, the actor explains, but the line implies that the opposition may come from the king. So, says Hutt, the silence must begin here.

Act I, Scene 3

This scene contained two parts, Scene 5, "The Riverside" (pp. 13-15) and Scene 5A, "Home Again" (p. 15). "The Riverside" scene inspired the use of the recorder and marked the occasion of its first use, under chilly gray light. To set the scene, the screen stage right which designated Wolsey's quarters flew out and one stage left for the river bank flew in. No light played on the cyclorama. This section begins with a conversation between More and a boatman and, despite the late hour, Thomas Cromwell soon enters and after him Signor Chapuys. Hutt says each of the characters in the play wants information from More, each pushing him as far as he dares. Fawkes says that in this scene his Cromwell has not yet arrived at a position of power, and so he is played without the ease and swagger the character will shortly acquire. The scene ends as it began, with More and the boatman negotiating the price: Even the boatman wants more from More than the established rate. Bolt says in his introduction to the published version that he used the land and water as symbols of the growing division in the play and singled out the Boatman's line about the channel in the water getting deeper as an example of how these symbols enrich the play. But the director emphasizes the impossibility of asking an actor to play a symbol. Learning praises the talented actors William Hutt and Douglas Campbell for bringing this image to life in this scene, saying that one has the feeling they are talking about more than just the channel depth. As the Common Man shifts the scene back to More's house, he removes this second tablecloth to reveal yet another one exactly like the one in the first scene already in place; clears away the props as the drape flew in; and changed tunics from boatman to steward. This time Frehner put some light, a very low level of blue light, on the cyclorama.

Act I, Scene 4

This scene contained three units: Scene 6, "A Passionate Lutheran" (pp. 15-18); Scene 7, "Levelling Talk" (pp. 18-19); and Scene 7A, "A Little History" (p. 19). More enters his home to confront Will Roper, the passionate Lutheran who wants to marry his daughter. Scott Wentworth, who played Roper, says the trick is discerning between the character's function and the lines he has to speak. Roper serves as a foil to More, says Wentworth, "but you can't play that." Instead, with that function in mind, he played each of the arguments with all the sincerity possible to give More a position to undercut. Hutt notes that the historical More burned heretics alive, and as this scene shows, the hero of Bolt's play, believing no less intensely, offers more compassion. But still he refuses to discuss a marriage between Roper and his daughter while Roper remains a Lutheran. Mitchell says that the arguments between them, in which she has very little to say, made her listen intensely to what the characters were talking about, backing with her intellect her father's position while portraying a young woman in love with a young man. The blocking placed her between the two; Mitchell solved her difficulty by coming down on More's side, a choice she describes as natural between father and daughter. Ultimately, she's "a daddy's girl," says Mitchell.

With Roper's exit, the "Levelling Talk" scene begins. During this scene, says Hutt, both Margaret and Alice ask what Wolsey wanted but More remains silent. The actor compares More's motives for his silence to his family with those of a Mafia member: "He does not want them to be involved...they will have more safety and security if they do not know what he does." For Galloway, the scene provided an opportunity for Lady Alice to show some of the concern and care for More that she wanted to build into the performance. In this scene, she fears he might have caught a head-cold.

During "A Little History," the Common Man rushes on stage in time to watch a history book, along with Cardinal Wolsey's robe and hat, fall to the floor on stage left. Campbell then reads from Bolt's account of the Cardinal's fall out of the book. The drape representing More's house flies out. and a screen representing Hampton Court flew in, along with a large seal of the realm depicting Cromwell's increased power. This time Frehner painted the cyclorama bright blue with clearly defined white clouds.

Act I, Scene 5

This scene played as one unit, Scene 8, "The King's Ear" (pp. 19-23). To make the point that this is the first view of Cromwell in power, Riddle provided a sharp, somewhat discordant fanfare instead of a more traditional fanfare of the period, written in thirds or fifths. As Cromwell tells Rich at the top of the scene, he came from the late Cardinal's service into that of the king, who accepts him after rejecting Wolsey. The actor explains the king needs insulation and someone familiar with the vast political and espionage structure Wolsey had created to serve the state. Indeed, this scene points up how complex the surveillance system has become. Cromwell buys information from More's steward, and so does the Spanish ambassador. But, says Fawkes, Cromwell must maintain a tight hold on this information network, as he does in this scene, where his speech to the ambassador about the detailed specifications of the new English warship simply tests the extent of his intelligence-gathering. Cromwell takes some measure of delight at the ambassador's corrections of Cromwell's "errors."

Act I, Scene 6

Act I, Scene 6 contained six scenes: Scene 9, "Where Is Thomas?" (pp. 23-25); Scene 10, "No Ceremony" (pp. 25-28); Scene 11, "My Brother's Widow" (pp. 28-32); Scene 12, "Joshua's Trumpet" (pp. 33-35); Scene 13, "Not Welcome Here" (pp. 36-38); and Scene 14, "A Stuffed Swan" (pp. 36-38). A screen with roses attached flew in to replace the one inside More's house, and blue sky and clouds played higher up on the cyclorama and appeared less clearly defined. "Where is Thomas?" begins amid the flurry of looking for More because of the king's "surprise visit." When he finally arrives from vespers service, he wears a simple black cassock, which Alice and Meg remove, leaving him in his usual attire. Originally Learning and Riddle had wanted to use the *Sanctus* under the scene as if it actually came from the chapel, but decided, says Riddle, that the music interfered with the blocking. Instead, Riddle used a series of fanfares, each played as if the ship were coming closer and each fuller than the last, reflecting the more traditional fanfares of the time. Learning, Hanson, and Hutt discussed putting More in the costume modeled on the Holbein painting that More wore at the beginning of the second act for this scene as well but decided against it. Learning saw More's costumes becoming more opulent as the gulf between him and the king widens, to underscore that More's stand will cost him the material comforts of which he is obviously fond. "No Ceremony" begins with the entrance of the king, in his white costume from *Henry VIII* but in muddy tights. Pownall says the Henry in *A Man for All Seasons* comes to More's home for the express purpose of having More give him approval for his divorce. Riddle explains that the script calls for instrumental music from the king's offstage musicians; he used a madrigal called "Oh My Heart," which King Henry had written expressing his "frustration at the love relationship." Riddle speculates that the lyrics related directly to the relationship Henry discusses with More in this scene. Because he chose the madrigal, Riddle explains, this production assumes that Henry has brought a boys' choir with him on board rather than an orchestra. Once the family exits, Henry cajoles and bullies More. Henry leaves the play after this scene, "My Brother's Widow," but Pownall considers that the king's continued manipulation of others to force More's "free" approval drives the play forward.

Hutt believes Henry "convinced himself that he had committed a horrendous sin by marrying his brother's widow." While conceding that Henry might have begun by using that "as an excuse so he could get rid of Katherine and get into bed with Anne Bullen," he eventually "convinced himself," says Hutt. But, he says, regardless of Henry's belief, More has no choice: For the lawyer, he explains, the law rules supreme. While More maintains his silence regarding his reasons for not giving consent, Hutt maintains that he cannot consider the appeals of the king or others who advocate his acquiescence in the divorce because, "If you are a lawyer you have no choice in that situation." More's line says, "And more to this, the immunity of the Church is promised both in Magna Carta and the King's own Coronation Oath." So even though Pownall's Henry moves skilfully back and forth between wheeling and threatening his host, the law, both earthly and spiritual, leaves Hutt's More no maneuvering room.

The play does not really begin until the scene with the king, Hutt continues. "Up until then it's laying groundwork....But there is real danger after that scene and I think he [More] knows it." Henry does not want More to see him off the property by the end of that scene, an event that "speaks volumes to More....He's on a very dangerous course now," Hutt explains. Lady Alice enters in time to hear the king make his excuses and leave without having eaten dinner. Once he has left, "Joshua's Trumpet" begins.

Now the play turns domestic, Hutt says, as More explains himself to his family. In this small scene with Alice, Hutt tries to show her that in this matter with the king he must rule himself. Richard Rich enters to begin "Not Welcome Here" and asks for employment that More denies him. Donaldson explains how desperately Rich wants to work for More, looking to More, a man of goodness, to save him as well. Rich pleads not just for employment but for his own salvation. During the scenes with Roper in "A Stuffed Swan," Hutt defines the primary issue, even in the domestic environment, as the law. Roper confesses that his views on religion have altered from founding a new church to reforming the old one. But More proclaims that laws cannot be set aside even in pursuit of the devil himself. Hutt says:

> It is a very small leap for More, but a very big leap for other people between the law of man and the law of God. If you believe firmly in the law of man it's a very small leap to believe in the law of God because at least you've got the groundwork of believing in laws and in believing.

Wentworth thinks Roper has changed in order to marry Margaret, not realizing how much his emotions have swayed his principles. Mitchell's Margaret works consciously to bring Roper back into the Church because she realizes that for her father the issue is his Catholicism. Roper understands that Luther set out to reform the old religion, so, says the actor, he uses that stand as a springboard back into orthodoxy.

Act I, Scene 7

Act I, Scene 7, consisted of Scene 15, "The Loyal Subject" (pp. 38-39) and Scene 16, "Lost Innocence" (pp. 39-43). Riddle put the recorder music again here to suggest the late night pub music and the idea of the "dark corner." Frehner played no light on the cyclorama. The Common Man at the end of "The King's Ear" says, "When I touch bottom, I'll go deaf, blind, and dumb." At the beginning of "The Loyal Subject" he does just that: To each of Cromwell's questions he replies that he does not understand. First, however, he hangs up a sign naming the pub, The Loyal Subject; carries off one of the chairs; drags the table to center stage; and arranges a chair on each side of it. When Rich enters for "Lost Innocence" into what Learning describes as a quiet, cozy setting, the conspiracy is launched. During

161

initial rehearsals the table separated Cromwell and Rich across its horizontal dimension, preventing that intimate feeling that Learning wanted. Later Learning moved the table along the up stage/down stage axis, thus separating the actors by only a few feet and breathing closeness into the setting. According to Learning, this scene presents the biggest challenge in the play to both actors and director because one can rationalize about why Cromwell behaves as he does, but he must still pose a formidable threat to More. The trick for Rich in the scene, says Learning, is to bring to it vulnerability from his rejection. If he comes across as a cork bobbing on the water in anxiety, his actions in this scene become understandable. He says that Cromwell cannot frighten Rich unless Rich first shows himself capable of fear. The full force of Cromwell's power to frighten him is shown in the ending of the scene, where he holds Rich's hand in the flame until it is burned. Riddle used a drum for emphasis under that moment, which led directly to the interval, and restored the full *Sanctus* to his score to carry the audience one more step in this progression of the mass.

Act II, Scene 1

Act II, Scene 1, contained five scenes: Scene 17, "The English Socrates (pp. 44-46); Scene 18, "Rumour Has It" (pp. 46-48); Scene 19, "Connection with Rome" (pp. 48-50); Scene 20, "A Noble Gesture" (pp. 50-52); and Scene 20A, "Even Stevens" (pp. 52-53). Riddle used another Henry VIII madrigal, called "Without Discord," to begin Act II, believing that the lyrics underscored the text for this scene. Learning points to Bolt's water imagery again in the Common Man's speech opening the scene. Again, he says, Campbell, through his reading of the lines, conveys a broader meaning than the words alone give him. Hutt sees More as finally coming to the place where he must take a stand. Indeed, the actor says, More has already taken the stand before the act begins: If the bishops agree to the creation of the new church by an act of Parliament More will resign as Lord Chancellor. While they wait for news from the convocation, More and Roper again fall into discussion about the law, but this time for a different purpose. If the intent of the law matters most to Roper, the wording of the law most interests More. Roper accuses More of legal quibbling when he refers to the wording of *The Act of Supremacy* to which More responds, "Call it what you like, it's there, thank God." Learning, saying the point reaches into the core of the play, stresses that More did not take an uncompromising stand in a pursuit of martyrdom. Rather, the director sees him as a person who actively tried to find ways to make things work, such as using the wording of the law, but who ultimately could not find a way to make a tradeoff. If More had sought martyrdom, he says, he could have found it much earlier.

The Spanish ambassador, says Kenneth Wickes, has not come during "Rumour Has It" simply to ask about More's potential resignation but to pour on pressure for More to make some kind of stand for Catholicism. Wickes' ambassador sees the threat to the Church in England as a threat also to the influence of Spain at the English court. Chapuys hopes that More will stand at least symbolically as a figure around whom the Catholic opposition can unite. But even with diplomatic immunity, says the actor, the ambassador cannot state his purpose openly, so the acting must convey nonverbally what cannot be spoken aloud. Hutt's More understands the ambassador's hidden agenda but will have none of it.

Norfolk walks in to announce the bishops' decision for Henry that begins "Connection with Rome." More asks Alice, Norfolk, and then Margaret to help him take off the chain of office. Hutt explains that the request for help is not realistic; More wants the support of others. Only Roper volunteers to help. Hutt recounts that Learning asked him in rehearsal one day why More refuses that help; Hutt answered that Roper is too anxious, Alice refuses for domestic reasons, and Margaret helps him because she realizes why he must resign. Roper calls More's resignation the "Noble Gesture," but More quickly refutes that idea. More makes no defiant gesture, in order to show he still seeks a way to compromise, says Learning, and Hutt finds the importance of the scene in More's protecting himself and his family, reminding them that "silence must be absolute." None of them must make any public statement about the king's divorce and remarriage. The Common Man's soliloquy composed the "Even Stevens" scene, in which the steward refuses to stay in More's service for a reduced wage. According to Campbell, the Common Man remains so because he never assumes the responsibility for taking an uncommon stand. His action resonates against the uncommon stand that More has just made.

Act II, Scene 2

Act II, Scene 2, played as one unit, Scene 21, "The Silver Cup" (pp. 53-57). Fawkes likes Bolt's careful sculpting of the play to establish points and counterpoints: To More, the lawyer and man of conscience, Fawkes counterposes Cromwell, the lawyer and man of pragmatism. When Henry applies pressure to More in order to ensure passage of *The Act of Supremacy*, More resigns his office; Cromwell all too readily responds by using the law to manipulate More. All of this, says Fawkes, forms the background of this scene. The actor emphasizes that the character understands the king does not want More harmed at this point, so Cromwell's job is to bring him around to the king's view. The device he had planned to use to frighten More, the accusation of taking a bribe, will not work; to do that "It's just a matter of finding the right law. Or making one.'' Fawkes invites a comparison of that idea with More's view that ''the law is a path a citizen can walk upon in safety.''

Act II, Scene 3

Act II, Scene 3, contained two scenes: Scene 22, ''A Letter From Spain'' (pp. 57-59), and Scene 23, ''Parsnips and Mutton'' (pp. 59-51). The Common Man again sets the stage for More's house primarily by removing the large globe brought on for the Cromwell scene. Wickes says the Spanish ambassador has brought from the Spanish king a letter urging him to take a public stand that might lead to rebellion. Wickes says that although the ambassador assures More of his elaborate precautions to make sure no one has followed him, spies are everywhere: No amount of precaution can prevent others from knowing what he has come to do. Wickes believes the character has more than one motive for this action. First, More has resigned and the ambassador worries that he will begin to lose his influence among Catholics who might still nourish hopes of rebellion. Second, the ambassador badly needs to show the Spanish king some measure of his own success at the English court. The last thing with which he concerns himself, says Wickes, is the danger to More. More is useful as a symbol of resistance--alive or dead.

During the ''Parsnips and Mutton'' scene, the mental and financial impact of More's resignation on his family becomes clear. Galloway explains that Alice never understands why he acts as he does. Using the ''overdone'' image again, she says that Alice has enjoyed her social position, and its loss is frustrating. Frehner used his lights at the end of the scene to point up the fracturing of the family unit by placing four beams of light on an otherwise dark stage to highlight More, Roper, Alice, and Margaret. As each character leaves the stage, the light goes out until More stands alone in a tight circle of light on his face. Silver appreciated Frehner's idea of using light in this fashion, calling it ''quite satisfying.''

Act II, Scene 4

Act II, Scene 4, played as one unit, Scene 24, ''There Are No Charges (pp. 61-64). Cromwell tells Rich that the king has appointed them to bring the More issue to some speedy resolution. Fawkes finds a parallel for Cromwell in the growing power of a formerly poor and hungry *mafioso*, who, long after he has gained status and comfort for himself and family, is still driven to acquire more. In this case, the king's appetite drives him on. He wants More's blessing or his death. Fawkes says underneath those instructions, his character understands the king's real desire is for More's blessing, so Cromwell carefully structures their meeting. Fawkes delineates the character's wit and charm, which he turns upon More at the beginning of their meeting to no avail. Then come the charges, which More easily brushes aside. The devastating blow is the king's own accusation of ingratitude that Cromwell reads to More. Fawkes' Cromwell respects More, even in the character's line at the end of the scene that he does not like More as much as he did. Nevertheless Cromwell fails to move More, and Fawkes characterizes Cromwell as returning home to face the wife and kids, "tired and deeply worried."

For Hutt's More the scene required that the character not be drawn into debating the merits of the charges against him and thus breaking his silence. He answers the king's statement with an expression of his grief, avoiding the debate Cromwell seeks to provoke. Hutt calls this strategy a lawyer's device to keep from answering a question.

Act II, Scene 5

Act II, Scene 5, contained two scenes: Scene 25, "Cease To Know Me" (pp. 64-66), and Scene 26, "Water Spaniels" (pp. 66-68). The Common Man serves as the bridge away from Hampton Court and to the riverside. More realizes how dangerous knowing him has become, so he tells Norfolk to stop befriending him, eventually starting an argument to cut off the relationship. To Schurmann, although More succeeds in angering Norfolk here --he hits him after persistent goading--he still cares for More. More's line reminding him that he has a son gives Norfolk impetus to reconsider the friendship when the anger cools, the actor says. As Norfolk leaves the scene, Margaret and Roper arrive to tell More of the new law requiring each person to take an oath about Henry's marriage, on compulsion of treason. More's enthusiastic explanation to Roper, that the oath means only what the words say it means and that man's business is to escape if he can, provides Wentworth's character with a reason for taking the oath. Riddle again used the recorder to underscore the riverbank setting. The melodic line comes from the *Credo*, scored for this instrument.

Act II, Scene 6

Act II, Scene 6, played as two scenes: Scene 26A, "It's a Job" (p. 68) and Scene 27, "The Commission" (pp. 68-74). The Common Man leads More from his cell to face the commissioners. Hutt says from then on, the question for More is survival: survival of principle, survival of self, survival of soul. More repeats the same idea he expressed in the resignation scene, that he will tell his reasons for refusing to sign the oath only to the king. Hutt believes the king's refusal to see him after the resignation scene is significant; perhaps, speculates the actor, Henry fears More will talk the king into changing his mind. Cromwell plays the lawyer's trick of asking a question by implication during this scene, while More carefully answers only the question asked. In this manner, Hutt explains, More keeps his silence, this time by using words. Schurmann says Norfolk's concern for More comes out in the way he plays the scene, both in his pleas to More and his antipathy toward Cromwell. And Fawkes explains that a North American audience may miss a dimension of the quarrel between Norfolk and Cromwell; Norfolk would use the accent of a country squire while Cromwell, the son of a farrier, would use a working-class accent. An English audience would immediately understand the animosity between the two simply by hearing the clash of accents, he says. By the end of the scene, Cromwell admits that if he succeeds in killing More rather than in getting him to sign the oath, he will have arranged for his own death as well. Fawkes believes Cromwell's eventual fall, outside of this play, begins with his inability to get More's signature on that piece of paper.

Archbishop Cranmer, played by David Brown, makes a late appearance in this play as well as in *Henry VIII*. Brown tried to turn this holy, sincere, humourless man into a believable human being, using the qualities he found in the Cranmer of *Henry VIII*, a man with narrowly focused dedication to his king, whose service he places ahead of that to his God. Brown says the role is drawn in only sketchily in this play. In this scene he concentrates, with complete fidelity to his monarch, on More's arguments. Brown concludes that no matter how devoutly the character wants to serve Henry, both the character and the disputation of More influence him profoundly.

Act II, Scene 7

Act II, Scene 7, played as one unit, Scene 28, "A Short Visit" (pp. 74-80), during which More's family have come to persuade him to sign the document and come out. Mitchell says that Margaret signed the oath because she thought if members of the family signed it would help get More out of jail. Despite attempts to change her father's mind during the scene, she does not want him to betray his principles. When he asks the family to go away from England to a place where they can find safety, Margaret has the courage to say "Yes" to him. More asks for Alice's understanding, but Galloway says, her character's honesty forces her to tell him she fears she will hate him for the stand he has taken. Hutt concludes that for him that most devastating accusation tells More of her extraordinary love for him. Galloway worked intently to put her love for More under her anger throughout the play, and Hutt says that as a result of her outburst, More recognizes a quality in her he has not previously identified. Hutt recalls that More has tried to interest Alice in the things in which he takes an interest--as exemplified in his offer to teach her to read. But the actor explains that she declines because she finds the idea frightening. Now before she leaves the stage following her outburst he knows her to be "a lion," which, he says, helps Alice defend herself in More's eyes and prevent herself from hating him. Having helped her to see her worth, More sees that after years of isolation within their marriage "They are as close as they are going to get."

Act II, Scene 8

Act II, Scene 8, contained two units: Scene 28A, "Coats of Arms" (p. 80) and Scene 29, "The Trial" (pp. 80-88). "Coats of Arms" consisted of Cromwell's appointing the Common Man, against his protestations, as foreman of the jury. Once again, says Campbell, the character does what someone tells him, just as Fawkes notes Cromwell's interest only in the trappings of the law. As "The Trial" begins, Norfolk informs More he has come before the court on a charge of high treason. More, dazed by his long imprisonment, does not immediately understand. A stage direction indicates that More senses the trial is rigged, so when Rich perjures himself to condemn More, Hutt says, his character feels surprise because he did not consider that Rich's intellectual dishonesty extended so far. Donaldson says by now Rich has become a very practical man and has learned the art of pleasing those in power. After Act I, Scene 7, "Lost Innocence," between Cromwell and Rich, Learning says, the latter will do whatever he has to do to prosper and will do it with relative ease. But More does win at least one convert in this production: Brown says that when his Cranmer questions More about his belief and finds him so sound, his character, who believed in himself and his king, now "begins to fracture" in the face of More's stand. Riddle used jagged, discordant, percussive fanfares for what he calls "this kangaroo court." He concluded the scene with a full choir singing the *Agnus Dei*.

Act II, Scene 9

Act II, Scene 9, played as one unit, Scene 30, "Secrets of My Heart" (pp. 88-89). In the blackout following "The Trial," removal of all furniture and the addition of the block produced the bareness that Silver and Learning wanted for the last scene. Frehner's bright blue cyclorama behind More as he went up the stage left staircase for his execution set him apart. Hutt elaborates that More needs the brief scene with Margaret that affords him the opportunity to tie up the relationship between them. Now she can carry on without him. "To the end of his life," the actor explains, "I am sure he is concerned with his family." Hutt says:

> *Nothing on God's green earth achieves life without something dying to give it life. Put a seed in the ground and something in that tiny seed*

dies before it will produce anything. Death and life are so inexorably intertwined, and I think he has to point that out to her.

While the execution took place, Riddle used a drum roll ending with a loud crack from the base drum at the falling of the axe.

Mitchell speaks of Margaret's courage in pushing her way through the crowd and soldiers to get one last moment with her father. She recounts the history that one night More's head disappeared from Traitor's Gate, and rumour reached Henry that Margaret had taken it. "Interestingly enough," Mitchell says, "according to legend, Anne Bullen (whom Mitchell portrayed in *Henry VIII*) told Henry to leave well enough alone and not bother Lady Margaret further." As the Common Man says, "Behold--the head--of a head," the last *Agnus Dei* plays through the speech. Riddle calls it a simple, beautiful arrangement.

Two years ago in Vancouver and again in 1986 in Stratford, Hutt worried that in his sixties he was too old to do justice to Sir Thomas More, who was in his mid-fifties during the time of this play. Hutt did not want to undercut the courage of the man by physically appearing as if he were going to his grave only a year or two before he would otherwise have done so. After playing some of the "great sufferers of the world--Lear, Titus Andronicus, Timon of Athens"--it was very important to his own spiritual development at this time to play More "to explore the simplicity of the spiritual experience for himself."

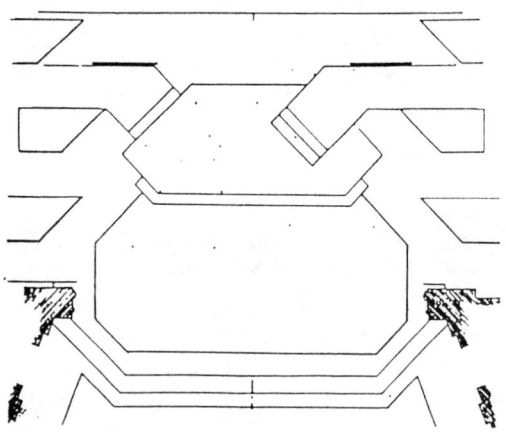

Illustration 7

Designer Phillip Silver's ground plan for *A Man for All Seasons*, the same as for *Henry VIII* except for the absence of the stage right staircase. This change makes the set asymmetrical for this production.

"There is the playhouse now, there you must sit."
Henry V II.pr.36

Act Two: The Festival Company

THE BOYS FROM SYRACUSE

MUSIC BY	RICHARD RODGERS
LYRICS BY	LORENZ HART
BOOK BY	GEORGE ABBOTT
	Based on "THE COMEDY OF ERRORS"
	by William Shakespeare

DIRECTED BY	DOUGLAS CAMPBELL
MUSICAL DIRECTION AND	
ADDITIONAL ARRANGEMENTS BY	BERTHOLD CARRIERE
CHOREOGRAPHED BY	MAX REIMER
DESIGNED BY	POLLY SCRANTON BOHDANETZKY
LIGHTING DESIGNED BY	MICHAEL J. WHITFIELD

The Boys From Syracuse is presented through special arrangement
with the Rogers & Hammerstein Theatre Library,
598 Madison Avenue, New York, New York, 10022.

THE CAST
in order of appearance

The Duke	JEREMY WILKIN
Aegeon	RICHARD MARCH
Sergeant	DALE MIESKE
Corporal	MARIA VACRATSIS
Antipholus of Ephesus	COLM FEORE
Dromio of Ephesus	KEITH THOMAS
Tailor	BRUCE SWERDFAGER
Tailor's Apprentice	ERIC McCORMACK
Angelo, the Goldsmith	NEIL FOSTER
Goldsmith's Apprentic	RICHARD MARCH
Antipholus of Syracuse	GERAINT WYN DAVIES
Dromio of Syracuse	BENEDICT CAMPBELL
Merchant of Syracuse	WILLIAM NEEDLES
Luce, Cook, wife to Dromio of Ephesus	SUSAN WRIGHT
Adriana, wife to Antipholus of Ephesus	ALICIA JEFFERY
Luciana, her sister	MARION ADLER
Maids	RENEE ROGERS
	LESLIE TOY
	CAROLINE YEAGER
Sorcerer	JEREMY WILKIN
THE Courtesan	GOLDIE SEMPLE
Fatima	KIM HORSMAN
Corutesans	WENDY ABBOTT
	TANYA RICH
Pygmalion	MAX REIMER
Galatea	WENDY ABBOTT
Amazons	TANYA RICH
	RENEE ROGERS
	LESLIE TOY

171

Merchant of Ephesus	BRUCE SWERDFAGER
Diogenes	MERVYN BLAKE
Seeress	CAROLINE YEAGER

Greek Chorus — WENDY ABBOTT, MARION ADLER,
BENEDICT CAMPBELL, COLM FEORE, KIM HORSMAN, ALICIA JEFFERY, ERIC McCORMACK, WILLIAM
NEEDLES, MAX REIMER, TANYA RICH, RENEE ROGERS, GOLDIE SEMPLE, BRUCE SWERDFAGER,
KEITH THOMAS, LESLIE TOY, SUSAN WRIGHT, GERAINT WYN DAVIES, CAROLINE YEAGER

Townspeople	EDWARD BALKA, PAUL BOND, ERIC COATES, DARCY GORDON
Stage Manager	NORA POLLEY
Assistant Stage Managers	LAUREN SNELL
	ANN STUART
Assistant Designers	WILLIAM SCHMUCK, GRACE NAKATSU
Assistant Lighting Designer	ELIZABETH ASSELSTINE

Chapter Eight: *The Boys From Syracuse*

At 11:45 a.m. on February 3 actor Bruce Swerdfager was battling the cold wind and temperature of the early February day as he made his way up the driveway to the stage door of the Festival Theatre to answer the first 1986 call for the actors in this troupe. Swerdfager had been a member of the original troupe in 1953 but had later gone into theatre administration and worked at the Stratford Festival during the 1970s. This year marked his return to the stage after a long absence. *The Boys From Syracuse*, like *Hamlet* at the Avon Theatre, got a three-week jump out of the starting gate over the other two shows with which it would share the spring rehearsal period. The first call for this company summoned them to Rehearsal Hall 3 at noon. The scene looked much as it had earlier in the day at the Avon, with signs at various stations about the room reading "Public Relations," "Payroll," "Accommodations," "Addresses," "Wigs," and "Wardrobe."

According to John Neville, *The Boys From Syracuse* was to be the first musical to be staged for an entire season at the Festival Theatre. He looked for a play with a Shakespearean equivalent in order to tie the musical to the long history of production in that theatre and to draw a distinction between the Gilbert and Sullivan operettas at the Avon and this new enterprise. Among the possibilities, given the small number of such Shakespeare-based shows--*Kiss Me, Kate* was considered but was unavailable--Neville's own favorite was *The Boys From Syracuse*.

At the first rehearsal, Neville welcomed the company, briefly explaining that with the assignment of company members to theatres, individuals must take every opportunity to get together to cement feelings that they all belonged to the same troupe. For this reason, he related, the informal Thursday night cabarets staged after the season opened in the Chalmers Lounge of the Avon Theatre by members of both companies would be just as important as any of the plays they would be doing. As in the opening talk at the Avon, he encouraged company members to enjoy themselves--pointing out that this was probably one of the reasons which had drawn most of them into the theatre as a career. Production stage manager Nora Polley, who also served as stage manager for this production, moved about the room distributing the information packets and scripts.

Director Douglas Campbell, who had returned to Toronto just twelve hours earlier from the American tour, in which he had played the title role in *King Lear*, was not scheduled to appear until rehearsals began in earnest the next day but came to the opening company reception that first evening; he was positive, upbeat, and showing none of the strain of the months on the road. He and others later moved on to Bentley's, a restaurant popular with company members, where he walked from table to table. Members of the tour told that Campbell had played his last performance on Saturday and stayed to cheer the company for the final performance of *Twelfth Night*. "He showed us how to finish like professionals," said Avon company member Nolan Jennings.

Campbell recalls having seen an Old Vic production of *King John* in Scotland during World War II and deciding that he wanted to spend his life in the theatre. He began by driving the Old Vic company truck and setting up scenery. Gradually he worked his way on stage as an extra before graduating to starring roles with several companies, including the Old Vic. He played in Guthrie's famous 1948 production of *The Three Estates* done in the Assembly Hall of the Scottish Kirk at the Edinburgh Festival. This is one of two productions usually cited as an influence on Guthrie's thinking about the open stage he and designer Tanya Moiseiwitsch later built at Stratford. Campbell remembers attending an Old Vic reception for a touring company recently returned from South Africa when he first heard Guthrie speak of the Canadian venture at Stratford. He wanted to go with the core of British actors who would make the trip. "And so you shall," Guthrie told him. The four actors Guthrie brought were Alec Guinness, Irene Worth, Michael Bates, and Campbell. Campbell has acted in or directed more than thirty productions in the thirty-four seasons at Stratford. He also went with Guthrie to Minneapolis for the first season of the Guthrie Theatre there, where he succeeded his mentor as artistic director. He travelled with the company to New York for productions of Guthrie's version of *The House of Atreus* and *The Resistible Rise of Arturo Ui*. Campbell also played the title role in *Gideon* on Broadway in 1961.

Each rehearsal for *The Boys From Syracuse* began with Campbell asking for "the smile for the day," something funny that a company member could relate. Thirty minutes of warmups included physical warmups led by choreographer Max Reimer and vocal warmups by musical director Bert Carriere. On the first day Campbell spotted performers having difficulty with Reimer's exercises. He would stand in front of that person, who placed hands on Campbell's waist and followed him as he followed Reimer. Campbell, Reimer, and Carriere started these warmups at a fairly relaxed pace and gradually turned up the intensity as sore muscles and unused vocal cords worked into fighting trim.

Reimer's career began in semi-professional lacrosse, until an injury sent him to dance class to strengthen his muscles. He had always enjoyed gymnastics and, he says, decided to launch a new career as a result of the dance and gymnastics training. He became a dancer because "There aren't many male dancers and the work is steady." Director Brian Macdonald hired him from the Citadel Theatre as dance captain for the 1985 production of *The Pirates of Penzance* at Stratford; he also had a small role in director David William's production of *She Stoops to Conquer* that season. When William wanted to inject humour using the servants on a bannister, Reimer was suggested to work out the mechanics of those stunts. He also worked with Campbell, who played Mr. Hardcastle in that production, and from that association came Campbell's invitation to choreograph *The Boys From Syracuse*.

Berthold Carriere hails from Ottawa and attended the University of Montreal, picking up a bachelor's degree in music while working in various musical jobs for the Canadian Broadcasting Corporation. He also began conducting the orchestra for musical theatre productions in the tradition of his high school teacher, later got his master's degree in music at the University of Western Ontario, and conducted musicals at the Grand Theatre in London. When the theatre asked him to do a musical score for some of the dramas, he "really got the bite" and accepted a musical position at the University of Banff for five summers. He came to Stratford in 1974 at the invitation of then director of music for drama Alan Laing and wound up doing the music for playwright Sandra Jones' children's theatre production, *Ready Steady Go*, at the Third Stage. Robin Phillips arrived that year, and the two of them began working on *The Comedy of Errors*. Carriere arranged the music written by Laing, who was then working in another theatre. Eventually Phillips appointed Carriere as his director of music, and Carriere recounts that most of his Festival experience was with Phillips. During the Hirsch years Carriere was musical director for the Gilbert and Sullivan operettas at the Avon. But, he concludes, he likes to practice both parts of his craft each season by composing the music for one show and conducting the orchestra for the musical. This year he worked with a fifteen-piece orchestra because of budget constraints. In other years, he says, the orchestra might total twenty members. But the fifteen-piece group represented an increase of five over the number he was originally given.

Following rehearsal warmups, Campbell made the design presentation, explaining the costume sketches and actually changing the scale model of scenery on a large layout of the Festival Stage under the watchful eye of designer Polly Scranton Bohdanetzky. While a student at the Ontario College of Art in Toronto, Bohdanetzky was taking drawing and painting courses that she says "couldn't be farther away" from the work of a designer. She remembers that someone in her class applied to work at Stratford, inspiring her to take the same course. She gained acceptance in 1958, when she worked as a design assistant to Tanya Moiseiwitsch and Desmond Heeley on productions of *1 Henry IV*, *Much Ado About Nothing*, and *The Winter's Tale*, directed by Campbell. She has worked at the Festival off and on over the twenty-eight seasons since, most recently when she again teamed with Moiseiwitsch as co-designer for the 1985 production of *The Government Inspector*. She has also worked in England, on Broadway, and all across Canada.

In early September 1985 she got a call from Campbell about *The Boys From Syracuse*; Campbell said Neville knew her work only for the 1985 season and wanted to see some preliminary designs. She began discussions with Campbell, who would leave Stratford in late October with the American tour, thereby speeding up their design process. Having read the script and heard the music, they came down to two choices. Campbell could see the show either as Shakespearean in period, set in Elizabethan England, or as Greek. Bohdanetzky says she had difficulty seeing these characters dressed in pumpkin hose while saying the lines and dancing the required steps, so she went for the Greek model with modern overtones. The time period was "broad, very broad," she says and chuckles; she added a Syrian influence in her treatment of the courtesan and her ladies of the evening as a harem and in the merchants' dress. She made some of the slaves look Egyptian. By combining these different cultures in the market place of Ephesus, she believes she achieved a more varied and interesting looking while not wandering too far from important influences that might have turned up in the center of a lively Greek city.

With the time period established, they turned their attention to the set. At the initial design presentation, Campbell had discussed the tent that originally protected the Festival Stage and restated his desire to capture some of the excitement "under the canvas." Bohdanetzky's parents had brought her to Stratford the first season, and she understood what Campbell wanted when he asked for a series of brightly coloured streamers to festoon the theatre as the audience entered and to ascend as each act's action began. In production, Campbell pronounced himself happy with the streamers; he says they increased the sense of excitement or expectation before the show. Bohdanetzky used them to fit the director's instructions to "keep the show bright, colourful, and fun" but to avoid the more muted "good taste pastels." He also asked her to place a ramp diagonally on the stage so that he could bring on a cart to carry Aegeon to begin the first act. He is rolled out of the stage left tunnel to plead for his life before the duke, who stands on the balcony of the permanent facade, and is then rolled off up right. Bohdanetzky also says Campbell wanted to give the city the feel of a seaport, so she worked a dock into the setting and used spouting fish for the fountain in the main square of the town. The next major scenic element, the entrance to the brothel, was conceived of as a gate leading to a veranda, but the cost of such a unit changed the idea to two tall torch lamps playing on the forestage at the down stage right tunnel. The script called for scenes inside and one scene outside of the home of Antipholus of Ephesus, for which Bohdanetzky had the idea of using shutters on the balcony. The characters inside the house could then interact with those outside in the wild exchange she and Campbell envisioned from the first time they read the script. The awnings used on stage during the market scenes also provided focus; they had similar lines but different colours. The designer says that as soon as the first odd angle was incorporated into the design, every angle took a corresponding departure from ninety degrees. Across from the ramp sat a set of steps with each level jauntily askew, leading up from the tunnel and out the up left exit. Bohdanetzky began the design process thinking of Egyptian style furniture, and since Campbell had specifically asked for a bench to go around the fountain (which came up into the market place on the hydraulic lift) and go off when the fountain did, she constructed it in sections and used them, pulled apart, for furniture in other scenes. She first showed this idea to Campbell when the tour reached Chicago at the end of November. He liked it because it saved time changing scenery and eliminated the need to bring on new pieces of furniture.

The designer says the director asked her to reread *The Comedy of Errors* to firm up her understanding of the characters in this show. This suggestion Campbell also made to the actors because, he told them, adapter George Abbott has been faithful to Shakespeare's original. Bohdanetzky remembers starting her costume research with the idea of adapting Greek shapes to all of the movement that had to be accommodated for the musical. Based on that research, she showed Campbell some of her preliminary designs, and she says he encouraged her to go further and be even more flamboyant. By early October they had presented some designs to Neville and she had won the job. Some designs continued to evolve as late as the rehearsal period; for example, she did not meet with Reimer to check steps for dances against the costume designs until rehearsals were underway. Some other costumes changed slightly when she knew what performers would play the roles. Also, cross-casting the shows put Maria Vacratsis in the role of the corporal. Campbell milked comedy out of using her in this traditionally male role by having her double as the belly dancer in the brothel scene of the first act finale.

After deciding on the proper line and shape, the designer went to the

177

colour scheme of rust and turquoise, unified by checkerboard patterning in the multicoloured costumes. She also used antique pleating, which, she says, allows the body shape to show through the costume but provides what appears to be yards and yards of fabric to move with the performers. Finally she had to consider that the costumes must take wear and tear of activity in a musical, where the actors would work up some perspiration and the number of performances was greater than for the other shows. She wanted to use man-made fibers to stand up under use and cleaning but wound up with cottons and silks because they moved more freely.

Swerdfager won the election as Equity deputy that first day of rehearsal on the basis of his experience on both sides of the footlights. During the read-through of the script, conducted as actors sat around wooden tables arranged in a rectangle, Carriere conducted musical numbers and rehearsal pianists Laura Burton and Marilyn Dollman provided music. Burton composed for both plays at the Third Stage later that season. Carriere jumped in at the rehearsal to help a performer with singing; if an actor appeared overmatched in this first meeting with the music, Campbell cancelled the rest of the song with a wave of his hand to Carriere. He kept the reading fast-paced by calling on performers who had not picked up cues fast enough, and he told Carriere how many bars of scene change music he thought the actors would require in selected places.

After lunch Reimer auditioned the company to see whom he would use in individual dances and the steps he would give them to do. Again due to the demands of cross-casting several shows, Reimer had not had a lot of say in which performers he had available. Campbell also attended the auditions, this large man dancing with the individual performers when necessary to put them at their ease.

Carriere had the last slot that day, to teach the company the first number. He explains that he generally likes to spend some time teaching the company to sing one number on the day before they will work on its choreography. If they already know the music, they can concentrate on dancing while working with Reimer. Once the company had mastered a song, Campbell, Carriere, and Reimer worked together. Campbell and Carriere did not allow the company to slack off on music while they were dancing, and Campbell and Reimer repeatedly emphasized the need to polish the choreography during rehearsals of the musical numbers. In rehearsal Campbell would often place the actors on the stage where he wanted them and then Reimer would teach them the steps. Reimer says he appreciated Campbell's knowledge of the requirements of the Festival Stage.

Although the show stayed in the rehearsal hall for the first three weeks, Campbell took the cast to the stage the second day of rehearsal to give them a chance to experience that space. In rehearsals he tried to make the show fit the grandeur of the theatre's architecture. He had a version of the fifth act of *The Comedy of Errors* prepared for the company to read in the theatre at one rehearsal. Campbell says he knew immediately that because of the differences in style he could not use it, but he found merit in the experiment. In Aegeon's speeches the company found comedy they transferred into the last scene of *The Boys From Syracuse*. In order to measure the play and the performers against the theatre, he says, one had to carry a conception of the theatre into the rehearsal hall. But Campbell faced three other problems against which he had to assess this production regularly: the break with the past Gilbert and Sullivan operettas, including the loss of popular director/choreographer Brian Macdonald (responsible for the last four of these productions); putting on the musical without a separate musical company; and a long layoff in the rehearsal process.

Campbell admits that he had other preferences for the 1986 season than directing a musical. But after Macdonald's withdrawal (see Chapter Three), Campbell accepted the responsibility. Neville believes that with his voice and musical talents Campbell could have had a successful career in opera. Campbell more modestly explains that he has been taking singing and dancing lessons since he was six years old. His ability and willingness to sing and dance with the company from the first day both delighted and relaxed them as they saw him taking the risks with them.

Neville emphasizes that a classical acting company ought to be able to do a musical as well, but this company had to come to believe in its ability to do so, since a separate musical company had been employed in the past. At the end of the season, actor Richard March (who began the season as Aegeon and ended it as Antipholus of Syracuse) said the real story behind this show was the company itself. The company began their work with uncertainty; as the show went before audiences in advance of opening, they quickly gained confidence in their work. In the early days of February, however, it was Campell who had to ignite their belief in themselves.

The problem with the rehearsal schedule was that this show got intensive work in the first three weeks but only occasional work as the first two romances, *The Winter's Tale* and *Pericles*, got underway. For the next six weeks the company had to keep *The Boys From Syracuse* fresh without the concentrated time in which to work at that. Campbell feared that the show would "go stale as a bun" over that time and that if too much was put in final form in the early rehearsals the energy would go out of the show toward the end of that process. He purposely put many ideas in motion in the initial three-week period without finishing or solidifying them until the final spring rehearsal period. Campbell urged the cast to go daily through the text, songs, and dances mentally--and physically if possible--to internalize the sequences so that the body could easily follow the mind's lead. Another timing difficulty was with dancing, since more time was needed than was scheduled for keeping those numbers fresh and polished. Polley rescued the situation by juggling schedules to find the dancers Reimer needed for an hour a day despite rehearsal requirements for the other two shows.

More problems developed when Campbell's son Ben, who played Dromio of Syracuse, developed back problems severe enough to take him out of rehearsal toward the end of the second week of work. He had part of a cracked disc removed from his back on 22 February and returned to watch rehearsals five days later. But by the time Ben Campbell actively returned to rehearsal, the play had entered the pause phase; he had to wait to work consistently on the piece until the final shaping period.

In rehearsals, Douglas Campbell worked hard to establish quickly the level of performance required in physical and vocal energy and the rapid pace needed to drive the show forward. Stopping a rehearsal one day, Campbell demonstrated the level of volume he wanted from a performer, who responded that he would go home, think about it, and find a way to do it. "I don't want you to think about it," responded the director. "I want you to do it." Campbell often explained that in this piece of musical comedy there were no great depths to be plumbed, so from the beginning he wanted the size and volume that he reasoned would sell the show to an audience. On another occasion, he stopped two other actors to explain that the line readings lacked colour and intensity. He explained again that there was no hidden meaning in the text and that he wanted a clear statement from the actors regarding their intentions, so that no one in the audience could possibly miss them. During the first week Campbell explained that in doing a musical, which involved no voyage of discovery comparable to that of working with Shakespearean text, to let the performers coast with less than an acceptable presentational style was a waste of everyone's time.

Veteran actor Butch Blake, appearing in his thirty-first Stratford season, complimented Campbell on this approach. "He showed them how big it had to be from the beginning and he never accepted less than that," Blake explains. Later in the summer, at a "Meet the Festival" programme, a series held in July and August that allows audience members to ask questions of performers, Dale Mieske (the sergeant) said he would always remember Campbell as giving the three directions "bigger, louder, and faster" for this production. The director responds to this comment by stressing that the rehearsal period consists of the exercise the performers need to throw themselves into the bewildering world of the characters in this play. "If the exercise is not strenuous enough to make the company discard all inhibitions, arrive at the truth of the characters, and play that truth with absolute sincerity, then the director has failed the cast and the piece," states Campbell. He also says that he never considered doing a "camp version" in which the actors comment on the characters or situation because such a smart aleck tone speaks condescendingly to an audience. He chose to stage *The Boys From Syracuse* for the values it still holds and to play them genuinely, with all the vim and vigor the company could muster. He pushes the point further: The comedy comes out of the "reality at the center" of an absurd situation, whereas putting a joke at the center--as in a camped version--robs the play of its comedy and makes it "just awful."

If the rehearsal period was not intended for an exploration of text, for Campbell it consisted of rehearsing every detail over and over again in text, song, and dance. "In a musical," he reminded the cast, "the crispness is all." Campbell also extracted humor by using veteran actors Blake, Swerdfager, and William Needles as a three-man chorus to punctuate the action frequently.

Without a history of musical production on the Festival Stage, Campbell did not know exactly what decoration or emphasis might be needed. For music, he instructed Carriere to write a medley of the songs from the show. On first hearing the company sing it, he asked Carriere to shorten it and eventually discarded it. The long rehearsal period, he says, gave him time to experiment with a number of options before deciding which solution to employ.

When not rehearsing, Carriere spent February and March redoing the musical score to accommodate a smaller orchestra. He rearranged the music, which called for five saxophones, to fit his three woodwinds; redid a score calling for the work of eight members of the brass section to be handled by four; and turned a string section into a string trio, a task he describes as "difficult." Doing the musical on the Festival Stage also required experimentation to fit the show to that space. For example, Carriere says they gave up the orchestra pit used at the Avon and placed the orchestra in the "heavens," a completely enclosed space located directly above the stage. In this situation the actors and conductor could not see one another, and, even worse, notes sung on stage bounced off the walls and were heard in the "heavens" about a quarter of a second late. Likewise, music from the orchestra reached the actors late. Carriere had to conduct using a headset and a monitor, and he pushed the orchestra so the actors had that quarter of a second to hear the note. He stresses that he told the actors to press ahead if they made a mistake, and he would catch up with them. Of the rehearsal schedule, he says that they drilled the singers hard to get the music to become as automatic as possible, but when rehearsals moved to the theatre from the rehearsal hall all the music had to be redone to adjust to that space.

181

Campbell and Carriere recall difficulties in running a cue-to-cue technical rehearsal on 22 March for a play that was not to open for nearly two months, on 19 May. Campbell tried to keep the cast up on technical changes following 22 March. For Carriere, getting the musicians who would actually play in the orchestra so far in advance of the time they would be needed regularly created added difficulty.

Lighting designer Michael Whitfield says he and Campbell decided on a brightly lit, very colorful musical comedy style for the look of the show. Campbell says the trick is to put bright light on that stage without a harsh reflection from the wood background. Whitfield solved the problem by controlling the direction of the light from high angles. Other problems included going from indoors to outdoors, moving from the marketplace to moonlit scenes for romantic numbers, and shifting the mood from the comic to the serious. He injected humor by means of gobos that spangled the stage facade with hearts for "falling in love at first glance" and with stars for an exaggeration of pain a character feels in running into a door. The final number provided opportunities for ingenuity in lighting, in which Whitfield switched the color from pink to blue as the company chanted "girls" and then "boys."

But once the show came back into rehearsal on a regular basis, Campbell made his final choices and polished individual segments. Actors complained about the long rehearsal period because it made them work with no audience from whom to elicit laughter: They did not know if the show would work until they took it before preview audiences. The show also played a preview performance for the Champagne Express, a trainful from Toronto who got an advance look at the show.

A cold drizzle punctuated the garden party at the opening of the 1986 season, but by evening on 19 May the rain had almost stopped. Earlier in the day Campbell held an "Italian rehearsal"--a practice session in which the actors speak lines in rapid-fire fashion. George Abbott, who wrote the book for The Boys From Syracuse, attended the opening night performance, sitting by John Neville, who introduced him by saying that it was not often the Stratford Shakespearean Festival could introduce the author of the play to the audience. When the play was over, Abbott visited with the cast backstage and expressed his enjoyment. Drama critics from the major Canadian and American media were temporarily housed in the administrative staff offices throughout opening week. As the shows ended each night, the critics made a mad dash up the aisles and out the doors, heading toward the offices to write reviews for the next day's papers.

Because so much of the story of the production of The Boys From Syracuse relates to the imagination and style of comic business, dance, and song, comments from the show's leading actors are included here in lieu of a

Feore as Antipholus of Ephesus
Goldie Semple as the Courtesan
THE BOYS FROM SYRACUSE.

1986 PRODUCTION PHOTOS
BY ROBERT C. RAGSDALE

Geraint Wyn Davies as Pericles in PERICLES.

Goldie Semple as Hermione, Kerry Dorey as a Sicilian Lord and Colm Feore as Leontes in THE WINTER'S TALE.

(Opposite) Joseph Ziegler as Posthumus,
Martha Burns as Imogen and Eric Donkin
as Cymbeline; (above) Nicholas Pennell as
Pisanio, Susan Wright as the Queen and
John Innes as Cornelius in CYMBELINE.

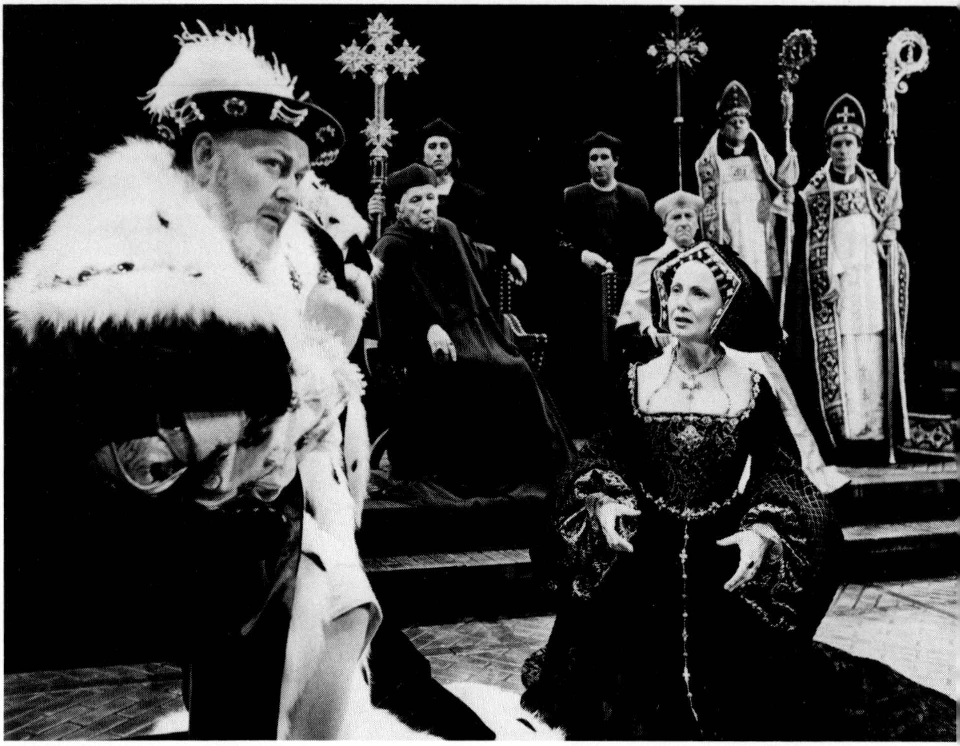

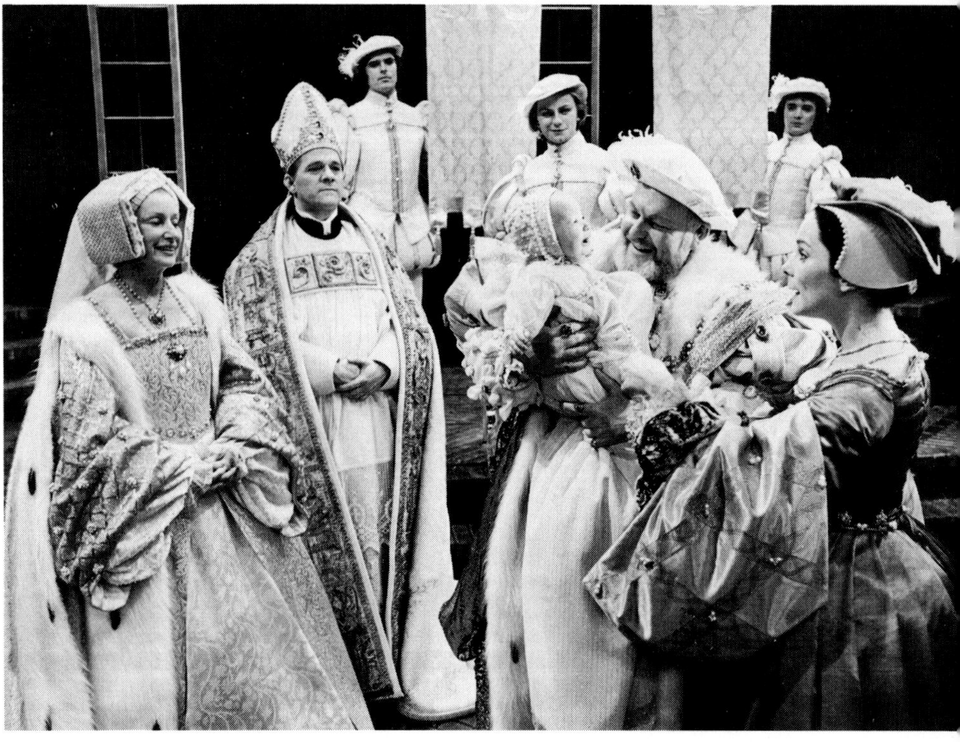

(Above) William Hutt as
Sir Thomas More in A
MAN FOR ALL SEASONS.

(Opposite) Brent Carver as Hamlet; with (above) Scott Wentworth as Laertes in HAMLET.

(Seated) Lucy Peacock as Ophelia, with Peter Donaldson
as a Tragedian, Lorne Kennedy as Horatio, Brent
Carver as Hamlet and Ian Watson as a Tragedian in
ROSENCRANTZ AND GUILDENSTERN ARE DEAD.

(...ve) Keith Dinicol as Guilden-
..., William Dunlop as Rosen-
...z, Peter Donaldson as a
...edian, Ron Hastings as the
...r, Eric House as a Tragedian,
...Pierre Fournier as a Tragedian,
...Watson as a Tragedian and
...Jennings as a Tragedian in
...NCRANTZ AND GUILDENSTERN
... DEAD. (Right) Marcia Kash
...dy Macbeth in MACBETH.

(Seated) Maurice Godin as Arturo Ui, wit
Jerry Etienne as Giuseppe Givola, Kim Co
as Ernesto Roma and Michael Hanrahan
Emanuele Giri in THE RESISTIBLE RISE C
ARTURO UI.

scene-by-scene analysis of the play's development. Actors agreed that if the rehearsal schedule had complicated the musical, performing it became an unexpected joy. It provided a welcome contrast to the serious matter of the rest of the Festival playbill. Colm Feore, who played Antipholus of Ephesus, points to the effect of individual audiences on this show. He says that the rewards of playing *The Winter's Tale* and *Cymbeline* came immediately and had far-reaching effects. While this show required "energy, energy, energy," on most days the audience joined in and had a good time, giving the cast real satisfaction. On the rare days where they did not, "It was a long day at the office."

Geraint Wyn Davies played Antipolus of Syracuse until the end of September, when he left the Festival to play in the new *Air Wolf* series on television; Richard March finished the season in the role. Wyn Davies says he appreciated the work in breath control the musical required and that it helped him in the title role in *Pericles*. He explains that almost all of the comic business in the show changed over the course of the summer as actors learned what got laughs. But, he says, because Campbell made the actors discover the truth in each character at the beginning of the process and use that as the basis for all the antics that evolved during performances, the show always retained those essential features to hold it on track.

Ben Campbell, who played Dromio of Ephesus, had the challenge of bouncing back quickly after his surgery. He wanted to protect his back but refused to give in to it, and found a way to do all his comic gestures and business without hurting himself. The doctor told him to be careful for six weeks after surgery: Campbell says that on the sixth week and first day he approached rehearsal at full tilt. If his back bothered him in doing some bits of business, he found other ways to accomplish them. By the end of the summer he had little difficulty, but he had to begin playing the role by bouncing on his toes, partly to protect his back. When Richard March took over as Antipholus of Syracuse, March often leaned on him and knocked him off balance. Campbell compensated by dancing around March in wide circles so that the latter could not unbalance him.

Keith Thomas, Dromio of Ephesus, says *The Boys From Syracuse* was the easiest show for him to do because of the audience response. For a long time he worked to add humour by doing specific things in a particular way. But once audiences began responding to the show, he learned to simplify his performance by playing the text without trying to force additional humour into it.

Jeremy Wilkin played a double role as the Duke and the Sorcerer, who was presented like the duke in *Measure For Measure*, who disguises himself to go about the town to spy on his subjects. According to Wilkin, he and

Campbell did not want to make too much out of this point, which might distract an audience from concentrating on the main story line. But their decision allowed him to present one consistent character from the two parts assigned to him.

Susan Wright, who played Luce, calls the playing style for this piece "close to Vaudeville," as typified by performers such as Martha Ray. "You have to go in big, with all guns blazing. It's big, big, big." Her main obstacle to mastering the role at first was holding back, a problem she overcame by allowing herself to "go whole hog." Comic timing, she says, makes or breaks a show done in this broad style. While she laments that such timing cannot be learned, she believes it can be refined. She points to some experimentation she did to discover "how to slide a line in for the biggest reaction."

Goldie Semple played the Courtesan. Like others who are not primarily singers and dancers, she compensated by doing what she can do best--act. She adds that doing musical comedy makes a performer supply personality to make a characterization work: The ad-libbed jokes and the humour in her character came from herself, she says, so much so that they exposed more of her own personality than did "saying somebody else's lines." She also treasured the opportunity to sing and dance, citing particularly the tap dance on a descending platform that she performed during the Diogenes number in the second act.

Alicia Jeffrey played Adriana, wife of Antipholus of Ephesus. Her role of wronged wife was not a comic one; she calls it a piece of "tragic relief" within the comedy. For that reason, she theorizes, "You don't get the payoff that everyone else gets." She says she started out much too heavily for the piece, realizing it was time to lighten up when the show was performed for the rest of the company and she got no laughs. She did have to give the character some weight in the big ballad of the show, she concludes.

Marion Adler, who played Adriana's sister, has a university degree in opera performance. In both classical theatre and opera, she says, performers need big scale, breath control, and a large and flexible voice. In Canada, performers are classified as either singers or actors, she admits, with few performers (Len Cariou is a notable exception) able to bridge the gap between the two groups.

The Boys From Syracuse, like *Hamlet* at the Avon, played more performances (65) than any other play at its theatre. A capacity crowd gathered for the final performance on Sunday afternoon, 19 October, including Neville and his wife. They attended as many of the closing performances as possible, since some of these finales were scheduled back-to-back at the Avon and Festival theatres. Following the last performance of *The Boys From Syracuse*, Swerdfager, his duties as Equity deputy and performer completed, walked jacketless out of the theatre through the front lobby and into the hazy brightness of an Indian summer afternoon, still whistling ''Falling in Love with Love.''

The Winter's Tale

BY WILLIAM SHAKESPEARE

DIRECTED BY	DAVID WILLIAM
DESIGNED BY	SHAWN KERWIN
MUSIC COMPOSED BY	BERTHOLD CARRIERE
LIGHTING DESIGNED BY	HARRY FREHNER
DANCES CHOREOGRAPHED BY	JOHN BROOME

Characters In The Play

Time	MERVYN BLAKE
Time's Children	MARION ADLER, ALICIA BUCK, SCOTT BURDETT, PATRICK HENRY, ADAM POYNTER, JENNIFER STEWART, ERIN TREISCHL
SICILIANS:	
Leontes, King of Sicilia	COLM FEORE
Hermione, his Wife	GOLDIE SEMPLE
Mamillius, his Son	ADAM POYNTER
Camillo	NICHOLAS PENNELL
Antigonus	WILLIAM NEEDLES
Cleomenes	GERAINT WYN DAVIES
Dion	JOHN BOURGEOIS
First Lord	JOHN INNES
Second Lord	KERRY DOREY
Third Lord	WILLIAM SAMPLES
Fourth Lord	DALE MIESKE
Fifth Lord	NEIL FOSTER
A Gaoler	MICHAEL SHEPHERD
A Mariner	BRUCE SWERDFAGER
Paulina, Wife of Antigonus	SUSAN WRIGHT
Paulina's Steward	WILLIAM NEEDLES
Emilia	MARIA VACRATSIS
First Lady	WENDY ABBOTT
Second Lady	KIM HORSMAN
Nurse	MARION ADLER
BOHEMIANS:	
Polixenes, King of Bohemia	STEPHEN RUSSELL
Florizel, his Son	KEITH THOMAS
Archidamus	BRENT STAIT
Old Shepherd	MAURICE GOOD
Young Shepherd	BENEDICT CAMPBELL
Servant to the Old Shepherd	BRENT STAIT
Autolycus	JOSEPH ZIEGLER
Perdita, Reputed Daughter of the Old Shepherd	MARTHA BURNS
Mopsa	ALICIA JEFFERY
Dorcas	KIM HORSMAN
A Bear	EDWARD BALKA

("Courtiers" brace groups Camillo through Nurse)

Sicilian Ladies, Bohemian Lords, Waiters, Guards,
Magistrates, Priests, Shepherds, Shepherdesses:
WENDY ABBOTT, MARION ADLER, EDWARD BALKA, PAUL BOND, ERIC COATES,
KERRY DOREY, NEIL FOSTER, DARCY GORDON, KIM HORSMAN, JOHN INNES,
ALICIA JEFFERY, RICHARD MARCH, DALE MIESKE, ADAM POYNTER,
WILLIAM SAMPLES, BRENT STAIT, BRUCE SWERDFAGER, ERIN TREISCHL,
MARIA VACRATSIS, PAULA WING

187

Stage Manager	CATHERINE RUSSELL
Assistant Stage Managers	LAUREN SNALL
	ANN STUART
Assistant Director	SUSAN FERLEY
Assistant Designer	ANDREA GRAINGER
Assistant Lighting Designer	KEVIN FRASER

Please Note: There will be a strobe effect used in this production.

THE PLAY WILL BE GIVEN IN TWO PARTS

PART I	PART II
The court of Leontes in Sicilia; the Oracle in Delphos; the Coast of Bohemia.	Bohemia; and again at the Court of Leontes in Sicilia.

188

"It is required
You do awake your faith."
The Winter's Tale V.3.94-95

Chapter Nine: *The Winter's Tale*

English director David William began rehearsals for *The Winter's Tale* on 24 February, 1986, in Rehearsal Hall 1 of the Festival Theatre, having directed for the Festival over 20 years: *Twelfth Night*, 1966; *The Merry Wives of Windsor*, 1967; *Volpone*, 1971; *King Lear*, 1972, which he restaged for the company's 1973 European tour; *Othello*, 1973; and *Romeo and Juliet*, 1977, for the Festival Stage; the Benjamin Britten opera *Albert Herring*, 1967, *Separate Tables*, 1984, and *She Stoops To Conquer*, 1985 at the Avon Theatre; and Sophocles' *Antigone*, 1985, at the Third Stage. These ten productions gave him credentials few could match. Among the 1986 directors only Douglas Campbell had directed over more seasons and only Robin Phillips had directed more Festival productions.

William's background also includes a degree in English literature from Oxford and work as both actor and director at the Old Vic, where, among other productions, he was asked to stage Judy Guthrie's play *Queen Bee*. He had extensive directing experience in Britain and the United States as well as in Canada and spent the winter of 1985-86 teaching at the Goodman School of Theatre in Chicago.

While Neville and William had known each other at the Old Vic when their tenures there had overlapped in the 1950s, they had lost contact after Neville came to Canada in 1972 and were not reunited until the 1984 production of *Separate Tables* in which Neville played Mr. Malcolm in "Table One" and Major Pollock in "Table Two" under William's direction. This Terence Rattigan play, William says, has acquired the difficult-to-produce label because it has already become "a period piece" presenting "a world whose shape and conditions and terms of reference we cannot restore" (William, David. "Reassessing Rattigan." *Separate Tables, Stratford Festival Souvenir Programme*, 1984). The highly successful production moved to the Royal Alexandra Theatre in Toronto following its Festival run.

During the 1985 season, artistic director designate Neville ran the programme for the Young Company and asked William to direct the production of *Antigone* scheduled for their Third Stage. But before William began work with the Young Company, Neville invited him to direct one of the romances scheduled for the Festival Stage during the 1986 season, an assignment which William immediately accepted. He asked for time to consider which romance he wanted to direct, asking later for *The Winter's Tale*.

Thus the production that William put into rehearsal on 24 February had benefited from a year's planning and study prior to the first read-through. William explains that the process by which he works on any play, including this one, revolves around "the images and key ideas" produced by an "exhaustive" reading of the play. These in turn point to "a guiding idea which the whole play embraces" and determine the selection of a visual style, which, once rehearsals begin, "fragments into all the detail that develops." He also explains that the difference between Shakespeare and most other authors lies in the quality of his verse, which produces a much more "myth-oriented world" in the works of Shakespeare.

The search for that basic concept for William's production was enriched by Neville's decision to do three of the romances in one season. In examining *The Tempest*, *The Winter's Tale*, *Pericles*, and *Cymbeline*, Williams notes one common demoninator: "a great wrong done within a family....The consequences of that wrong can only be put right by some kind of experience which can only take place through the passage of time...." William believes that the Elizabethans were much more conscious of the passage of time and of their own mortality than are moderns because the only way of remembering someone who had died was either through "word of mouth" or what someone wrote about the departed. Film and records, he concludes, dilute "our sense of time" and make it "less intense, less passionate."

William also decided that he wanted the audience to sympathize to some extent with the plight of Leontes, so he needed a young Leontes, Hermione, and Polixenes. Very often, he explains, these characters are played by the company's leading actors, who might be middle-aged; he recalls seeing a middle-aged John Gielgud in a moving performance as Leontes. But the rash judgments Leontes makes are more understandable in a younger man, says William, and the kind of sexual attraction Leontes and Heromine will feel after a sixteen-year separation will be completely different for a couple who begins the play in their early thirties than for one who begins it in their late forties.

William made another major decision prior to beginning rehearsals, to emphasize the healing power of time by enlarging the role of the character called Time, who appears in IV.1, to include a prologue. Reminiscent of the story of Sleeping Beauty, in which time is made to stand still, William had the auditorium wrapped in gauze to represent a moment frozen in eternity. As the prologue begins the lights come up on Time standing on the balcony under the gauze, and he speaks a line from *Pandasto*, Shakespeare's source material for this play, about the healing power of time. At the same moment that Time releases the spell with a gesture, William put the light on eight children, dressed in costumes from different ages, symbolizing the children of the world, who dance in the spirit of youthful innocence. Three of those children will become Leontes, Heromione, and Polixenes, says William, while conceding that few members of the audience will understand this point. But to emphasize the idea, the children exit up the stage right staircase toward Time, who beckons them gently to him while a line of characters including Leontes, Hermione, and Polixenes enters with hands joined to start the play. By use of this device William wished:

> *to create a sort of envelope in the beginning in which you place the message that you are trying to send the audience....And it struck me you could do this by both combining something you hoped would be spectacular and at the same time relevant to the ultimate meaning of the play and link it with some kind of imagery that continued through the play.*

William chose as his costume and set designer Shawn Kerwin, who had previously designed sets and costumes for four plays presented at the Third Stage during the 1978 season--*Ned and Jack*, *Stargazing*, *Medea*, and four one-act plays by Samuel Beckett---as well as designed costumes for *The Glass Menagerie* during the 1985 season. She served as design assistant to Desmond Heeley for the 1981 production of *The Misanthrope* and the 1983 production of *The Country Wife* and as design assistant to John Ferguson for his 1981 production of *The Visit*. Kerwin, who had learned her trade by working as an apprentice in England and the United States, had designed for small theatres in Toronto before realizing that the art of design had a name. She took one year of formal education in design in England from Margaret Harris, who had worked as a designer at the Old Vic.

While working on the *The Glass Menagerie*, she was exhausted at the end of "a long day" when producer Peter Roberts asked her what, if anything, she would like to do during the 1986 season, and she replied, "Just give me a job in the box office." Roberts did pique her interest in designing *The Winter's Tale*.

In October 1985, she got a call from Roberts asking if she could meet with William in Toronto in a few days to test their compatibility as director and designer. Kerwin, working on two other shows at the time, sat up reading the play the night before the meeting but fell asleep before finishing it. She went into the interview telling herself, "You're going to have to bluff your way through this, too." One of the first questions William asked her concerned the period in which she would set the show. She told him that in her view a play as difficult as this one could not go too far back in time because the further back in time the play was set, the more difficulty a modern audience had telling what kind of character a costume signaled or the position this character held in the world of the play. Therefore the more recognizable the costume silhouette, the easier the audience finds telling "the bad guys from the good guys" and "the wealthy guys from the poor guys." Moreover, she says, an audience will not start to listen to the spoken text of the play until it has succeeded in making these basic kinds of distinctions. The problems of portraying the different worlds of Bohemia and Sicilia and of personalizing the character of Time headed her list of problems, but did not exhaust it.

For that reason Kerwin liked the Edwardian period because it would bring a grace and elegance but also an innocence to the piece. William, however, saw it set a bit earlier because the rural world of Bohemia, including the sheep-shearing scene, made better sense to him if it were set prior to the Industrial Revolution. The world of Bohemia, William believes, was really England, and the peasants, he suggested to Kerwin at their meeting, might be very little changed from those depicted by Northern Renaissance painter Pieter Brueghel. William and Kerwin then discussed a "Thomas Hardy world", but on reflection Kerwin felt that its kind of women's silhouette, "nice round, poufy dresses," would look funny with the women saying lines of the weight and gravity of the ones Shakespeare wrote in this play. If the time period were backed up a bit, she suggested, they could take advantage of the "credible and simple" neoclassical line, which Kerwin advocated because it would allow the women to say the words of the text without having the clothes get in the way. So in one three-hour meeting, Kerwin explains, the basic period was set with the stipulation that liberties would be taken where necessary. Dressing the peasants of Bohemia offered the most substantial opportunity for breaking the conventions of period dress, it was agreed. By the end of the meeting, according to Kerwin, William said it was clear to him that they should do the production together.

Another meeting was scheduled in Toronto for which Kerwin was to think about how to do the statue scene, her "final exam question." Again her busy schedule precluded her being able to address as much time as she wished to staging the final scene prior to the meeting, but she came and explained over grilled cheese sandwiches that the solution to the scene had to be "very simple" and "uncluttered," which to her meant somehow bringing the statue of Heromione up through the trap door.

After conclusion of these preliminary discussions, Kerwin thought about how to use the stage as a neutral area and define each scene by means of props. About a week before a November meeting, she began to make a stack of "very rough drawings" that demonstrated her solutions to the basic problems in each scene. She asked herself, for example, how on that stage to tell an audience they are in a palace in Sicilia as opposed to a palace in Bohemia or a Bohemian seacoast. "You put down what you know," she explains and "one thing leads you to the next." The director-designer conferences she used to confer with William about what she saw as the intention of each scene and what she would use to illustrate it. To her this process is the one "where all the important groundwork gets done." She illustrates the process by talking through II.1.

The scene begins with Hermione and Mamillius, mother and son, talking together innocently and in a very sheltered environment into which Leontes brings violence with his accusations against Hermione. Kerwin set the scene in a nursery complete with crib waiting for the child with whom Hermione is very pregnant. A Christmas tree-like structure being trimmed with ornaments also establishes a tone of expectancy; a single bench, for the very practical reason that Hermione must sit down, finished the list of materials Kerwin would use for the clear, uncluttered appearance she believed to be so important for the scene.

After working out the flow of the show by determining the staging requirements for the intention of each scene, just as she had for II.1, Kerwin worked back through, asking herself what each piece of furniture looked like. For example, "You want this crib. Now what do you think it looks like?" Questions such as: How tall is it? How wide is it? How deep is it? What color is it? and What style is it? make up this process, which she calls the second phase of hard work. Kerwin and William met again in Chicago in December and in Stratford in January. In each case she kept bringing him work "to react to," most of it in that second phase.

Designing the costumes required working out a basic vocabulary. They decided the text called for the scenes in the first half, which occur mainly in Sicilia, to take place during the winter and the scenes in the second half of the play, which with the exception of Act V take place in Bohemia, to occur during the summer. Winter colours were chosen for the court of Sicilia: Lords were to wear coats of a dark gunpowder gray with cream-coloured breeches, while the ladies were to dress in various pastel shades of cool colours, such as purple. Kerwin explains that designing the show in the winter in Toronto helped because the stores were featuring their winter fashions and she realized anew how many different colours winter can wear. The Bohemian lords were to wear coats of green, trimmed in gold, with cream-coloured breeches. During the scenes in Sicilia in the winter their coats were to be a bright Robin Hood green. During the summer months in Bohemia the intensity of the colour of their coats was to be much more muted. The other large group of people in the play, the Bohemian country people, were to be dressed in light, warm earth colours. With this vocabulary in place, Kerwin could then begin to create individual touches to distinguish the characters from one another.

The costume for the character of Time went through a number of revisions. Kerwin began with the idea that she did not want him to look like a refugee from a New Year's Eve calendar. She had made several changes in her concept when she learned that actor Mervin (Butch) Blake would be playing the role. This time Kerwin based the costumes on the qualities she believed Blake would bring to the role. Kerwin and other designers often cite the difficulties of designing a costume before knowing which performer will be wearing it. In the end Kerwin decided to put a transparent mask on him so that in effect, "It was his own face and yet not his own face," the mask serving as "a second skin for him." He was costumed in an early Nineteenth Century cream-coloured coat, vest, and breeches and wore a white face under the mask. In this manner, she believes, she avoided stereotyping the character yet set him apart as functioning in a different manner from the other characters in the play. While he was obviously distinctive, the cream colour tied him to the rest of the men in the show.

A third member of William's design team was Festival director of music Bert Carriere, who had composed the music for *She Stoops To Conquer*, which William had directed in 1985. Carriere, who had enjoyed working with William, had thanked him for that opportunity and had expressed a desire to work with him again, to which William had replied, "Very, very soon." Carriere smiles as he recollects that "Obviously he knew something I didn't." During the first week of September, Neville called to tell Carriere that William would be directing *The Winter's Tale* and had asked for Carriere to compose the music, an invitation he immediately accepted. William then told him that he would be in touch about "what he heard in his head as far as the music/sound was concerned."

Carriere then received a letter from William in early January with all the music cues noted. Carriere cites William's musical preparatiion because the list of cues subsequently changed only to include a few additions. William had listened to Schumann's *Kinderszenen*, Opus 15, and had recommended using that piece. Carriere asked William about doing an original piece in the same style as the Schumann, but William really liked that particular music and so Carriere decided to use it. Because *Kinderszenen* is a series of musical pieces for children, an individual selection had to be made. William like a variation entitled *From A Distant Land*, which Carriere used. To William this selection brings "a marvelous evocation of the innocence and simplicity of childhood." There is also a certain mystical element about it for him that its title suggests. Carriere says working with a director as secure in his musical tastes as William presents no problem. He says, "I can give him exactly what he asks for plus a little more." Carriere then decided to use different variations of this theme in each sound cue, thereby achieving a unified musical structure for the play. The same fifteen-piece orchestra was to record the musical sound tapes used for *The Winter's Tale* and *Cymbeline* as was employed to provide live music for *The Boys From Syracuse* and *Pericles*. Under the terms of an agreement reached with the musicians, which makes coming to Stratford financially viable, the members of the orchestra are paid each time the sound tape is played. Therefore Carriere was free to compose variations on the Schumann theme for any instrument or combination of instruments from a single piano to a 15-piece orchestra.

Carriere explains that music in the theatre makes a point and then must leave it alone. Music must not overpower, says Carriere, who prefers not to underscore each scene because then the music would become obtrusive. The musical choices should always enhance the dominant emotions, he continually stresses. All things considered, he says of his career, "It's a nice way to spend a lifetime."

William had also worked with lighting designer Harry Frehner during the 1985 *She Stoops To Conquer* production, and Frehner says William asked for him as designer for *The Winter's Tale*--the first time in his Stratford career that a director had asked specifically for him. His early conferences with William established the specific time of day, season of the year, and dominant mood for each scene.

The Winter's Tale was the second show to go into rehearsal at the Festival Theatre. Some performers (Martha Burns as Perdita, Maurice Good as the Old Shepherd, Nicholas Pennell as Camillo, Stephen Russell as Polixenes, and Joe Ziegler as Autolycus) were answering their first 1986 call, while others (Butch Blake as Time, Ben Campbell as the Young Shepherd, Colm Feore as Leontes, Goldie Semple as Hermione, Keith Thomas as Florizel, and Susan Wright as Paulina) had already been in rehearsal for three weeks for *The Boys From Syracuse*. Blake had appeared as the Old Shepherd in Douglas Campbell's first production of *The Winter's Tale* in 1958. He also appeared along with two other 1986 cast members in Robin Phillips' 1978 production. In that second production Blake played Time, as he did again in 1986; William Needles, who had played Camillo then, now played both Antigonus and Paulina's steward; Alicia Jeffrey, who had played one of Hermione's ladies for Phillips, now played Mopsa for William.

William began in rehearsal by explaining the design decisions that had been made. In apology to the actors for having made these decisions without them, he gave some background and cited the need for long-range planning by the Festival. The job now involved bringing the actors on board as quickly as possible, he said.

He then explained that because the Festival would produce three of the four romances as well as *Henry VIII*, itself perhaps the last play Shakespeare wrote, taking a few minutes each day to get in touch with some of the last thoughts expressed by this artist in dramatic form would be a useful exercise. With that introduction he appointed all actors to what he called Cabinet Posts or Ministries with Portfolio in his *Winter's Tale* government. Because he also thought dealing with the actors' conceptions about the play's weaknesses would prove a valuable exercise, he first appointed a Prosecutor, Nicholas Pennell, to bring the play to trial the next day. He was to present the last thoughts of a tired old man, bored with life. He then appointed a Defense Attorney, Colm Feore, to defend the play against these charges. In a similar manner actors were appointed to Cabinet Posts: Attitude to Women, Apollo and Religion, Art versus Nature, Just Desserts, Tyrant and Tyranny, Sicilia and Bohemia, Prose versus Poetry, Childhood, Parents and Children, Courts and Courtiers, Comedy, Final Plays, Love--Earthly and Spiritual, Myth, Country Life, Doing the Classics, and Shakespeare's Sources and Choices. He asked each Cabinet Post to give a report representing the work of all members (between one and three persons) and that with the exception of the minister dealing with Shakespeare's sources the play be used as the primary research material. The actors quickly asked if they might consult him privately regarding their preparation and he assured them that they might. In addition, he appointed assistant director Susan Ferley as Prime Minister with the responsibility of assisting the others. He assured his cast that he would have much to say about the play, but the most important task consisted of having them coming to it first for themselves. He explained his concept of the prologue as well as an additional scene at the beginning in which Leontes gives a party for Polixenes. ''Characters have life before and after the play in which they appear, and we will sample some of that life before the play begins.'' He asked the company how many of them had seen a production of the play and seemed genuinely pleased that over half the cast had not seen it on the stage.

The scripts which the stage management team distributed to the actors already contained the cuts which William described as ''negotiable''--although by ''hard-edged'' negotiations. The remainder of the morning was given over to a read-through of the play. After lunch William and Kerwin explained the costume designs and William shared with the cast some of the problems involved in establishing a chronology and time period for the play. He explained that the references in the text to the Delphic Oracle were Pre-Christian, while those about the crucifixion were obviously Post-Christian.

The Italian Renassiance painter Julio Romano referred to in V.2 died ten years before Shakespeare was born. So William and Kerwin chose a period knowing they would have to live with the consequences. They also bore in mind the specific references to time and place which, with the exception of the character of Time, dictated a naturalistic approach to sets and costumes. Because there are references to both day and evening, William wanted a time period that would reflect a difference in day and evening clothing, which necessitated a choice after about 1810.

The next day Nicholas Pennell rose for the prosecution. He leveled several charges at the piece, but the most damning blast by far was the charge that it was turgid and inaccessible to modern audiences. He concluded by arguing against its performance. Colm Feore rose for the defense. He defended the play as a part of the Shakespearean canon, which the Festival Board of Governors has mandated to be performed in its entirety. *The Winter's Tale* had been scheduled for the season and should be performed, he reasoned. As William must have hoped, the members of the company jumped in, debating the merits of the play, when the trial concluded. When the rehearsal hall again grew silent, William summed up the morning's work. Fifty percent of the vocabulary of this play is unknown to a modern audience, he began. That problem compounds itself in that there are no speeches from it that people know by heart. Therefore, continued William, the company must find in it that which is eternally modern and which helps to make it accessible. Eventually he conceded that the company must get down to the business of blocking the play, but first the cast must understand what a challenge the play would be to perform successfully so that actors could concentrate their skills on the process of making it eternally modern. To that end he said, ''We will put each scene under the microscope and then throw it out into the arena and have a go at it.'' He illustrated his point about making the play understandable with a story about an actor speaking the words so quickly that they were not understood; what the audience did comprehend was the torrent of emotion whipping the actor about which helped the audience understand the scene even more than did the words.

Then the actors spoke again about the play. One claimed to dislike it because all the honest and virtuous suffer. Another admitted that he wanted to believe in the redemptive quality of life so essential to William's reading of the play, but he simply couldn't. William listened intently to both comments and told each of the two actors that we live in such a world as they had described. But he went on to say that beyond the random suffering of the innocent there is an order that at least imposes seasons on the earth in a cyclical fashion, even if man is not orderly. Pennell, who three weeks earlier had returned from an American tour which ended a year of work on

King Lear, remarked that it was a relief to go from the dead bodies in that play and in *Hamlet* to this play about redemption, love, and forgiveness. All traces of the Prosecutor dropped away as he spoke admiringly of the play. William remarked that for the very reasons Pennell had just named, the scale of passion and the intensity of emotion in this piece force an audience to deal with them. Several times William quoted Hamlet's line, "The native hue of resolution is sicklied o'er with the pale cast of thought." He explained that this play requires in its presentation the "native hue of resolution." Academics have in his view too frequently intellectualized about Shakespeare's plays "with the pale cast of thought." There is nothing pale or sickly about the nature of forgiveness or reconciliation, and these emotions would call for all the "native hue of resolution" which the actors could muster, William frequently reminded them.

William wished to establish a vocabulary to use in working on the text with the company. He asked each person to write down three adjectives that best described the concept "male" and three that best described the concept "female." All the responses were read and catalogued. Words receiving more than one vote were noted while words with similiar meanings were voted on by the company to get the one that the group felt best described the particular gender. The three words emerging for "male" were: 1.) active, 2.) dominant, 3.) direct; the three for female were: 1.) enfolding, 2.) receptive, 3.) flexible. William continued throughout the rehearsal process to use those words. He explains that men and women carry inside them a balance:

of the masculine and feminine elements. A happy psyche life is one in which they live in a good equipoise together, but when one or the other takes over to a certain degree and dominates beyond its proper range, then difficult things are apt to happen.

The words, he says, are generally used in an emotional or decision-making situation, and carry no judgmental value, but rather allow the director to describe the actions of a character in a scene as masculine or feminine; as active, dominating, and direct or as enfolding, receptive, and flexible.

William blocked the individual scenes into which he had divided the scripts after gathering everyone in a scene around a table and having a reading. Often he would ask an actor a basic question relating to the character being portrayed, such as, "How old is Archidamus?" He would explain the significance of the scene and would then block it, sometimes using several variations before choosing the one he wanted. He usually conferred with the actors to be sure they were comfortable with movements they were asked to execute. If several days had elapsed since a scene had been practiced, William brought the actors back to the table to read it and then talked it through with them, reminding them of what the important issues in it were before beginning to work it in earnest. As a scene was being rehearsed, he called for the report of the Cabinet Ministers responsible for the issue that the scene raised. Actors were, therefore, unsure when they might be called to report, but the procedure did allow the cast the spontaneity of dealing with these important issues as they arose during rehearsal rather than in a predetermined order. During the early rehearsals, actors continued to inject opinions when the reports were concluded and sometimes lengthy discussion periods followed these presentations, in which actors measured the validity of the play's themes against their own experiences.

Throughout the rehearsal period William preferred to work intensely on the individual scenes rather than running larger sections. *The Winter's Tale* also profited from extensive rehearsals held on days when it was not designated as the primary rehearsal. Due perhaps to sheer luck, it seemed to be the one Festival Theatre show which could pull enough actors together not needed for the other two plays to make meaningful work possible. During these small scene rehearsals, he worked first on blocking and then on character and interpretation, delving at times into the psychology of the dominant characters in the scene, as for example when he explored the sixteen-year gap by asking the characters in V.1, before each speech, such questions as "Why?", "What do you mean?", or "Explain." In this manner he kept digging deeper and deeper into a very small section of text. Toward the end of this phase of rehearsals, he worked on some of the more important scenes to see if anything else could be gleaned from each of them. Then came the refining process in which he blended the elements together, giving each scene its own pace and showing concern that the actors used enough different pitches to make the scene move off the page as a distinctively knit unit. He had a very clear idea that he imposed on each of those units and then, within the specific limits he had set the actors, helped to make the work their own.

The run-through for lights held on the Festival Stage was the first of the play and did not occur until 31 March, marking William as the director who waited longest before running the entire play in sequence. Because of the detailed work of that rehearsal, there were minor interruptions from time to time. As a result, interest in the 5 April run-through scheduled for the more intimate atmosphere of Rehearsal Hall 1 ran high. Actor Bruce Swerdfager later spoke for many of those present in calling that experience "a knockout."

The Winter's Tale that opened on 21 May contained thirty titled scenes into which William had divided the play. Page numbers refer to the New Penguin paperback edition used for this production.

Prologue

This prologue, not contained in Shakespeare's play, contained two parts, Scene 1, "Prologue," and Scene 2, "Party." On opening night the house opened about half an hour before performance. The stage was completely draped in the gauze, which appeared as a massive ice block cascading from the heavens above the stage balcony down onto and over the forestage area. The sound of ocean waves gently breaking on the shore was played just prior to beginning the show. The house lights dimmed down and as Scene 1, "Prologue," began, a strong light came up on Time, standing on the stage balcony, and on the eight children seated in various positions under the balcony, while Time spoke the opening line from *Pandasto*: "Although by means of sinister fortune truth may be concealed, yet by time it may be most manifestly revealed." Carriere, using the Schumann theme played by a string quartet, added what he and William called "a colouring" to Time to set him apart. Actor Blake believes using Time as William did in a prologue and epilogue to the play gave the character a beneficence which he liked playing. As he raised his hand at the end of the speech, the the gauze suddenly and magically withdrew into the heavens. The light spread across the stage as the children did a slow and deliberate waltz in their different period costumes before walking up the staircase, hands linked, toward Time, who led them out the balcony door under a flashing strobe light while a line of actors walked on stage for Scene 2, "Party." The music of the quartet swelled to the sound of an orchestra as the lights came up for the scene. The orchestra sounded as lavish as the rest of Sicilia's entertainments, with fanfares ringing out with the unmistakable sounds of the timpani over all.

Four triple-tiered candelabra with lighted candles dominated the scene: two on the balcony, as well as one on each balcony landing and one additional two-tiered candelabrum in front of each vomitorium. Three matching benches with gray cushions rested at the steps of the forestage, one in front and one on each side. The scene set at the Court of Sicilia opened on a party being given by Leontes for his friend Polixenes.

One of William's Oxford dons, Nevill Coghill, had written an article about the jealousy of Leontes having begun before the play starts, since Polixenes is concluding a nine-month visit as the play opens. Indeed the production William had seen starring Gielgud had opened with a tableau in which Leontes was staring with some hatred at Polixenes and which had the first scene cut to support this reading of the play. But William believed that an action as important to Shakespeare's plot as the breakup of the friendship between these two kings who had been childhood friends must take place on stage, and to set up that rupture he began the play by first affirming that friendship. Given the decision to stage the incidents which aroused Leontes' jealousy, the problem for the actor consists of finding a way to move from feelings of great friendship for Polixenes to those of intense jealousy as quickly as the text dictates he must. Feore explains the starting point for Leontes: "I am playing...great love, warmth, and affection and complete and absolute contentment for the first three and one-half minutes. The next two hours are hell," he laughingly acknowledges, and only partly in jest.

But in those opening minutes, Leontes moves in a world of his own making among his court, with his friend and his wife. Realizing that the character's view becomes warped and twisted later on by anxiety, hatred, and jealousy, Feore stresses his desire to start the play at the other end of the scale. Not to do so, he says "would weight the dice in everybody else's favor and nobody would go along with you." Because so much had to be shown about the relationship between Leontes and Hermione in so little time, Feore started with the powerful negative emotions which Leontes displays and then worked backward to the beginning of the play, believing that one cannot hate without having loved. With this theory in mind he talked with William and Semple about the nature of the husband/wife union. Together they decided that they enjoyed a very "intense, physical, alive, sexual relationship," which bore positive if somewhat extreme connotations:

> Only a man who is capable of such things can believe that others are indeed so capable and could for a moment believe that if he felt this way about her it is not unbelievable or impossible that someone else would. In fact it is entirely possible. If you are thinking like that, you go from intense love to intense hate in about thirty-five seconds.

Thus Feore believes that the transition the character must make is difficult only if the actor has insufficient subtext to accomplish it. The actor also sees the character as a warm, sensitive man who gets himself emotionally entangled in a situation that he is in no way equipped to handle, rather than as petulant --and thus impossible to portray sympathetically.

The scene opens with a dance already in progress and, after a brief interval, Leontes, Hermoine, and Polixenes leave the stage by the right vomitorium. Servants stand by with trays of champagne glasses, some of which are distributed during the scene. William believes the scene, a pantomime to music, strengthened the line in the next scene about the lavishness of the Sicilian court. The scene also replaced Shakespeare's as the audience's introduction to the main characters. Leontes and Polixenes wore costumes tied by color to those of their lords but cut in a more formal manner, while being different from one another. Hermione wore a very simple peach-coloured dress cut in the Empire style to emphasize that she was seven or eight months pregnant. That costume made her stand out against her ladies, dressed in winter colours. Kerwin wanted her to stand apart on her own strength and not to undercut her inner resources by putting her under a crown or other gaudy accessories. Hermione's costume must be the simplest one on the stage, Kerwin explains. William wanted her to stand out because she is the character who makes the entire play happen. "Another woman might not have survived and enabled others to survive. She is an enabler." Semple says of the role:

> Everything that's good about being a woman is in Hermione. She has a sense of humour, she's sexy, she's got warmth, honesty, integrity, understanding, and spirituality.

The first scene pictured her in this glow, so it remained a favorite one for Semple and one she described as feeling like a warm bath. "It's the high place to fall from as well," the actress asserts.

Act 1, Scene 1

Act 1, Scene 1, contained only one scene. As the main characters exit from the "Party," Scene 3, "Our Bohemia, Your Sicilia" (pp. 53-54) begins with Archidamus, played as a young Bohemian lord just beginning his diplomatic career, most impressed with the lavish entertainments of the Sicilian court. Camillo, on the other hand, embodied the qualities of a smooth, older, seasoned statesman. The champagne which flowed so freely at the party helped to establish the happy, almost euphoric mood of these ambassadors and served as a sharp contrast to the atmosphere of disruption which looms so near. William chose to emphasize the friendship of the two kings by breaking the scene after Camillo's speech about their being childhood friends. He brought the three back on stage for Leontes to present Polixenes with a medal that he hangs around his neck, to the applause of the court. The gesture was perhaps inspired by Leontes' later reference to Polixenes as:

> ...he that wears her like a medal, hanging About his neck....
> I.2.307-308

At the mention of Mamillius, he appears on the balcony in the care of Paulina and her husband, Antigonus, who, however briefly, thereby have their relationship visually established. Paulina, as Wright played her, has a sharp eye for character and something of the psychic about her at times. Wright theorizes that Paulina had known Hermione since childhood, although Paulina is the elder. She has been drawn to Hermione by the latter's character, which Wright believes to be exceptional "in her beauty--not only physical-- but her warmth, her stature, her class." Wright's Paulina lacks the inner peace and calm which make Hermione so attractive to her. At the beginning

Hermione believes Paulina knows Leontes less well because she makes the terrible mistake later in the play of bringing him the newborn princess. But Wright concludes her assessment by asserting that Paulina can also see nobility in him.

Act I, Scene 2

Act I, Scene 2, contained three scenes: Scene 4, "Bawdy Planet" (pp. 54-62); Scene 5, "Some Severals" (pp. 62-68); and Scene 6, "The Urgent Hour" (pp. 68-71). "Bawdy Planet" begins with Leontes pleading in front of the entire court with Polixenes to remain, thereby putting all of his prestige on the line, and failing in his endeavours despite the holiday atmosphere of the scene. When Hermione accepts his invitation to intercede with Polixenes, she asks with a gesture to Leontes that they have some privacy, and Leontes obeys her request, clearing the room with a sweep of his arm and then leaving himself. Semple explains that she believes Hermione and Polixenes each loves Leontes very much. She and Polixenes enjoy each other's company, and there is between them an easy banter characterized by her asking him to relate stories of growing up with Leontes. Semple played these requests as if she were asking him to repeat one of her favorite stories still another time. Hermione sits on the stage left bench, at times holding Polixenes' hand and at others allowing him to touch her protruding stomach.

But the director and these two performers decided after a certain degree of experimentation in rehearsals that no hint of impropriety exists in this relationship, although Semple believes that in this production Polixenes' decision to make so hasty a departure may hinge on his attraction to her. Even if her reasoning proved accurate, Semple maintains, his decision to leave speaks for his integrity. But she acknowledges that her Hermione has no such suspicions. For his part, Russell says, his Polixenes indeed feels a strong attraction for her. He bases that opinion in part on the character's choice to leave his own wife for nine months, which Shakespeare allows to correspond with the term of pregnancy. Russell and his wife experienced the birth of their first child, Andrew, during the spring of 1986. He recalls the special warmth and glow of a pregnant woman and he remembers his feelings about who should and who should not be allowed to touch his wife's stomach to share their sense of expectation. Nonetheless, he says, Polixenes behaves in an honorable fashion toward Hermione despite their lively and occasionally flirtatious behaviour.

Feore believes that Leontes' somewhat emotionally upset frame of mind, caused by his friend's announcement of his impending departure, helps to explain his faulty reasoning in the rest of the scene. He describes the steps in his thinking, none of which taken in isolation would lead Leontes astray, as 1.) Hermione's willingness to let Leontes stay in Bohemia an additional month if Polixenes will stay another week; 2.) her speech ending with the lines:

Th'offences we have made you do we'll answer, If you first sinned with us, and that with us you did continue fault, and that you slipped not with any but us. I.2.83-84

that he re-entered to hear while missing the rest of the speech; 3.) her success in getting Polixenes to stay, which Leontes could not achieve; and 4.) their physical familiarity, which, Feore posits, Leontes has encouraged. Leontes then becomes trapped in the circumstantial web he himself has spun. As Feore says, "By this time he has gone round the bend, and there is no help for him." The actor explains that if there is the slightest suspicion that any truth lies in these charges then the sympathies of the audience "will be unblanced, and they must never be."

The audience first sees that Leontes' imagination has led him to a loss of control in the speech that begins "Too hot, too hot!", a speech occasioned by the sum of all the bits of evidence rather than by any new physical action between Polixenes and Hermione. William chose to play the speech as a monologue by bringing the lights down to spotlight Leontes and to isolate him from the social context of the scene by darkening the rest of the stage. For the duration of the scene, Leontes cannot break free of his fears, and Feore used the scenes with Mamillius to mask his thoughts from the others present by hugging and carrying the boy about:

Are you so fond of your young prince as we Do seem to be of ours? I.2.164-165

and as a means of kindling new doubts:

...Mamillius, Art thou my boy? I.2.119-120

William used the scenes between the two to demonstrate the strong bond between father and son. These moments also contain one the last chances to show Leontes as a loving and admirable human being before his fall. As Mamillius leaves the stage, Camillo, having first checked with the nurse, provides a treat which the boy immediately pops into his mouth.

Semple begins Hermione from that same warm, loving, and passionate base that Feore describes. She believes that she can charm Polixenes into staying, as indeed she does. Her Hermione is well aware of her charm when she wants to turn it on. Some nights, explains Semple, Feore will show her by his face that there is something wrong at the conclusion of this scene and some nights he doesn't, so that on those occasions his entrance into the nursery is the first clue she has that something has gone wrong.

During "Some Several" Leontes goes through several stages of emotional turmoil before asking Camillo to kill Polixenes. Feore enumerates his subtext in those phases as: 1.) You were my father's right-hand man and I have advanced you even further than he did. You know everything that goes on. Now tell me that which I will not name because you owe it to me. 2.) You are my closest friend, Camillo. Have you not seen what happening? Of course you have. Feore acknowledges that Leontes is laying himself open as a way of raising the stakes. 3.) Finally, because Camillo still has no idea what Leontes is talking about, he tells Camillo. Feore says, "Now that those words have passed my lips, I'm committed and committable...." Leontes "becomes certifiable at that point. He is beyond the judgment of anything but a very odd lucidity that still allows him to manipulate Camillo." Feore detects in Leontes' twisted conception of honour and in the indirectness with which he asks for the murder a certain Godfatherish tone that he describes as "Take Freddy fishing."

Once Camillo agrees to do the deed, Feore explains, Leontes doesn't want to stand too close because he believes he has polluted Camillo. Leontes also hopes this distance will show Leontes as none too happy about having to order the murder of his friend. The actor stresses the necessity for the character to appear anxious, unsure, and struggling, so as not to stand condemned as a tyrant by those judging his actions. William interprets Camillo's acceptance of this loathsome task as his realization that there is no other way to deal with Leontes at this moment. William at first called Camillo's assent "a little white lie." Then he explained it in terms borrowed from the *The Merchant of Venice* IV.1.216, "To do a great right, do a little wrong."

Pennell explains that Camillo acts as a senior advisor to Leontes and to his father before him (as this production makes use of a younger-than-usual Leontes). The actor considers that in this exchange between the two characters, Leontes acts as he has never before behaved in his life, a behavior that upsets and confuses Camillo. As the summer progressed, Pennell says, Feore's Leontes' got louder and more demanding in this scene, suggesting to Pennell that Camillo's best response was to become more confused; he understated his lines to show that Camillo agrees to Leontes' plan because he can find no escape while in such a state of shock. The actor stresses that his character never has any intention of killing Polixenes, despite the two assurances he gives Leontes:

> ...*I must believe you, sir. I do; and will fetch off Bohemia for't: Provided that when he's removed your highness Will take again your queen as yours at first.* I.2.333-336

and

> *...I am his cupbearer. If from me he have wholesome beverage,*
> *Account me not your servant.* I.2.345-347

The first commitment, according to Pennell, is to get Polixenes out of Sicilia in hopes that Leontes will be restored to a more rational frame of mind and will not harm Hermione. In the second, Camillo does not swear to commit the murder. Instead his only choice lies in switching his role to that of Polixene's servant. Pennell quotes the lines:

> *...I'll put My fortunes to your service,...* I.2.439-440

to explain his motivation.

"The Urgent Hour" began with Camillo debating his plight and briefly hiding behind the center balcony post when Polixenes returns to the stage. Russell says Polixenes believes Camillo not only because of the integrity of his character but also because he has seen friendships of long standing break apart over the mere suspicion of one friend's having slept with the other's wife. Russell muses that perhaps the "male butch ego" invests this taboo with such significance. At any rate Polixenes instantly recognizes that because this charge has been laid at his door, he must flee. His first impulse to go to Leontes and say, "What is all this nonsense about?" becomes pointless, considering that the very charge often produces an irrational response.

Act II, Scene 1

Act II, Scene 1, was composed of two parts, Scene 7, "A Sad Tale's Best" (pp. 72-76), and Scene 8, "Three Great Ones Suffer" (pp. 77-79). During the scene change into the nursery, Carriere turned the second part of the Schumann theme around to provide a varied but united sound. For "A Sad Tale's Best" a nursery setting provided what Kerwin described as a very protected environment for the scene into which Leontes would bring such violence, as described earlier. William believes that the intimacy depicted in this scene would make Leontes' shattering of it more painful; Leontes' single presence there would be quite natural but his presence with his array of lords about him makes a very different impression.

When Leontes enters the nursery, Antigonus and five Sicilian lords come with him. In this production only the lord who brings the news about the flight of Camillo and Polixenes has any inkling that anything disruptive lurks beneath the surface. The entrance of the men made the situation somewhat awkward for the queen and her ladies, dressed in their night clothes. Feore describes Leontes' actions in the scene: "He staged it...staged it as a vicious, absolutely vicious infiltration and violation of her chamber...her women, her pregnancy and her children....He violates her chambers as he feels she has violated him.'' He has stage managed his own shame, Feore explains. If he is to suffer the pain of being humiliated by this woman over whom he has made such a great show of affection, ''He's going to do it in public and it's going to be a grand show.'' He explains his subtext by asserting that since Leontes knows he has no facts to support this charge, he has to stage it in a grand fashion to force a corroboration from Antigonus, Paulina, Hermione, or any of her ladies. Because Leontes loves Hermione so much, Feore has decided, he dares not confront her privately because he knows she will charm him all over again and he will proceed no further with these charges. ''He is a deeply sensitive man,'' says Feore, ''who is now afraid of his own vulnerability.'' Despite the charges Leontes makes against Hermione, the performer found that thinking ''I hate you'' didn't help him. He then switched the intention to ''I love you, I love you, I love you,'' a motivation on which he builds his relationship to her in every scene in the show. ''When I should hate her most, I love her most.'' He goes on to explain that with that feeling the actions in the play could at any moment be redeemed, as the sensible characters constantly beg him to do.

For Semple the scene presented the difficulty of providing her with very few lines with which to explain herself. The very sleepy or drowsy quality of the scene as she sets about putting her son to bed is jolted by Leontes' entrance. She feels a sense of personal violation when he walks in with his lords and keeps trying throughout the scene to tell him not to go too far with his accusations lest there be no way to undo the damage he has done. During his accusations she goes from embarrassment to an understanding that his rational mind has left him. In this manner she sets up her attitude for the end of the play: She believes he has suffered from a mental sickness which has passed, and she can therefore forgive him.

''Three Great Ones Suffer'' was also played in the nursery. William wanted the Lords to try to talk Leontes out of this rash action but to argue no harder than their continued good favor with the king would permit.

Act III, Scene 1

Act III, Scene 1, was transposed to follow Act II, Scene 1, and played as one unit, Scene 9, ''Oracle'' (pp. 90-91). William maintains that Shakespeare presents a man who transgresses against the Oracle and pays a terrible price, but who after his time of exile can come back healed. But ''in a largely unbelieving age, a secular age, the importance of the Oracle is very undervalued,'' he insists: ''The authority of the Oracle dominates the entire play; you may say it's what supports Paulina's faith to the very end.'' William buttresses his argument by citing Mamillius' death coming as soon as Leontes defies the Oracle. For this reason he wanted to transpose the first part of the Oracle scene to follow the scene in which the Oracle is first mentioned.

Both to imbue the scene with that sense of religious importance, which is so difficult for a modern audience to grasp, and to show a glimpse of the life of the spiritual community at Delphos, which he saw as a "different culture," William wanted twenty-three priests in this scene. But, as he explained to the cast in rehearsal, the days when one can get twenty-three extra costumes for one scene are dead and gone at Stratford. He continued, "I had been planning my production for a year and I wasn't about to give up my priests. Therefore, when costumes from a production of *The Magic Flute* done at The National Arts Center in Ottawa became available, they were quickly accepted and treated by the Stratford wardrobe staff to look Byzantine, according to Kerwin. William confessed after the first rehearsal in costume under performance lighting that he had been holding his breath wondering what the priests would look like. As he staged the scene, the Sicilian ambassadors were led onto the set to chanting and given the Oracle's reply in very low lighting so that the stage appeared to be filled with priests--but one couldn't be sure. As soon as the Oracle's answer had been given, the priests, exited across each other through the vomitoriums, leaving the Silician ambassadors amazed. Even though the borrowed costumes represented a victory for William, Frehner says, designer Kerwin asked him to put as little light on them as possible because they never looked proper to her eye. As a result Frehner had some light stream from the mouth of the cave (the up stage center entrance), and four or five hand-carried torches caused a moving pattern of light that to Frehner recalled Prometheus the Fire Giver. Carriere's choice of music here, Russian Orthodox Church music, broke his pattern of using the Schumann.

Act II, Scene 2

Act II, Scene 2, was composed of one unit, Scene 10, "Prison" (pp. 79-82). The sense of spiritual peace and joy just established in the "Oracle" was meant to contrast sharply with "Prison." The music turned heavy and sombre for just a moment and the sound of a key in a lock and the slam of a heavy door introduced the scene. The stage was set very sparsely, with only a rough-hewn table and chair. This prison setting, William noted in rehearsal, should make the point that Leontes has not placed Hermione under house arrest but has rather sent her away: The person the audience cares very most about is being treated very shabbily. The birth of the baby, he added, has come at the hands of a quack.

Act II, Scene 3

Act II, Scene 3, was composed of two scenes, Scene 11, "Tryannous Passion" (pp. 82-87), and Scene 12, "Brat" (pp. 87-90). William and Kerwin set the scene in Leontes' bedchamber because, as William explains, so much of this play is about what does or doesn't happen in a bed. The chamber contained only a double bed set to stage left of the area under the balcony. Leontes was dressed in a partly unbuttoned white shirt and dark trousers. An elegant dressing gown was laid across the end of the bed for him to put on as soon as Paulina entered. William says that the scene title, "Tyrannous Passion," uses words that have lost much of their power. After the Cabinet ministers for Tyrant and Tyranny reported during the rehearsal process, the company defined a tyrant as "one who does horrible things." William stressed in rehearsal that the cast must work to recapture the meaning and to communicate it to an audience.

Wright explains that although Paulina had to be frightened in bringing the baby to Leontes, she is confident that he will accept her--that the baby would be the means of redeeming them all. But when Leontes not only denies his paternity but orders the baby killed, Paulina quickly reminds him that he is acting as a tyrant and leaves the scene very frightened at his madness. Even though Paulina could not have known Antigonus would be sent away with the baby, Wright believes Paulina psychic enough at this point to know somehow that her relationship with her husband has ended. Her "farewell" at the end of the scene is directed to Antigonus rather than to Leontes or his lords.

Feore's Leontes fights against Paulina's coming to him because he recognizes that she speaks the truth. He fears being left alone with her because he knows her virtue will force him to recant. In the middle of the summer season, Feore says, he was still questioning why not backing down, even in the face of truth, was so important to Leontes. Also of importance to the actor were the pains Leontes took to deny that he is a tyrant, since in his own mind he does not commit horrible deeds. Feore says that on the one hand, somewhere in his subconscious mind, he recognizes that Paulina speaks the truth, but on the other he consciously believes so entirely in the justice of his cause he can honestly disclaim the title "tyrant."

Needles as Antigonus begins the scene trying to keep Paulina out, but after her entrance, he says, he realizes that the more she talks the more he knows that she is right: The baby must not be killed. For Needles the conflict between duty and honor is paralleled in Camillo and Antigonus.

An event from one of the first rehearsals onstage shows how committed the actors became to the integrity of the scene. Wright had laid the bundle of muslin representing the baby too close to the edge of the bed and during the course of the scene it rolled off. Wright and Feore were facing away from the bed and could not see the six attending lords who came rushing forward in a futile attempt to catch the bundle before it hit the floor.

After the exit of Paulina, "Brat" begins. Feore says he used the moment in the text where the king decided the baby would live as the place to show the audience how close he has come to accepting Paulina's truth. He believes, he says, that Leontes must raise at least a chance of reversing his position to make his change at the end of the trial scene viable. But once Leontes realizes how vulnerable he has become, he immediately turns hard and resolute in his desire to regain control. Feore believes that in reasserting an extreme position, that the baby be left unattended in a deserted place, his character ventures even further into madness. If Paulina cannot coax him back to reasonableness, what chance have the attending lords, concerned that their stock at court not suffer?

For the end of this scene, William asked Carriere for a sound effect to show Leontes' mental condition to the audience. Carriere blended four sound tracks to achieve the desired effect, a somewhat stylized version of the sounds of two lovers. Band one contained Semple and Russell breathing heavily, band two a stock sound of two monkeys copulating, band three some high-pitched string and parrot sounds, band four a repetition of high piano notes. Carriere explains that he added lots of reverberation, as well as stock sound of wolves howling at the beginning of the sequence. At the end of it, Russell yelled and then the reverberation took over. As staged, the lights then came up on the balcony on Leontes' chair for the trial scene. Feore likes the sound cue because he believes audiences would think, "Oh, so that's what he's been feeling." William says the sound cue helps remind us that we all have savage feelings.

Act III, Scene 2

Act III, Scene 2, was composed of two scenes, Scene 13, "Trial" (pp. 91-97), and Scene 14, "Shame Perpetual" (pp. 97-100). Moving the Delphic Oracle scene allowed Leontes to go directly from the highly agitated frame of mind of the bedroom scene, reinforced by the sound tape, into the trial scene, where the staging suggested he plays the dual role of prosecutor and judge. His throne sits highlighted alone on the balcony, above Hermione and the delegates to the Oracle. Clearly William wanted this effect, for he wished Hermione to look as if she had been judged already. Kerwin dressed her in a rough-textured grayish-brown linen sack, her face smudged with dirt and her hair unkempt.

Semple explains that the trial scene is the the most technically difficult one for her. William blocked the scene by putting her immobile in the middle of the stage. Semple appreciates the need for this blocking, but it offers her no place to hide. To make matters more difficult, she says, Hermione comes into the court bearing the guilt for what has befallen her daughter. If she can clear her name, she might be able to find the baby before it dies. This guilt and worry further exhaust her, and she must stand emotionally naked and vulnerable, pleading her case to deaf ears. Semple explains that while Hermoine trusts the gods implicitly, any number of human hands may have gotten hold of the Oracle between Delphos and Sicilia. Until Hermione hears it she cannot be sure of its truth. Finally, when Apollo clears her, the situation she must have feared occurs: Leontes rejects Apollo's truth and Hermione wonders, "What's going to happen now? Can it get worse?" When she grasps, in addition to her husband's accusing her and her daughter's being unaccounted for, that her son has died, the weight crushes her. Medically, Semple says, Hermione may be in shock, but in any case she looks dead.

Feore believes that Leontes thought he was providing a just and fair trail in which his actions would be vindicated. During Hermione's defense, he says, his emotions ranged from the pettiness of a wronged husband to the patience of a prosecutor looking for the confession that will seal his case. But underneath he also loves her and wonders how she could possibly have done this shameful deed to him. Because he loves her he is shocked to see how badly she has fared in prison, as attested to by her harrowing appearance.

By the time she arrives at the long list of injuries which made her content to die, Feore's Leontes has steeled himself by silently saying over and over, "I don't care." Semple attests to the difficulty of pleading her case to that brick wall, while fully supporting Feore's choice for the scene. Feore believes that once the Oracle's answer is read aloud, Leontes subconsciously registers that portion which says, "And the King shall live without an heir, if that which is lost be not found." Leontes then rushes down from the balcony to deny not only the truth of the Oracle but also the premonition of impending disaster. With the death of the son, Feore explains, the bottom has fallen out physically and emotionally for the now-repentant Leontes. Hermione's collapse into what he believes to be her death must show him being damned, muses Feore; he's stuck at the absolute bottom.

"Shame Perpetual" begins with Leontes face down upon the ground, a position Feore acknowledges may seem extreme but which he reassumes more sympathetically in V.1, set some sixteen years later. Leontes is then discovered in the chapel where he believes his wife and son lay buried. William explains that the critic Stark Young described a production of *Oedipus Rex* in which the full knowledge of what he has done compels Oedipus to prostrate himself upon the ground "as if wishing to return to the land he had defiled. And that

211

image of seeking, as it were, to relate so intensely that it becomes physical to the most basic part of the soil out of which you were created seemed to me what Leontes would do at that moment.'' When Paulina returns to the stage, after having left when Hermione was carried out, to announce her death, the text calls for her to turn on Leontes, listing all of his faults. Leontes' next line, addressed to her, reads: ''Go on, go on....'' He turns to the one person who has insisted on telling him the truth even at risk to herself, Feore explains contemplatively, even though to his conscious mind she must be the ''most unlikely character in the world to say, ''Sir, there is a way out.' '' William explains the shift in Paulina's conduct from her speech ending:

> ...*A thousand knees, Ten thousand years together, naked, fasting, Upon a barren mountain, and still winter In storm perpetual, could not move the gods To look that way thou wert....* III.2.208-212

to the speech less than four lines later beginning: ''I am sorry for't.'' He points out the difference between the conventional form of repentance that she thought he had put on and the posture and words, ''Go on, go on,'' which show him to be truly penitent. Feore says he hears Paulina tell him, in effect, ''I know that I exacerbated your problems, but I am the only one who can help you. I can see you understand; I didn't think you would....They are dead...let's go on and see what we can do.'' Feore explains that Leontes cannot face that truth yet accepts her help.

For Wright, the problem during this scene is having to remain silent for so long. Paulina makes ringing declarations at the conclusion of the scene but can say nothing until after Hermione faints. Wright explains Paulina has no power against the injustice of Leontes but she feels anger toward him and trusts that the Oracle's answer will eventually make everything right. Using the sense of the anger pent up inside Paulina, during one rehearsal Wright called the ladies together and told them the men assigned to carry out Hermione should not be allowed to. So the women asserted themselves by rising up as if to protect the queen and then lovingly bore her out themselves. William approved the business and left it in.

Feore, Semple, and Wright had independently reached the same conclusion about the offstage action that occurs next, in which this unlikely pair has gone to see the bodies. They reasoned that Hermione's revival from her death-like swoon occurs at some later point. These speculations affected Wright's performance, because as Paulina she believed Hermione dead during her confrontation with the king. The transition from a cursing to a supportive Paulina proved a very difficult one for Wright. She can explain it in terms of bawling somebody out until that person breaks down and starts to cry, and then, Wright explains, ''You say to yourself, 'What have I done?' ''

She says she came to the realization as Paulina that making Leontes suffer was not her job. "I should not be the instrument to give this man this agony."

Act III, Scene 3

Act III, Scene 3, was composed of two parts, Scene 15, "Antigonus' Dream" (pp. 100-102), and Scene 16, "Lucky Day" (pp. 102-104). "Antigonus' Dream" begins on a bare and foggy stage with the *Kinderszenen* theme music greatly distorted. Antigonus and the Mariner enter from the stage right vomitorium. Needles finds significance in Antigonus' willingness to carry the baby ashore in Bohemia despite a prophetic vision of his own death in a dream. He says that although Perdita would have perished when the ship went down, Antigonus places her in dreadful circumstances and pleads with earnestness to the gods for her survival, keeping true to his duty and his honour. After Antigonus has revealed his dream, he encounters the murderous bear. As brief and dark as the moment was, it almost always drew a laugh.

"Lucky Day" drastically shifts the mood of the play as it introduces the Old Shepherd (Maurice Good) and his son (Benedict Campbell), who find the baby. Good explains that while the Old Shepherd comes in to look for his lost sheep, the actor inside always reminded him to make every word clear to all parts of the house. (Several of the actors note this concern for technique above the demands of the characterization.) Good also posits the similarity of the Old Shepherd to Lord Cerimon, whom he played in *Pericles*. Both characters come on just before the intermission and pose a new challenge to the audience that the actor must solve by telling at once and in generalities the character's chief concerns.

Intermission follows this scene. Once the Old Shepherd finds the baby and the gold, Good says, he loses interest in finding his sheep, but the gold does not change him, as the second half of the play reveals. Campbell had to temper the Young Shepherd's joy at finding the baby and the gold with his sympathy for the men on the ship who have drowned and his horror at seeing Antigonus eaten by a bear. At the end of Part One, William said one day in rehearsal, the audience ought to think that with the birth of the baby, perhaps this circle of violence, jealousy, and crime can be broken and a new order established. To reinforce this feeling of hope, Carriere provided a moment of the theme music followed by a chord in what he describes as a very Wagnerian, Parsifal-like manner to move out of the storm and into the bright light. William asked Frehner to provide lighting reminscent of a "ray of hope."

Act IV, Scene 1

Act IV, Scene 1, played as one unit called Scene 17, "Wide Gap" (pp. 104-105), composed entirely of the character Time's soliloquy beginning,

"Imagine sixteen years have passed...." Carriere reintroduced the string quartet for Time but with the theme rearranged and reorchestrated to give it a different sound. Blake explains that William had cut much of Time's speech--including the joke Shakespeare may have written about his own acting ability, if he played Time as legend accords--to pare the speech down. These lines include:

...Of this allow If ever you have spent time worse ere now; If never, yet that Time himself doth say He wishes earnestly you never may.
IV.1.29-32

Act IV, Scene 1

Act IV, Scene 1, played as one unit, Scene 18, "Thoughts of Sicilia" (pp. 106-107) which opened with what William called a moment of reflection as Camillo looked upon the portraits of Leontes and Hermione, desiring to return home. To underline those feelings, Carriere provided a very soft version of the theme with the clarinet as the dominant instrument. Pennell says that he completely understands the character's need to "return to his roots" as he gets older. Besides, he adds, the son of Polixenes, Prince Florizel, has grown up, and Camillo's duties have lessened. The scene opens with Camillo reading a letter from Leontes asking him to return. Feore, not having spoken to Pennell about the matter of the letters, acknowledges that he does not know how many Pennell's Camillo has received, but he does know his Leontes has sent quite a number of them. Pennell agrees and adds that the letters have grown steadily more pleading in their tone as they urge Camillo to return home.

As Polixenes listens to Camillo, Russell says, he is hurt that his old friend Leontes has not written to him as well. Although Sicilia has receded in his thoughts in the intervening years, there remains some torment for Polixenes. Russell believes that his queen has died and he alone must take responsibility for his son, whom he sets out to find at the sheep-shearing. Memories of Sicilia lead to his harsh actions once the wayward prince is located.

Act IV, Scene 3

Act IV, Scene 3, was composed of one part, Scene 19, "A Merry Heart" (pp. 107-111), which was set simply on a road. The scene begins with a soliloquy by Autolycus, whom William describes as the vinegar of the piece. Actor Joe Ziegler remembers auditioning for the part in November in Toronto for William, who asked him to tell some jokes--but Ziegler could not remember any. As the audition progressed William asked him if he knew the work of English comedian Max Miller. The comedian uses a lot of double entendres and calls the audience dirty- minded when they respond. Ziegler understood that William wanted from him "the word patter of the comedian."

Ziegler says that the character has to play to two audiences, that on the stage and that in the house. The soliloquy of the first scene gives him a chance to establish those relationships and show himself to be a consummate con artist. The Young Shepherd's sincere desire to help sets up the comedy of Autolycus' robbing him. Campbell and Ziegler, who worked together previously, say they enjoy playing off the creativity of each other.

Act IV, Scene 4

Act IV, Scene 4, was composed of seven scenes: Scene 20, "Unusual Weeds" (pp. 111-113); Scene 21, "Flowers" (pp. 113-118); Scene 22, "Ribbons" (pp. 118-123); Scene 23, "Your Divorce" (pp. 123-127); Scene 24, "A Course More Promising" (pp. 127-132); Scene 25, "Exchanges" (pp. 132-135); and Scene 26, "Fardel" (pp. 135-140). "Unusual Weeds" takes place during the sheep-shearing celebration, as does the whole of Shakespeare's Act IV, Scene 4, in this production. A huge straw statue of the harvest goddess dominated the scene from atop the balcony, and tables loaded with food covered the area underneath it. Harvest baskets brimming with ripe produce, from which protruded shepherds' crooks tied with bright bows, lined the steps around the forestage.

The scene introduces Prince Florizel, who has fallen in love with the Old Shepherd's daughter, Perdita. Burns says the key to her performance as Perdita in the beginning of this scene is the mixture of being in love and being in love with a prince of the realm--the excitement tinged with danger. "You can't just play one and then the other," she comments. "You have to play them both all the time." For example, she says that Perdita truly loves but at the same time fears this arrangement will not work; "It breaks my heart, but it isn't going to work." Burns admires Perdita's ability to remain practical in the midst of being in love, commenting that she demonstrates that strength in her first appearance in the play. Keith Thomas (Florizel) remembers the acting exercises in which William had the performers look into each others' eyes and grow faint with love for one another. He too understands that this romance will have drastic consequences, for a prince cannot marry a commoner. But, says Thomas, Florizel's love for Peridita overrules everything else at this moment.

The large Bohemian crowd enters in costumes of light brown, tan, or green. Kerwin says most costume items were pulled from stock if in the proper colours; they could fall fifty years on either side of the period and still be used. She notes that costumes were not pulled straight into the show but were altered to match a skirt with a different bodice or add new trim. William's idea for this sheep-shearing party was that these people wore what they

215

would have worn every day but decorated themselves by adding bits of coloured ribbon to their clothing, their harvest goddess, and even their everyday implements.

In "Flowers" the Old Shepherd presides over the harvest festivities. Good explains that while he now leads the life of a country squire, it is not from the gold he discovered with Peridita. The actor sees his character as going about his work of planting and harvesting as he always has, and he takes joy in his daughter's serving as hostess. For the dance in this scene, Carriere and choreographer John Broome focused on combinations of the theme, repetitions of it, and the tempo of each. Broome selected a polonaise, and Carriere created the sound of a country band using the same fifteen-piece orchestra he had used so regally for the Sicilian court. Carriere emphasized acoustical guitar and woodwinds in this dance that begins slowly but soon erupts all over the stage.

Once Polixenes and Camillo arrive at the celebration, Russell believes, Polixenes becomes enchanted with Perdita to the point that he almost forgets that he has come here to see how Florizel spends his time. Once he sees the strong attraction between the prince and Peridita, he decides to watch and see how serious this affair has become. The two lovers walk to the top of the balcony for some privacy, characterized by Burns as Perdita tossing aside her practicality by assuring Florizel, "Yes, I do love you, and I'll do anything to be with you." Thomas says that by this point in the play his prince has made up his mind to marry Peridita, no matter what the consequences. "From that point on he never looks back," concludes the actor.

"Ribbons" begins with a peasant rushing in to announce the approach of the peddler, Autoylcus, in a disguise Ziegler describes as like those "of those people who kidnapped Pinocchio." Autoylcus drives on from up center a cycle-cart, which caused a considerable bang as it rolled off of the step and onto the top platform. At a flick of the wrist the back of the cart flew open to expose an elaborate display of trinkets and ribbons for sale. But this peddler keeps his eyes on wallets to be picked later. The Young Shepherd spies his father and Polixenes in conversation, and the crowd carries cart and peddler off stage. "Your Divorce" begins with Polixenes calling Florizel down from the balcony. He explodes, saying rash things and hurting Florizel just as Leontes hurt Hermione. According to William, Polixenes' tyranny here is a "moral" one, whose consequences are not so devastating.

"A Course More Promising" begins after the Old Shepherd has also denounced Perdita. Thomas belives Florizel and his father have shared an excellent relationship; that history impels him to cement the relationship with Peridita. Burns says that when the worst befalls Perdita, when Polixenes discovers their secret and threatens her and her family, Perdita does lose courage momentarily. But she takes her strength from Florizel. Burns had to work through the sweetness and innocence of the character on the one hand and her great strength and determination on the other. Pennell sees the plan hatched by Camillo to send this pair of lovers to Leontes as more than a selfish plot to help Camillo attain his own purpose of returning home. The actor cites motivations of the heart rather than those of the intellect in planning the match of Florizel and Peridita and the rematch of Leontes and Polixenes.

The "Exchanges" scene simply provides the means of escape for Floziel and Peridita by Camillo's forcing the exchange of clothes between Autolycus and the prince. But Autolycus fears discovery of the stolen purses hidden under his clothing. William suggested in rehearsal that he react like an old maid taking off her clothes in front of someone else. Ziegler worked out a routine of comic squeaks and hysterics that forced Camillo, Perdita, and Florizel to turn their backs while the exchange took place.

In "Fardel" the shepherds decide to take the fardel and gold that came with Perdita to Polixenes. Autolycus waylays them: Dressed as as gentleman, he impresses the shepherds and trades information that the king has boarded a ship and intends to sail to Sicilia for some of the shepherds' gold. Ziegler adds that his character's real purpose is to help his former master, Florizel, but because Shakespeare does not make that point clearly he played the character as an opportunist. His last line encourages them to head toward the boat: "I will but look upon the hedge, and follow you." (IV.4.819-820) As they leave Autolycus turns and relieves himself on the upstage center post of the theatre. Ziegler says that the action fit the character in that Autolycus acts somewhat sacrilegious at times, and "nothing could be more sacrilegious than peeing on a stage pillar of the Stratford Festival Stage!"

Act V, Scene 1

Act V, Scene 1, was composed of two scenes, Scene 27, "Saint-Like Sorrow" (pp. 140-145), and Scene 28, "The Daughter of a King" (pp. 145-149). "Saint-Like Sorrows" opens in the chapel that Leontes had promised to build for his wife and son at the end of the trial scene (III.2). William explains that Leontes has spent the intervening sixteen years in a philosophical mood:

> What all religions have in common--never mind dogma or ritual,
> but what they all seem to have in common--is the understanding that
> we are capable of good and we are capable of evil, but when we have
> performed evil it is possible not to unperform it but...to make some
> kind of amends in society's eyes and, more importantly in God's

eyes, for the wrong one has done.

Feore says metaphorically that Leontes has moved "to the winter palace and packed lots of sackcloth." He believes the character has turned religious, read the Oracle's answer many times over, and written repeatedly without reply to Camillio in Bohemia. He theorizes that immediately after the trial Leontes wrote official proclamations clearing Polixenes and Camillo, but that for several years no other communication was possible. Now he has begun to write to his old friend again because he wants to see him.

He also thinks that if Leontes has repeatedly sent out emissaries to try to find the daughter his repentance has more credibility than if he has simply made inquiries or, worse yet, done nothing. Feore acknowledges this point can't be played, but if Leontes hasn't been persistent, forgiveness can't come yet because, as painful as his repentance has been, "It isn't enough yet."

Paulina has been his companion and has prescribed much of the course that Leontes follows. But Paulina also has the relationship with Hermione, who has lived secluded for sixteen years. Semple speculates that Hermione has taken this long time to get over the physical and psychological hurt. She believes that Hermione has had some say in when she will be reunited with Leontes but that obviously she must rely to a large degree on Paulina's reports of his pilgrimage of repentance.

The chapel where the audience again sees Leontes and in which Leontes receives Perdita and Florizel contains two rectangular marble monuments with the recumbent likenesses of Hermione and Mamillius carved on the tops. Kerwin says that William wanted the audience to think Hermione has died: Seeing the carving of her would contribute to that illusion as well as setting up the "statue scene" at the end of the play. A row of nine lighted candles on a railing appeared in front of the monuments. Three other railings that held nine simulated candles created the atmosphere of a chapel. Cleomenes and Dion, worried about the succession, have pushed Leontes to marry again, and Feore imagines that they have a number of princesses lined up for him. Wright believes that although Paulina doesn't show it, she is worried because revolution is brewing over the issue of succession. She says that Paulina has even had to force Leontes to swear he will not marry again without her consent. To Wright the necessity for the vow indicates that things are getting out of hand. If news had not come of Prince Florizel and his "princess" very quickly, Paulina might have had to produce Hermione sooner. William says simply, "The curse of the Oracle is lifted; Perdita has come home."

At the moment of the announcement that Prince Florizel has arrived, Feore believes, Leontes has faced the painful consequences of his rash actions in the solitude of the chapel but has not yet found a way of atoning to

Polixenes. Now he can meet him through Prince Florizel but must also face the ghost of another young prince, whom he is similiarly unprepared to meet, his own son. But Paulina speaks of him, thereby provoking the confrontation, although Leontes asks her to cease. William reminded the cast that "Purification comes when the wounds bleed afresh," and somehow Paulina knows that, Wright says. William marvels that without knowing any modern psychology Shakespeare was unerringly right in his choices for his characters. Feore explains that his Leontes wants Paulina to cease asking about his son because he has a hard enough task confronting him, welcoming Florizel and confessing to him the wrong he has done Polixenes.

"The Daughter of a King"(pp. 145-149) begins with the entrance of Florizel and Perdita at which Leontes nearly breaks down in gratitude after hearing the message of love from Polixenes--which Florizel has made up. William notes that even though the prince speaks untruthfully about himself, Polixenes' affection for Leontes emerges as truth. When Leontes then learns that Polixenes and Camillo have arrived he is thrilled, says William, because for the first time he can hope for a reconciliation which, if he can effect, he feels reasonably sure he can extend to the the young lovers. William points to Leontes' willingness to help this pair as an indication that "he has learned a lesson." Then because the lines in which Leontes sees Hermione in Perdita were cut, Feore built in a look at Burns in which he silently says: "Don't I know you? Haven't we met somewhere?" Thomas says that when Florizel hears of the arrival of Polixenes and Camillo, he immediately realizes that Camillo has betrayed them but cannot understand why "honest Camillo" would do so. Florizel now sees the prospect of marriage slipping away. Burns says Perdita, who wants this marriage as much as Florizel does, senses danger in the approach of Polixenes.

Act V, Scene 2

Act V, Scene 2, contained two scenes set in a street, Scene 29, "An Old Tale Still" (pp. 149-153), and Scene 30, "Gentleman Born" (pp. 152-154). During the first of these scenes, Ziegler says, Autoylcus tries desperately to find someone to tell him what has happened in the off stage action when the two shepherds showed the two kings the empty fardel and the gold, which establish Perdita's identity. Pennell compares *Pericles* with *The Winter's Tale* to note that the audience does not get to see a reunion scene. But this play does show the reunion between husband and wife which, Pennell says, *Pericles* does only briefly and therefore less satisfactorily. John Innes, who played one of the lords pestered by Autoylcus for information, explains that he began playing the role in rehearsal as if he wanted to get rid of Autoylcus by telling him whatever he needed to know to make him leave. But gradually that

219

interpretation changed as the character became so caught up in the wonder and power of that reunion that he could not wait to tell about what he had seen. Thomas also expresses sorrow at not discovering Perdita's true parentage in an on-stage scene:

> He calls her a queen so many times during the course of the play that it's a shame I don't get to play my joy in seeing my judgment affirmed by all.

"Gentleman Born" is a comic scene placed by Shakespeare just before the final scene in which he pulled together all the treads of the play. The Old and Young Shepherds--dressed in three-piece suits with vests of the worst of nouveau rich taste, complete with top hats askew and canes pointing in all directions--are attacked for information by Autolycus. Zielger decided to play Autoylcus as penniless and therefore with everything at stake. Campbell established the Young Shepherd as a character who always had a flask in his pocket, beginning this scene "wobbly." The shepherds recognize Autolycus and forgive his part in their deception, perhaps to foreshadow the forgiveness to come in the next scene. Autolycus returns the forgiveness with a hearty embrace of his own while picking the watch from the Young Shepherd's pocket--the opportunist to the end, says Ziegler. At the end of the scene Carriere provided the sound of a distant carriage pulling away with the court party on the way to see the statue.

Act V, Scene 3

Act V, Scene 3, played as one unit, Scene 31, "Statue" (pp. 155-160). The music for the statue scene repeated the theme, this time with the oboe dominant over the strings and piano. The music underscored the scene for two minutes and twenty seconds and played very softly under Wright's first speech. Before "Statue" begins, Feore explains, Leontes has been joyously reunited with his daughter, Polixenes, and Camillo. But great sorrow underlies the offstage scene because the three people aren't there who ought to be: Hermione, Mamillius, and Antigonus are absent because they died as a result of Leontes' actions. So, says Feore, "He is torn between joy and grief....He is absolutely torn....The pins are very loosely marked and when he [Shakespeare] pulls them out Pinocchio falls apart....All of that has to be borne before we can walk into that room...sort of a running undercurrent. That's how we begin the scene."

He considers that Paulina has very recently had her steward put out "the Julio Romano rumours", and therefore Leontes has only recently heard of the statue. He says he comes to show Perdita her mother but acknowledges that in his joy he wants to see it and yet does not want to. He describes the

states through which his Leontes passes in the final scene. At first believing
absolutely that the statue is a statue, he gradually gives play to emotion and
wishes it were real so it can chide him for having done wrong. The longer
the scene goes on the more emotionally confused he gets, so that he thinks
he can see the statue moving. Paulina increases the stakes as she can see
he is receptive by saying, "I can make it move," until he believes himself
to be having a mystical experience and expects Hermione to speak to him
from beyond the grave. Finally, having gone through the sins of the past
and this time feeling forgiveness, he is ready when Paulina says, "It is required
that you do awake your faith." He answers very faintly under his breath,
"Yes." Feore remarks that after the statue comes to life he has almost no
lines which establish a relationship between them but rather must tie up the
loose ends by introducing Florizel and uniting Paulina and Camillo. He says
of Leontes's absence of speech to Hermione, "There is nothing to say that
I haven't already told the statue." But there is significance for the actor in
Leontes' call to Paulina to lead them hence just as he called on her to lead
him from the end of the trial scene. Paulina leads them arm and arm up the
balcony steps, where Time receives them as he received the children after
the prologue.

For Wright's Paulina, the last scene also contains several mood shifts.
She starts the scene with a mixture of joy undercoated with sorrow because
"It is too profound just to be joy." She has come to believe that "We are
giving the audience this incredible treat," and therefore she can hardly wait
for the scene to come. She rubs her hands together with great relish just
recalling her satisfaction in underscoring the reunion scene. She credits William
with helping her find the wide vocal range necessary to do the last scene
and find something in Paulina that made her a kind of priestess. "She is herself
transported. Her life's pilgrimage is nearing its completion."

But once Paulina has bestowed her wonderful gift, Wright says,
Shakespeare brings her right back down to earth again by giving her a line
that says in effect, "Don't worry about me; I'm just going out under the tree
and cry." Pennell's Camillo reached out for Paulina just after she passed him.
Though he never made contact, the movement helped make Leontes' gift of
her to Camillo plausible. Wright says she and Pennell had built nothing into
the play earlier to suggest this kind of union but she had noticed that in
performance Pennell had started to look at her more intently in the first act.
Wright did not find not the transition from priestess to neglected old aunt
a difficult one. She believes that Paulina, who had built a meaningful
relationship with Leontes and a secret and wonderful relationship with
Hermione, does not realize until the moment after the reunion that she now
has no place to turn. "I'm not a member of this family and I am suddenly

very lonely." The Paulina/Camillo union had originally been cut, but Wright, who had been moved by it when she first read the play, reinserted it into rehearsal one day and William restored it to the text. Pennell also wanted the scene restored. These two are the "wise people" of this play, each working in his/her own way to make the reunion between husband and wife a reality, and the actor believes that their union at the end is worth the risk of an occasional laugh to heighten the level of reconciliation that he finds "rising like yeast" and reinforcing the mythic qualities of the play in this moment.

The miracle of making a statue come to life owes something to stagecraft, in addition to acting. Usually Semple was raised to the forestage on a hydraulic lift, in statuesque position and carefully lit, but in a June performance the lift would not operate through the trapdoor. Semple hurried up from the underworld and stood under the balcony, where assistant stage manager Ann Stewart placed the covering over her. Paulina, Leontes, and the others had taken their places on the upper portion of the balcony, and there was no way to relay to them that Semple was standing under them rather than out on the forestage. So when Paulina led the others down from the balcony and began to deliver the line, "But here it is," she suddenly realized Hermione was not there at all. Wright stretched the word "is" into several syllables before finally locating the statue--a few seconds that felt like an eternity, Wright says.

Semple finds Shakespeare's choice of Julio Romano as the possible sculptor of the statue an interesting one because some of Romano's contemporaries were doing paintings in which the statues looked like people and the people looked like statues. The question of Paulina as a white witch who has the miraculous power to turn a statue into a person presents another question: Does the miracle occur in Leontes because he is now ready for it to happen? The actor see the miracle as internal in Leontes and hinging on Paulina's line "It is required that you do awake your faith." But word of mouth periodically reached the cast that audiences believed Paulina responsible for bringing her to life. During the statue scene, Semple says, she often wondered if Hermione had to suffer for sixteen years for loving a mortal thing, Leontes, too much. As for being a statue, she points out that Hermione may be used to posing because she may have, according to lines cut from the script, resided in Romano's house for all those years. Semple practiced standing still by keeping her position in rehearsal even when the scene was run several times. Sometimes, she says, she did not move for as much as twenty minutes, longer than she needed to remain motionless in this scene. Another problem she cites is concentrating to avoid becoming so involved in the scene that she cries when Perdita speaks to her. As she played the scene, Semple first noticed how changed Leontes was after so many years. What Semple felt from Feore was shame, inspiring her desire to comfort him. While she is reunited with Leontes, the first and only line is to her daughter, about whom she has worried and wondered for so long. There is great joy at the end, but Semple believes the life these characters will lead must of necessity be very different. She thinks they do attain the state of grace again--expressed by linking arms and walking up the steps as the children did in the beginning.

Burns used to sit in the auditorium watching and rewatching Part One of this production--in which she does not appear except as one of William's twenty-three priests--for clues from Leontes and Hermione about who she is. There she found the stubbornness and innocence that Perdita exhibited in Part Two confirmed in the characters of Part One. The final scene for her offers an opportunity to find out who she really is. Although reunited with Leontes, her Perdita knows the minute she looks at the statue that it is her mother. Her line to the statue ending with "Give me that hand of yours to kiss!" Burns interprets very realistically. She points to the manner in which children engaged in a game suddenly become intent on the truth in the fantasy. She says Perdita similarly knows Hermione is real, and her search for self has ended.

For Russell's Polixenes the ending is bittersweet. He finds himself restored to his old friend, but Camillo will certainly stay in Sicilia with Paulina, and Florizel will leave home when he marries. Perhaps to allay such particular concerns William chose to elevate the ending to embrace the universal rather than just this particular set of circumstances. At the end of the scene the adults join hands and walk up the stairs toward Time, who leads them upward. Carriere, having associated Time with strings, began the ascent with the underscoring by a piano, which swelled into a full complement of strings. Time, says William, ushers them "out of the balcony door and into the presence of God."

PERICLES

BY WILLIAM SHAKESPEARE

DIRECTED BY	RICHARD OUZOUNIAN
DESIGNED BY	PATRICK CLARK
MUSIC BY	CHARLES AND JOHN GRAY
LIGHTING DESIGNED BY	HARRY FREHNER
FIGHTS DIRECTED BY	JEAN-PIERRE FOURNIER
DANCES CHOREOGRAPHED BY	JOHN BROOME

THE CAST

in order of appearance

Gower	RENEE ROGERS
Antiochus, King of Antioch	NICHOLAS PENNELL
Pericles, Prince of Tyre	GERAINT WYN DAVIES
Daughter of Antiochus	TANYA RICH
Thaliard, a lord of Antioch	STEPHEN RUSSELL
Messenger	SHANE KELLY
Helicanus Lords	JOHN INNES
Escanes of Tyre	WILLIAM SAMPLES
First Lord of Tyre	MICHAEL SHEPHERD
Second Lord of Tyre	BRENT STAIT
Third Lord of Tyre	DALE MIESKE
Cleon, Governor of Tarsus	JEREMY WILKIN
Dionyza, wife of Cleon	CAROLINE YEAGER
Leonine	JOHN BOURGEOIS
First Fisherman	MICHAEL SHEPHERD
Second Fisherman	KERRY DOREY
Third Fisherman	WILLIAM SAMPLES
Simonides, King of Pentapolis	WILLIAM NEEDLES
Thaisa, daughter of Simonides	GOLDIE SEMPLE
Lychorida, nurse to Thaisa	MARTHA BURNS
First Lord of Pentapolis	JOHN BOURGEOIS
Second Lord of Pentapolis	NEIL FOSTER
Knights	ERIC COATES, KERRY DOREY, ERIC McCORMACK, MAX REIMER
Sailor	DALE MIESKE
Cerimon, a Lord of Ephesus	MAURICE GOOD
Poor Man	MAX REIMER
Philemon	SHANE KELLY
First Gentleman of Ephesus	NEIL FOSTER
Second Gentleman of Ephesus	ERIC McCORMACK
Marina, daughter of Pericles	KIM HORSMAN
Philoten, daughter of Cleon	LESLIE TOY
First Pirate	DALE MIESKE
Second Pirate	MAX REIMER
Third Pirate	BRENT STAIT
Pander	WILLIAM NEEDLES
Bawd	MARIA VACRATSIS
Boult	NICHOLAS PENNELL
Lysimachus, Governor of Mytilene	JOSEPH ZIEGLER
Lysimachus Soldier	KERRY DOREY
Diana, Goddess of Chastity	LESLIE TOY

Gentlemen, lords, ladies, attendants, servants, sailors, pirates, priestesses, courtesans:
WENDY ABBOTT, TANYA RICH, LESLIE TOY, PAULA WING, EDWARD BALKA,
PAUL BOND, ERIC COATES, KERRY DOREY, DARCY GORDON, SHANE KELLY,
ERIC McCORMACK, DALE MIESKE, MAX REIMER, BRENT STAIT

Stage Manager	HILARY GRAHAM
Assistant Stage Managers	ANN STUART
	LAUREN SNELL
Assistant Director	CHARLES McFARLAND
Assistant Designer	JESSICA BLACKMORE
Assistant Lighting Designer	KEVIN FRASER

Please Note: There will be a Strobe effect in this production.

"Now blessings on thee! Rise; thou art my
child." *Pericles* V.1.

Chapter Ten: *Pericles*

Rehearsals for *Pericles* began on 4 March, 1986, in Rehearsal Hall 3 in
the basement of the Festival Theatre in the same space where four weeks
earlier *The Boys From Syracuse* had begun its odyssey. Director Richard
Ouzounian, the only freshman to direct on the Festival Stage in 1986, began
his journey to Stratford with an M.A. degree from the University of British
Columbia in Vancouver. His thesis production, *Much Ado about Nothing*,
featured four actors who appeared at Stratford during the 1986 season: Goldie
Semple and John Innes of the Festival Company and Lorne Kennedy and Brent
Carver of the Avon Company. Ouzounian met Neville when the latter attended
a performance of *Jacques Brel Is Alive And Well And Living in Paris* that the
former had directed at the Citadel, where Neville had been appointed artistic
director but at the time had not yet taken over. The two spent an evening
in conversation following the production, and two weeks later Ouzounian
received a call from the theatre administrator at the Citadel asking him to
join the staff for the year as Neville's assistant. He was to direct *The Caretaker*
and serve as assistant director under Neville for *Much Ado about Nothing*,
with the rest of the season to be worked out.

The night before rehearsals for *Much Ado* began, Ouzounian explains,
Neville confided that he would be quite busy playing Benedick and directing,
so asked Ouzounian to direct the comic scenes. When veteran actors such
as Eric Donkin (Stratford's 1986 Cymbeline) and Douglas Chamberlain (who
spent 1986 at the Shaw Festival) showed up for their scenes expecting Neville,
a 23-year-old Ouzounian greeted them instead. That year Ouzounian also
directed Neville in a production of *Child's Play*, which Neville describes as
"a rather good thriller." Ouzounian explains that he learned much about
producing Shakespeare from Neville, who taught him his willingness to take
a risk and a faithfulness to the text. Those statements may sound
contradictory: Ouzounian explains the seeming dichotomy by saying that he
learned from Neville to begin by thinking about the best way to get
Shakespeare's message across to an audience, pointing to a production of
The Taming of the Shrew in modern dress that Neville did in Halifax

when artistic director at the Neptune Theatre. But once the period and style are chosen, he says, the emphasis must be put on a faithful production of the text.

Still Ouzounian confesses surprise when Neville sat down with him to go over the Stratford Festival's 1986 season and offer him a directing slot. Ouzounian read the shows and was attracted by several of them but eventually chose *Pericles*, remembering Gascon's 1972 production with Nicholas Pennell as Pericles, a production popular enough to warrant repeating during the 1973 season. Ouzounian confesses being "drawn to those father, mother, daughter things" that for him composed "the emotional heart of the play." And in the final analysis, he says, "It's a damn good play." So in late April he told Neville he thought he was the man to tackle *Pericles*. In late May, Neville came to Toronto and had dinner with the Ouzounians and as he was leaving told Ouzounian that he began rehearsals on 4 March. "That," says Ouzounian, grinning, "was how I found out."

When they began to discuss the production, the first thing Ouzounian told Neville was that he wanted the narrative speeches of Gower set to music and sung by a black woman. Neville, who had done a production of *Measure for Measure* at Nottingham Playhouse in the mid-Sixties with music by Johnny Dankworth and Cleo Lane, immediately understood what Ouzounian wanted. But he confesses:

> Before everyone thinks this is so revolutionary, Tony Richardson did a production of Pericles in the late Fifties in England...where Gower...was kind of chanted by a black Calypso singer....So the whole idea of Gower being done a little off center and being done interracially was not new. But I felt it was crucial because of the climate of the play that it be something non-Anglo-Saxon. And I also felt because of the strong female currents in the play that it be a woman....The next choice was John Gray to do the music.

That was the point from which the production began. He had known John Gray for 15 years from the same UBC group and had directed many of Gray's plays in the years since university, but what he most repected, he says, was Gray's "ability to write story songs"--in some ways he is considered a balladier in a rock music vein. Gray, author of a number of successful shows--among them *Billy Bishop Goes to War*, *Rock and Roll*, *18 Wheels*, and *Don Messer's Jubilee*--read the play at Ouzounian's suggestion with the reaction, "Richard, what are you going to do with this?" Ouzounian replied that he wanted "a pop epic for our time" which might look as if Cecil B. DeMille had done it. As the ideas formed in his mind, Ouzounian explained the parameters of the production to Gray over the telephone. He didn't want the production to sway toward the frivolous on one hand or the lugubrious on the other. Nor did he want it to dip toward "camp" at one end of the spectrum or toward "oratory" at the other end.

At Christmas 1985 Gray met Ouzounian in Calgary to review designer Patrick Clark's costume sketches to help give Gray a feel for the show as he saw it. He laughs about the sight the two of them must have presented in the bar where they met, on the Saturday before Christmas, listening to "weird Middle Eastern music" on a tape recorder and giggling at sketches they showed one another. For nearly four hours they talked through the position and content of each sound cue. Gray provided three pieces of music at that initial meeting, two of which played in the show: the themes for Antiochus' entrance and for the brothel scene. He had also provided a theme for Pericles, but that piece proved " too camp." Eight weeks later, just before rehearsals began, the sound tape arrived from Gray with all the music cues for the instrumental numbers and most of the music cues for the vocals, only three of which had to be redone. Because Gray had written music he himself could sing with the piano, some small reworkings of Gower's numbers proved useful for this production that featured a woman singer. These rearrangements were done by the actress playing Gower, Renee Rogers; the pianist, Laura Burton, who is herself a composer; and Ouzounian. Gray accepted these slight alterations. Eventually Gray composed the music that his brother Charles orchestrated, earning them dual credit for the musical score.

Neville suggested designer Patrick Clark because he had a classics major at the University of New Brunswick and had assisted Desmond Heeley with the 1981 production of *Coriolanus* done in a Roman style, which had favorably impressed Ouzounian. He believed another of Clark's advantages lay in his knowledge of the Stratford machinery. Clark had also worked as a design assistant to David Walker in costumes for *Blithe Spirit*, 1982, and *Romeo and Juliet*, 1983, as well as design assistant to Susan Benson for *The Pirates of Penzance*, 1985. In addition he had designed sets and costumes for the Third Stage production of *A Midsummer Night's Dream*, 1982. During the 1985 season he presented his résumé to Neville and asked to be invited to design a show the following season, hoping at best, he says, to be given the small late season opener at the Avon, which during the 1984 and 1985 seasons had been Tennessee Williams shows with "nine costumes," Clark recalls. Instead he was offered *Pericles*, which he immediately accepted.

The design process began with a search for the proper time period. Ouzounian at first thought of showing the timelessness of the piece by doing each of the six countries in which the play takes place in a different epoch-- e.g., Tarsus as Depression-era America, Antioch as Berlin of the 1930s, and Mytilene as the brothels of Victorian England. He later realized that such a decision would draw attention to itself and not the play, but he and Clark did some initial work along this line. Clark then came back with what Ouzounian calls an intellectual approach, which involved staging the play as if Eighteenth Century aristocrats were watching a play being performed, an approach Clark had seen in the staging of the Handel opera *Xerxes*. An Eighteenth Century style would have helped Clark meet his mandate of pulling twenty-five percent of the costumes from stock, but the director felt this approach had very little to do with the emotions he wanted and the look of *The Ten Commandments* being done today. He suggested Clark rent the video of this 1950s production; he wanted to find a way for this production to take itself as seriously in the 1980s as that one had taken itself thirty years earlier. Clark says that the idea caused him to readjust his thinking a bit because he came from the English tradition of doing research to see what fabrics were in use at the time. If they were to begin from a DeMille base, says Clark, that meant "shoulder pads, push-up bras, and sequins," the ancient world as it never existed outside of American movie lots.

During their second conference they agreed to use of the ancient world setting because all of the locations Shakespeare names existed in classical times and the names are vaguely Greek. By medieval times, those place names and character names had begun to disappear. Clark thinks of the period as 500-600 A.D. because there are both Christian and pagan references in the play--a time of transition. As an example Clark points to the statue of Diana in the last scene. The virgin goddess, he says, is easily confused with the Virgin and the actual statue he designed was chaste enough in appearance to resemble either. Clark also liked the period because it gave him the opportunity to pull costumes from the Roman shows done over many seasons and from some productions of the Scottish tragedy. Both Ouzounian and Clark stress the fable or story tale element of the play, yet both wanted to ground this story in time and place rather than letting it wander off into "Never Never Land." Clark stresses that because the audience doesn't know the fashions of these six different locations during the Sixth Century A.D., enormous liberties could be and were taken with some of the costuming but that the production started from this larger-than-life techicolour concept, yet a "real base, all the same."

The first designs Clark brought in depicted Antiochus' soldiers. Ouzounian said, "That's the court of Antioch. That's the spirit. It's very theatrical. It's larger than life. It's operatic." "But," says the director, "I think there is nothing wrong with bold classical theatre being operatic." Once the concept was established in their minds, they worked on each character and scene to assure that the production "wasn't all flash, but had something underneath it." Once they hit on the concept, Ouzounian says, he hardly ever rejected a design. By August 1985 they had arrived at the style of visual presentation desired, and by mid-October final designs for most costumes had been approved by the director and submitted to the Festival. Lighting designer Harry Frehner, who lives in New Brunswick, travelled the short distance to Halifax to meet with Ouzounian in February 1986. That conference took two directions: a scene-by-scene discussion of the look he wanted as well as a review of specific techniques which Frehner had previously used in the 1975 production of *Measure for Measure*. Ouzounian explained his goal for the visual style of the show as "an operatic tour of the Middle East." That Frehner should reinforce the colour coding with the lighting represented a more important consideration for Ouzounian than did the specific time of day of any scene. In addition, the director explained the desired mood of each location in the play.

In casting, Ouzounian asked for Goldie Semple to play Thaisa and Kim Horsman to play Marina. Fortunately both were available. For the title role Ouzounian originally wanted a star, and his first choice was Richard Chamberlain, whose *Richard II* Ouzounian had seen in Seattle, but Chamberlain was not available. The next choice was Mel Gibson, "to play a Mad Max subtext in places." Ouzounian says that over the years he has found that pop culture production values work best to:

> *inform from underneath...and if we think Mad Max, Tina Turner, and Mel Gibson, that gives us some of the energy we need to enliven it, but if we put that literally on the stage, it can cheapen it.*

The tournament scene came easily to his mind as one in which such a subtext could enrich the scene. But Gibson was also unavailable, as was William Hurt. Geraint Wyn Davies had originally been offered smaller parts for the 1986 season but had turned them down because he had a television series. But in mid-December the series was cancelled, and he accepted an offer that included playing Pericles. While Ouzounian had never directed Wyn Davies, he had hired him as well as seen his work, and he felt they would be "emotionally compatible. The fact that I am cheerful, and big, and blond, and Ger is cheerful, and big, and blond is more than a coincidence."

Ouzounian explained that the casting system used for the 1986 season involved the pairing of principal roles to be played by an actor or actress. For example, the actress who played Thaisa in *Pericles* had to play Hermione in *The Winter's Tale*. Given that role division, the directors affected could ask management to engage whatever principal player they wanted: Both Ouzounian and William wanted Semple. But if directors had almost total say in casting the leads, they had almost no say in casting the secondary roles, which were also paired using the company members hired.

In preparation, Ouzounian reread the play for the images it presented, with some of his initial images that were eventually discarded nonetheless helpful in staging the important concepts. His first image of the storm scene was one in which actors would trail bits of silk up the aisles in a Kubuki-style presentation of wild wind and rain but eventually understood that the appealing idea was motion. From there he decided to use in some scenes a sail with wind machines to fill it up. Not all scenes immediately presented an image, he says, recalling that in the first scene in Tarsus he thought of Cleon and Dionyza walking outside the palace, surrounded by the starving populace begging for food until pursued inside. The rulers could begin talking about the siege of starvation with much more urgency than if the scene began with them lounging around the palace discussing starvation.

Ouzounian says that to do a good job with a major play, "You must let scenes haunt you and lines stick in your head. You deal with the show in the manner in which it presents itself." Another consideration for him is that the important issues in the production should coalesce at the placement of the first act curtain. To accomplish that unity in this production, he hit upon the idea of taking two scenes, neither of which was enough in itself--Pericles saying good-bye to Lychorida and Marina at Tarsus and Thaisa bidding Cerimon goodbye--and playing them simultaneously on opposite sides of the stage. For the end of the scenes, he thought, "What if...Lychorida was there with the baby and Pericles and Thaisa violated the time-space continuum, which you can do on a thrust stage, and passed each other?" He admits the idea came to him shortly after the birth of his own daughter during the planning period, and in that moment he knew this production would center on Pericles, Thasia, and Marina as father, mother, and daughter. As long as that support held fast, the director believed, everything else would fall into place.

But he stresses the importance of time in making these decisions. Stratford, at its best, allows a director the time to think the production through and work on many possible solutions to a problem before finding the proper one. He planned this production from May 1985 to March 1986. In most other situations, he says, a director might be called to do a production three to six months in advance and meet with a designer almost immediately; he contends this approach will lead to a series of "freeze dried" solutions to problems, made to meet deadlines.

The company that assembled to put the play into rehearsal on 4 March, 1986, contained two actors from the 1973-74, production: Nicholas Pennell, who played Pericles in both early productions, played Antiochus and Bolt; and William Needles, who had played Simonides in 1974, played Simonides and Pander.

On the first day of rehearsal, the director began by talking about the

232

dramatic structure of the play. The play doesn't follow a straight-line progression, he said; it gets from A to B by digressions and by degrees in the fashion of an episodic fable. Each episode would become important as it was blocked, costumed, lighted, and given musical identity. A friend, he relates, capsulized the play: "Isn't this really about a rather green guy who is a little bit arrogant and a whole bunch of s*** happens to him and in the end he is a better guy because of it?" To that version Ouzounian adds his contention that the play is a very good one, conceding that it might not be considered today as one of Shakespeare's best but still better than anything outside the Shakespearean canon. Festival education assistant Jeffrey Marontate calls it the most popular of Shakespeare's plays in the playwright's lifetime.

Next Ouzounian tackled the joint authorship dispute, arising from that popularity of the play in the early 1600s. The acting company went to great lengths in those days to keep its copy from getting out, he explained in rehearsal; consequently one or more scribes may have sat in the Globe Theatre and copied down as much as they could. Later this rough rendition of the first half of the play was added to what scholars believe to be a second half that is almost entirely the work of Shakespeare. Yet, he said, from the remarks of friends who have produced the play, the lines of Shakespeare carry the play over those rough patches during the first half. Regardless of the authorship dispute, he concluded, the company must play the text that it had with strength and integrity.

To that end the text that Ouzounian brought into the rehearsal process was the New Penguin edition with some changes suggested by the Arden edition, the Gascon production promptbooks, and Wilkins' account, *The Painful Adventures of Pericles, Prince of Tyre*, published in 1608, which quotes nearly one-third of Shakespeare's text verbatim. Beyond the changes and insertions, he had cut the existing script "ruthlessly," explaining that the cuts were not "set in stone" but open for discussion in consultation.

He explained setting the speeches of Gower to music by saying that no matter how brilliantly an actor spoke those six eighty-line speeches a chance existed that the audience would "nod off at times, and nodding off is not an option in this production." The lines Gower would sing were 85 to 90 percent those of Shakespeare, with some of the obscure language removed. The one line Ouzounian asked Gray to change was in the first song where the lyric "Wanna take you from Ontario, Wanna take you all to Syria" was eventually changed to "Wanna take you from this wooden O, Wanna take you all to Syria." In the choice of a style of music that combined Middle Eastern music and the sound of rock, he confessed he sought a contemporary sound for the production. As the play centers more and more on the human family values and grows "less and less about epic spectacle, the scale of music grows smaller and smaller as well," explains Ouzounian. To match the music the visual style starts out very boldly and, except for the scenes set in Mitylene, the visual boldness decreases until the final scene, set in the Temple of Diana at Ephesus and coloured with blues and creams, provides "almost a rest for the eyes," says the director.

For the design presentation he explained that because he had always wanted to direct on the Festival Stage, he intended to leave it as "bare as God and Tanya Moiseiwitsch had designed it." Neville, who sat in on all opening rehearsals and who had issued a plea for directors and designers to use the bare stage whenever possible, smiled broadly at this point. This decision meant the costumes would carry the visual emphasis of the production, each location using different colours, "big, bold, and technicolour." Red had been selected for the court of Antioch, blue and orange for Tarsus, burgundy with gold trim for Pentapolis, and bright orange for Mytilene. Only Tyre in beige and ivory and Ephesus in sea green would be less colourful. Neville would later joke that one could always tell in which location the play was set at any particular moment because "all the teams were colour-coded." Gower's costume contained all of the colours in a spectrum arrangement, a costume that started as white silk that was pleated and dyed.

Ouzounian reminded the company that in acting they were working with a combination of Shakespeare's language and the Festival Stage's 220-degree thrust stage, both of which demanded stature and size rather than small conceptions or executions, "cardboard cutouts, or ham acting," he warned. He confessed to the cast his belief that this production at its core would center on the relationship between parents and children and particularly on the relationship between fathers and daughters. This theme not only suited the play but the director and leading actor as well, since the Ouzounians' first child, a daughter named Katherine, had been recently born and the Wyn Davies' first child, a boy named Gaylan, was to be born in mid-April.

Ouzounian blocked the play very quickly; if a scene presented special problems, he asked the actors if they wished to read it before beginning work on it. Generally they preferred to work it rather than read it. In the early blocking rehearsals, a review of large portions of previously blocked scenes was frequently included. On 7 March, three days after rehearsals began, he scheduled "a stagger-through" of Part One that, he reminded the actors, was more for his benefit than a check on their progress, to see if he was over- or under-using particular blocking configurations and/or stage areas. He recognized, he reminded them, that actors work in different fashions and that for the purposes of the stagger-through each should maintain an individual pace: Some might work quietly and inwardly while mumbling their lines with their heads in their books while others might project loudly, perhaps shouting. Gower's speeches he read in the appropiate spots because actress Renee Rogers was not yet familiar enough with the music to sing them.

Given the rapid pace of rehearsal, the interpretation of each scene developed quickly, and the rest of the rehearsal period was spent refining it. Ouzounian thus worked more swiftly than any other Stratford director. While he did not impose an interpretation on a scene, he did take what the actors gave him and shaped it quite speedily. In other productions more time was spent in exploring a scene before the final interpretion developed. Ouzounian explains that he prefers to work in this fashion and that the episodic nature of the play caused him to concentrate on the sweep of events.

Major textual changes occurred during rehearsal when University of Leichester Professor Roger Warren brought a photocopied version of the play that Oxford University Press was soon to bring out in a new one-volume edition of the works of Shakespeare under the editorship of Stanley Wells, adding some of the material from the Wilkins novel in verse form in the first half of the play. Since Ouzounian was only two weeks into rehearsal and the changes consisted of additions to scenes where he and his principal actors felt they needed more text to portray the emotional content, he embraced about eighty percent of them. In the relationship between Pericles and Thaisa, Ouzounian added twelve new lines for Thaisa and ten for Pericles, but as he says, "It shifts the balance. It suddenly stops it from being a cardboard storybook to being almost believable people having a love affair." Another addition put Pericles on the balcony of the Festival Stage singing a song to Thaisa in the stage right doorway after Simonides had Pericles escorted in honour to his chamber following his tournament conquests. For that song Ouzounian lifted the second verse of the song that Wilkins reports Marina sang to Pericles aboard ship in V.1. Ouzounian used the first verse of the song in this spot, but the second verse he gave to Pericles to sing to Thaisa at the end of II.4. By setting both verses to the same music, he hoped to link Pericles and Marina in the latter scene.

After getting off to a good start, Ouzounian says, rehearsals hit bottom about halfway when nearly a week's rehearsal time had to be cancelled on account of illness. "We all began to doubt that the show as conceived would work." Following his illness he asked the company to give the show its all and after one week of very hard work, the momentum of the show steadily increased.

Wyn Davies, who had never worked at Stratford before, says that coming into rehearsals very few actors except Pennell and Needles knew the play and that much of the criticism labeled it as a weak text. His own negative feeling was displaced by Ouzounian's confident rehearsals, and he was amazed at the quick blocking. He remembers occasions after running a scene when Ouzounian would put his arm around him and walk him apart from the others, with a cloud of the director's pipesmoke trailing after them, so they could check their reactions. A feeling persisted, says Wyn Davies, that "we were the rookies," because *Pericles* had a director who had not tackled any Stratford stage before and because it had the fewest number of veteran actors in the company. At the same period that Ouzounian felt the rehearsals hit rock bottom, Wyn Davies says, he began to worry that this show would be one of the worst productions with which he had ever been associated. Scheduled for ten student matinees, the play's rock songs and Pericles and Thaisa's struggles as young lovers seemingly separated by a disapproving father found favour with this audience and cheered the cast.

When Wyn Davies accepted a role in the televison series *Air Wolf*, Joe Ziegler played the role of Pericles during the month of October and Stephen Russell added the role of Lysimachus, who appears only in the second half of the play, to his part as Thaliard, who appears only in the first.

The production that opened on 25 May, 1986, contained twenty-seven scenes, subdivided and titled as a joint effort by Ouzounian and stage manager Hilary Graham. All page numbers refer to the New Penguin edition used for this production.

Act I, Scene 1

Act I, Scene 1, was divided into two scenes, Scene 1, "Incest" (pp. 49-50), and Scene 2, "Deathlike Dragons" (pp.50-56). "Incest" contains Gower's song with Gray's rewritten lyrics and music in place of Shakespeare's speech, and constitutes what the New Penguin edition calls "I Chorus." It was set in Antioch at the court of Antiochus. Gower appears on the balcony to sing the first song, accompanied by a dance showing Antiochus and his daughter in incest. A suitor comes to study the riddle on a scroll handed him, cannot answer it, and is pushed up stage to the chopping block. The executioner raises the sword while the lights dim, and when they rise the head of the suitor is displayed. The business of the dumb shows was established by Ouzounian and choreographed by John Broome. Renee Rogers, who played Gower, says she did not know about the music until Carriere called her on 28 January and explained the musical concept behind Gower's speeches. She did not hear the music until a week after rehearsals had started in early March. She did some of her own musical arrangments and worked on two or three songs at a time. Because her background consisted of night club acts and musical comedy in which she had given her arms free reign, she and Ouzounian worked out a system whereby she set the stage for the dumbshow that played while she sang and at times cued the lights to come up by pointing in their direction. She spent a great deal of time working to control and then refine those arm gestures. She explains that the first number introduces the relationship between Antiochous and Pericles, the result of which causes Pericles to flee Antioch and Tyre to escape his henchmen for first half of the play. She describes the song as beginning in a typical musical theatre vein but then switching to a heavy rock sound. That number, one of the most theatrical in the show, often elicited clapping from student audiences that she found distracting.

Following the song, "Death-like Dragons" begins with Antiochus' soldiers in place on the balcony and in front of each of the side doors on the Festival Stage, one of the boldest looks in the show. Ouzounian and Clark agreed immediately about the look they wanted: red, savage, and barbarous. The colour-coded costumes help to explain Shakespeare's language and clarify each location: the operatic technique. In Antioch, Clark explains, people have red hair, red clothing--often skimpy--trimmed in gold to show them "a nasty, decadent people, which ought to be apparent to Pericles just by the look of the place." These costumes were lots of fun, he explains, because of the touches that could be added without breaking the established conventions, and in some cases, the actors contributed to the costume ideas. For example, Pennell asked Clark about using the built-up shoes used in classical Greek tragedy that added several inches to Antiochus' height. He also wanted very long fingernails. Both of these affectations played on the pride and sense of self-importance of the character, and director and designer readily approved the ideas.

Pennell says that Antiochus' evil must radiate from the character from his first entrance and yet the actor thinks that making the character an empty pit of wickness is incomprehensible. Rather, the actor chose to play off the character's line that Pericles shall not live to "tell the world Antiochus does sin in such a loathed manner" (I.1.147-148). First, maintains the actor, Antiochus represents the fulfillment of the Old Testament prophecy that sin will be visited upon wrongdoers down the generations; he comes from abusive parents and has abused his own daughter. But he also sees in the lines the character's arrogance and pride that he uses to cover his shortcomings. Pennell maintains, too, that the "corrupt" script makes his lines sound very formal; he attempted to give them a more modern form by elongating the vowels where possible.

Frehner explains that the basic lighting plot for the Festival Theatre covers the entire stage in white light, specific colours being added as needed for each show. This system differs from the American style of lighting that combines a number of different colours to produce white light or coloured lighting when used individually. To achieve the effect he wanted in the court of Antioch, Frehner used the white light in the center of the stage and surrounded it with a perimeter of red wash through which the audience viewed the scene.

The director explains the presence of Pericles in this incestous court by saying that Antioch is geographically the closest major kingdom to Tyre and doubtless he has heard that King Antiochus has a beautiful daughter to woo. When he arrives he learns why this court is dangerous, the discovery that launches the play. The character of Pericles, he says, has no tragic flaw; by playing him as a young man, too, he can be shown to confront evil for the first time. Wyn Davies says that he plays a young prince of increased responsibilities, seeking a wife who can give him an heir. But, says the actor, the character is a little too cocky. The court of Antioch represents his first slap on the wrist by the gods, who are saying to him, ''Be a little more careful about what you want.''

Act I, Scene 2

Act I, Scene 2, was composed entirely of Scene 3, ''Time to Fear'' (pp. 56-60) and, set in Tyre, shows a cool world of peace. Its lords do not wear helmets, shields, or swords, but tunics of brown and cream colours in a Coptic design. A marble throne of Greco-Roman style stands center stage. The court of Tyre is lit almost entirely in white light, only one light added to the basic plot in order to highlight the throne. When *Cymbeline* director Robin Phillips saw a preview of the show he commented to Ouzounian that he liked everything but the court of Tyre scenes because in those he did not know where he was. Ouzounian and Frehner, both of whom admire Phillips' eye for detail, changed the lighting design to make those scenes appear as if they occurred in an interior throne room. One of the most difficult jobs on that stage, explains Frehner, is achieving changes in location. In the original concept of that scene the lighting covered too much of the stage. To achieve a more definite atmosphere he confined the light to a smaller area, added a gobo to achieve the look of light entering the room through a window behind the throne, and brought down the intensity of the level of light.

The court of Tyre looked more severe than lavish, concludes the designer. When Pericles enters, Wyn Davies says, he is very much disturbed by the evil that he has encountered at Antioch and concerned about the war Antiochus is sure to wage from his position of strength against this weaker state. In counsel with his trusted advisor, he decides to exile himself to spare his kingdom Antiochus' revenge. Wyn Davies began rehearsals playing this scene with some pent-up anger,'' a bit like Richard III,'' he confesses, but over time became more mellow as he sought the best course for himself and his kingdom. John Innes' Helicanus showed concern for both the man and the state, arguing that Pericles should flee to avoid the cost of war to his people. Innes found that the character of this trusted statesman grew over the course of the run from a character who did what the lines indicated he should do to one whose view of goodness expanded to allow him to deal with the other courtiers in a firm manner in order to achieve that good purpose. In that sense Innes says that while the role began within him, it grew as if to ask, "All right, this is who I am. Who are you?" Because so few roles expand to teach the actor, Innes asserts, he found special pleasure in this one.

Act I, Scene 3

Act I, Scene 3, consisted entirely of Scene 4, "Unknown Travels" (pp. 61-62), and subsumes all of Act I, Scene 3, also set in the court of Tyre. Once Pericles has left, the lords of the court enter to ask what has happened to him. Innes says Helicanus must decide whether to tell them all he knows or only to give part of it, the choice he eventually makes. Thaliard of Antioch enters on the balcony. As confrontation looms, Helicanus invites Thaliard to dinner. Ouzounian says that the statesman Helicanus understands the best way to find out why Thaliard has come is to wine and dine him and see what he will let slip about this mission. Russell enjoyed this opportunity to put all the energy into the fourteen lines of Thaliard's text that he would normally put into a much longer role, such as his Festival performance of Richard II in 1979. Perhaps the arrogant attitude of the actor toward the character made him arrogant as well, Russell says, questioning if any other actor could get five laughs out of Thaliard's monologue in this scene.

Act I, Scene 4

Act I, Scene 4, consisted solely of Scene 5, "Misery of Tarsus" (pp. 62-66), set in Tarsus, a city that Ouzounian says from the days of St. Paul enjoyed a reputation for decadence, later slipping into poverty. As the director and designer considered the look they wanted the costumes to communicate, they agreed on a description of rich and lazy for the rulers Cleon and Dionyza, whom the director described as weak characters. Again director and designer went for a bold look. The dark blue basic colour was coolly dignified, but the bright orange trim and undergarments hinted at the passion which that colour would later lend to the brothel scenes of Mytilene. Ottoman and medieval styles were mixed, not for lack of care but to emphasize the fable-like story. Ouzounian explained that hot colours in this production were evil, used to underscore the excesses: incest at Antioch, attempted murder at Tarsus, and prostitution at Mytilene. These colours are contrasted with the cooler colours of reflection at Tyre, love at Pentapolis, and spiritual renewal at Ephesus. Clark began with the idea of oriental carpets gone to seed and, based on the colours from an old blue and orange carpet he owned, the designs took shape.

The opening sequence of the people begging the rulers for food suggested to Frehner that the scene be bathed in pale green and blue light to make flesh to appear pale and sickly and complement the costumes. Light from steep angles darkened the stage in contrast to Pericles' entrance, to suggest hope that has come to Tarsus in his person. Wyn Davies found Pericles' motivation in going to Tarsus to aid them a gesture to appease the gods for the difficulty his foolish choice of the daughter of Antiochus had caused. Jeremy Wilkin sees Cleon as a well-meaning but ineffective character. He feels for the people of the city but cannot find a way to help them. Caroline Yeager, who played Dionyza, found the character's chief function in this scene was reacting to Cleon. The famine has gone on for a long time and she wants to support him, but she also wants him to do something about the problem. The actress says the continued starvation of the people has hurt Dionyza and the audience should recognize in her a sympathetic response to the plight of the people in this scene.

II Chorus

This scene played as Scene 6, ''Thunder Above'' (pp. 66-68), and contained the rewritten lyrics and music for Gower's second speech. Rogers directed traffic in the dumb show on the stage during a song that recaps the action and tells what will happen next. All of this Gower accomplished to a beat Rogers describes as ''modern contemporary.''

Act II, Scene 1

Act II, Scene 1, consisted only of Scene 7, ''Finny Subjects'' (68-73), and was set on the coast of Pentapolis. According to legend, says Ouzounian, the three fishermen played the three bawds in the scenes in Mytilene during Shakespeare's time. But because each trio is distinctly different, this director decided to cast each separately. Also, it gave him a chance to hear from the common people for the first time, although Ouzounian used them comically to contrast with the raging storm that has thrown Pericles upon their shore. He broke up long speeches into short, choppy ones given to more than one actor and had the third fisherman echo the speeches of the other two for a comic effect.

Gradually increasing warmth of light in this scene, explains Frehner, hints at Pericles' increasing good fortune. He also explains why he chose to use gobos by citing psychological research that shows light broken up into patterns is reassuring--for example, the light on waves. For Wyn Davies the scene demonstrates some of the problems of playing the character: The clash with Antiochus is one of the few conflicts the character has with another person. Usually he's buffetted about by the gods, responding by accepting what has happened and moving forward to the next hurdle. Playing persistent patience and optimism in the face of continued adversity in a varied and interesting fashion constitutes a challenge for an actor. When the armour comes ashore, the actor notes, the character comments that he got the armour from his father. He believes that the incredible quest on which the character has embarked is one to fill his father's shoes. "Until you are a father yourself, you can't replace your own father," this new father remarks.

Act II, Scene 2

Act II, Scene 2, included all of Scene 8, "The Triumph (pp. 73-76), set in the court of Pentapolis. Ouzounian says that in setting the atmosphere for Pentapolis, he and Clark worked against geography for the only time in the production, since the ancient kingdom of Pentapolis lies in modern day Libya and calls in some interpretions for the characters there--Thaisa, Simonides, and courtiers--to be black. Designer Clark contends that Pericles' route would land him in Constantinople. The director instead wanted to focus on the contrast between the good court of Simonides and that of Antioch, building on a healthy relationship of love between father and daughter. Smiling, unveiled faces live and thrive here.

Clark chose a Byzantine flavour to highlight this court rather than a North African one. The basic burgundy colour suggested royalty, and the gold trim (also used for for a gaudy effect in the red Antoich court) this time added a lustre of nobility to the scene. Most of the costumes and banners used in this scene (and in many others as well) were personally finished by Clark with a paint brush or coloured marker: He says, "It was nearly impossible to describe to someone else what I wanted, and I was not quite happy with a costume until I had taken it into my hands and accented it the way I wanted it myself. Thus the epic scale visual style creates much more work for the designer than would one which features frock coats." He found more than enough compensation for the extra work in the increased freedom from traditional limitations which the style also gave him. Pentapolis was the home of Theodora, the mistress to the Roman governor before she married the Emperor Justinian and moved to Constantinople, thus providing ex-classics honor scholar Clark with his link between Pentapolis and Byzantium. Since the Roman Empire continued in the East until the fall of Constantinople in 1453, Clark sees Simonidies as a continuation "of the Roman emperor." The two thrones on which the king/emperor and his daughter sit for "The Triumph" were inspired by those in some of the cathedrals of

Ravenna, Italy, which Justinian and Theodora dedicated between 500 and 600 A.D. The small figures that adorned the thrones were based on Syrian models traceable to that time.

Ouzounian decided very early in his preparation period to stage the tournament, which in Shakespeare's text takes place offstage. He had Pericles win three battles, and fight director Jean-Pierre Fournier made each of the three rounds more realistic. The defeated combatants are disarmed, not killed, so as Pericles bows to Thaisa, the last knight rushes at him with a knife Pericles then uses to kill him. He is revealed as Thaliard, a device Ouzounian claims as a first. In another textual addition, the director also had Simonides translate the mottos on the shields of all the knights rather than just the three which the text provides for him to translate.

Act II, Scene 3

Act II, Scene 3, was composed solely of Scene 9, "Men In Arms" (pp. 76-81), set at the court of Pentapolis. For Goldie Semple, the differences between the roles of Thaisa in *Pericles* and Hermione in *The Winter's Tale* are more interesting than their shared revival from the dead. She played Thaisa "as young as I can get away with," she says. The respect, love, and genuine humour William Needles brought to his portrayal of the king helped to show both characters as stubborn enough to stand up for their points of view without giving offence. Semple believes that since Simonides has no son, he has educated his daughter, who in the previous scene could translate the Latin and Spanish mottos as well as he. For Thaisa, says Semple, Pericles is a fairy tale prince with skills as a knight, good looks, and excellent humour. Yet, says the actress, there is a sense of loss about him, an air of melancholy, which Thasia also finds attractive: love at first sight. She points to the difficulty of expressing feelings with so little text to express her feelings. One early speech taken from Wilkins and one later which she believes to be Shakespeare's deal with feelings. The rest, she says, is "hostessy talk." To help express the relationship called for in the text, Ouzounian added a kiss to the end of the dance between the two which prompts Simonides' line beginning "Unclasp, unclasp!" and his breaking off of the festivities, sending all to bed. Semple credits the dance choreographed by John Broome with giving the two performers a chance to express their love that the text does not provide.

Needles describes Tony Van Bridge as the model from which his Simonides takes its basic structure, since because of Van Bridge's other commitments Needles took over the role during the 1973 tour and the 1974 season. Needles recollects that Van Bridge brought to the role much of "the heavy set man's bubbling goodness and twinkling humour. Tony can blow up a storm very easily, and his anger seemed terribly real." But, says Needles, he could switch in an instant to say, "I'm only kidding." These then constituted the building blocks Needles used in constructing his character. He was helped when his director immediately accepted the character that Needles brought him early in the rehearsal process. If anything, Needles explains, "Richard aided and abetted me in what I was about."

His Simonides cares deeply for his daughter and wants to find her a husband who will suit her and challenge her. After all, the actor says, she is a strong person, too. Needles believes that the tournament is staged by the father to please his daughter, perhaps on her birthday. Their verbal sparring delights them both and provides a way the father can push the daughter toward Pericles by seeming to push her away from him.

Scene 9A, "Instant Solace," suggested in the Oxford edition and set in the court of Pentapolis, gives Pericles a song. Thaisa enters from one door to listen while Simonides enters from the other to watch. Ouzounian explains that this moving moment on the stage makes little impression on a reader from the page. Ouzounian emphasizes that earlier in the play Pericles says, "My education hath been in arts and in arms." The tournament scene shows off his education in arms, and this scene completes the sequence. It also gives the young lovers a few more moments to concentrate on one another. Even if Pericles doesn't know she can hear him, no doubt exists that he is singing about her.

Act II, Scene 4

Act II, Scene 4, contained Scene 10, "Noble Subjects" (pp. 81-83), again showing the lords of Tyre pushing Helicanus to accept the crown. Innes explains that Helicanus firmly rejects the offer to take power officially as opposed to ruling in the absence of Pericles. But by this scene Helicanus no longer receives instructions from Pericles and he must act on his own without in any way undercutting Pericles' power, explains the actor. That tension explains the fact that he grows a bit short-tempered with these three would-be tempters.

Act II, Scene 5

Act II, Scene 5, contained only Scene 11, "Get You To Bed" (pp. 83-87) set in the court of Pentapolis. The text of the scene calls for Simonides to pretend disapproval of Thaisa's plans to marry Pericles, and Needles relished this opportunity. Wyn Davies points to the early part of the scene in which Simonides, as part of the deception, calls Pericles a traitor who has come to his court to capture his daughter by witchcraft, one of the few occasions where Pericles confronts adversity in the form of another person. The actor explains that the character has learned something since he fled from Antiochus because this time he stands his ground to acquire Thaisa. Semple contends that both father and daughter like Pericles from the start, and audiences could not get enough of this double meaning. Needles says that if the conception isn't large enough the character can't sustain the lines he must speak, and if the conception gets too far the scene slips into farce.

III Chorus

III Chorus contained Scene 12, "Neptune's Billow" (pp. 87-89), with the reworked lyrics set to music of Gower's third speech called by the New Penguin edition "III Chorus." Rogers says her job that of bridging time in "a funky rock and roll" song to introduce Thaisa, who will very shortly give birth.

Act III, Scene 1

Act III, Scene 1, contained the single unit, Scene 13, "A Little Daughter" (pp. 89-92), and played throughout Act III, Scene 1, aboard ship. A huge sail drops from the "heavens" and quickly fills with the breeze of the wind machine while sailors clasp the ropes on each side of the ship. Both Ouzounian and Clark acknowledge the similarity of this sail to the one that opened the 1982 production of *The Tempest* directed by John Hirsch and designed by Desmond Heeley, but Clark's sail was smaller and could not be tossed violently about because the scene contains essential text not related to the storm.

Like Clark, Frehner had to battle the sail, originally having planned lots of light for it. But that took the focus away from Pericles; the director had asked for a sense of motion in the scene, so several lighting instruments equipped with motion wheels to which gels alternating between blue and green were added. Frehner says that while they do not look like waves they do give a sense movement, heightened by having the motion wheels for the instruments focused on one side of the stage turn in a different direction from those of the other side. Because of the terrible storm and its effects on the sailors, Frehner again decided on the blue green-wash to illuminate the actors' faces.

Wyn Davies visualized that storm-blasted deck as the waiting room at a maternity ward in a hospital. In contrast to the way he began rehearsal, full of rage, he moved into a more plaintive attitude in which his pleas to the gods contrast with the harsh reality of the storm. Likewise, where once he raged in anger at Lychorida, he moved into an attitude of grief as she announced the death of Thaisa and the birth of Marina. This change meant that Martha Burns' Lychorida had to progress from recoiling at his anger to reaching out to support him in his grief.

There existed no text from which Burns, Semple, and Ouzounian could construct the relationship between the two characters, so, Burns relates, they filled in one: that Thaisa and Lychorida had been raised as mistress and maid. Thus at the moment Lychorida comes forward to tell the news to Pericles of the death of his wife, she has just experienced the death of her closest girlhood friend. Wyn Davies says that Pericles becomes angry with the gods for the first and only time in the play when he asks for the life of his wife and for the storm to abate. He gives in to the sailors' demands to put the queen's coffin overboard, Wyn Davies says, in honour of their religious beliefs, again reconciling himself to the will of the gods.

Act III, Scene 1

Act III, Scene 1, contained only "Golden Slumber" (pp. 92-97), set in Lord Cerimon's home on the coast of Ephesus. Ouzounian stayed with his original plan for this scene, in which he envisioned it starting with torches coming out of the darkness of the blackout, with a little wistful music underneath and eventually a little light introduced on stage revealing the people dressed in sea foam blue-green. Non-speaking characters were deployed around the stage symmetrically so that the audience could see faces clearly and thereby have access into the scene. Ephesus, says Clark, represents the Greco-Roman world at its best: everything looks washed clean by the sea. Maurice Good says Cerimon represents another good man introduced late in the first half of this play, as is the character Good played in *The Winter's Tale*, the Old Shepherd. Warm lighting comes from the torches, amplified only by one light focused on Thaisa as she revives, says Frehner. Semple takes the fairy tale quality of the show quite literally because she believes that her character's revival is magical in *Pericles*, whereas the revival in *The Winter's Tale* occurs because the character has simply fainted. Semple says she had done some coffin acting previously when she played Camille and had to be encased for nearly fifteen minutes. Luckily, she says, she is not claustrophobic, but did appreciate the numerous air holes provided. The only bothersome part, she says, was having her face covered. She could not see any of the scene where she is revived, but she says she enjoyed listening to it.

Act III, Scenes 3 and 4

Act III, Scenes 3 and 4, were combined into Scene 15, "No Tears" (pp. 97-99), set respectively in Ephesus and Tarsus. Wyn Davies notes Pericles' ability to look forward in the midst of his own grieving and direct the ship to Tarsus, to which they can take the baby before they could reach Tyre. Caroline Yeager, Dionyza, describes her character as truly sorry she had not met Pericles' queen before her death. The actress believes she welcomes the opportunity to raise his daughter to show her gratitude for past favours

Pericles has done for them. She chose to show none of the malevolence that would later surface in Dionyza. Pericles, says Wyn Davies, believes that what the gods have done is past worrying about and directs his attention to the child, which shows that he understands what is most important.

When this action was over, the characters moved to one side of the stage while Thaisa and Cermion entered from the other to play their short scene. Then Pericles and Lychorida crossed center stage while Thaisa crossed behind them, each turning to look at the baby. After they exit, Lychorida stands in the only pool of light, with her head turned upward in supplication.

Frehner explains how he went about staging the lighting for the implication of two worlds presented simultaneously on stage. In the end he decided to light each world separately so that the scene had two sources of light, a sun for each world. At the end of the scene Lychorida stands in a different pool of light that represented neither world as Pericles and Thaisa each exit away from Marina.

IV Chorus

IV Chorus played as Scene 16, "Monster Envy," beginning Part II. Gower rises from the trap door singing the rewritten lyrics and music to the scene the Penguin edition calls "IV Chorus." Frehner lit Gower from underneath through the trap, rigging three lights, one gelled in each of the primary colours, to shine straight up through the floor and to mix on Gower. Smoke was added to the scene through the floors, to catch the various rays of light and to create the colours around her. Above, Dionyza enacts a pantomime, bribing Leonine to kill Marina. Rogers describes the music for this text about Marina's childhood as "blues music with a base beat."

Act IV, Scene 1

Act IV, Scene 1, contains only Scene 17, "Goodly Creatures" (pp. 101-105); that is, all of Act IV, Scene 1, and is set at Tarsus. As Yeager says, when the scene begins Dionyza has already decided to have Marina killed. She explains that "jealousy is such an irrational emotion" she played the text in that Marina grew up favoured by her peers over the daughter of Cleon and Dionyza. Yeager says that Dionyza is younger than Cleon and determines to do something, as he never has, to help their daughter over Marina. She has the affair with Leonine to help ensure he will carry through with the plan to murder Marina. Kim Horsman, Marina, says she began by trying to find a clear path through the role. She reports that what she read said the part was difficult to play because it centered on values like the maintenance of one's virginity, that do not carry the same value in the modern world. So Horsman set out to make her a very pragmatic character: If she loses her virginity, she is as good as dead, reports Horsman.

John Bourgeois played Leonine, servant to a very weak ruler, Cleon. The actor sees the character as bound by his oath to kill Marina, an oath that he hopes will bring advancement to ruler…"a reluctant murderer." Ouzounian wanted to see someone leaning over the Festival stage balcony with a knife at the throat ever since he first walked into the Festival Theatre, so he "trapped" Marina on the balcony. Yet, as Pennell pointed out to Ouzounian, while the balcony is a very strong position, people going up and down are basically invisible; the effect of most lines delivered on the steps is lost. Consequently the director had Marina and her attacker stroll arm and arm up the stairs before beginning the scene. As Leonine bends her over the balcony to cut her throat, the pirates rush in and carry her off. Leonine escapes out of the balcony door and reappears from under the balcony on the stage level, thus avoiding having to come down the stairs. Yeager believes Dionyza poisons Leonine once he has "botched" the murder. She has to deal with each newly exposed raw nerve, asserts Yeager, as it appears.

Act IV, Scene 2

Act IV, Scene 2 was composed only of Scene 18, "Present Practice" (pp. 105-110) which was set in a brothel in Mytilene. Ouzounian saw Mytilene as hot, dusty, and sweaty, with orange colour to make it appear overripe and suggestive. Clark says that when it came time to do the brothel scene, he and Ouzounian had already used the colour red for Antioch so they looked at yellow as another bright colour; but, Clark says, yellow reminds one of a wholesome sun-splashed kitchen. So by process of elimination they come to orange, which is also an unpleasant colour to a Western European eye, says Clark. Pander's costume evolved from that of a pasha, and Boult's began by designating him as a "Seventh Century motorcycle gang member with orange spiked hair." Bright orange pillows with lewd scenes on them suggested the brothel, and brought a large number of personnel through the part of the warbrobe shop where they were under construction to "check on their progress" during the early spring.

The costumes looked so vibrant that Frehner had to kill some of the orange light he had planned for the scene, even though he had been told that "he could go over the top." To emphasize the dusty and dirty atmosphere, smoke caught the particles of dust flowing in the air. Light came onto the stage from angles as off center as possible.

Needles says the part of Pander contains only seventeen lines, and so the impression he creates must come immediately and vividly. The image that worked best for him was the Sidney Greenstreet character in the film *The Maltese Falcon*: "a very bland old man seemingly harmless but absolutely venomous underneath.'' Since he's ''absolutely hag-ridden'' by the bawd, his desire is simply to retire. Boult, Needles says, is smarter and a better businessman. These brothel scenes, he says, contain much cruelty and yet they come at a point in the play where humour is called for. It took playing them several times in front of an audience to get the balance right. According to Horsman, Marina probably did nothing but cry on board that ship, gets to the brothel, and sizes up the situation. Her best course is not to submit in order to cause real trouble in this house.

Pennell says Boult, like the fool in *King Lear*, comes from the lower classes and as an actor he wanted the opportunity to explore what choices the poor have in order to stay alive. Once cast in this role, he went to Clayton Shields of the wig department to get the wig that Brian Bedford wore in the 1983 and 1984 productions of *Tartuffe*. He says he suggested the large arm holes in the costume to Clark because they give the character a more contemporary look. Vacratsis sought to make her character, the Bawd, convey the darker element in the play along with the humour. The Bawd, she says, runs this house, and believes that the job of woman is to serve man. Marina's rejection of this principle confounds her. Because of the age difference between Vacratsis and Needles, they decide she must be his third wife and she hen-pecks him relentlessly.

Act IV, Scene 3

Act IV, Scene 3, plays as one unit called Scene 19, ''Eagles' Talons'' (pp. 110-112). This scene was one of the few that Ouzounian could rehearse during days when *The Winter's Tale* was designated as the primary rehearsal because neither actor in the scene, Wilkin or Yeager, was cast in that production. Ouzounian finds the impact of this scene at the point when Cleon, having finished his angry oration to Dionyza, realizes he will have to be her accomplice in Marina's murder. Yeager sees Cleon as coming unglued in this scene and she therefore has to hold it together. In doing so, the actress stresses how difficult she finds playing the scene with a sufficiently varied voice. Wilkin points to Cleon's inability to see the true character of his wife until this one moment.

Act IV, Scene 4

Act IV, Scene 4, was composed of one unit, Scene 20, ''The King's Daughter'' (pp. 112-114), which contained the rewritten lyrics and music for Gower's fifth song. Rogers says this piece was the softest in the show and had a jazzy ''Muzak'' sound. During a dumb show, Pericles comes back to Tarsus to visit his daughter only to find out that she had died. Wyn Davies says that after wrestling with the questions of what has happened in Tyre for fourteen years and why has he not come for the child before now, he has come to the conclusion that any answer is not important to the issues that he must play in the scene. Pericles, a mature and wiser man, has little chance to show that quality in the dumb scene that he has to play when he learns of Marina's death.

Act IV, Scene 5

Act IV, Scene 5, played as one very short scene, Scene 21, "Hear the Vestals" (p. 110), in which two men outside the brothel swear to give up their sinfulness after Marina preaches to them.

Act IV, Scene 6

Act IV, Scene 6 played, as Scene 22, "Deeds of Darkness" (pp. 114-120), and was set in the brothel. Lysimachus, governor of Mytilene, comes to the brothel specifically to claim Marina's virginity, says actor Joe Ziegler, who found the demands of the role balanced by the virtues he must possess when he marries Marina at the end of the play. He believes the character has a history of "coming to the brothel each week looking for a virgin." The banter between his character and the Bawd shows that on each visit he gets cheated, but Marina is real: an honourable wife to give his life meaning and direction. Ziegler concedes that "looking for a wife by searching the local brothel for a virgin of worthy birth might be considered very odd." Vacratsis says that the Bawd, Pander, and Boult fear the power of Lysimachus and are anxious to please him--especially this time when they have a real virgin to offer him.

Ziegler talks about three versions considered for the scene that it went through in rehearsal. One had him take a very passive role with the expectation that the woman would initiate the action, and another made Lysimachus very aggressive. The approach finally adopted takes a middle ground between the two extremes but Ziegler hopes that the sense of danger which his character poses to Marina doesn't dissipate until the end of the scene, when he becomes convinced of her worth. Ziegler cautions that as interesting as the speculations about his motivation become, the essential element in the scene is Marina. The choices made have to be the ones that best tell her story. Ouzounian believes that the key which unlocked the scene for the actors was the moment Marina listened to Lysimachus' talk about sex and then turns her back on him, showing an intelligent young woman who cannily uses Lysimachus' psychology to her advantage. Horsman agrees. She says that listening intently and playing on the qualities of the gentleman she finds in Ziegler's Lysimachus show Marina the way to win him over. When Clark costumed Lysimachus he had some of the same problems with the boundaries of the role. In theory as the governor of Mytilene, Lysimachus should be dressed in the orange oriental costumes of that city, but to show him worthy he chose much less intense browns and beiges in a Greco-Roman look.

Once the governor has left, Marina still has to deal with Boult, who throws her to the floor to mount her and suddenly he pulls her atop him; the actors changed position so that their faces could be seen as they spoke the lines. Pennell was especially helpful in suggesting effective moves for this scene, says Ouzounian. Pennell gives two reasons for Boult's transformation. First he quotes one of Boult's lines:

> *What Would you have me do? Go to the wars, would you? Where a man may serve seven years for the loss of a leg, and not have money enough in the end to buy him a wooden one?* IV.6.170-172

Boult does what he has to do to get along. But just as Marina has won Lysimachus, she wins Boult where no other woman might have succeeded, Pennell believes. She has converted Lysimachus and Boult in this scene: winning over Pericles in the next scene then the becomes a possibility.

V Chorus

V Chorus played as one unit, Scene 23, "An Honest House" (p. 121), containing the rewritten lyrics and music for the scene the Pengiun edition called "V Chorus"; Rogers says the song has a definite Spanish feeling and mood.

Act V, Scene 1

Act V, Scene 1 played as Scene 24, "Music of the Spheres" (pp. 122-132), set aboard Pericles' ship just off the coast of Mytilene. Clark wanted a very austere cabin augmented both by Frehner's bright white light and his use of two gobos to throw light in the shape of the ship's windows on the back wall of the stage. A simple drape, in front of the area under the balcony, masked Wynn Davies lying on a cot. Ouzounian agrees with Wyn Davies' contention than the text does not supply answers as to why Pericles has waited so many years to come back to Tarsus to claim Marina, but he does believe that the text supports his decision to use the blow of hearing of Marina's death to drive Pericles over the edge into despair. He remarks that no matter how much losing Thaisa hurt, Pericles, over the intervening fourteen years, has continually said to himself, "I still have Marina." But thinking his daughter lost sends him into the deep grief in which he is described to Lysimachus shortly after the scene opens. The governor very quickly produces Marina, but of course she and her father do not recognize one another.

Ziegler points out that according to lines cut from the script, he and his entourage are in the process of celebrating the feast of Neptune when he sees the sails of Pericles' ship and comes on board. Assistant director Charles McFarland told him that such an important feast would certainly offer a time of good will, and from this impetus Lysimachus comes aboard the ship and acts decisively to help Pericles. Ziegler surmises that his ability to produce Marina so quickly may mean that she was a part of a celebration in progress on the beach, having used his gold to buy her freedom from the Bawd. But he is not sure if she has gotten her place in reputable society with her "companion maids" through his offices or through those of Boult.

Ouzounian says the scene where father and daughter discover one another is the most difficult scene in the play to make work because each has been hurt and is reluctant to trust. The director believes that watching them make that choice necessitates sharing that pain. But once Pericles goes through that process and decides to trust again, he also realizes that the gods will do him good and that he can now be healed, says Ouzounian.

Again Wynn Davies' thinking about the scene changed over time. He used to start the scene as a very bitter man but sees himself now as having become a good man overcome by his sorrow. He fully agrees with his director about the pain inherent in the scene; it became for him "the most wonderful scene in the whole play" nevertheless. He chose to play the ending as a fragile interior joy, accented by the heavenly music of Diana.

Horsman approached this scene by seeing Pericles as another character who has been through a great deal. After she touches him she begins to tell him her secrets as she supposes people do sometimes after having known one another for only a short time. She played the scene as if she does not know that Pericles is her father until he tells her so at the very end of their encounter.

Act V, Scene 2

Act V, Scene 2, was made up solely of Scene 25, "Feathered Briefness" (pp. 132-133), and contains the rewritten lyrics and music to Gower's speech that Rogers describes as Greek in feeling, away from the heavy rock sound.

Act V, Scene 3

Act V, Scene 3, played as two units, Scene 26 "Present Kindness" (pp. 133-137), and Scene 27, "Joy at Last" (p. 137) and was set at the Temple of Diana in Ephesus. Ouzounian explains that whereas the reunion with Marina was played in very hot white light, the reunion with Thaisa was played in very cool mood lighting, within the temple, in front of twenty-four people. Some of the priestesses carried torches because the scene was conceived as "a ritual, exorcism, healing" of the wounds that have been opened in the reunion scene with Marina.

With the return of location to Ephesus, Clark notes, the colours change back to sea foam and cream. But he explains that because this time the location lies in the Temple of Diana, an additional coolness comes from the marble statue of the goddess on the balcony and altar on the stage. The six cream-coloured priestess costumes, some of Clark's favorites because of their simplicity, evolved from Greek models. Both the statue and the altar are Roman in look, based on research on the House of the Vestals in Rome and the altar in Rome.

Wyn Davies explains his character's feelings on being restored to the wife that he believed he had lost fourteen years ago. "One of these vestal virgins turns out to be, alongside Marina, the most beloved thing in his life." He addressess the gods in an interior monologue as he says, "Stop, stop. You can't better this one....But if you want to take me away now I'm ready to go." The closing tableau, with Pericles on his knees and Thaisa and Marina standing beside him, was suggested by Wyn Davies, who says that it is an appeal to the gods that this family unit will remain as one.

Semple explains that the script is in many ways a scenario which must be filled in by an actress in order to make the last scene effective. In her version the goddess Diana has had a busy night because she has appeared to her as well as to Pericles and has told her that she has been in service in the Temple long enough. Semple reflects for a moment to recount how young Thaisa was fourteen years ago when she met Pericles, married him and had a child. She sees the major difference between the revival scenes for Hermione in *The Winter's Tale* and Thaisa in *Pericles* in Leontes' the culpablity in the former play. As in *The Winter's Tale* she is bothered by how few lines she has to share with her daughter but believes that the final tableau with the three of them together makes up for some of the lack of words. "Scene 27, Joy At Last" (p. 137), contained the rewritten lyrics and music for what the new Penguin edition calls the epilogue, during which Gower summarizes (in a song "with a strong gospel bent," says Rogers) what has happened while a lone light shines on the final tableau.

Ouzounian says that at its heart the play remains very primal, "If you scrape away all the countries and the costumes." On the printed page the play ends with all the characters leaving, but Ouzounian's tableau focuses on the family. "If one can't buy that final tableau one will have trouble with this production," says Ouzounian. But he also admits having a very strong subjective interest in the play because its events happen in life. He says:

People get battered, they get bashed, and there is no reason. You can either say, "It's fate" or you can say, "It's the will of the gods." But whatever happens, happens, and the question is, "How do you

emerge from it--embittered or ennobled, weakened or strengthened?'
It's like tempering steel. You put the red hot steel in ice cold water.
If you put faulty red hot metal in ice cold water, it shatters. If you
put decent red hot metal in ice cold water, it tempers it forever. We
are all tested like that.

Cymbeline

BY WILLIAM SHAKESPEARE

DIRECTED BY	ROBIN PHILLIPS
DESIGNED BY	DAPHNE DARE
LIGHTING DESIGNED BY	MICHAEL J. WHITFIELD
MUSIC BY	LOUIS APPLEBAUM
FIGHTS DIRECTED BY	JEAN-PIERRE FOURNIER

THE CAST

LONDON, ENGLAND

Pisanio	NICHOLAS PENNELL
Gamekeeper	WILLIAM SAMPLES
Curate	KEITH THOMAS
Cymbeline, the King	ERIC DONKIN
Imogen, his daughter	MARTHA BURNS
The Queen, Imogen's stepmother	SUSAN WRIGHT
Cloten, the Queen's son	BENEDICT CAMPBELL
Posthumus Leonatus, Imogen's husband	JOSEPH ZIEGLER
Cornelius, a physician	JOHN INNES
Helen	ALICIA JEFFERY
First Lord to Cloten	ERIC McCORMACK
Second Lord to Cloten	DAVID KIRBY
Lord to Cymbeline	MICHAEL SHEPHERD

ROME, ITALY

Iachimo	COLM FEORE
Philario	JEREMY WILKIN
Frenchman	WILLIAM SAMPLES
Spaniard	MAX REIMER
His partner	TANYA RICH
Caius Lucius	JOHN BOURGEOIS
Philarmonus	MERVYN BLAKE

MILFORD HAVEN, WALES

Belarius	STEPHEN RUSSELL
Cadwal	BRENT STAIT
Polydore	KEITH THOMAS
1st Gaoler	WILLIAM SAMPLES
2nd Gaoler	ERIC McCORMACK
Jupiter	JEREMY WILKIN
Father	MICHAEL SHEPHERD
Mother } to Posthumus {	CAROLINE YEAGER
Brother	KERRY DOREY
Brother	RICHARD MARCH

Lords, Ladies, Grooms, Maids, Footmen, Nurses and Soldiers:
MARION ADLER, EDWARD BALKA, PAUL BOND, ERIC COATES, KERRY DOREY, ANDREW DOUGLAS,
DARCY GORDON, SHANE KELLY, DAVID KIRBY, RICHARD MARCH, ERIC McCORMACK,
PETER POWNALL, MAX REIMER, TANYA RICH, RENEE ROGERS, SCOTT SHARP, BRENT STAIT,
LESLIE TOY, PAULA WING, CAROLINE YEAGER

Stage Manager	NORA POLLEY
Assistant Stage Manager	HILARY GRAHAM
Assistant Stage Manager	ANN STUART
Assistant to the Director	MARTHA HENRY
Assistant Designer	ALIX DOLGOY
Assistant Lighting Designer	HUGH CONACHER
Choreographer	MAX REIMER

256

"Never was a war did cease
Ere bloody hands were wash'd with such a peace
Cymbeline V.5.485-486

Chapter Eleven: *Cymbeline*

Rehearsals for *Cymbeline* began in Rehearsal Hall 3 of the Festival Theatre on 3 June, 1986, making that the most utilized of the theatre's rehearsal spaces. Because the show was a late-season opener, many observers-- performers from the Festival and Avon companies--congregated with the cast at the tables to watch Robin Phillips begin directing his first show for the Festival since *Long Day's Journey into Night* at the Avon in 1980. Phillips invited the cast to move into the rectangular arrangement of tables and for an hour worked through the design for the production in order of scenes, giving detailed information about Daphne Dare's costumes and the time of day and location of each scene. Cast members then understood the precise location of major areas of the palace and the relationship of these locations to one another.

He then took them to the Festival stage to talk about using the space. First, he said, "The real importance of the Festival Theatre comes from putting actors and audiences together in the same room." Also, he noted that tunnels and steps around the forestage were areas to pass through to get on or off the stage, rather than areas in which to stage scenes. Finally, he reminded them that for a speaking actor to achieve the variety of body positions necessary to make him or her visible to all parts of the house, the actor listening would have to move often so that the speaker would have a reason to adjust his position. After this narration and demonstration, Phillips returned to the rehearsal hall, where he had actors read selected speeches aloud. He stopped at words that linked ideas; he said he did not see a useful purpose in having the actors read the script through "without any understanding of each other." In the first rehearsal he also concentrated some attention on Act I, Scene 6, the first scene set in Italy, instead of Act I, Scene 1, because he thought it one of the most difficult scenes in the play. Most of the observers sat until the end of rehearsal and watched as each direction was given.

Robin Phillips was appointed artistic director of the Stratford Shakespearean Festival in 1974 for 1975-80. Trained as a director, actor, and designer at the Bristol Old Vic, he had directed for the Royal Shakespeare Company and the Chichester Festival,and had done a West End production of *Heloise and Abelard* that toured in America and was done again during the 1978 Stratford season. Phillips has played several roles for television and has film credits on both sides of the camera. Following his resignation from the Festival in 1980, he served as artistic director for the Grand Theatre's 1983-84 season and directed a film version of Timothy Findley's *The Wars* among numerous other credits.

While Phillips and Neville have enjoyed a long-running working relationship, Phillips says he initially turned down an opportunity to direct two shows during the 1986 season. Neville lined up his season with other directors, and all appeared to be on track until Phillips ran into Neville on a Saturday afternoon looking "ashen gray" and the latter told him that Alan Scarfe had withdrawn as director for *Cymbeline* when unable to resolve a casting difficulty. By the end of a conversation the following Monday, Phillips had agreed to take over, but remembers thinking, "Holy cow! What do I do now?" Phillips says Neville "couldn't have been more sympathetic toward my fear...about coming back."

Phillips had only made one official appearance at the Festival since his 1980 departure when he and *Cymbeline* assistant director Martha Henry accepted the invitation of board president Oliver Gaffney for opening night of a 1984 production of *A Midsummer Night's Dream*. Phillips admits that he has slipped in to see other shows, but that official occasion made his heart pound so hard after stepping into the lobby he wondered if he might suffer a heart attack. Because of that experience, he says, he knew he would react physically to coming back to direct *Cymbeline*:

> It's very difficult (to return to a place where)...you have given a major part of your life and a major part of your theatrical experience. They were formidable years for me, those seven years, and compared to everything else I've done, a major part of my career because I did so much during those years....I knew the place incredibly well, every corner of it.

When it was time for his first day of conferences at the Festival Theatre, Neville picked him up at the Belfry, a Restaurant above the Church Restaurant, and drove him to the Festival. Phillips says Neville intuitively understood his unease and stayed by him without either of them acknowledging that anything out of the order was happening.

Phillips says he has wanted to do *Cymbeline* for a long time. He thought initially about a Jacobean production because each time he read the play he pictured the furniture and gardens of that era. But he switched periods

258

even after Dare had begun her designs; he gets such a strong feeling about period from his reading that he seldom makes such a change. But his research showed him that a new port was under construction at Milford-Haven during the time the piece played at the Globe, and he suddenly got a sense of what it must have been like for Shakespeare's audiences to see their own period clothing walking around on the stage and hearing references to topical subjects even though the play was set at the time of Julius Caesar. He and Dare eventually chose to set the play in the time period from the late 1930s through the middle 1940s. Phillips also wanted young people who come to the theatre to find a modern resonance in the production; if a play's setting goes back beyond the "Pilgrim fathers," he says, young audiences will fail to find this essential ingredient.

Phillips and Dare have done a number of productions together, and he believes their design process works much the same way each time. He says those discussions begin with his very explicit descriptions to her of the people, places, era, season of the year, and time of day in each scene. He also includes textures and colours in these early discussions. He explains that when he does make changes about people, times, or places, his changes are made just as explicitly to the designer as were his original choices. He often uses a minimum of decoration on stage but begins from a very elaborate, detailed plan of the whole environment. In his 1976-77 production of *A Midsummer Night's Dream*, built around the idea of using Queen Elizabeth I at different ages, he used only a few pillows onstage but he gave the action vivid detail so that the actors could supply much of what was not physically present.

The director believes that the design process starts with the treatment of the floor. In 1986 Neville asked directors not to use special floors on the Festival stage in order to save money. But Phillips sees the design for the floor in that space helpful as a backdrop for so many people in the auditorium and as a way to mitigate the effect of the number of right angles in the stage facade. Once Phillips and Dare finish the detailed plan of what the location "looks like in life," they describe what it ought to look like on the stage. This process includes evaluating what carries over from life, what is transformed into something, and what gets left out. That process, says Phillips, must start from the shape and emotional feel of the floor treatment.

But the design plays an important part in the process to this director for another reason. A script calls for both an intellectual and an aesthetic response, says Phillips, and he incoporates both reactions into his design. "Birth, death, rebirth," he emphasized over and over again in his opening night remarks to the cast. The use of the wood and the steel in the set design incorporate his idea that the man-made world constantly asserts in its iron gates and tall buildings that it can keep out everything. But nature replies, "No, you can't. I am stronger than anything man-made,'' explains the director. For example, at the beginning of the production, crosses marking grave sites had been placed about the up stage area with grass already growing up around the graves. Phillips wanted such overgrowth on the cannon in the last scene, too. Designer Daphne Dare says she located William Turner's painting of *Tintern Abbey*, used in the Stratford Programme, which served as a starting point for the design. The painting depicts the remains of the abbey overgrown by nature. She says they also found pictures of Highgate Cemetery in London, which, even though closed to the public view, portray a landscape almost entirely overgrown.

Dare also made her return to Stratford in 1986; she had served as head of design for the Festival from 1975 to 1980. She chose a career in art over one in dentistry when she decided she could not spend all of her professional life looking down people's throats and took a four-year curriculum leading to an interest in three-dimensional form. Her first job took her to the Birmingham Repertory Theatre, the old tiny theatre, she points out, ''with the steep rake.'' Next, at the Bristol Old Vic, she painted scenery and designed ''alternative theatre productions.'' She met Phillips when he was a student there and remembers that the relatively small company traded ideas freely. She and Phillips began working together in this fashion. Then, she remembers, he set out to become an actor. Some time later he asked her design the first play he directed in London, at the Hampstead Theatre Club. Dare then worked at the British Broadcasting Corporation as a costume designer, where among other things she did the first two years of costumes and monsters for the *Dr. Who* series. When Phillips became associate director of the Northcott Theatre in Exeter, she accepted his invitation to design for him there and then did several productions in the West End with him. After becoming artistic director at Stratford, he asked her to ''redo or redesign a permanent surround setting'' for the Avon Theatre. Her work became the first black box setting there, to which designer Phillip Silver acknowledges his debt in creating the 1986 Avon black box. Phillips made a position for Dare as permanent head of design, to provide some continuity. During his tenure wardrobe began to build costumes for the next season just after the close of the previous one, says Dare. She denies that she and Phillips have developed any particular style or look to their productions, saying that they approach each script as an individual experience. She does not even adopt a consistent style of sketching from one show to the next, she says.

Dare says she got a call from producer Peter Roberts in the winter of 1985 asking her to design *Cymbeline*, but she asked some questions about dates and budgets:

If budgets are too small and there isn't a lot of time, I don't feel that it's worth doing something because you have either got to have time or you have got to have money. It's amazing what you can do with almost nothing, given a lot of time to do it in. But if you have no time and very little money, there is not too much you can do.

Once she had accepted the assignment, she talked to Phillips to get his ideas after having read this play, to which, she says, she brought an open mind because she had never seen it. Her early outlines stayed in the production even though, as with most shows, more design sketches were tossed out than remained.

Dare opened the playing area by exposing the space behind the balcony, painted black, while leaving the balcony in place. In addition to depth, the look creates an interior and exterior. The original designs called for a river with real boats floating on each side of the balcony during the first Italian scene, abandoned to stay on budget. A large tree played on the balcony, and its tiny lights were turned on for that scene. A great deal of furniture played during the show, a consequence, says Phillips, of not having an individualized floor. Dare credits Phillips' organizational skills, saying "he almost choreographs" large-scale changes of sets and props.

The forestage area was to be raised to the level of the stage under the balcony entrance to help actors maintain concentration while stepping out onto the forestage from that entrance. Festival Theatre designer Tanya Moiseiwitsch says that while the step was incorporated into the original design for many reasons, she agreed with Phillips about eliminating it.

In explaining the choice to execute the setting in wood and metal, Dare says that the idea for the wood came from the Festival stage itself. The colour of the existing wood so dominates that setting-- especially from the balcony, she explains--that she adopted that colour for her wooden accents, arches inspired by the *Tintern Abbey* drawing and furniture. But the steel also makes its presence felt from the very first scene in the gates that seal off the area under the balcony and in the barrel of the gamekeeper's gun. In addition, she explains that the wood and steel were combined in some of the furniture used in the show, including the railing around the top of the desk in Imogen's bedchamber.

In costume choices, the designer says, everything gets "khakier and khakier" as the show progresses. Imogen starts out in a bright blue, then appears in a cream-coloured nightgown, a "stone-coloured" outfit in the scene in Pisanio's office, and finally in men's khaki clothing for a disguise. To stay within the restriction that twenty-five percent of the show's costumes be pulled from stock, she took the men's evening clothes from designs she had originally made for plays by Coward and some of the tweeds from designs for Chekhov's plays. But, the designer stresses, everything that was pulled from pre-existing stock was altered in some form for this show; she had the advantage of altering her own costumes from storage, rather than those of another designer.

Phillips began the rehearsal process by detailing for actors the ambience of time and place for each scene and then began to wed the text to the atmosphere created. While he does not usually proceed in this manner, he chose to do so with *Cymbeline* because he wanted to unify this company, whom he did not know well, and to immerse them in the late 1930s world of prewar Europe. He often likes to work by creating an environment without exploring either the play or the period in which he has chosen to set it: "part playground and part laboratory," he calls this approach. By the time he gets to the text, "We have started to set rules and create a quality of the stuffing," he says. During the rehearsal of this play, he sometimes began rehearsals of certain scenes by whistling popular war tunes to set a specific atmosphere. The cast followed his example and carried that mood into the rehearsal of the following scene.

In working through individual scenes Phillips prefers to work out the moment-by-moment discoveries and choices that the characters make, rather than reading a scene abstractly and deciding about its shape in relation to the whole text. At the beginning of rehearsals, he says, the script is "as shapeless as life and as long." Nor does Phillips dictate choices to the actors. For example, during rehearsals for Richard Monette's 1976 *Hamlet* at Stratford, he kept saying to the actor that his line, "Where is your father," sounded as if it were merely the next line in the script. One day Monette read the line as, "Where is *your* father?", as if playing off of the idea that his own father was dead. "You can't plan those choices that come out of rehearsals," says Phillips.

Another example shows how Phillips worked scenes through for this production of *Cymbeline;* he chose the first scene between Caius Lucius and Cymbeline, and he asked a series of questions: How well do they know each other? What do they think of one another? Did their fathers know each other? He and the cast in this way shaped each scene without thinking of the overall shape. In his 1976 production of *Measure for Measure*, the actors made clear choices from moment to moment. As a result, he says, they suddenly realized they had "something huge sitting out there." He admits this approach drives the technical people crazy; it takes a strong director to say, "We must wait." In 1986 he was already thinking about the shape of *School for Scandal* for 1987, but, he says, once rehearsal starts he will throw out all the plans and encourage the actors to take that moment-by-moment journey.

Lighting designer Michael Whitfield comments on Phillips' eye for detail. He can see the look he wants as he composes the scene in his mind, Whitfield explains; his mental picture is complete even in terms of lighting. Phillips' concepts formed Whitfield's starting points for designing each scene.

This production also reunited Phillips with composer Louis Applebaum, with whom he had worked extensively at Stratford and the Grand Theatre. Applebaum, who describes himself as a "very bad piano student," attended the University of Toronto's School of Music. He remembers composing love songs to court the lady who is now his wife of forty-six years. During the New York World's Fair of 1939, he became interested in doing music for films and later served as director of music for the newly formed National Film Board. in 1941 eventually becoming Director of Music. From 1946 to 1950 he did music for a number of American movies and radio productions. He recalls working in Ottawa in 1952, when he received a call from Cecil Clarke, Guthrie's assistant, explaining that a Shakespearean Festival would open the next year in Stratford and asking him to compose the music and conduct the orchestra for *Richard III* and *All's Well That Ends Well*. Applebaum wrote the fanfares still used to call the audience into the auditorium but cannot recall if they were lifted from his score for *Richard III* or were written especially as calls to the audience. These two fanfares have been used since the opening season, although he has frequently rescored them to fit the instrumentation available to the Festival in a particular year. For the past few years, he says, four brass instruments and a drum have been used. He composed dozens of versions of "God Save the Queen" to reflect the mood of the production to follow. That custom was abandoned in 1968, as Pettigrew and Portman report:

> because there was no way in which the Festival could reconcile the demands of those who wanted "O Canada," those who wanted "God Save the Queen," those who wanted no anthem, and those who objected to varying arrangements. (Pettigrew, John and Portman, Jamie. Stratford: The First Thirty Years, *Macmillan of Canada, Toronto, 1985, Vol. II, p. 2.*)

Applebaum recalls that artistic directors Gascon and Hirsch also planned to get rid of the fanfares but the ensuing uproar from Festival patrons quickly restored them.

Applebaum has composed more than fifty original scores for the Festival, at least one during nearly every one of the thirty-four seasons. The composer believes the Festival must be one of the very few theatres in the world composing for each production. Some directors know how to use music effectively and others are baffled, he says; Phillips "has one of the finest ears in the business." The first question Applebaum says he asked Phillips concerned the latter's approach to the play. "There is no point in thinking on your own "until you have checked with the director," he says. Once he had Phillips' time frame in mind, he drew up a long list of popular tunes from the "big band era." The one piece of set music consisted of a rendition of what Applebaum calls "a fairly famous lyric" from Shakespeare's works called "Hark, Hark, The Lark." Because Cloten serenades Imogen with this song, using a record player complete with horn rather than singing himself, Applebaum did seven versions of the song before hitting on the 1938 "ricky-ticky version sung by a Rudy Vallee-type crooner." Brent Carver, who played the title role in *Hamlet*, actually recorded the song.

After the one set piece of music was completed, Applebaum explains, the rest of his job was to write musical bridges from scene to scene. But until the length of time for the scene changes could be determined, Applebaum could not write that music. For example, when the scene shifts from England to Italy for the first time, a lot of furniture has to be moved, so Phillips inserted a rumba for Applebaum to write, performed by Max Reimer and Tanya Rich. This dance provided something for the audience to watch while the shift in location took place. (After Reimer pulled a hamstring muscle during the annual Labour Day cricket match against the Shaw Festival, Colm Feore took his place in the rumba.) An important production consideration, Applebaum says, is the question of using live or recorded music. Since Cloten requires a record and Phillips wanted the sound of bands in the distance, the composer and director decided they needed the kind of control that recording the score provides.

The composer explains that a director counts backward to arrive at the recording date; by 15 July the director had to give the composer the times for the scene changes so Applebaum could write the music and have it copied in time for the recording session on 18 July. But because the rehearsal schedule for *Cymbeline* had to be worked around the performance dates of the productions already in repertory, Applebaum says, he had not seen the entire production by the time the musicians recorded the score. Under such circumstances, says the composer, he had no choice but to record many music cues in case the ones he had written did not work properly. In one instance, Applebaum relates, he had eleven different cues from which Phillips took his choice. Having to review such a large number of alternatives is to some extent unfair to the director, he explains, because of the amount of time it takes to listen to them all and make choices.

Once selections have been made, the music cues must be edited, and once rehearsals moved to the theatre, the director and composer spent a day selectiing directions from which they wanted the sound to come and another day working on sound levels. Then the sound cues were played underneath the action of the play until the actors accomplished their moves in the required amount of time. While he was working on the music cues, with which he spent most of his time, Applebaum says, sound engineer John Hazen worked with Phillips on soundscapes that included wild sounds of nature and sounds of battle.

The actors whistled or sang the war tunes under parts of scenes as the recorded hymn ''Dear Lord and Father of mankind, forgive our foolish ways'' was sung by a boy soprano. Phillips had sung it as a boy soprano, reports Applebaum. The phrase also seems to comment on the director's idea of war in this play. Applebaum calls the completed work for this play one of the most complicated that he has worked with, since it included live and recorded sound, musical sound, soundscapes, and cues run through a synthesizer or a reverberation machine.

The production that opened on 1 August, 1986, was divided by Phillips into thirty scenes. All page numbers refer to the Arden paperback edition of the play, edited by J.M. Nosworthy, used for this production. The Festival had presented this play only once before, in 1970, with then artistic director Jean Gascon using Powys Thomas in the title role, with Maureen O'Brien as Imogen, Kenneth Welsh as Posthumous Leonatus, and Leo Ciceri as Iachimo. Two members of the 1986 cast participated in that production, billed as the first in North America. Eric Donkin, who played the title role for Phillips, played one of the British lords for Gascon, and Mervyn (Butch) Blake, who played the soothsayer in 1986, played Belarius in 1970.

Act I, Scene 1

Act I, Scene 1, played as one unit, called Scene 1, ''Stuff Within'' (pp. 3-6) and was a daytime scene set on the grounds of Cymbeline's palace. Two of Posthumous' followers appeared from stage left, engaged in casual conversation and dressed in military uniforms. Then the house lights gradually dimmed to begin the production. When the lights gradually came back up, those characters began the opening dialogue, entering up center. Whitfield describes the picture Phillips wanted from the light as containing woods, and soft shadows, located on a country road. Phillips chose to break up a speech given by Shakespeare's two lords among three, and so added to this scene Pisanio, Nicholas Pennell. Pennell explains that by dressing the first lord as gamekeeper, complete with shotgun; the second lord as a priest; and Pisanio as a lawyer, Phillips introduced three great institutions of early Twentieth Century England: the military, the clergy, and the law. The politician, says Pennell, is Cymbeline. Phillips often creates a full biography for each character for the actor to call upon; Pennell says that when he saw the designer's sketch of his lawyer's robe, he understood what the director wanted from the character, remembering his own family lawyer in England. Pisanio contains a good bit of that lawyer, says Pennell, who even sees a physical resemblance between the two in production photographs.

Act I, Scene 2

Act I, Scene 2, played as one unit, Scene 2, "Dearest Husband" (pp. 7-13), which immediately followed "Stuff Within" without changing time or place. Martha Burns, Imogen, says her journey in playing this heroine really began when she was a thirteen-year-old girl sitting in the audience for the 1970 Stratford production. Images from that production still remain vivid with her. The chance to play Imogen during the Festival's second staging presented a special challenge--so special that she considered the offer for nearly a week before accepting it. Her Imogen, she says, grows in strength as the play progresses, but the character begins with hurt so acute that it completely dominates the mood of this brief farewell scene. She suggests that she and Joe Ziegler, Posthumous, began the performance at an emotional height usually reached only at the end of a play. The agony of her impending separation from her husband overrides all other thoughts and emotions, the actress explains:

> It's something that hits you in the gut with a thud, and you don't think you're ever going to recover. We have to begin this play having one of the greatest disappointments life has to offer.

Ziegler says Phillips began rehearsals by stressing to him that even though his character lays a bet on his wife's chastity and arranges for her murder by a faithful friend, Posthumous does those things out of the extremity of his pain. The director helped him develop a number of specific referents, for example, to recall times when leaving his wife for extended periods of time hurt him the most. Ziegler would go to the underworld, the area beneath the Festival Stage from which he makes his first entrance, fifteen minutes before the show began in order to work himself into physical agitation at the thought of that pain from separation from a loved one. After this very short scene, Posthumous bolts down the tunnel; in Phillips' words, he must feel as if "I have to get down this tunnel before one of us breaks up."

Eric Donkin disagrees with scholars who call Cymbeline a part not worth playing and worked with Phillips to create a fully developed human being whom he characterizes as believing himself a king by divine right, misguided and besotted by his wife, and willing to do his duty. Donkin defends Cymbeline's banishment of Posthumous; doubtless, he says, the present queen sat down "one day with Prince Andrew and said, 'Now, Andy, none of this

Koo Stark business. We'll find you a nice girl.' And they did, too."

For Susan Wright, the queen, the character's motivation to get the throne of England for herself and her son Cloten by any means possible made her intentions quite clear. Phillips asked her not to play the character as "really evil." She agrees with Donkin that she manipulates Cymbeline, yet the character has very few opportunities to show an audience the degree of that domination. Speculating that the queen's bitterness comes from emotional bitterness in rearing a young boy alone, Wright explains that the character obviously has some ability since she has made herself queen. Wright explains that she has stage managed this last meeting of the lovers so she can make sure the king discovers Imogen and Posthumous together. This ensures that the king will issue Posthumous a "ticket out of town," leaving Imogen free to marry Cloten, deduces Wright. The angrier the king becomes, she reasons, the easier time she will have in bending him to her double purpose.

Act I, Scene 3

Act I, Scene 3, played as one unit, Scene 3, "Shift a Shirt" (pp. 13-15), and played as a continuation of the first two scenes. Pisanio tells the queen that her son has drawn his sword on Posthumous as he left the court. Ziegler had to rush down the tunnel for a quick change from his military to his civilian clothes, where Benedict Campbell, Cloten, waited for his entrance to this scene. Campbell spontaneously drew his weapon as soon as Ziegler entered the tunnel, forcing him to defend himself briefly before he could change. This bit of creativity became ritual, so that as soon as Ziegler exited he ran into Campbell, who sprang into action at the sight of him.

Campbell says he wanted to play down the buffoon in Cloten, seeking to make the threats he poses plausible. He decided to play the character as excitable by temperament, losing control in one situation after another. The first three times Cloten appears he has lost at something, here a fencing match with Posthumous. On his next entrance he has just lost a bowling match and on his third a card game. Campbell points out, however, that Cloten can fence, bowl, and play cards with some skill until he loses his temper. Campbell needed three to four minutes backstage to calm down from that level of intensity of anger each time; he cannot remember having a similar experience as a performer. In rehearsals, he adds, he used a broad accent and harsh sounds that Phillips asked him to refine for sophistication in the character.

John Innes, Dr. Cornelius, noting that the production combines the characters of the doctor and Cloten's second lord, appreciates that the lord's lines show he is uninvolved in the action and comments on Cloten's foolishness. In the two scenes involving the doctor, the first shows him in conference with the queen (I.6) and the second announcing her death (V.5).

To establish the connection between the doctor and Cloten, Innes and Phillips decided that Cloten suffers from hemophilia and thus bears close watching. Innes developed his characterization by thinking about the comfortable life of the court doctor, punctuated only by attendance on Cloten when he goes out. Innes had his character register disgust at the brief fight in the underworld that the audience never even saw.

Act I, Scene 4

Act I, Scene 4, played as one unit called Scene 4, "Senseless Linen" (pp. 15-17), later at the palace. At Posthumous' departure for Italy, Pisanio returns to tell Imogen about it in an "extraordinary" speech filled with images of a ship growing smaller and smaller, says Pennell. This scene plants the idea that their relationship will grow; "You see how close they become very, very quickly," says Pennell. He speculates that they have been friends previously and the loss of Posthumous brings them even closer. When offered his parts for the season, Pennell had told Neville that he feared Camillo in *The Winter's Tale* and Pisanio in *Cymbeline* might turn out very much alike. Neville encouraged him, and the parts became distinct fairly quickly, Pennell admits, especially because of this relationship established in the script for Pisanio and Imogen. No counterpart exists for it in *The Winter's Tale*. Burns sees Pisanio's return as a link to her husband; she does not break down until much later in the play, maintaining here a stoic, royal attitude to all but Pisanio.

Act I, Scene 5

Act I, Scene 5, played as one unit called Scene 5, "No Lay" (pp. 18-26), at Philario's house in Italy. Ziegler remembers that Phillips blocked this scene first during rehearsals, explaining that Posthumous comes late--probably still distressed--and so the Italians can talk about his banishment and separation from Imogen. Once at the party, Ziegler explains, Posthumous finds the other guests openly discussing his wife just as he wants most to embrace her memory privately. He tries to end that line of conversation in a way that defends her virtue, but Iachimo (Colm Feore) baits him further. For the first time he loses his self-control, telling the Italian, in effect, "Listen....She is not some kind of thing for sale," and making another attempt to withdraw. But Iachimo will not let him alone, says Ziegler, openly proposing a wager he does not want to accept. Posthumous cannot, however, let this challenge to Imogen's chastity go unanswered, says Ziegler, who compares the wager to a "cock fight." According to the terms, if Iachimo does not seduce Imogen he must fight a duel with Posthumous, whose threat to kill him must resonante with "force and truth."

Feore sees his character as a shallow, cowardly "lounge lizard," although Phillips' choice of period allowed him that attribute. He puzzles out loud about an Elizabethan counterpart. In this scene, Iachimo arrives at the party to find Posthumous the focus of conversation. Feore asserts that Iachimo belongs to the Italian nobility and resents the ascendancy of this commoner; he is threatened on his own turf. Iachimo banters with Posthumous until he discovers his vulnerability on the subject of his wife, so he strikes at his rival's weakness. Posthumous' anger makes the latter ploy easy, says Feore: "He's malleable enough to be bent to my purposes." Zielger played the scene by trying to hold back, then losing his temper. Feore's rhythm was to attack, pull back to a taunting cynicism, then assault again in the guise of insinuation. In the chilly light of reality, Feore believes, Iachimo might realize that the wager and possible duel have carried him beyond the limit he intended.

Jeremy Wilkin deduces that the name "Philario" comes from the Greek root word meaning "a love of something." Believing that Shakespeare wanted to convey a particular quality in choosing that name, Wilkin played the character as a loving host friendly to both of the feuding men. Wilkin says that Philario tries to mediate between them. Even by the end of this scene, throughout which he has tried to maintain a position as peacemaker, explains Wilkin, the character cannot bring himself to take the bet "completely seriously."

Act I, Scene 6

Act I, Scene 6, played as one unit called Scene 6, "Lingering Poisons" (pp. 26-31). The palace during the day provided the place and time. Innes says the episode comes at the end of a long line of incidents in which the queen has barged into his laboratory wanting supplies, information, or both. This scene takes place in a wing of the palace kitchen in which she has set up shop temporarily. For the first time she asks the doctor for poisonous drugs that he's reluctant to give this evil woman. To placate her, he gives her a sleep-inducing drug instead. To reinforce this scene as one of posion and death, Dare says, Phillips suggested carcasses of the large animals hanging in the background.

Wright confirms Innes' fears. The queen wants to poison both Cymbeline and Imogen, says the actress, so that the throne will belong to her and she can pass it on to Cloten. To this end she needs the poisons and Pisanio's help in giving them to Imogen. If Pisanio also takes the drug, so much the better for the queen, perceives the actress. To Pennell, the scene is like *The Dog That Barked in the Night*: The point is that the dog failed to bark. In receiving the poison, Pennell remarks, Pisanio says only two words at the end, "I will." Such a scene with an actress like Wright is "a treat," the actor says, because so many layers describe the relationship between the two. She makes sexual advances toward him and he "twinkles" right back, Pennell says; this deliberate ambiguity makes the scene more exciting because neither of the characters knows exactly where it will go. Taking the box from her to pass on to Imogen when he knows the malicious character of the queen becomes a bit tricky, he says, but he points to the good things she does for the kingdom by helping Cymbeline, such as aiding his decision in Scene 13 to refuse tribute to Rome. Taking her statements at face value is easier, then, when she tells him the drugs she gives have five times restored the king to health.

Act I, Scene 7

Act I, Scene 7, played as one unit called Scene 7, "Bound to Wonder" (pp. 31-44), in a garden party at the palace. Pisanio introduces Imogen to Iachimo by telling her the latter has a letter for her. The interesting facet of the brief scene for Pennell is the contrast between what is private and what is public. Without any words Pisanio reminds her of the presence of others, that she does not have privacy to enjoy the letters. Feore says that as soon as Iachimo sees how enthusiastically she accepts the letters, he immediately realizes that the strong bond that exists between husband and wife will make his job harder. The actor posits that winning at any cost has become the supreme goal for Iachimo; just in case he cannot successfully lure her, Feore suspects, the character has laid out other plans in his mind before his boat "docks in Dover." He tries to win the wager first by straightforward seduction, an attempt that became more pathetic to Feore the longer he played the role. The language in the rest of this scene, explains the actor, may be difficult to understand in hearing, so he and Phillips introduced seductive physical contact.

Once Imogen understands his sexual motive, Feore realizes, he must change course 180 degrees--"a bit too calculatedly"--perhaps reverting quickly to alternative plans with which to win the bet. Feore perceives that the duel with Posthumous is more important to Iachimo than the diamond ring he stands to win. "Without truth, justice, or honour on his side," the actor deduces, the character may very well lose his life: He must win the wager. Yet Feore remains unconvinced that even a character as outrageous as Iachimo could have planned the trunk device in advance. As Iachimo tries to appear smooth, telling her his real purpose was to test her to report her virtue to Posthumous, he is scheming desperately for a winning plan, finally hitting upon the idea of hiding in a trunk.

To Burns, it is noteworthy that several months have passed since Posthumous' departure, yet her character still suffers. Her soliloquy at the top of the scene, she explains, shows her desire to escape her father's domination, as if reasoning:

> *This is my life. I have a cruel father. I have a false stepmother. A horrible step brother. My husband is banished. What can be worse? But it's my burden and it's a sweet burden because I know whom I am waiting for.*

She finds in this way that the character possesses a sense of humour. Iachimo's presence at first excites Imogen because he has come from Posthumous, she explains, but the stories he tells of Posthumous' carefree life without her hurt her all over again. "She takes a quick dive and then pulls herself up," says Burns. Imogen almost believes Iachimo until she discerns that his goal is to seduce her. Imogen's faith in herself allows her to survive:

> *It's a wonderful show of her strength, manners, and dignity to be able to go through that kind of assault and to come back with that speed and that grace. She is rattled to the very core of her being, but she is able to exit a princess. It's wonderful, all the stuff that Shakespeare gives you, to keep you on top. Otherwise you'll think this poor girl can't survive.*

Act II, Scene 1

Act II, Scene 1, played as one unit, Scene 8, "Cock and Capon" (pp. 45-48). In Campbell's research for the play, he found some scholars who considered the scene unnecessary. Yet, the actor explains, for Cloten this scene is essential to reveal: his frustration at losing at bowling, which reinforces the idea of his temperament; his jealousy of Posthumous; and his insulting manner with interiors, which seems to point up his own inferiority. If the scene were not written, the character would have to build all of what is discussed here into other scenes without benefit of words, says Campbell.

Innes' doctor dislikes attending Cloten at bowling as much as having had to stand by during the earlier round of fencing. This time he has brought his lunch (in place of his doctor's bag), and to fit the title, "Cock and Capon," the items in his basket were narrowed to poultry products, an egg and a chicken leg. One day during rehearsals, when Innes first got the hard-boiled egg, he attempted to crack it on his forehead--producing gales of laughter from the others in the rehearsal hall. He and Phillips worked out the bit so he hits the egg three times against his forehead to punctuate the end of one of his lines.

Act II, Scene 2

Act II, Scene 2, played as one unit called Scene 9, "Pick'd the Lock" (pp. 48-52), set during the evening in Imogen's bedchamber. A large bed dominates center stage, with a capacious trunk at its foot. When Imogen kneels to pray, she looks under the bed before climbing into it and has her lady put on top of the trunk the book she has been reading. When she has fallen asleep, the upstage half of the lid of the trunk begins to open slowly; Iachimo reaches out to find and secure the book so that both halves of the trunk can open. He moves like a snake around the room, noting the details he will later recite to Posthumous. The lines are delivered breathily into a body microphone, heightening the tension. Feore defends the sinuous movements he makes against a friend's charge that they are "overdramatic":

> Well, of course it all is, but you have to realize that Iachimo is a guy who dramatizes himself to himself...and in fact is vaguely disappointed that she is not awake to see what a brilliant performance he is giving.

The actor believes Iachimo will go back to Italy and brag about this performance to selected friends. He decided to kiss the mole while exposing her breast because the character brags to Posthumous in a later scene that he has done so; the kiss is the one truth he will tell. He adds that the director has heightened the scene with a soundscape, the microphone for whispering, and low lighting that makes each member of the audience a voyeur. He describes the impact on the spectators as having their eyes pinned open so that they have no choice but to watch. Although Imogen sleeps through the scene, Burns explains, the character twists and turns, and her movements make her an involuntary participant in the scene. This action adds an important degree of sensuality to the scene and demonstrates that Imogen, despite her nobility and high moral character, shows her passionate, sexual nature in sleep. She calls the opportunity to show this side of the character "a gift."

Act II, Scene 3

Act II, Scene 3, played as one unit called Scene 10, "Heaven's Gate" (pp. 52-61), set in the morning at the palace. Cloten has just lost at cards and enters with a demonstration of his temperament; Cymbeline and the queen enter, and she gives Cloten tips about how to romance Imogen. Campbell thinks that Cloten takes these suggestions to heart and tries to woo Imogen in a genuinely loving and gentle manner, but the problem lies in the character's inability to understand these concepts. Throughout the scene between the two, says Campbell, he tries his best despite repeated rebuffs. But by the end of the scene the character succumbs to utter frustration when he fails to make any headway. The character, says Campbell, believes Cymbeline will make Imogen marry Cloten whether she wishes to or not and even reminds her she is his for the asking. She taunts him by telling him she does not care and that he should report her behavior to his mother. The actor describes his character's response to her as, "What? You're not supposed to react like this!"

According to Burns, the scene took a long time to develop in rehearsals. In having lost her bracelet--Iachimo slipped it off her arm unknown to her in "Pick'd the Lock"--she has lost "an important link to my husband." In the midst of searching for the bracelet she must deal with "the worst kind of antagonism" from Cloten, who calls Posthumous a commoner. Burns says the character understands Cymbeline has encouraged Cloten to come after her and for the first time comprehends the depth of the great undercurrent of wrong at her father's court. In the final scene of the play, when Belarius tells Cymbeline that he kidnapped his sons and took them away from the court, Imogen can appreciate why. Near the end of the exchange between Cloten and Imogen in this scene, Pisanio enters for yet another brief scene. According to Pennell, Pisanio has now seen Cloten press his suit physically and verbally on Imogen and, more importantly, he has seen the state into which Cloten's advances have thrown Imogen. None of this information comes from the lines, Pennell says, but it relates directly to Pisanio's later decision to give Cloten Posthumous' uniform and send him off to Milford-Haven.

Act II, Scene 4

Act II, Scene 4, contained two scenes: Scene 11, "She Stripp'd...She Pluck'd" (pp. 61-71); and Scene 12, "No Way for Men" (pp. 71-73). These contiguous scenes take place in Philario's house in Italy. The first begins with a conversation between Philario and Posthumous, which Ziegler played as if he knows that Iachimo is in the house and that he must wait for his appearance. Iachimo enters later in a yellow terrycloth robe and light blue swim trunks, confirming that he has "obviously not just arrived in an airport limo." Even Philario appears in lounging attire, in contrast to the conservative suit and sweater Posthumous wears that make him feel hot and ill at ease as he waits. Philario opens the scene with a discussion of politics, upsetting Posthumous' determination to focus his energies on his adversary, says Ziegler. This distraction explains the slight edge in Posthumous' voice during the opening dialogue. When Iachimo does enter, Ziegler explains, Posthumous wants to get this encounter over with quickly, despite the complete trust he places in his wife. When Iachimo gives him letters from Imogen, Ziegler says, the fact that she has used this Italian as a messenger despite what he believes she must have learned of his purpose in coming to Britain gives Posthumous his first clue that something has gone awry. Ziegler allowed some time to pass while waiting for Iachimo to broach the subject Posthumous wants to discuss, and when no mention is made of it, Posthumous must raise the issue himself. As the Italian claims to have enjoyed Imogen's favours, Ziegler says, his Posthumous becomes entangled in the torture of the thought that he must remain friends with this man by the terms of the wager between them. As Iachimo recites the proof, moving from a description of the tapestry to that of a chimney frieze--each detail more intimate than the last--he can take advantage of the likelihood that Posthumous has spent little time in this room. When Posthumous hears a description of the room's roof, Ziegler says he thinks, "I don't even know what the roof of that chamber looks like" and is heartbroken that his rival knows so much more than he does. Such a mental state, while not obvious to an audience, prepares his character to take the next step.

Ziegler understands the playwright's purpose in using the word "honour" so much in this scene is to underscore the serious consquences of what seems like a game to Iachimo. Posthumous appeals to Iachimo by granting that he has seen the chamber; Iachimo then produces the bracelet--a personal bond between the couple--and Posthumous assumes the worst. Ziegler and Phillips experimented with several ways of having Posthumous react to the bracelet. They finally decided not to allow him to erupt fully at that moment but rather to start the build and then let Philario's interjection bring the character back to reasonableness. Ziegler describes asking Iachimo to give him some sign that he has slept with Imogen as one of his character's most desperate remarks. Because Iachimo can swear by the god Jupiter that he had the bracelet from her arm Posthumous again believes him. Phillips wanted the two characters to break out of the conventional mode of arguing at this point, relates Ziegler, so Iachimo knocks Posthumous down and gets on top of him, only to have Posthumous roll him over to take the top position. Ziegler understands that since he can physically feel Feore's body at that point, he can believe in his physical union with his wife. Iachimo then tells him about the mole on the left breast, but by this time Posthumous' world has already come down, according to the actor.

Feore sees Iachimo at this point as a character with "several chips on his shoulder and a couple of major psychological flaws." But having collected the information to win, he controls the scene and the tempo, building slowly to the point where he devastates Posthumous. Philario, Wilkin notes, believes at the top of the scene that Iachimo has carried the joke a bit far even for him but becomes alarmed when he sees the depth of the passion between the two men. Wilkin thinks Philario is a balance between a devilishly malicious (if likable) Iachimo and a pig-headed (if likable) Posthumous.

Ziegler says of the soliloquy that composed "No Way for Men" that he does not remember Phillips' method for communicating its basic structure, but he does recall that after going well in rehearsals the scene turned troublesome around the technical/dress rehearsal stage. At that point, he remembers, Phillips told him:

The thing that you as an actor are saying with that speech is...I feel like a bit of an ass..out here talking to you people...I have done some terrible things in this play for which you may not forgive me and I am going to do some more terrible things....But please understand that I hurt so much right now that nothing makes sense.

Act III, Scene 1

Act III, Scene 1, played as one unit, called Scene 13, "War and Confusion" (pp. 74-78), set at the palace at tea time. Cymbeline refuses to pay the tribute demanded of Britain by Caesar, but Donkin points to his gentlemanly reception of the Roman general, Caius Lucius. The actor says he sees in this officer those attributes of character absent from Cloten; in fact, no one at the court, except banished Posthumous, can match the quality of Caius Lucius. John Bourgeois, Caius Lucius, found this a bittersweet scene with Cymbeline. The bitter part is delivering such a harsh message and the sweet is showing this "adopted father" that he can do a responsible job well. Phillips used as his model for the scene the relationship between British Prime Minister Harold Macmillan and President John F. Kennedy, a friendship based on mutual respect. Wright says that the queen, whose patriotism springs from her desire to run the country, supports Cymbeline's decision. In this production Cloten spends much of the time lounging on a down stage sofa listening to the conversation before rising to make any contributions. Campbell agrees with Donkin that Cloten, although of the same mind, shows none of the refinement of a prince, but rather "acts like a yahoo."

Act III, Scene 2

Act II, Scene 2, played as one unit, Scene 14, "Milford Way" (pp. 78-83), set in the palace barrister's office. Pennell observes that this scene turned out to be the only one in which Pisanio comes close to being like Camillo in that both characters receive orders from superiors to kill someone and both decide not to carry out those orders. Pennell believes that the very human qualities of Pisanio make him wonder, "What can Posthumous think of me that I would do such a deed?" Then Pisanio must face Imogen and her excitement over the letter Posthumous has sent her through Pisanio asking her to meet him at Milford-Haven. Pennell posits that the only sense Imogen can make out of his demeanor is that he thinks she ought not to leave the palace.

Burns as Imogen treasured that scene because it gives her "a ticket out," and she does not care if she never comes back. While Imogen notices Pisanio's reluctance, Burns played her desire to see Posthumous strongly to set up the irony for the audience of having learned the truth from Pisanio earlier in the scene.

Act III, Scene 4

Act III, Scene 4, played as one scene, Scene 16, "I am a Soldier" (pp. 89-l00), set in a railway station. Both Burns and Pennell point to Phillips' transposition of Act II, Scene 3 (the scene which introduces Belarius, Guiderius, and Arviragus), to follow Act III, Scene 5, making this scene much easier to play because the energy built into the first carries Pennell immediately into the second. The location made him feel nostalgic about little country stations in England in the middle of nowhere; this setting brings with it an image and feel of distance, even alienation that the actor found useful. Preparations for war are visible, Pennell notes. When Pisanio and Imogen appear, he pushes a fully loaded wheelchair, an unusual prop; Pennell explains that since the pair probably traveled out of Paddington Station and thus risked being seen by their upper-class peers, the wheelchair, scarf, and dark glasses provided a disguise.

The transposition also helps, Pennell says, because Pisanio hasn't had time to think of a plan. He has probably had to chat with Imogen on the trip and talk with her, without a chance to give the plan more than a first thought. Phillips decided that Pisanio loves horse racing, so he carries a groom's clothing, a pair of binoculars, and a swagger stick that hides a sword. Pisanio has left the palace announcing he's to spend the day at the track. The plan itself tells more about Imogen than Pisanio, Pennell explains, because he will not propose any plan that he does not believe her fully capable of executing.

Burns says that Shakespeare has laid out in this scene the stages through which people pass when they have experienced rejection, since Imogen hears from Pisanio that Posthumous has in fact asked him to kill her. It takes most people a long time to pass through those stages, Burns explains, but Imogen recovers from despondency so quickly that five minutes after Pisanio has told her the truth she stands ready to search for Caius Lucius. The scene contains some of the character's most anguished moments, even bringing her at one point to hate Posthumous; Imogen then jumps at the opportunity to observe her husband while disguised as a boy, which shows her "great strength of character" in Burns' opinion. The interval occurred here.

Act III, Scene 5

Act III, Scene 5, played as one unit, Scene 17, "War for Britain" (pp. 100-108), and played at the palace. Donkin posits that royalty cannot always display emotions in public, so Cymbeline courteously refuses to pay tribute. Donkin sees Cymbeline's own judgment and that of his subjects in this refusal. According to Bourgeois, Caius Lucius has resigned himself to the inevitability of war but worries about what will help to his mentor, completely under the sway of the queen and her son. With Caius Lucius dispatched to Rome, Wright says, the queen considers that even if events have not gone as she planned, they have gone well enough for her. Both Imogen and Pisanio have disappeared, the obstacles to putting Cloten on the throne. But Campbell's Cloten has another motivation: Imogen. He has tried gentleness and now he decides to collect her. He demands Posthumous' clothing from Pisanio, arrogantly shoving him. Pennell finds his motivation in this encounter by working at self-control, not even daring to look at Cloten for fear of striking him. Campbell relates that Pennell told him he thought the wimpy gesture indicative of Cloten's character, in contrast to a brave action like a slap. Pennell acknowledges that Pisanio finally gives Cloten both the uniform and news of Imogen's destination because he believes she will have met Caius Lucius by the time Cloten arrives and will escape any danger he might have posed to her.

Act III, Scene 3

Act III, Scene 3, transposed to this spot, played as one unit, Scene 15, "Safer Hold" (pp. 83-88), set in a cave in Wales. Stephen Russell says that because Belarius stole the king's two sons and raised them here in the wild he has kept them away from the inverted values of Cymbeline's court. Russell wants the audience to see that the environment in which he has raised these boys:

> is an incredibly natural, wonderful situation, better than court life, where honesty prevails, where truth prevails, where all the things that seem to be mucking up the court are not happening here....until the court interrupts and...ends it all.

The bonding between Belarius and his "sons," says Russell, exceeds that of any group at court. Russell notes that despite their closeness the boys long to see a larger world, a natural desire but one that hurts this "father." Keith Thomas, Guiderius, recounts that Phillips rehearsed this scene at the beginning with the actors as gorillas, a table serving as the only prop. The performers jumped on and over it, using it as the cave. Phillips then introduced

Imogen into the scene without anyone knowing what would happen. Still without benefit of speech, the three actors had to decide what to do with Imogen, says Thomas: "Kill her or keep her." Then Phillips allowed the use of patterned sound and finally speech, which within five minutes had progressed to Shakespearean verse, Thomas recounts. The two boys, he says, have both animal and human qualities; the animal characteristics don't demean these youths, but allow them heightened senses of the wild, traits superior to those of refined persons raised at court. In addition, the boys' princely nature must shine through, as in Thomas' line, "What air's from home" (III.3.29), with a double meaning that he does not know what the air is like away from home and that it puns on "heirs," describing the boys.

Act III, Scenes 6 and 7

Act III, Scenes 6 and 7, played as one unit, called Scene 18, "Stay and Eat It" (pp. 108-114), still in the cave at Wales. Imogen, who never before "ventured outside the palace gates except in an armoured car," now sets out alone, overland, on foot, from Milford-Haven, with a bicycle that does not work, according to Burns. Imogen has two things working for her: a release from the confinement of court and a charge of energy to get to Posthumous. Her hunger drives her into the cave, but her sense of humour allows her to get through discomfort and terror. Russell says that finding Imogen disguised in the groom's clothes as Fidele simply adds one more member to the family, once they see Fidele means them no harm, a condition that again contrasts to the machinations of the court. Thomas says his reaction centers on the animal instincts of one creature toward a strange one, a sensual reaction that shows him this boy represents something extraordinary. Thomas did not see this heightened natural sense in the production done by the British Broadcasting Corporation in the recent series.

Act III, Scene 8

This production cut Act III, Scene 8, originally called Scene 19, "Incite the Gentry" (pp. 114-115). Phillips experimented with the scene before deciding to cut it, for example trying it set in a club in Rome.

Act IV, Scene 1

Act IV, Scene 1, played as one unit, called Scene 20, "Spurn Her Home," set in Wales. In this scene, Cloten, who has now reached Wales, delivers his soliloquy. Having succeeded in nothing else, the character sets out to kill Posthumous, rape Imogen, and force her home, where his mother can intercede for him with Cymbeline. As close as the queen believes herself to Cloten, the latter views their relationship in terms of using him to fix

the problems he creates for himself.
Act IV, Scene 2

Act IV, Scene 2, played as three units: Scene 21, "Come to Dust" (pp. 117-134); Scene 22, "Wren's Eye" (pp. 134-136); and Scene 23, "Cry Out for Service" (pp. 136-139), all of which played in front of the cave. Burns describes Fidele's illness, which leads to her taking Pisanio's restorative drug, as resulting from the long walk, having had very little food, and her desire to see Posthumous. When the boys talk about their love for her and their father, the memory of her own provides a painful experience. As Fidele goes into the cave, Cloten arrives. Campbell says Cloten attacks the man standing in front of him for no reason except temper. Thomas, using his animal instinct, fights because Cloten attacks. Had Cloten acted reasonably, he, too, would have gotten a good reception. In killing Cloten, says Thomas, Guiderius realizes that he has killed a fellow creature, now having stepped out of his Garden of Eden. Phillips says, "Killing a human being is a new concept, something that has not entered their universe." Once Guiderius comes back with Cloten's head, Belarius also sees the end of their pastoral world. When Arviragus brings in the "body" of Fidele, under the spell of the sleep-inducing drug, Russell reads the situation as some sort of cosmic justification: "You took a life, you lose a life." He leaves the boys with Fidele's body to give them time to adjust to the reality of death while he goes to get Cloten's body. Leaves fell from the ceiling on stage left for the rest of this scene. Phillips wanted them to cover the entire stage, but they could only fall from one point from which a stagehand already stationed there could drop them. The leaves presaged the falling of soldiers like leaves in the war, shortly to be evinced on stage. Phillips contends that the falling leaves forced the audience to listen more closely to the lines the characters spoke.

Phillips speculates that it is possible to use the same actor to play Cloten and Posthumous, since they have no scenes together in the play. If he had done so, he says, the audience could have been genuinely fooled about which one had died--as is Imogen--because of having to stop and think at each appearance of one or the other, "Who is it?" Imogen's soliloquy over "Posthumous"/Cloten composed "Wren's Eye." Burns says that here Imogen maintains her control even when she wakes up; she and Phillips talked about those first moments of this crisis and discovered that in such a situation people do not usually lose control until later. The first reactions are calmer, focusing on an understanding of what has happened and why, so here Imogen wonders if Pisanio has betrayed her. She feels "absolutely alone."

When the Italian army comes along in "Cry Out for Service," she says, she goes with Caius Lucius because he may take care of her, although she wishes only for death at that moment. According to Bourgeois, Caius Lucius enters tired and world-weary; he knows the stupidity of war, that it can usually be avoided but seldom is. When he sees the body of an enemy soldier, he wants to bury it. Bourgeois recounts that Phillips told the actors that a body during war time could even be booby-trapped. Nonetheless, in the face of so much inhumanity, this character performs humane acts by burying the body and taking Fidele under his protection.

Act IV, Scene 3

Act IV, Scene 3, played as two units, Scene 24, "Amaz'd with Matter" (pp. 140-141); and Scene 25, "Perplex'd in All" (pp. 141-142). These scenes played continuously and were set in the palace. Cymbeline wants to know Cloten's and Imogen's whereabouts: Pennell points out that Pisanio, the one person who has set everything up, does not now know where to find anyone. Shakespeare has clearly located everyone but nobody has communicated with Pisanio, who during "Perplex'd in All" has a soliloquy expressing his concern at this development.

Act IV, Scene 4

Act IV, Scene 4, played as one unit, called Scene 26, "Action and Adventure" (pp. 142-144), set in Wales. Belarius cannot dissuade the boys from fighting in the war, deciding in the end to join them.

Act V, Scene 1

Act V, Scene 1, played as one unit, called Scene 27, "Every Breath" (pp. 145-147), and was set inside the Italian camp. Posthumous enters with a column of Italian soldiers and lags behind as they march offstage. Pulling off his uniform, he begins what Ziegler calls "the bloody scarf speech," the essence of which is his repentance and longing to atone with his own life by fighting for Britain. Pisanio had never considered really killing Imogen; he sent her scarf, dipped in blood, to Posthumous as proof of her "death." Ziegler also believes it important that Posthumous repents of arranging for her murder while still ignorant of her constancy.

> …You married ones If each of you should take this course, how many
> Must murder wives much better than themselves For wrying but a little.
> V.l.2-5.

As if to make amends, he seeks death by fighting for her country; Ziegler understands that banishment prevents Posthumous from asserting any connection with Britain in his own right. Technically, Ziegler says, the speech was one of the more difficult ones for him perhaps because he delivers it immediately on entering after an hour-and-a-half absence from the play.

Act V, Scenes 2 and 3

Act V, Scenes 2 and 3, played together as one unit, called Scene 28, "Those That Would Die" (pp. 147-154), and was set in the field. Iachimo enters with an Italian army column; resident lighting designer Michael Whitfield's lighting clarified Feore's distinctive profile and manner of holding his cigarette to identify him immediately in this group. Posthumous comes upon him and for a moment their personal battle takes precedence over the larger war. Feore considers that his character must now face that fight with Posthumous that he has worked so treacherously to avoid. As he feared earlier he loses and fully expects Posthumous to kill him. Ziegler thinks that Posthumous does not kill him in order to deny him the end Posthumous himself wants, death.

Following this confrontation, Belarius, Guiderius, and Aviragus enter to make their stand against the Italian army. A group of British soldiers, perhaps including Cymbeline himself, retreat despite the pleas of these three to stay and fight. Donkin says that in the dark of the scene, one cannot identify the character with certainty as the king; Phillips explains that modern warfare keeps leaders out of the front lines. Posthumous joins Belarius and his sons as they make a stand. Fight master Jean-Pierre Fournier choreographed three waves of enemy soldiers from the tunnels onto the forestage area held by the four actors. Work on these fights began very early in rehearsals, with a whole evening given over to the first one. As the fights developed, the enemy soldiers attacked and fell or rolled backwards down the tunnels to re-form for the next assault. Light concentrated on the main stage area made such a design possible by focusing the audience's attention on a small area filled with activity and allowing the regrouping in darkness.

Act V, Scene 3

Act V, Scene 3, followed immediately as if part of the same scene, beginning with a long soliloquy by Posthumous. Ziegler looked for personal reasons for Posthumous to make that long speech and, when they did not spring to mind, Phillips broke up the speech among about eight people, giving each a reason for speaking his or her portion. One person spoke into a field microphone, another into a tape recorder as if doing a piece for the evening news. Ziegler recounts that Phillips told him a week before opening to learn the speech because he would probably be doing it. Ziegler cannot point to any motivation that helped him understand the speech, but he can say that the "arc the character has to complete in the second half of the play somehow lacked that completeness" until he began doing the speech. Two points of the speech interest the actor. First, Posthumous credits Belarius and his two sons with making the stand that stemmed the tide of battle without referring to the part he himself played, which was at least as significant. Second, he notes the number of times the word "slaughter" is used in the writing. He remembers the 1984 production of *1 Henry IV* done at the Third Stage in which he played Hotspur and which concluded with enough talk about the battle as "slaughter" for him to believe that perhaps Shakespeare's point in writing it lay in Falstaff's view, "What is honour?" Giving up on the possibility of dying a glorious death in battle for Imogen, Posthumous lets himself be led off by a British soldier to an ignominious death. Once imprisoned, he wants only to unfetter his soul so he can go to Imogen, Ziegler perceives.

Act V, Scene 4

Act V, Scene 4, played as one unit called Scene 29, "Rise and Fade" (pp. 154-164), set in the field. Posthumous, mistaken for an Italian soldier, is now in prison, assured of death. In sleep, however, he sees his father, mother, and brother, who tell him he comes from noble blood; that knowledge gives the character hope, Ziegler notes. Jupiter's arrival to tie up the final strands of the play, Phillips says, is a masque, an elaboration of the English tradition of mummers. In its form as a dance or pantomime, as in *The Tempest*, Phillips maintains, it wastes time to "watch people skipping around like little Morris men." For *Cymbeline*, Phillips decided to present this masque for all of the spectacle and shock value he could get out of it. "I want to alert them, startle them awake for the Fifth Act," he says.

Jupiter appears as an *avatar* in *Cymbeline* in a World War II bomber, a literal *"deus ex machina,"* says Wilkin, who played him. He puts a "beneficence" on the situation that man has fouled up beyond his ability to fix. Wilkin appeared on the balcony in the cockpit of the plane while two huge propellers roared from the floor; he spoke into a microphone for his "radio." Jupiter tells Posthumous that he crosses people to make his blessings to them the sweeter and promises that he shall be the lord of Lady Imogen.

Act V, Scene 5

Act V, Scene 5, played as one unit, called Scene 30, "Such a Peace" (pp. 164-187), set in the field hospital. Feore recalls that Phillips wanted scene changes accomplished in seven seconds, the time it takes the eye to adjust from light to darkness and back to light again. So when the lights came up on this scene, a massive tank dominated the set, sticking out from under the balcony, a long barrel and an enormous pair of wheels. Phillips calls it "a destructive element" that he wanted to stage as being swallowed up by nature, with weeds growing over it. The final image on stage, without the weeds, was "incomplete" to him. The principal characters are dressed in military uniforms, and wounded soldiers lie on the floor, some on stretchers. Whitfield tried to suggest with lighting that the scene of devastation stretched as far as the eye could see; the director wanted the shock value of the scene multiplied and for the audience to wrestle with the disconnected fragments.

The scene contains a number of discoveries, all but one of which the audience already knows. Therefore, the dynamic of the scene consists of watching reactions of people who do *not* know, says Pennell. Cymbeline has the most to learn; by setting up the field hospital around the king, Phillips takes some of the burden off of the actor to sustain the audience's attention throughout all those discoveries. Cymbeline begins by knighting Belarius and the two boys. Then later he asks about Cloten, and Guiderius steps forward to admit he has killed the king's stepson. Thomas explains that the character has always told the truth, and Russell says that his Belarius takes his cue from Guiderius. "If this son can speak the truth, then so can Belarius," says Russell, who admits that telling the truth ends his hope for returning with the boys to their natural world. "Now that he has told Cymbeline that the boys are his long-lost princes, what does Belarius have left?" he asks, speculating that he will take an apartment over the palace garage. "Not my garage," quips Thomas; "Not until he takes a bath."

The only discovery for the audience is the queen's death, announced by the doctor. Innes says that the doctor, conscripted for service, feels uncomfortable about his part in the war. In his announcement, his voice was blended with Wright's, who overrode him to describe her hatred of the king from an offstage microphone. At the end of that speech the doctor's voice again became the dominant one as the queen's faded away. In this manner actor and director avoided having Cornelius stand there and make one more announcement, Innes says. Then Cymbeline's attentions turn to to Caius Lucius and the Italian prisoners, on whom he pronounces a death sentence. Bourgeois says that his character had not looked for death at the hands of his old friend and says so. He also notes that his character asks only for the life of his page, Fidele.

Burns says that she does not think Imogen would have revealed herself as Cymbeline's daughter in the camp, preferring to accept death, had she not spotted the ring she gave to Posthumous on Iachimo's finger. Feore says that Iachimo has come to the point where he, too, wants only to die and enjoys this opportunity to unburden his conscience. The sound of Iachimo's voice brings Posthumous to his feet; Ziegler says the story that Iachimo has told publicly further humiliates him because he was still deluded by the lie. Upon hearing that Imogen proved faithful, he wants even more to die and by the fastest means possible, says Ziegler. In his pain he sees Imogen come toward him but does not recognize her and forcefully tosses her to the stage floor. To Phillips, that devastating blow is very important: "After what the characters have been through to rid themselves of the aggression of war, notice how quickly aggressive acts erupt again. How do we reach the point at which we can live in a different kind of communion with one another?" he asks.

Burns also keyed off of the recognition of a voice, but for her it belongs to Posthumous. At that point she realizes that everything she thought she had lost comes back to her, and that realization staggers her. Despite knowing that Posthumous has given Iachimo her ring and that Iachimo has taken her bracelet--the outward symbols of her marriage to Posthumous--Imogen wants to exchange these tokens with Posthumous as a sign that they will begin anew. At that moment, the actress says, Imogen stands between her father and Posthumous, the two men who have betrayed her, not judging them but moving forward in new relationships with each of them. She says of Imogen's relationship with Posthumous:

> We are damaged people but we will try to rebuild what we lost. I have a feeling that because we are two extraordinary people we will make it, but it will be a very, very delicate, fragile thing to reconstruct.

In that sense she describes the ending of this production for Posthumous and Imogen in terms of a "real" instead of "happy" ending.

Ziegler says that his Posthumous forgives Iachimo because he needs forgiveness from Imogen; he believes he has begun to obtain it when she puts his bracelet back on her arm, causing him to put the ring back on his finger. The actors explain that the strength these two characters have had to build within themselves will see that relationship rebuilt. While Burns agrees that Imogen comes through this experience a stronger person, she also says that, given a choice, if painful experiences build strength, she would rather have done without them. But now that she has acquired that strength, along with the increase of love and faith that also sustain Imogen, she has many of the qualities necessary for starting again in the marriage. Burns, however, remains more skeptical than Ziegler about their characters' future together.

Pennell finds significance in the red poppy petals that rained down on the final tableau. On Remembrance Day in England, he says, the queen lays a wreath at the cenotaph, and a concert is given at Albert Hall. At the conclusion, the following lines from Lawrence Binyon's *For the Fallen* are read:

They shall not grow old, as we that are left grow old:
Age shall not weary them, nor the years condemn.

At the going down of the sun and in the morning
We will remember them.

During the moment of silence that follows, thousands and thousands of poppy petals fall from the ceiling over the hall, creating quite an emotional moment. Those bright red petals, representing the poppies of Flanders Field, also fell at the end of this production.

Jupiter, Donkin says, admits the gods have wrecked havoc and yet now everything will turn out all right. The soothsayer's last line, given in this production to Cymbeline, says Donkin, reiterates what the god has said:

The fingers of the powers above do tune
The harmony of this peace. V.5.457-468.

Phillips believes the lines quoted at the top of this chapter are Shakespeare's tribute to James I, and ring hollow; he cannot see universal peace in this scene. Cymbeline, he surmises, has probably learned nothing at all and, "like the duke in *Measure for Measure*, Cymbeline remains a king of dark corners."

Following each performance the cast exited to the lobby through the aisles of the house to greet the audience with a medley of popular wartime tunes: "The White Cliffs of Dover", "We'll Meet Again But I Don't Know Where", "Lilli Marlene", "Mademoiselle from Armentieres, Parlez-Vous?", "Pack Up Your Troubles in Your Old Kit Bag", and "It's a Long Way to Tipperary". Richard March accompanied the cast on the piano, and company manager Ron Nichol set up glasses of beer for the cast to drink. Although only cast members got beer, the attraction became so popular that toward the end of the run large crowds who had not attended the performance waited in the lobby for the cast to begin the sing-along. The addition, put in place by Phillips at 4:30 p.m. at opening-night rehearsal, was the last bit of business added to the show. Some in the audience would sing and others preferred to listen, but few left the theatre until the cast had departed from the lobby and March had played his last note.

Act Three: The Young Company

"Tyrant, show thy face."
Macbeth, V.6.24.

Chapter Twelve: *The Resistible Rise of Arturo Ui* and *Macbeth*

The Young Company met for the first time on 14 April in Rehearsal Hall 1 of the Festival Theatre. Tom Kerr, director of the company, not only had overall supervision of the company's activities but also directed both *The Resistible Rise of Arturo Ui* and *Macbeth*. Kerr was making his Stratford directing debut but was no newcomer to directing or to Canadian theatre. He was born in Scotland in a theatregoing family and came to Canada for what he originally expected to be a short time, "but stayed for the rest of my life." After graduation from the University of British Columbia, he taught in high school there while spending some of his vacations in London. Michael MacOwan, whom he met while studying there, advised him that the Canadian theatre "desperately needed directors," so Kerr followed that advice. He says he found the professional theatre in Canada in a state of development, "where one could direct amateur or professional, teach or adjudicate. It wasn't like an established European culture, where you had professional and amateur." After working on workshops and contests, with an occasional professional offer, he did a season of Equity summer stock that Tyrone Guthrie happened to see in Alberta in the early Sixties. Guthrie invited him to Minneapolis for the first season at the Guthrie Theatre, and a year later he was Guthrie's assistant. Following that eighteen-month stint, he directed *The Caretaker* for the Glasgow Citizens Theatre. Although he continued to work with Guthrie until his death, he also insisted on living and working in Canada.

Kerr first met Neville during the latter's tenure at the Citadel Theatre in Edmonton. He first directed Neville in a production of *Pygmalion* and again as Shakespeare in a Canadian Broadcasting Corporation production of another of Shaw's plays, *The Dark Lady of the Sonnets*. When Neville moved to Halifax, Kerr directed him as Othello. "I have seen Canada develop. It was unheard of to have Canadian plays at one time and...(as director of the

Neptune Theatre in Halifax) half my season was Canadian.'' While teaching in British Columbia, he was invited to become head of the drama department at the University of Saskatchewan in Saskatoon in 1975. Kerr continued his own development by studying at the Bergdorf Studio in New York and at Trinity College in London, where he worked extensively on the oral presentation of literature from Medieval times to the present. John Neville says he believed Kerr an ideal choice to head the Young Company because of his extensive work as a teacher.

Once Kerr accepted, he talked with Young Company founder Robin Phillips, who said that he ''started the Third Stage with the intention of putting about six old-time, settled, wonderful actors with about six bright, new, chipper, talented young ones and seeing what fireworks would happen...and do that with experimental plays. ''Several days before he resigned, to be replaced by Robin Phillips for 1987, Kerr asked himself if the Young Company's purpose was learning or being seen in roles in Stratford. Only if the purpose is learning, he says, does the ensemble become the most important element. When the plays are critiqued, he believes, reviewers make little distinction between productions at the three theatres. If the most important element is good performance, then the Young Company, he thinks, must recruit and cast as at the rest of the Festival, using powerful individual talents. He also points out that the actors in the 1986 Young Company ranged in age from 26 to 31, and asks, ''What do actors in that age range need to accomplish as members of the Young Company?'' Kerr says the question of purpose has troubled the Young Company for a long while.

Kerr chose to stage *The Resistible Rise of Arturo Ui* and *Macbeth*; he and Neville were intrigued by the connection between the two in the theme of lust for power. Kerr has liked the convention of using white face in *The Resistible Rise of Arturo Ui* to convey the facelessness of the mob that followed Hitler, yet was concerned about doing the last scene, the rally, with only fourteen actors. Once into the production, that difficulty proved solvable with sound and movement. As Kerr reminded the cast, the final scene, in which the mob embraces the new dictator, is ''as fresh as tomorrow's news.'' That idea also made *Macbeth* seem contemporary to him. The actors finally cast to play Macbeth and Lady Macbeth were aged twenty-eight and twenty-six, in roles that young actors in Canada seldom get the chance to play. So Kerr began with the concept of two young people at the height of their powers who make wrong choices. He concludes that this starting point has to be flexible in order to include the qualities and strengths of the actors.

John Neville and Richard Dennison met the company with Kerr at the first rehearsal. Neville welcomed the cast, explaining why it was a company "close to my heart" by telling them that his first professional association with the Stratford Festival had been as a senior member of that company in 1983 and that he had run the company in 1985. The Festival's Board of Governors could save half a million dollars by doing away with the Young Company, he said, but he promised them that he would resign first. He told them he considered the company a part of the entire Festival, not an isolated unit in a separate building. To that end the original schedule called for them to rehearse in the Festival Theatre for two weeks and then in the Avon Theatre before moving to their summer quarters at the Third Stage, located in the Kiwanis Building on Lakeside Drive. Neville cautioned that the company would need to stay together and function as a group over a longer time than the normal season (mid-April to August) usually allowed in order to reinforce the intense training programme its members undergo.

In fact, the Festival's option in their contracts included two possibilities for an extension of the season, and both were exercised. The first was for a six-week residency from 2 September to 12 October at the University of Waterloo, to work with students and redo *Macbeth* for performance there. The actors afterwards expressed their delight at the chance to interact with students. The second option, a tour of small towns in Ontario and the United States from October to February, depended upon a provincial grant approved in mid-July. They left waving a special goodbye to resident director Bob Beard (who had restaged *Macbeth* at Waterloo) on 13 October as scheduled; then the first of many feared breakdowns of their bus stopped them an hour north of Toronto.

Richard Dennison explained that the Young Company serves as the Festival's research and development division. Indeed, several members of the Festival and Avon companies--Colm Feore, Joe Ziegler, Keith Thomas, Lucy Peacock, and William Dunlop--have worked in the Young Company since 1983. Therefore, Dennison told them, their potential loss would do the Festival greater harm than the potential loss of any other section. He told them then that the tour would bring the Stratford Festival to many small communities that could not afford to bring in a larger company, such as the one that toured the United States in 1985. That company had consisted of fifty actors, with corresponding supply requirements in sets, costumes, and props; it required a guarantee of $110,000 a week. This tour would fit into one bus: actors, technicians, sets, costumes, props, and personal luggage.

Kerr added that once the two plays had opened in repertory, the company would be involved in projects and workshops, opportunities to explore individual development. To expose company members to other directors and working methods, Kerr invited Douglas Campbell, Robin Phillips, Martha Henry, and Guy Sprung, among others, to conduct summer sessions with the company. Having explained the rhythm of the season and as much as was known about the tour, Kerr turned his attention to the two plays that would form the first phase of their work, warning that thoughts of the tour must not take over other considerations at this point. He believes, however, that having to wait from April to July to find out about employment contributed some discontent to the rehearsal process as performers made individual decisions about pursuing auditions for other work.

Kerr, having combined in his career both academic and professional theatre, centers his concern on the study of the actor's speech, so he had both a movement and a voice coach assigned full-time to the Young Company for the first two months before the openings. Movement coach Paula Thomson studied dance and movement at the Jose Limon School in New York under Libby Nye and Jennifer Scanlan; at the Dance Circle in New York under Alfredo and Andrea Corvino; at the Centre of Movement in Toronto under Frau Til Thiele; and at the Richard Sugarman Dance Studio in Toronto. She is a faculty member at York University and a movement teacher at Equity Showcase in Toronto. She worked with the company in three ways: workshops for the entire company, choreography for dances, and individual sessions with actors to build the physical aspects of their characters. In the workshops, she led warmups each day during rehearsals. Because this is a young group, she says, they can "work a lot," and she was not afraid to demand a lot of them. She and Neville have worked together since 1983 and he shares her belief that the best movement for an actor is dance. Thomson choreographed the opening sequence with the barker, the tango, the whitewash song, and the final rally in *The Resistible Rise of Arturo Ui*. In *Macbeth*, she did the dance at the banquet. Finally, she worked with every actor on a physical approach to characterization. She says that a person generally leads with a certain part of the body, often a useful beginning in her work of developing a character. Or she developed a definite movement pattern, as for Clark, using his head and neck as if they were a periscope. After the productions opened, the Young Company joined the Festival workouts with John Broome, but Thomson came back once a week to work with them.

Voice coach Dorothy Ward, who prefers to be called a speech teacher, says that speech chose her, rather than the other way around. She began her career teaching gifted students in high school, then was trained by Kerr at the University of Saskatchewan. She has taught at Dalhouse University and the National Theatre School, among other places. She says that her approach is to work on sounds related to the text, emphasizing that an actor should take as few pauses for breath as possible in speaking. Her work with the company focused first on where breaths should be taken in the text. This kind of planning, she says, frees the actors to perform and experience the text more fully. She first saw Neville perform at the Citadel Theatre in Edmonton, remembering him as "the actor with breath forever, who seemingly never had to replenish."

Four members were returning to the company for a second season: Donald Adams, Kim Coates, Richard Gilbert-Hill, and Maurice Godin.

The Resistible Rise of Arturo Ui

At the first rehearsal, after a read-through of this play, stage manager Peter McGuire passed out packets of information about it. Berthold Brecht ostensibly wrote about a Chicago gangster, but the play is a thinly veiled allegory about the rise of Hitler in Germany. Most of the characters and events in the play have counterparts in history:

Arturo Ui, gangster leader .... Adolph Hitler, Chancellor
Ernesto Roma, friend of Ui .... Ernst Roehm, friend of Hitler
Emanuele Giri, gangster .. Hermann Goering, Natl. Socialist leader
Giuseppe Givola, gangster ..... Joseph Goebbels, propaganda chief
Old Dogsborough .... Paul von Hindenburg, President
Mr. Clark, trust leader .... Franz von Papen, former Chancellor
Ignatius Dullfeet, editor .... Dollfuss, Austrian Chancellor.

Place names also have counterparts: Chicago is Germany and Cicero is Austria. Kerr has directed this play often, and enjoyed fielding questions from the actors about these parallels, but avoided forcing an interpretation on any actor or scene at this early stage.

Also on the first day designer Stephen Degenstein, who had met Kerr at the University of Saskatchewan when Kerr headed the drama program there and who had become resident designer at the Neptune Theatre while Kerr was its artistic director, presented his concept of the production. Kerr and Neville, he says, talked to him about designing the play well ahead of time, in the summer of 1985. He adds that while the amount of money relative to the amount of space that he had to fill was not large, the most important restriction he faced was the half-hour changeover time between the two shows. Fourteen cast members play fifty-seven roles, so he could not give every character a completely different costume. Often, he explains, a hat or apron was added to an existing costume--as for the grocers. Most costumes were pulled from stock or borrowed: Only the women's dresses and Young Dogsborough's suit were built. Degenstein expected to have to build more

The Resistible Rise of Arturo Ui

BY BERTOLT BRECHT

DIRECTED BY	TOM KERR
DESIGNED BY	STEPHEN J. DEGENSTEIN
MUSIC BY	LAURA BURTON
LIGHTING DESIGNED BY	LOUISE GUINAND
CHOREOGRAPHED BY	PAULA THOMSON

THE CAST

in order of appearance

The Barker	DANIEL KASH
Old Dogsborough	RICHARD GILBERT-HILL
Giuseppe ("The Florist") Givola, gangster	JERRY ETIENNE
Ernesto Roma, Ui's sidekick	KIM COATES
Emanuele Giri, gangster	MICHAEL HANRAHAN
Arturo Ui, gangster boss	MAURICE GODIN
Dockdaisy, a singer	ANNE WRIGHT
Flake, Businessmen,	DONALD ADAMS
Butcher, leaders of the	DAVID McKNIGHT
Clark, Cauliflower Trust	LEE MacDOUGALL
Sheet, a shipping tycoon	DANIEL KASH
Young Dogsborough	DAVID MARR
Dogsborough's Manservant	DANIEL KASH
Ted Ragg, reporter on The Star	JERRY ETIENNE
Bowl, Sheet's treasurer	DONALD ADAMS
O'Casey, chairman of the investigating committee	DONALD ADAMS
The Actor	LEE MacDOUGALL
Goldman, wholesale vegetable merchant	DAVID McKNIGHT
A Wounded Woman	SALLY SINGAL
The Defendant Fish	RICHARD GILBERT-HILL
The Judge	LEE MacDOUGALL
The Court Physician	PEGGY COFFEY
The Defense Counsel	DONALD ADAMS
The Prosecutor	DANIEL KASH
Young Inna, Roma's boyfriend	DANIEL KASH
Ignatius Dullfeet	RICHARD GILBERT-HILL
Betty Dullfeet	MARCIA KASH

Reporters, Gunmen, Grocers of Chicago and Cicero, Bodyguards, Molls, Policemen:
DONALD ADAMS, KIM COATES, PEGGY COFFEY, RICHARD GILBERT-HILL
DANIEL KASH, MARCIA KASH, LEE MacDOUGALL, DAVID MARR,
DAVID McKNIGHT, SALLY SINGAL, ANNE WRIGHT.

Stage Manager	PETER MCGUIRE
Assistant Stage Managers	JANET SELLERY
	ANNE L. THOMPSON
Assistant Director	JORDAN MERKUR
Assistant Lighting Designer	KEVIN FRASER
Assistant to Laura Burton	MARILYN DALLMAN

that gangster on all sides of his crate. Guinand says Kerr wanted the look of a police lineup in this scene, so to give that illusion she top lit the crates. The flashing lights that other actors carry were focused on the gangsters on their crates; the sounds of blaring sirens reinforced the cops-and-robbers feeling of the scene.

Scene 1

Scene 1, "Cauliflower Trust" (pp. 12-18), takes place at night outside their building and was lit with just a bit of blue to preserve the feeling of a neutral space, Guinand says. The Cauliflower Trust (a parallel to the Prussian Junkers) has hit hard times and badly needs credit. As they fall to discussing methods of solving their crisis, word comes that the gangster Arturo Ui has come to "offer his services." Mr. Clark, head of the trust, sends word to throw him out and turns to a discussion of how a trusted city official, Old Dogsborough, opposed granting them a city loan. Kerr staged the scene with the trust members on the balcony, watching Ui being tossed out "politely." The text does not introduce the character at this point; the director chose to bring Ui and his strong-arm friend Ernesto Roma onto the dimly lit main stage while news of his presence is carried to the balcony. When the messenger comes down and pantomimes dismissing Ui, he leaves quickly to cover his embarrassment. Roma waits a few seconds before retreating after his boss.

This staging allowed a visual comparison between Clark and Ui; actor Lee MacDougall's Clark is sophisticated, a sharp dresser, and good with words, against Ui, who has none of these attributes but will acquire all three. Maurice Godin, as Ui, agrees that his character begins the play "on the down and out" and explains Ui's eventual rise to power as a result of his "compelling forward drive" stemming really from his fear and insecurity. Godin concludes from reading of history that Hitler's compelling personality helped him to draw a large following. Once he had that following, he kept attention focused on himself by temper tantrums that gave him time to think while he caught everyone's attention, Godin supposes. When Hitler became calm and began to talk again, everyone listened intently to what he said, a technique Godin used later in this play.

Kim Coates, Roma, sees his character as the muscle behind Ui's scheming; he is Ui's closest friend, relishing the opportunity to stay at his elbow. Coates recognizes that since Ui has most of the lines, Godin's habit of focusing his attention on Roma helps Roma seem to be a "larger character." The looks between the two cement their friendship.

Scene 2

Scene 2, "The Tango" (pp. 18-21), which Kerr set in a nightclub rather than in front of the Merchandise Mart, contrasted the strength of the trust--in taking property with which to bribe Old Dogsborough--against Ui's inability to exert pressure, even to dance socially. To highlight the sleazy nightclub Guinand designed a "purple and red" colour for the stage areas, with the sparkle of a mirror ball. She picked up Ui in a follow spot when he enters; the lighting board operator had no cues coming up immediately and so could man the spot. Guinand says the lighting focused on Ui, who here literally takes the spotlight away from others.

Scene 3

Scene 3, "Dogsborough's Saloon" (pp. 21-26), shows trust members giving Dogsborough the property "acquired" in the previous scene, supposedly in appreciation of his public service, but actually as a bribe to get the city loan. Lighting covered the stage for a neutral backdrop, says Guinand.

Scene 4

Scene 4, "Pool Room" (pp. 26-35), also begins in a neutrally lit space, with light from a window on the other side of the stage to make this scene different. Ui laments his inability to sell protection to others since he has not yet bought it for himself. Into his hideout comes the proof, in the person of Mr. Bowl, that Ui needs in order to prove Dogsborough has voted city money to the trust while sitting on it. Until this point, Godin explains, the incredible forward motion of the character has not latched onto anything with which to focus power on himself. Once he discovers the corruption of Dogsborough, the actor says, he has a place from which his rise to power can begin.

Scene 5

During the Country House" scene (pp. 35-46), set outdoors, Guinand covered the full stage with a "leafy white light...open, rich, and elegant" against the starkness of the rest of the show. Dogsborough, repentant at accepting this country house, is now vulnerable to Ui's demands for help. At the scene's close, Clark announces an investigation into the loan and suggests that Dogsborough find someone to clarify this matter.

Scene 6

Scene 6, "City Hall Inquiry" (pp. 46-57), introduces Ui as the man who will succeed in getting Dogsborough through the investigation--by killing two witnesses. Godin thinks that here Ui cannot function smoothly within the system, once having wedged his way in. His tactics have saved Dogsborough, but his speech fails to hold any listeners save his fellow gangsters. Roma applauds, but that audience Ui already owns. It is as if he has been shown the doorway to power, Godin theorizes, but does not yet have the key to open it. The scene represents the first time Clark has to deal with Ui, MacDougall notes, creating a shift in their relative strengths. A strobe light with red gels showed machine-gun fire for Bowl's murder.

Scene 7

Scene 7, "Acting Lessons" (pp. 57-63), takes place at the Mammoth Hotel, lit by Guinand's hotel window down stage left. Ui here realizes that he lacks the polished speech and physical dominance that mark the men of the trust, Godin notes. Against the advice of some of his gangsters, he takes voice and movement lessons from an old actor. Movement coach Thomson says that, while these new mannerisms seem awkward and unnatural--and thus very funny--in this scene, by the time Ui has perfected them he will have become a much more powerful man. Godin explains that now Ui has the facade that will make him credible, just as Hitler gained power while for a time no one took him seriously. For Godin, the false front Ui can now project helps him to gain power in ways that do not attract the notice that raw violence does. MacDougall, who played the old actor, relates that Godin watched movies of Hitler and picked out the moves he wanted MacDougall to exaggerate and give to him. He adds that it was rumored in rehearsals that John Neville would come in to play the role of the actor, but when that did not work out he and Godin got together in Godin's apartment one Sunday afternoon to work out all the business. Kerr made some modifications to this action, which turned out to be one of the biggest crowd-pleasers in the production.

Scene 8

"Ui Meets the Grocers" demonstrates his rising power. After offering the grocers protection, Ui burns the warehouse of one dissenter. The fire scene, Godin believes, shows that Ui can act provocatively but does not yet know if he can get away with it; the fire fuels Ui, too. MacDougall notes here the beginning of a shift in the balance of power from Clark to Ui. The decision to put Ui into the scene from the balcony both foreshadowed the end of the play and separated him from the people below. Guinand raised the light level on Ui as he increases the stakes; the offstage fire punctuated the scene, an effect created by off stage lights.

Scene 9

In Scene 9, "The Wounded Woman" (p. 72), that character comes out alone into a pool of dim light, begging for help after Ui's violence against her husband. The light comes up on Ui and Roma in discussion; Roma moves toward her, holding out one hand as if to help her, while concealing a pistol in the other. Just as Roma squeezes the trigger, Guinand put red light in the gunfire, followed by a quick blackout.

Scene 10

During Scene 10, "The Trial" (pp. 72-81), the location shifts to the courtroom, with light from two downstage gobos providing a window effect. A second gobo, Guinand recounts, revealed the same window but with much distortion. As "events get madder and madder," the window effect becomes increasingly more distorted. Here the trust successfully prosecutes a defenseless, innocent man for the fire--a trial manipulated by Ui's men. Ui does not appear in this scene in Brecht's script, but it gives him important information, Godin says. His name does not come up in reference to the crime, so he realizes he can get away with this one and even sees bigger targets ahead. So that he could demonstrate Ui's growing power in this scene, Godin asked Kerr to allow him to appear occasionally on the balcony, pantomiming the action of conducting to Gotterdammerung as if orchestrating the trial. Above the main stage, Ui swept across the balcony miming to the music while the lower stage lights dimmed and witnesses were changed in the box under cover of darkness.

Scene 11

Scene 11, "The Song of Whitewash" (pp. 81-82), includes singing by the judge and members of the prosecution team to cover the scene change. The script calls for Givola to sing alone, but Kerr gave the song boasting of the gangster's power to a group in order to accent the idea of the mob's mindless parroting of Ui's line. Guinand says she gave this action "a torrid look."

Scene 12

Here in "Dogsborough's Testament" (pp. 82-83), indoors at the country house, Guinand used two gobos to depict a window and leaf shadows. Old Dogsborough has suffered a stroke, but before he dies he makes out his will and confesses the evil deeds for which he and Ui's gang have been responsible.

Scene 13

Scene 13, "Testaments Cont'd" (pp. 83-98), takes place in a hotel room at night, shown by colder light to reflect both the night and the growing split between members of the gang. Dogsborough's will has been intercepted and a new one forged in which he "appoints" various gang members to posts in city government. The gangsters quarrel, Ui intercedes, and trust members urge Ui to dump Roma "to improve his reputation." Godin says that Ui is frustrated by the gangsters' failure to see the larger picture of his increased prominence and his new ability to act unopposed. Over the next few scenes, he says, the character begins to lose his hokey accent and develops the ability to handle things when others oppose him. At the end of the scene Ui deliberately lies about the involvement of the police--the beginning of even bigger lies.

Clark, who now advises Ui on business matters, wants to merge with Dullfeet, says MacDougall, and he pushes Ui to reassert control over his gangsters and get rid of Roma. But Ui takes matters into his own hands by killing Roma, and eventually Dullfeet, and forcing the merger on his own, says MacDougall.

Coates says that Roma senses a difference in his relationship to Ui at the beginning of the second half, when Ui does not spend as much time with the gang. Roma sees a possible double-cross by members of the gang and forces a split by drawing his revolver. But Ui has his mind on the larger goal and tells Roma to quit worrying about tensions within the gang. Coates adds that his Roma finds this rebuke the most empty moment in the play, adding that Godin also senses Roma's pain. Ui reaches out to him; they lay plans together just as they did "in the good old days."

Scene 14

Scene 14, "Garage Massacre" (pp. 98-103), was kept very dark to show the garage late at night, Guinand says. Roma assures his impatient men that Ui will come. Through one of the entrances the headlights of a car and the sound of its engine come closer. Backstage two lights representing the headlights were fastened to a light pole equipped with wheels that was pushed closer and then pulled back as the car leaves at the end of the scene. Guinand appreciated the chance to play with lighting for this special effect: "It's nice to be able to do something like that," she says. When Ui gets out of the car and comes into the garage, he has Roma and his faction shot. Godin explains that Ui's forward drive means sacrificing anyone in order to move ahead, with the character thus becoming "more and more insular."

That Ui would bring rival faction members to Roma's hideout in the garage constituted for Coates the first hint that things are not going right for his character. But his loyalty to Ui is such that in one of his first lines he inquires if Ui is all right--and then gets shot. Coates saw a production of *The Resistible Rise of Arturo Ui* in Edinburgh in which the homosexuality of the character "came out of the blue" in this scene, as Roma comforts a young man frightened by Ui's lateness. Coates explains that Ernst Roehm was homosexual, so he tried to build clues into some scenes. He kissed

Dogsborough's son in Scene 5 and held hands with other men at other times, to display this aspect of Roma's character.

Scene 15

Scene 15, "The Florist Shop" (pp. 103-111), was lit from a window down right that Guinand describes as similar to that in Act I; here, though, the intensity of light was lower because the mood of the scene is not as friendly. The trust, wanting to annex the town of Cicero, must first win over its crusading newspaper editor and his wife, Mr. and Mrs. Dullfeet. They meet Ui and reluctantly agree to merge, provided Ui holds down the violence for which he is now noted. After Dullfeet leaves, Ui decides to kill him. Now, says Godin, Ui moves to major public lies in an attempt to show the Dullfeets that he shares their goals and successfully concludes the negotiations.

Scene 16

Scene 16, "The Funeral" (pp. 111-119), is described by Guinand as "cold, rainy, and filled with doom and gloom." To achieve this effect she used full-stage cooler-colour washes, employed much more extensively throughout *Macbeth*. Ui, in his best Richard III style, begins in this scene to woo Mrs. Dullfeet--at her husband's funeral. During the long confrontation scene, Godin says, his character confronts her with the facts as Ui sees them: "You have nowhere else to turn but to me." Despite her rejection, no one tries to stop him. Two scenes later the announcement of the merger is made.

Scene 17

Because the locale for Scene 17, "Roma's Ghost" (pp. 119-120), returns to the hotel room, the window again provided the major light source. Guinand explains that the doors of the Cauliflower Trust Building (set on the balcony and constructed of scrim) could, when lit from behind, clearly show the approach of Roma's ghost. A fog penetrated the open doors even before the ghost stepped through them. Once the ghost enters, he crosses from Guinand's white back light into a red light spilling over the balcony to catch Ui sitting below. The effect, Guinand points out, linked both actors by confining them within it. The ghost's message, that Ui has killed a part of himself when he killed members of his own gang, so upsets him that he awakes from his dream and orders his men to shoot the phantom.

Coates liked playing the ghost scene, he says, because the light and fog create a powerful environment; also, lines cut from the production have the character complaining that he feels cold. Coates reread the script in the last month of the run, found those lines, and began playing the scene as if he were freezing.

Scene 18

Scene 18, "The Rally," needed still more special lighting effects, Guinand recalls. Kerr asked her to silhouette shapes on the main stage but not light the actors sufficiently for the audience to recognize individuals. She gradually built the intensity of light on Ui on the balcony, with a strong backlight, so that he took on a glow or aura as the scene progressed. Spotlights crowded to within six feet of his neck, in ever-increasing intensity. Such a bright profusion of light set Ui apart in an almost halo-like effect. The character, who stood on the balcony, now master of all he surveyed, grew more intense as he delivered the closing monologue. The faceless crowd marched on the stage below him, two of them carrying Degenstein's banners with the symbol for the Cauilflower Trust on one side and the Nazi swastika on the other. As Ui's speech grew more passionate, the marching columns of actors responded with more precision in the noise of stamping their feet in unison. Hours of marching practice, begun by Thomson in the first week of rehearsal, produced a definite crispness, which, with Guinand's contrasting light levels and Burton's selective but clear use of Ui's theme music, created the chilling spectre of Nazi power about to be loosed on the world. Godin removed his Hitleresque moustache as he descended the staircase and delivered his final lines to the audience as the actor rather than the character; the playwright warns that although Hitler was defeated, "the bitch that bore him is in heat again."

Macbeth

The second Young Company production, *Macbeth*, went into rehearsal on 16 April in Rehearsal Hall 1 of the Festival Theatre, two days after the start of *The Resistible Rise of Arturo Ui*. Laura Burton and Louise Guinand relate that the vast difference in style between the two shows dictated differences in their approaches. Burton, who seems to work best when a large bag of cookies resides on the piano, says that in an early meeting Kerr stressed that he wanted a primitive, earthy production. She sought a "through line" similar to the use of Wagner's opera in *The Resistible Rise of Arturo Ui* around which to compose, and she came across a Twelfth Century collection, "The Growth of the Tiobairreachd and Its Preservation," a Highland bagpipe chanter's scale that was, strictly speaking, outside of the Tenth Century setting for this play but not inconsistent with it. In selecting fanfares and creating six recurring thematic strands, as well as writing music for the coronation scene and dance before the banquet, she studied these and other Gaelic

MACBETH

BY WILLIAM SHAKESPEARE

DIRECTED BY	TOM KERR
DESIGNED BY	LESLEY MACAULAY AND
	WILLIAM SCHMUCK
MUSIC BY	LAURA BURTON
LIGHTING DESIGNED BY	LOUISE GUINAND
FIGHTS DIRECTED BY	JEAN-PIERRE FOURNIER

THE CAST

in order of appearance

Three Weird Sisters	MAURICE GODIN
	ANNE WRIGHT
	SALLY SINGAL
Duncan, King of Scotland	RICHARD GILBERT-HILL
Malcolm, Duncan's Son	DAVID MARR
Bleeding Captain	KIM COATES / JERRY ETIENNE
Lennox, Thane of Scotland	MICHAEL HANRAHAN
Ross, Thane of Scotland	DONALD ADAMS
Macbeth, Thane of Glamis,	
Later of Cawdor,	
Later King of Scotland	JERRY ETIENNE / KIM COATES
Banquo, Thane of Scotland	DAVID McKNIGHT
Lady Macbeth	MARCIA KASH
Messenger	LEE MacDOUGALL
Fleance, Banquo's Son	PEGGY COFFEY
A Porter	MAURICE GODIN
Macduff, Thane of Scotland	KIM COATES / JERRY ETIENNE
Donalbain, Duncan's Son	DANIEL KASH
Seyton, Macbeth's armour Bearer	DANIEL KASH
Two Murderers	DAVID MARR
	MICHAEL HANRAHAN
Lady Macduff	PEGGY COFFEY
Son of Macduff	PATRICK FINNIGAN
A Doctor	DAVID McKNIGHT
Gentlewoman Attendant on Lady Macbeth	ANNE WRIGHT
Seyward, Earl of Northumberland	LEE MacDOUGALL
Young Seyward, his son	RICHARD GILBERT-HILL

Messengers, Thanes, Soldiers, Servants, Attendants:
PEGGY COFFEY, RICHARD GILBERT-HILL, MAURICE GODIN, MICHAEL HANRAHAN, DANIEL KASH,
LEE MacDOUGALL, DAVID MARR, DAVID McKNIGHT, SALLY SINGAL, ANNE WRIGHT

Stage Manager	HEATHER KITCHEN
Assistant Stage Managers	JANET SELLERY
	ANNE L. THOMPSON
Assistant Director	JAMES GUEDO
Assistant Lighting Designer	KEVIN FRASER
Assistant to Laura Burton	MARILYN DALLMAN

tunes and then composed her own music for the instruments available to her. In the dance Burton wanted to use the Gaelic words, so she asked native Scotsman Douglas Campbell for help. He spent one morning walking around the auditorium of the Third Stage plugged into a portable tape recorder by means of earphones; he provided her with a phonetic transcription of the Gaelic to use in composing her music and teaching the cast the words.

Macbeth also required soundscapes, run through the synthesizer for distortion, as for the eerie voices underneath the witches' scene. Burton prefers to use a synthesizer, she says, for changing sounds rather than for reproducing the sound of a specific instrument. Production stage manager Heather Kitchens and Peter McGuire assisted Burton, sound coordinator Wendy York, and sound engineer Jim Stewart in working on the recorded composition, assigning directions and sound levels. Kitchens relates that sound cues had to be introduced during technical rehearsals because the cue-to-cue rehearsal had been cancelled.

Guinand says she was surprised at the degree of difference she was able to achieve between the two shows using the same basic lighting plan. She and Kerr talked through the time of day and specific location of each scene in *Macbeth*. The special effect used for the witches, Guinand believes, always creates expectation for an audience; in this case, four lights washed the stage in the blue inkiness of a nearly moonless night. She laughed at hearing Kerr's instructions to her after seeing the scene under light for the first time: "Make it darker." Many directors, she observes, are afraid to make extensive use of darkness, but she likes contrasts of light in scenes played in relative darkness. In lighting the rest of the show she relied heavily on the four different colour washes used to cover the entire stage rather than on individual areas of light, as she had used in *The Resistible Rise of Arturo Ui*. She acknowledges that the window gobo in Macbeth's castle was out of period, but she did not like the "square hole of light" effect that she would have gotten from correct window treatment for the period. The battle scene provided another challenge: Kerr had to make fourteen people look like two armies, so he staged two-person battles on different areas of the stage. Guinand lit them and then dimmed them as individual fights.

Macbeth codesigner Leslie Macaulay consulted with Kerr about the production until she was forced to withdraw because of illness. William Schmuck, design assistant to Polly Bohdanetzky for *The Boys from Syracuse*, took over the design chores for *Macbeth*. Grace Nakatsu replaced him. Schmuck, a graduate of the National Theatre School, had enrolled later at the University of Waterloo. He says choosing a career in design helped him combine his interests in theatre and art. He has designed some of the Grand Theatre's studio productions and costumes for one of its main stage shows. He enjoyed that assignment because, he says, he likes to work with the entire design process. He first came to Stratford for 1985 to ready sets for the American tour and was asked to work on the musical in 1986 before taking on *Macbeth*. Macaulay gave him designs for each character and visited the warehouse to find costumes to be modified for this production.

Schmuck says that Kerr wanted the production to look barbaric, for which they borrowed images from the Roman Polanski film version, including the rough, homespun look of the costumes, the barnyard atmosphere, and the savage look of the characters, costumes, and settings. Kerr allowed frequent departures from the Tenth Century setting so long as the look remained primitive. Because of the limited costume budget for Young Company productions, a large number came from stock. Schmuck says he pulled primarily from two Desmond Heeley-designed productions, the 1981 *Coriolanus* and the 1984 *1 Henry IV*, and the 1978 *Macbeth* designed by Daphne Dare. The show had also been produced on the Festival Stage in 1983, and some of designer Susan Benson's costumes were available for use but had to be greatly modified because they were very large on these young actors.

The requirements of the projected tour formed the basis for designing the rest of the production. Neville was determined to fit the entire show on one tour bus, says Schmuck, so all the costumes had to fit on two racks and be constructed for easy care. The designer solved this problem by making the costumes out of "leather and rags." He also designed a set that could be set up easily in any performance space the tour might encounter. Kerr asked him early in the process about using the brick wall Degenstein wanted for *The Resistible Rise of Arturo Ui*; originally Degenstein had envisioned a cartoon blood-red wall. The wood on stage, Schmuck explains, has a warm-to-hot yellow tint, a "hot" stage floor that from the raised seats is the backdrop for much of any play staged there. With Degenstein's textured brick wall in place, Schmuck decided to leave the floor a neutral space out of which would emerge the cooler colours he and lighting designer Guinand designed for the show. He particularly liked Guinand's design for its haze in front of the setting through which the show was viewed.

Kerr suggested that he consider covering part of the brick wall, and he began thinking about possible coverings while talking with Kerr about the witches, since Kerr did not want them to seem supernatural but very much connected with nature. With some of the Polanski imagery in mind, he worked with the idea of cocoons, seed pods, and natural objects found in hay or grass. From this concept, he decided to cover part of the brick wall with "erosion cloth, thickly woven to give the appearance of a macramé hanging or hanging moss in pale earth colours." He then had the three wierd sisters use their heavily woven shawls to create a compost heap from which steam would emerge, in place of the usual boiling cauldron. A voodoo doll was to materialize out of the mists of the heap. Schmuck then faced the difficulty of making smoke appear from the bare stage, over which the sisters had spread their cloaks, to form this smoldering mound. Technical director Allan De Luca built a system of hoses under the stage, leading to a small plug on the forestage that could be raised to emit the smoke. When the plug was not raised, its presence could not be detected from the audience, but it was opened after being hidden by the shawls.

Because most of the actors played at least three roles, Schmuck says, he gave each a basic costume to which bits and pieces were added or subtracted to make the costume appear as versatile as the performer. The same idea was used with performers playing major roles when the designer wanted to vary the look of the costumes. For example, Lady Macbeth wore the same dress with detachable sleeves and corset; her dress was to look like a patchwork of very soft leather. This is an important unifying factor, the designer holds, since these characters scavenge from the dead in roving bands after a battle. The element unifying them as belonging to the same tribe was the shaggy leather look. The same principle applied to the old, heavily scarred leather coronation robes; the designer wanted them to look as if they had been in tribal ceremonial use for generations. In this way Macbeth and Lady Macbeth looked as if they belonged to the upper echelons of this band of wandering barbarians, but they did not stand apart from it. "She might be queen, but I think she still feeds the chickens," Schmuck deduces.

Two weeks into rehearsal, actor Jerry Etienne, scheduled to play Macduff, was asked along with other cast members to audition to play Macbeth. Kerr explains that he had worked with actor Kim Coates, originally cast as Macbeth, at the Neptune Theatre during the spring of 1986 and had begun to doubt that the actor could handle the role vocally. At that point, Kerr says, he told Coates of his doubts. Coates, on the other hand, remembers talking with Kerr in Halifax and hearing Kerr tell him he would have to work hard, but he does not remember Kerr's expressing any doubts about his ability to master the role. According to Kerr, after two weeks of rehearsal he still felt uncomfortable opening the show with Coates playing Macbeth and decided to make the switch then. But because Coates still wanted a chance to play the role, Kerr promised him that once the production opened he would go into rehearsal and that he and Etienne would alternate the roles of Macbeth and Macduff at remaining performances.

Etienne opened as Macbeth and Coates as Macduff on 18 June. Beginning 18 July, when Coates opened as Macbeth, the two actors began to create different characters and thus different productions. Kitchens prepared separate prompt books for each show to accommodate blocking and script changes.

In place of a scene-by-scene description this chapter highlights the different interpretations of the roles of Macbeth by Etienne and Coates and the reaction of Marcia Kash, Lady Macbeth, to her role and the experience of playing it opposite two Macbeths.

Once Etienne had taken over the principal role, he sought to put the other actors at ease with him by learning the lines as quickly as possible; he was off book for Part One three days after being cast. He had played in *Macbeth* before but not as Macbeth or Macduff. Accepting that his Macbeth would be different from Coates', Kerr did not try to force him into the established blocking. Etienne says they spent the early days after the switch trying to find out "what kind of Macbeth I had in me," beginning with the Macbeth/Lady Macbeth scenes, which Kerr considered some of the most important in the play. The director had explained on the first day of rehearsal that he saw them as two young people at the height of their love for one another who make the wrong choices. Kerr and Etienne, the actor says, saw Macbeth as "both poet and barbarian--even if he was a general in the barbarian army." The actor found playing the poet easier than playing the general since, as he says, "I am not a huge person." He began by accepting Macbeth as a man who takes pride in his nobility. Indeed, in a scene with Lady Macbeth, he read the line, "If we should fail?" (I.7.59) to question the consequences of failing to keep his nobility; the actor explains Macbeth fears that more than simply failing. From the idea of nobility in this poet/general Etienne built his Macbeth.

When the audience first sees Macbeth, he enters fresh from battle, Etienne says. Furthermore, he has emerged as a hero and expects some reward for his services. Yet Macbeth senses as soon as he sees the wierd sisters that something not quite right hovers over this meeting. When the sisters predict he will become Thane of Cawdor and then king, Etienne's Macbeth assumes the king has been killed in battle. When Ross enters and greets Macbeth as Thane, Macbeth is confused by the prophecy. Etienne thinks Macbeth accepts his promotion without considering having to kill Duncan until the idea "just comes out of his mouth" without being consciously formed in the soliloquy "murder yet is but fantastical" (I.3.138). Once the thought has been spoken, he cannot get rid of the idea. It becomes the "parasite that gnaws his mind to pieces by the end of the play," says Etienne.

By the time Macbeth returns home, the actor explains, he has had a long ride and a long time to think about killing Duncan. In fact, the actor speculates, the soliloquy which begins:

If it were done, when tis done, then twere well
It were done quickly. I.7.1-2.

might have been mulled over on his way home. He has looked forward to his reunion with his wife, in whose embraces he hopes to forget the perplexing matters raised by the prophecy. Instead, explains the actor, his wife will not allow the idea of the murder to be dismissed. Macbeth carries the responsibility for murdering Duncan, he admits; she does no more than prompt him to do what he yearns to. His character is startled by the eagerness with which she pursues Duncan's life. Although Etienne's Macbeth loves his wife very much, he murders Duncan because he is carried away by ambition. Just as importantly for the actor, the murder proves a mistake for which he has to commit more murders in a vain attempt to cover up the first one. Ironically, if he does the first murder out of ambition to advance himself and Lady Macbeth, his crime costs him that very relationship. As he sheds more blood, he becomes increasingly estranged from her, relates Etienne, citing Act II, Scene 2, as an example. In this scene, which comes just before Macbeth engages the murderers to kill Banquo, the actor says Macbeth attempts to bridge the gap between himself and Lady Macbeth. He played the scene as if failing at closeness, feeling that she has slipped even further away.

After exploring the possibilities for playing the nature of the relationship between Macbeth and Banquo (David McKnight), Kerr and the actors decided that the two began the play as best friends. Etienne explains that establishing so strong a bond of friendship requires that Macbeth's decision to kill Banquo be a desperate attempt to protect himself and his queen. Macbeth cannot even tell his lady that he has done this; as she takes him by the hand to lead him out of the banquet, this murder has created more distance between them, the actor asserts. By the end of the play, Macbeth, still trying to cover up, has even killed Lady Macduff and her son. As Macbeth himself dies at the end, Etienne feared the audience would remember only those last two murders. But all four are important, he says, especially the initial murder of Duncan because it began the cycle of destruction.

Macduff serves as Macbeth's foil, says the actor, representing everything Macbeth has lost. While he may not be a poet, he is a man of strong action, as well as a general. He may act impulsively--as when he leaves his family unprotected to go to England--but he remains fiercely loyal to his native land. After defeating Macbeth, he offers the tyrant's crown to Duncan's son Malcolm, serving the state rather than protecting his own interest, Etienne concludes.

Once the production had opened, rehearsals reopened for the Coates *Macbeth*. Coates says John Neville did much of the directing--at what Neville calls Kerr's invitation. Coates had continued to work on the role since mid-April with assistant director James Guedo in the evenings. Before he even came to Stratford, he had visited Duncan's castle in Scotland, preparing for the role. He had worked with a coach in London who compared the progress of the character through the play to that of a leaf in a stream: At first it moves slowly, then picks up speed in preparation for the final spill over the waterfall, which ends in destruction, Coates recounts. Neville told him to consider that by the end of the play the character has become a trapped animal, lashing out at all who come within reach. For the first third of the play Coates elected to act as if struggling to choose between good and evil forces. Once having chosen evil, his Macbeth spends the last half "burning in hell to pay for his sins," the actor asserts.

Coates attempted to play the relationship between Macbeth and Banquo as the pivotal one for the first half and that between Macbeth and Macduff for the second half. The continuing relationship that ties both halves together, he says, is the marriage. Coates and Neville, like Etienne and Kerr, began with the idea of a strong physical attraction between husband and wife. Kash notes that the relationship with Coates was more sexually charged but less caring than the one with the gentler Etienne for her Lady Macbeth.

According to Coates, Neville encouraged him to play the poet during the first half and the warrior later. He took his starting point in developing the role from Macbeth's first line, "So foul and fair a day I have not seen" (I.3.37). "Where has he been and what has he been doing?" asks the actor. "He has fought a bloody battle and done it very well...so he feels both extremes as he comes in to the encounter with the sisters." Once he has heard the prophecy, he revives thoughts of murder to achieve the crown, on which, Coates believes, he has not before dared to act. Nor would Coates' Macbeth have been incited to murder if Lady Macbeth had not urged it. Kash says that while she could coax Etienne to do the deed, she almost had to insult Coates' manhood by calling him a coward to urge him to murder. Coates, like Etienne, believes the willingness to murder is forwarded by ambition.

Coates points to the turns in the play: Lady Macbeth urges him to murder, but he eventually initiates murders of which he cannot even tell her. The turning begins, Coates says, when they were crowned rulers of Scotland. It is a scene with no lines but one in which Macbeth demonstrates without words that he has taken command. By the time he engages the murderers, Macbeth has so thoroughly established himself as leader that Lady Macbeth kneels to him. At the end of the first part, Coates says, Neville told Kash she should look at Macbeth on his line "We are yet but young indeed" as if she were asking herself what kind of monster she had created. "Monster" provided an image for the second half of the show. When Macbeth visits the sisters again and discovers that despite his actions Banquo's son will be king, Macbeth has heard "the worst thing." History tells that he purged the land for the next seventeen years. Coates believes that because of the dual prophecies--that he would survive until Birnam Wood remove to Dunsinane and that he could not be hurt by any man born of woman--Macbeth comes to think of himself as some kind of superman. Once he loses Lady Macbeth, "the bone-weariness of the character begins to show."

Coates also stresses Macduff's role as a foil for Macbeth. He goes to England to bring back Malcolm, around whom his forces can rally an army to overthrow Macbeth. He shows himself a highly emotional man in risking everything to rid his country of Macbeth, says Coates, and eventually serves his country better than the "poet and warrior" Macbeth.

Macbeth began for Marcia Kash as she reads the letter explaining the witches' prophecy, creating an anticipation tinged with danger. She says:

At the line "Hail, king" (1.5.8) my mind starts to race. How are we going to achieve that....I don't think I plan on murder from the start, but I know we are going to have to do things differently.

The character comes to believe that the end justifies the means, she concludes, as soon as Duncan's arrival is announced. Lady Macbeth is ambitious for her husband "while not being entirely selfless." Her blinding love causes her to push him, the actress considers, and it took different techniques for her to motivate Etienne and Coates' individual Macbeths. Coates' size called for a stronger and bolder approach than she used with Etienne. Etienne was more vulnerable, more boyish, she says, and "I didn't have to push so hard to make him do it." She notes "a weak link in there somewhere, and I know it and go for it." It was more of a fight to convince Coates. Since they each gave her something different in their roles, she had to play it moment-by-moment to follow appropriately, she says. Explaining that she manipulates them both sexually, she finds more of the mother or madonna quality in her relationship to Etienne. That quality came out from her toward Coates only after the banquet scene, where a stunned Macbeth requires her aid.

In Act I, Scene 6, welcoming Duncan to their castle, she perceives that the character offers genuine respect for his office even while conspiring against him. By the time Macbeth commits the murder in Act II, Scene 2, the actress has created a very methodical character to demonstrate that she is fearful underneath but confident on the surface. "I think you can overcomplicate Lady Macbeth," she says of this approach. Macbeth's jitters at the murder bring out the no-nonsense side of the character, she says. The audience "ought to be almost as excited as we are," she imagines, "but ought to be horrified that we might succeed." She took Macbeth's bloody hands and could feel the liquid "squishing between my fingers" yet guided him carefully to the next step. Etienne's reaction she characterizes as quiet and brooding, involved with the blood on his hands; Coates was louder, making her more anxious to quiet him before he causes a commotion.

Between Act II, Scene 4, and Act III, Scene 1, Kerr inserted a coronation scene and procession. Without lines, the actors had to rely on each other to create a sense of what is happening. Kash recalls that Etienne made her feel that Lady Macbeth "has really contributed to his success." She almost felt as if she were leading him, she says. With Coates, however, "the pride I feel is in him, not us....I am not an equal partner." In both cases she sensed "a lot of love coming back." At the discovery of Duncan's body (Act II, Scene 3), Lady Macbeth begins "an acting job she continues until the banquet scene." By that time (Act III, Scene 4) her false front breaks with the realization that Macbeth no longer needs her; her *raison d'être* has disappeared, she is exhausted, and she fears he will break and reveal everything. At the banquet, she saw Etienne was more tortured, more aloof from the others at the event. Coates she saw as more social and confident until the ghost shatters him. Her reaction to both of them was, "What have I done to this man?"

Lady Macbeth's sleepwalking scene (Act V, Scene 1) terrified Kash at the beginning of rehearsals. She decided to play the scene as if Lady Macbeth has gone mad, "with guilt tumbling out," because of the murders but also because of the loss of her relationship with her husband. To emphasize her lunacy she sang line 41, "The Thane of Fife had a wife; where is she now?" In conclusion, she recounts that a night or two before opening she saw a soldier in costume on the back of stage left, under the macramé of the set; Anne Wright thought she saw him in a dressing room mirror, but turned around and he was gone. Every night during the sleepwalking scene Kash looked for him...and one night in early August he was there again.

"...it is an epilogue or discourse, to make plain
Some obscure precedence that hath tofore been sain.
I will example it....
Love's Labour's Lost, III.1.81-83.

Epilogue

"Love, to labour and effect one thing specially."
The Taming of the Shrew, I.1.118.

Chapter Thirteen: The Stratford Touch

What is the mix of ingredients that contributes to the renown of the Stratford Shakespearean Festival? What goes into making this theatre unique in Canada and eminent among theatres of the world? At various times during the season a number of the theatrical professionals who have worked across the country and at times across the continent and the world have wrestled with that question. "It all comes down to time and money," *Henry VIII* director Brian Rintoul reiterated when returning to Stratford in October. Other directors, designers, actors, and coaches point to Stratford's commitment to excellence in theatre, evident in time and money but also in depth of support and talent.

Time makes a difference in the thoroughness of preparation in rehearsal, Rintoul contends. A four-week rehearsal is usual, but in the Stratford repertory the six plays that opened in May were rehearsed over two and a half to three and a half months, although none was rehearsed continuously. Each show readying for the Festival stage was typically positioned for two primary, two secondary, and two tertiary days in rehearsal a week. The Young Company had two months of rehearsal in which to prepare their two plays. The two late-opening shows, *A Man for All Seasons* at the Avon and *Cymbeline* at the Festival stage, had seven and eight weeks of rehearsal time, respectively, although neither could rehearse a full work week because their actors played in other productions.

"When I am directing a play in four weeks, I have to arrive with a plan in my briefcase that will be seventy-five percent operational by the end of the first week," Rintoul continues. Such restrictions require the "lecture approach" in place of a collaborative rehearsal process. The latter, he says, opens up interesting choices not only for him but for the actors and audience. At Stratford he had the time to explore a number of options for various characters as they were engaged in different scenes before deciding which one to choose. Outside of the Festival, he says, he has "to cut off the creative process" to avoid dead ends from which the production will not have time to redirect itself. Even if the company hits a brick wall, Rintoul holds, the time taken for the side trip will generally be well spent in providing at least one insight for at least one performer. In May, he said that *Henry VIII* should be stronger in August because the cast had time to try out many ideas in rehearsal.

Rosencrantz and Guildenstern Are Dead director John Wood and *Pericles* director Richard Ouzounian agree. Wood used the days between primary rehearsals to think actively about the production or simply let it simmer while he worked on another project. To Ouzounian, the extra time meant remaining flexible about the interpretation of a scene until he had a better sense of where the entire production was heading. *The Boys From Syracuse* director Douglas Campbell recalls Shakespearean productions from the beginning of his career that took two weeks from start to finish: The first week was devoted to blocking and the second to interpretation and dress rehearsals. He explains, "That seemed like all the time in the world to us back then." Yet Campbell appreciates the extra time Stratford afforded him, in which he was able to experiment with different musical endings, juggle the timing for various musical numbers, and rechoreograph the opening sequence, among other tests. David William, director of *The Winter's Tale*, told his cast that half of the language in the play was inaccessible to a modern audience and that they must use the time to make the piece understandable. Several directors comment, too, that Stratford's mandate to perform all of the Shakespearean plays requires allowing time and money not often available at regional theatres.

Designers at Stratford fit the time period to the requirements of their assignments and styles of working. For designer Shawn Kerwin of *The Winter's Tale*, more time also means more work. "It's like eating your way through a huge cake," she says. "You eat it little by little." With five other shows being built at the same time as *The Winter's Tale*, the shops needed the extra time. *Hamlet* and *Rosencrantz and Guildenstern Are Dead* designer Sue LePage had to design both shows quickly and then took advantage of time later to rethink her approaches before rehearsals started. Even if very little change resulted, she says, the redesigning venture at least validated her first instincts and permitted minor adjustments. For lighting designer Louise Guinand, the extra time meant that she could continually refine the lighting over the course of the rehearsal period for her three productions. In a corresponding length of time, she says, she might light fifteen to sixteen plays at other theatres. Using *Hamlet* as an example, she explains that she sometimes reconstructed the lighting for a particular scene a number of times before she and director John Neville got the desired result. Another situation might not have provided the time or equipment to fix the problems, she adds.

Rintoul believes that money also makes a difference in the end product. Shakespeare's plays call for large casts and demand a large scale of visual presentation in order to be appreciated, he says, noting that the Festival is one of the few theatres able to maintain such production standards. Producer Richard Dennison adds that even under budget limitations imposed this year, the Festival still allows directors and designers more resources than do most other theatres. Among those resources, Rintoul says, are the quality of the actors and the length of the season. In another setting, he says, a director might well wind up with as many as a dozen actors who cannot handle the verse structure of Shakespeare's plays adequately. It works both ways, he says: One of the Festival's drawing cards for good actors is the long season over which to refine and polish their roles. The issue of resources also interests resident director Bob Beard, who explains that he was attracted to Stratford in part by a 1981 production of *Coriolanus*. He remembers the excitement of his friends in the theatrical community that the Festival could put its resources into production of one of the lesser-known Shakespearean plays. In fact, the 1986 season was a season of lesser-known plays with Neville's selection of the three romances.

The choice of productions is tied to money, explains media relations manager Bob Allen. About seventy percent of the Festival's annual budget comes through the box office, and that figure accounts for almost all of the production budget. Even with a mandate to do the entire Shakespearean canon, including the less popular plays, the Festival survives by its box office. The remaining thirty percent of the budget comes from fund-raising and government grants, and Neville observes that the federal government has lagged behind the province in supporting the Festival. So even as production standards must remain high, the financial structure that ties this state theatre so closely to its box office remains precarious. The dean of the Festival critics, Jamie Portman of the Southam News, states the problem graphically in describing Neville's first season. Portman thinks of the artistic director as the captain of a modern-day *Titanic*, asking if Neville can steer the huge vehicle, with its $14 million budget, away from the icebergs of financial disaster. So far, says Portman, he has made a gallant try of it. But if Neville's seamanship provides a short-range answer to the problem, a more permanent solution has yet to be found.

A third plus of working at Stratford, say members of the company, is the support system; specifically, the actors talk about the additional help they get in working with body and voice. The work of Paula Thomson and Dorothy Ward with the Young Company was noted in Chapter Twelve, and members of the Avon and Festival companies had the service of movement coach John Broome and voice coach Anne Skinner for much of the season. Broome, who came to this job from a background in dance, became interested in working with actors after recruiting a number of them for a dance program. He says that the actors did not move with the accuracy of the dancers but that they brought an element of interpretation to their roles that made them more interesting to watch. After a long career in England, which included a residency at the Royal Shakespeare Company, Broome came to North America and to Stratford, working with the company in several ways for increasingly longer periods. First, he works with directors, who may assign him a particular actor with a movement problem. Or as for *Henry VIII* the director may ask him to hold a class on period movement for the entire company. Second, he looks for movement problems while shows are being rehearsed and then approaches the director involved, asking to work with a particular actor. Third, he is available to actors who sometimes seek him out for cures for specific problems, ranging from pulled muscles to peculiarities of difficult dance steps. Actor John Innes says that Broome approached him about Dr. Cornelius, whom he played in *Cymbeline*, explaining that Innes was "curved, but the doctor has to be more angular." Innes used the observation to help develop the physical side of his character presentation, thrusting out elbows and knees when he moved. Having Broome available to the company not only during rehearsals but also for almost two months after the last production opened allowed actors to check with him any physical problems they encountered during the run. It also gave him the chance to work with individual performers over a long period to combat some of their more resistant movement problems.

Both physical and vocal warmups are held for the actors before each performance. Broome tries to individualize his warmups, gearing them toward the demands of specific productions. Voice coach Anne Skinner agrees that putting the physical warmup before the vocal one readies the actor to speak. She studied in the United States under Kristin Linklater and later in England under Patsy Rodenburg, taking voice to enrich her training as a director. After working as a director with scripts built around particular sounds, she chose to work as a voice coach. Very few theatres have the funds to hire a voice coach, she explains, but the Festival does. Otherwise, coaches work out of acting studios in large cities--where actors can concentrate on sharpening their skills between jobs--or as part of a university programme. Few people have credentials as voice or m ovement coaches, so few professional companies can engage their services, according to Broome and Skinner. Skinner used the long period after the last show had opened to work intensively with actors on passages of their choosing perhaps unrelated to specific lines they spoke, but work that deepened their overall performances. Voice coaches, she says, are concentrating today more on textual interpretation than merely on the vocal mechanism. Directors would assign her an actor with problems to correct, or she might suggest to a director that she could help a particular actor and ask for permission to do so. She also worked with actors at their request on specific problems. Geraint Wyn Davies, who played the title role in *Pericles*, found his work with Skinner particularly helpful. Because he had not played a Shakespearean lead before, he and Skinner worked for about an hour and a half before each *Pericles* performance on integrating voice and text, with director Ouzounian's blessing. To round out the tutoring, company members were offered additional work in movement in Alexander Technique classes taught by Kelly McEvenue and singing lessons with Carol Forte.

Designers cite Stratford's support system, as well. Polly Scranton Bohdanetzky, who did *The Boys From Syracuse*, says the Festival's workshops give a designer literally anything, even with budget constraints, because the talented people know how to build anything. That kind of expertise can be taken for granted at Stratford, she explains, but is not usually available outside the Festival. The wardrobe (including, among others, tailors and cutters), jewellry, millinery, dyeing, costume painting, costume decoration, wigs, and shoe departments build costumes; the scenic and prop departments are responsible for the settings. Guinand likes to design at Stratford because the people there can create any device she designs for lighting. And when William Schmuck wanted fog coming from what had been a bare floor for the Young Company production of *Macbeth*, the technicians at the Third Stage found a way (see Chapter Twelve). The large body of professional crafts people employed at the Festival have years of solid experience in which they take pride, says the designer.

The Festival has depth in this support system, hiring design assistants for most of the designers. Louise Guinand, Harry Frehner, Sue LePage, and Shawn Kerwin first came to Stratford to assist other designers before being given shows of their own. Third Stage production stage manager Heather Kitchen began her career at Stratford as a production assistant at the Festival Theatre in 1975. And the Young Company is a training ground for Festival actors, making young artists familiar with the aesthetic demands of its theatres and the requirements of working within a large administrative structure. The Festival provides itself in this way with a pool of acting talent that sustains itself and serves other Canadian and international theatres.

The smooth functioning of each theatre at Stratford is helped by the work of the stage managers and their two assistants for each show and of the production stage managers for each of the three theatres. One assistant stage manager has responsibility for text and one for props. The latter sets the properties during rehearsals and performances and supervises their storage; the former keeps an accurate daily record of cuts and blocking. They give actors written notes explaining what lines or bits of blocking or business did not go properly during performance. In taping each production for the archives, the assistant can settle questions about lines or blocking by reviewing the tape. The stage manager calls the show and controls cue lights (used in all three theatres) for the actors, since the architecture of the Festival stage does not allow actors to wait in the wings and listen for their cues. Nora Polley, Margaret Palmer, and Heather Kitchen at the Festival, the Avon, and the Third Stage, respectively, drew up daily schedules for their theatres, balancing the competing demands of directors. At the same time they scheduled actors for wardrobe fittings; classes in Alexander Technique; singing, voice, and movement classes; fencing and fighting classes; and, in the Festival Theatre, for the tanning machine, needed for two shows with Middle Eastern locations. Kitchen points out that her responsibilities do not differ markedly from those at other theatres in which she has worked, but they differ greatly in complexity because of the demands of repertory theatre.

No accounting of the Festival's unique place in Canadian theatre would be complete without including a note about the open stage architecture of the Festival Theatre, which, when first built in 1953, created the close, surrounding actor-audience relationship of Sheakespeare's theatre in a modern design. As Douglas Campbell explained to his cast in February as rehearsals began, the design employed the blocking patterns for which Shakespeare wrote his plays, so the design can never grow old, as each generation of actors discovers that basic plan. He invited his cast to take their turn with the three or four generations that had gone before them in that theatre. That design calls for speaking the words of the playwright on a practically bare stage. The emphasis, then, is on the actor, enhanced by the lighting and the costumes. The unique space necessitates an elaborate system to create lights and costumes that keep the focus on the actor and the spoken word.

The costuming system, for example, required thirteen cutters, each of whom supervised a team of five or six sewing assistants. They began work in January on the more than six hundred costumes needed for the 1986 season, according to assistant head of wardrobe Gayle Larson. A costume pattern might be traced on brown wrapping paper and then be adjusted; be transferred to muslin, of which a mockup of the costume would be built; and be adjusted again before the pattern was transferred to the actual fabric. The six shows scheduled to open the first week were the ones for which costumes were first built. The costumes for the Young Company went into production about 1 April, and costumes for the last two shows were begun in late April, Larson says. Larson explains that each of the thirteen groups works from start to finish on the costumes assigned to it, with the exception of adding trim or final decorative accents. The designer interprets sketches, brings in research to show the correct historical line of the period, and answers questions for the team. The wardrobe's goal is to fit a costume on the actor three times-- up to 1,800 fittings; with such a production schedule, costume fittings frequently got priority even over rehearsal. At its height at the end of February, Larson explains, the wardrobe employed between eighty and ninety people for the seasonal work. As the load lightened during the season, so did the wardrobe staff.

In November or December, Larson says, wardrobe manager Anne Elsbury meets with her to evaluate cost overruns or underruns and determine personnel needs before hiring for the next season. Dennison says this large number of actors and wardrobe staff needed makes the Festival a "labour-intensive organization." According to Larson, the design assistant keeps a "bible" for each production: a photocopy of each design; a photograph of the finished costume; a sample of each fabric; samples of the dyeing, painting, spraying, or other technique used; a note of the quantity of fabric purchased and how much was used; the size of each article of clothing in a costume; the cost of the costume; and a list of accessories--gloves, hats, and jewellry. She says that the Festival is among the first to keep such detailed records.

The scale of the enterprise at the Stratford Shakespearean Festival of course accounts for its budgetary and personnel needs. The depth of its resources-- its richness in talent and support--requires a commensurate commitment in money and time. The creative side of this process is arguably among that of the best of world theatres. The depth of talent and resources attracts to Stratford new generations of talent and new varieties of resources. The Festival combines the classical theatre tradition with what Professor Ronald Bryden calls essentially the English repertory system of production. But the Festival defines and particularizes both the tradition and the system with the sensitivities and experiences of the primarily Canadian artists, designers, directors, and administrators employed by it. This resulting Canadian stamp has been carried by those who have worked there to all parts of the country. But ensuring the contuinance of its influence will require a stable financial base, which in turn determines the scale of its operations.

322

Chapter Fourteen: The Season In Review

On Monday, 20 October, just a few hours after the close of the 1986 season, John Neville sank into a sofa in the artistic director's office, relaxed for a moment, and then offered his assessment of the season just ended. In his interviews with the board before assuming his position, Neville had stressed that he would seek to restore both the artistic and financial footing of the Festival; at season's end in 1986, he believed he had made a significant beginning in accomplishing both. Recognizing the difficulty of measuring precisely the qualitative aspects of the season, he expressed satisfaction that the four plays at the Avon Theatre did what he hoped they would do; that is, sell one another. The three romances at the Festival Theatre proved harder to sell, but, Neville says, such an arrangement will always be "a hard sell." Moving the musical to the Festival Theatre was a calculated risk, he admits, but the gamble paid off because the production did the business predicted for it in that larger theatre and so provided a kind of self-subsidy.

As for the company, he says he takes pride in "the huge stride forward" that it took during the season:

> *First of all, it has enormous confidence in itself now, which is what I have tried to instill. It doesn't have too much fear, which it had in large quantities before because the fear was frankly instilled into it. Fear was a condition of the place. It doesn't have that fear any more. We can now go head to head with any company in the world, in my opinion. So the company has that confidence and with that confidence have grown the talent, the means, the ability to do these great plays, and I think that is a great, great sign for the future and bodes well for next season....*

In addition, he notes, the company has begun to sit "more easily" in the community. After all, he acknowledges, if it had not been for the community's involvement thirty-four years ago, there would not be any theatre here today. In building a bridge to the town, which he has considered vital since he first worked as an administrator at the Nottingham Theatre, Neville played an active and visible role in the life of the community during the 1986 season. He did public readings, made speeches, appeared at openings, and met with local leaders regularly.

The season was also a financial success. Total paid attendance dipped by 10,429 to 426,135 in 1986 (from 436,564 in 1985), but the gross box office receipts rose by $33,069 to $8,825,358 from the 1985 total gross of $8,792,289. The Festival's accounting system requires subtraction of the total value of discounts from the gross box office to determine the net box office amount; total discounts in 1986 dipped by $355,570 (to $548,282) from the 1985 figure of $903,852. Fewer discounts, added to the high gross box office, meant a $388,639 net increase over 1985. The season's ten productions played 493 performances; box office receipts, shown in percentage of revenue capacity for the productions, were:

Festival Theatre

The Boys From Syracuse	65 performances	69.4 percent
The Winter's Tale	47 performances	51.5 percent
Cymbeline	38 performances	46.1 percent
Pericles	48 performances	40.7 percent
	Total:	55.2 percent

Avon Theatre

Hamlet	66 performances	83.5 percent
A Man for All Seasons	43 performances	80.2 percent
Rosencrantz and Guildenstern Are Dead	43 performances	76.1 percent
Henry VIII	49 performances	65.1 percent
	Total:	76.1 percent

Third Stage

Macbeth	47 performances	79.4 percent
The Resistible Rise of Arturo Ui	46 performances	52.4 percent
	Total:	66.8 percent

Total for all three theatres: 62.0 percent

These performance numbers do not include previews; figures were supplied by Festival marketing manager Christopher Blake.

General Manager Gary Thomas calls the overall financial health of the Festival "much improved" as a result of the 1986 season. Acknowledging a shortfall at the box office from the $9.9 million projection, he points out that the season came in under the costs budgeted for production. According to Thomas and producer Richard Dennison, Neville cut costs--among other ways--by requiring less elaborate settings. This requirement in turn cut time needed to change sets between performances and, again in turn, cut labour costs. Making some cost savings, as for sets, creates others, Thomas and Dennison point out.

Dennison reported a growing saving to the board each month from production costs' coming in at less than the budget. With $14 million to plan for, he says, if projections are off by only one percent, the budget is off by $140,000. Budgets had to be laid out to accommodate problems and still stay ahead of projected costs. For example, costume projections for *Henry VIII* and *A Man for All Seasons* turned out to be too low, but there was room for adjustment. The budget was constructed to allow for such extra expenses, another example being overtime labour costs. When it is time to take photographs for the season programme, Dennison says, overtime may be required to get costumes ready by that deadline.

Media relations manager Bob Allen says that even though the box office revenues are at least to some extent out of the Festival's control, limiting expenses is a way to stabilize the financial result. Several reporters, he says, have wrongly interpreted the $1.1 million box office shortfall as a $1.1 deficit for the season, not considering the saving in expenditures. Most of the $392,924 surplus reported at the end of the 1986 season came from the increase of $290,572 in the fund-raising campaign over the amount budgeted. To this amount was added $270,683 of the $447,315 realized from the sale of stock that the board held during the year, to produce a net income of $663,607 during fiscal 1986, ending 31 October. The stock came to the Festival from the Jackman Foundation; Hal and Eric Jackman served on the Board of Governors. In 1983 the foundation gave stock to some of the major arts organizations, and Stratford got about 3,300 shares. With the matching funds (at that time two dollars for one dollar raised) from the province, the money helped pay the portion of previous losses from the American tour. Neville, opposed to the tour from the start, considered that debt one more legacy that limited his manoeuvering room in this already difficult season.

In addition, through its president, William Sommerville, the Festival received a $1 million grant from the province to clear up the remaining debt on its "building expansions and renovations undertaken in 1984." The remainder of the grant was used to clear up accounting for old inventories and cover expenses from the 1983 establishment of the Stratford

Shakespearean Festival of America. The generosity of the province, Thomas says, means that the Festival no longer faces capital debt on any of its property and can operate without bank loans for the first time in several years. The figures here were supplied by Thomas.

According to the report of finance chairman Murray B. Frum to the Stratford Shakespearean Festival Foundation of Canada at its 6 December, 1986, annual meeting, the Festival had on 31 October, 1984, an operating deficit of $3,309,594. Thomas, who gave these figures, says the board decided to use some of its assets to reduce that total and used $524,998 in funds it had raised to make a payment that year. In 1985, it used $876,000, and in 1986, $473,616, which matured in the Wintario arts challenge grants after five years and was awarded to the Festival in the amount of $2,876,000 in the early 1980s, says Thomas. In addition, the $24,901 surplus from the 1985 season and the $663,607 surplus from the 1986 season were applied against the deficit, reducing it to $746,479.

Allen takes comfort in both financial and artistic achievements made during 1986. He and resident director Bob Beard conclude that the Festival received in 1986 more positive reviews than it has seen for a number of seasons. These, he believes, are instrumental in increasing attendance; they help advertising and promotion for future seasons. In 1986, even without a recent history of good reviews, restauranteurs and hoteliers reported increases in business, figures he interprets as meaning that people came from farther away and stayed longer. People from closer markets "hadn't gotten the word that it's worth coming here," he says. Nearby Toronto offers competing arts activities and entertainment. Leisure dollars go to Canada's Wonderland and other attractions, and the Festival has to compete heavily for the entertainment dollar from that area.

Beard points to the positive attitude that prevailed in the company in 1986, and, while admitting the difficulty of measuring such a quality, he believes people generally do better work when they are happier. Allen concurs. He says that whether an artistic director must be an actor to be successful can be debated, but what cannot be debated is that the acting company readily understands and identifies with an artistic director who shares their craft. Allen also sees the progress of young performers such as Colm Feore and Martha Burns as an important artistic achievement, one on which no clock or timetable can be imposed. But, just as importantly, Allen calls 1986 a season in which artistic consistency from production to production was very high--a "successful beginning for the 1987 season."

Southam News critic Jamie Portman notes that before 1986 he saw a slippage in the quality of productions at Stratford. He credits Neville with reversing the Festival during 1986 in three important ways: economically, artistically, and by a renewed commitment to classical theatre. According to Portman, returning classical theatrical productions to the Avon Theatre breaks the five-year tradition of housing the Gilbert and Sullivan operettas there. Portman also appreciates the manner in which Neville went about binding up some old wounds by bringing back talented people such as William Hutt and Robin Phillips "from exile."

Lastly, Portman says that Neville's plan to do the three romances worked better than many had expected. They gave his season a definite signature. Beard adds that from very early in Neville's tenure as artistic director designate, he played with the idea of building his first season around those three. Neville himself concludes:

> *The fact about those three plays is that I personally will never stop being proud of the fact that we did them, and I think this theatre will remain proud forever that we did them all in one season, which no one else has done in our lifetime or in our memory. It may well be a long time before anyone else does.*

Index

I would like to add a note of appreciation to Margaret Chase for her dedicated help with the index.

Bob Gaines